nickelodeon™

降击神通

AVATAR

THE LAST AIRBENDER™

IMBALANCE

Created by
BRYAN KONIETZKO
MICHAEL DANTE DiMARTINO

script
FAITH ERIN HICKS

art and cover
PETER WARTMAN

colors
RYAN HILL
ADELE MATERA

lettering
RICHARD STARKINGS &
COMICRAFT'S JIMMY BETANCOURT

DARK HORSE BOOKS

publisher
MIKE RICHARDSON

editor
RACHEL ROBERTS

associate editor
JENNY BLENK

assistant editor
ANASTACIA FERRY

designer
SARAH TERRY

digital art technician
SAMANTHA HUMMER

Special thanks to Linda Lee, Joan Hilty, and James Salerno at Nickelodeon, to Dave Marshall at Dark Horse, and to Bryan Konietzko, Michael Dante DiMartino, and Tim Hedrick.

Nickelodeon Avatar: The Last Airbender™—Imbalance Omnibus

This book collects *Avatar: The Last Airbender—Imbalance* parts one through three.

Published by
Dark Horse Books
A division of
Dark Horse Comics LLC
10956 SE Main Street
Milwaukie, OR 97222

DarkHorse.com
Nick.com

To find a comics shop in your area,
visit ComicShopLocator.com

First edition: August 2023
eBOOK ISBN 978-1-50673-392-0
ISBN 978-1-50673-381-4
T# 1013797

1 3 5 7 9 10 8 6 4 2
Printed in China

FSC
www.fsc.org
MIX
Paper from responsible sources
FSC® C109093

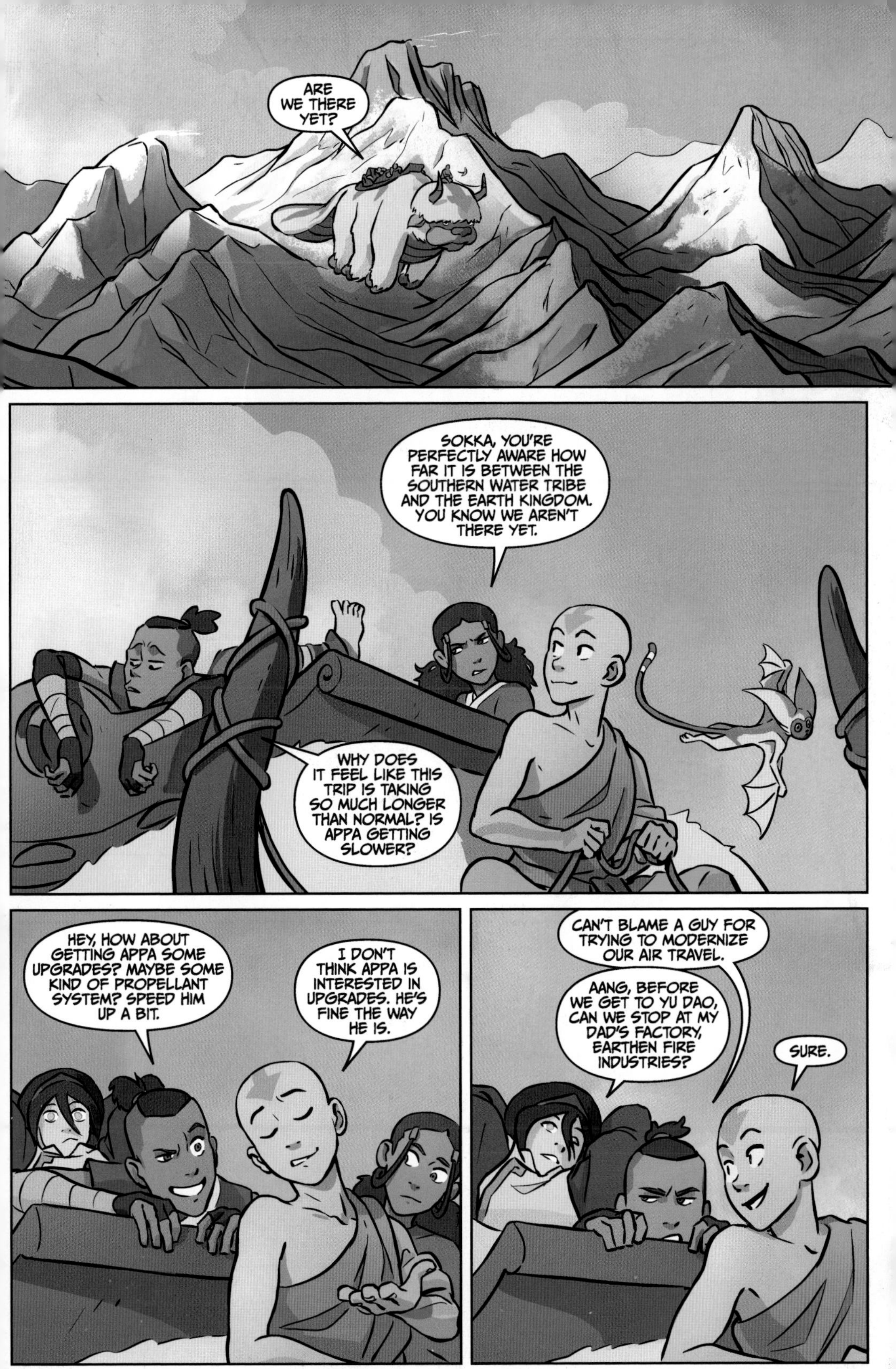
ARE WE THERE YET?
SOKKA, YOU'RE PERFECTLY AWARE HOW FAR IT IS BETWEEN THE SOUTHERN WATER TRIBE AND THE EARTH KINGDOM. YOU KNOW WE AREN'T THERE YET.
WHY DOES IT FEEL LIKE THIS TRIP IS TAKING SO MUCH LONGER THAN NORMAL? IS APPA GETTING SLOWER?
HEY, HOW ABOUT GETTING APPA SOME UPGRADES? MAYBE SOME KIND OF PROPELLANT SYSTEM? SPEED HIM UP A BIT.
I DON'T THINK APPA IS INTERESTED IN UPGRADES. HE'S FINE THE WAY HE IS.
CAN'T BLAME A GUY FOR TRYING TO MODERNIZE OUR AIR TRAVEL.
AANG, BEFORE WE GET TO YU DAO, CAN WE STOP AT MY DAD'S FACTORY, EARTHEN FIRE INDUSTRIES?
SURE.

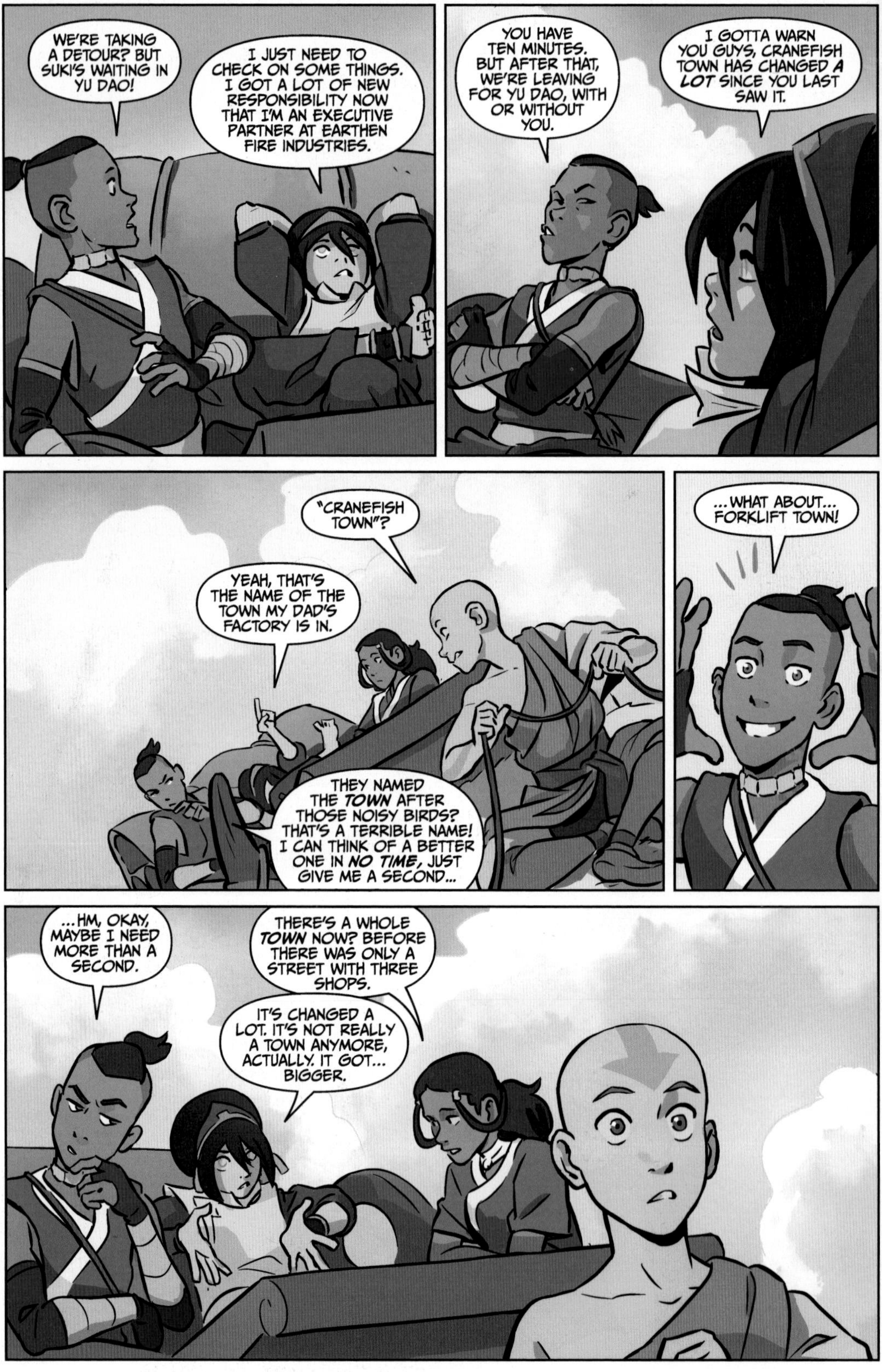
WE'RE TAKING A DETOUR? BUT SUKI'S WAITING IN YU DAO!
I JUST NEED TO CHECK ON SOME THINGS. I GOT A LOT OF NEW RESPONSIBILITY NOW THAT I'M AN EXECUTIVE PARTNER AT EARTHEN FIRE INDUSTRIES.
YOU HAVE TEN MINUTES. BUT AFTER THAT, WE'RE LEAVING FOR YU DAO, WITH OR WITHOUT YOU.
I GOTTA WARN YOU GUYS, CRANEFISH TOWN HAS CHANGED *A LOT* SINCE YOU LAST SAW IT.
"CRANEFISH TOWN"?
YEAH, THAT'S THE NAME OF THE TOWN MY DAD'S FACTORY IS IN.
THEY NAMED THE *TOWN* AFTER THOSE NOISY BIRDS? THAT'S A TERRIBLE NAME! I CAN THINK OF A BETTER ONE IN *NO TIME*, JUST GIVE ME A SECOND...
...WHAT ABOUT... FORKLIFT TOWN!
...HM, OKAY, MAYBE I NEED MORE THAN A SECOND.
THERE'S A WHOLE *TOWN* NOW? BEFORE THERE WAS ONLY A STREET WITH THREE SHOPS.
IT'S CHANGED A LOT. IT'S NOT REALLY A TOWN ANYMORE, ACTUALLY. IT GOT... BIGGER.

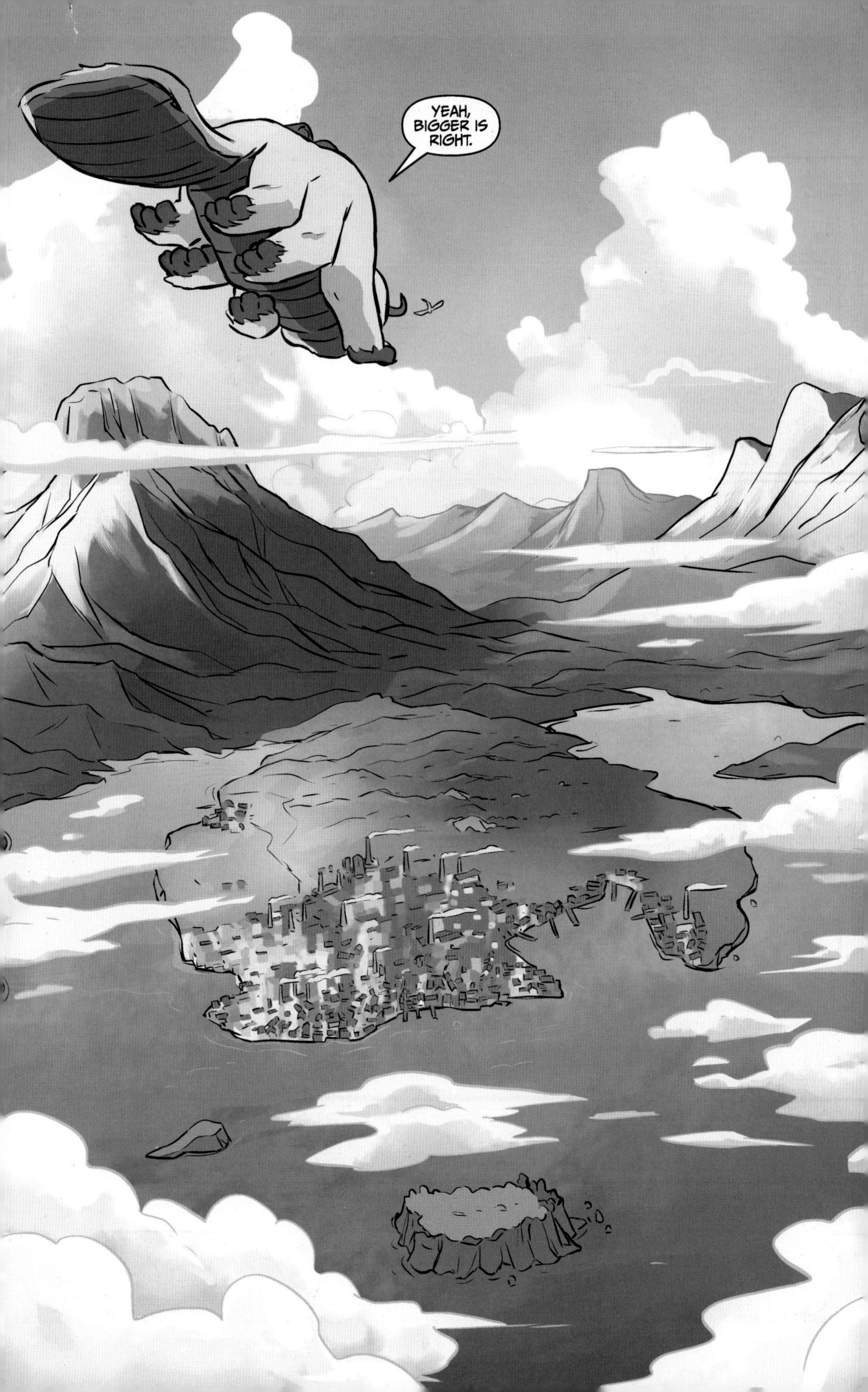
YEAH, BIGGER IS RIGHT.

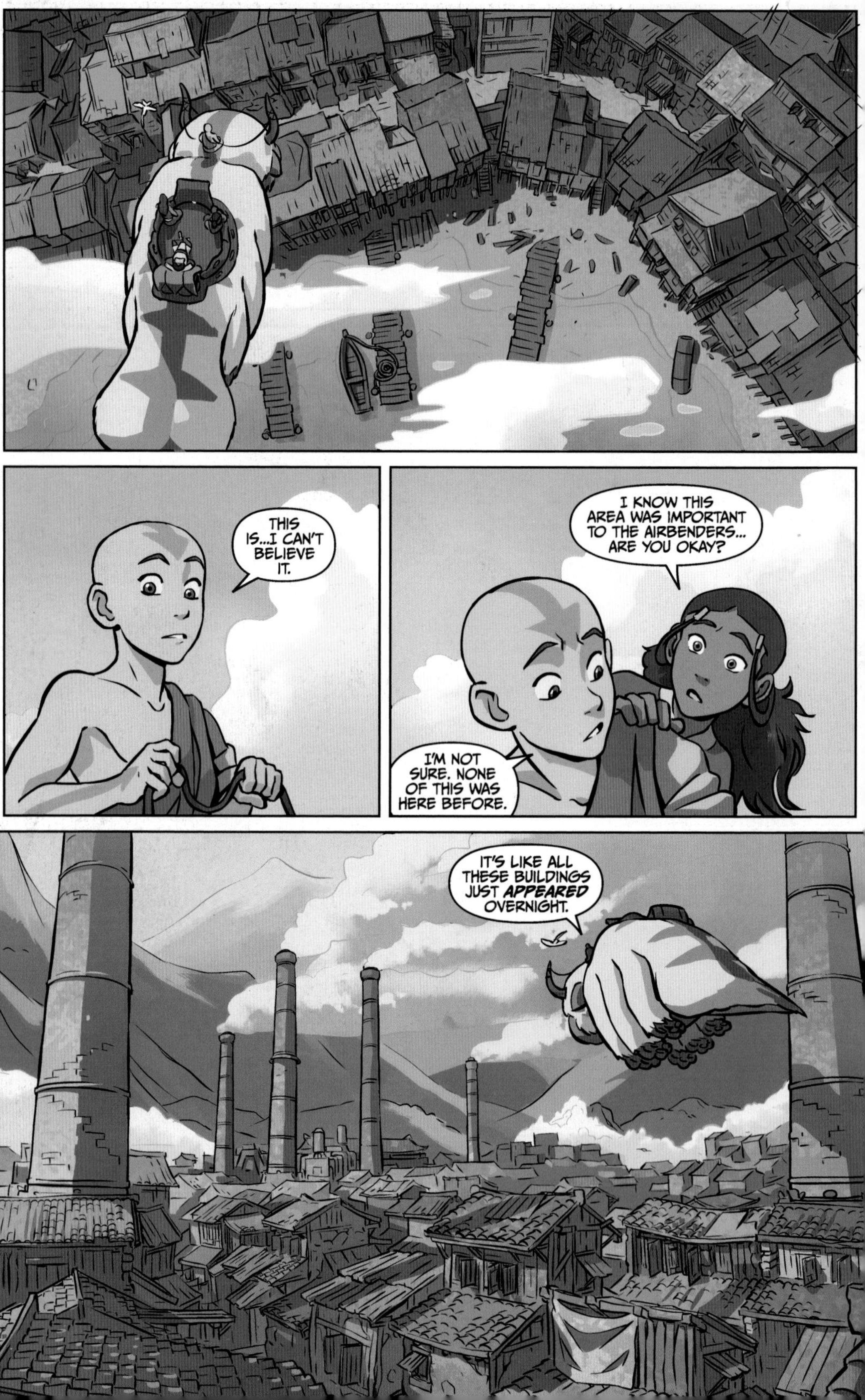
THIS IS...I CAN'T BELIEVE IT.
I KNOW THIS AREA WAS IMPORTANT TO THE AIRBENDERS... ARE YOU OKAY?
I'M NOT SURE. NONE OF THIS WAS HERE BEFORE.
IT'S LIKE ALL THESE BUILDINGS JUST *APPEARED* OVERNIGHT.

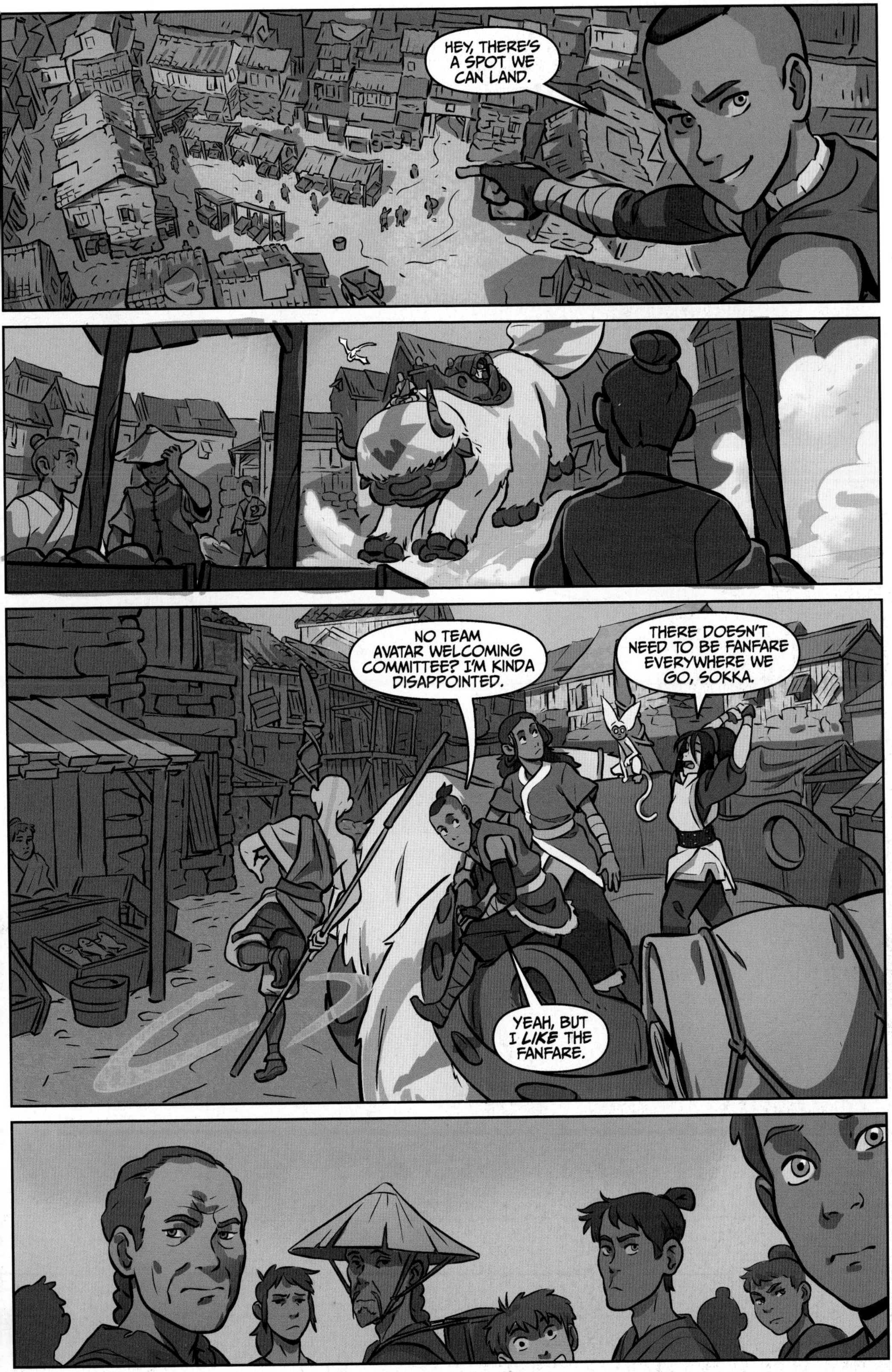

HEY, THERE'S A SPOT WE CAN LAND.
NO TEAM AVATAR WELCOMING COMMITTEE? I'M KINDA DISAPPOINTED.
THERE DOESN'T NEED TO BE FANFARE EVERYWHERE WE GO, SOKKA.
YEAH, BUT I *LIKE* THE FANFARE.

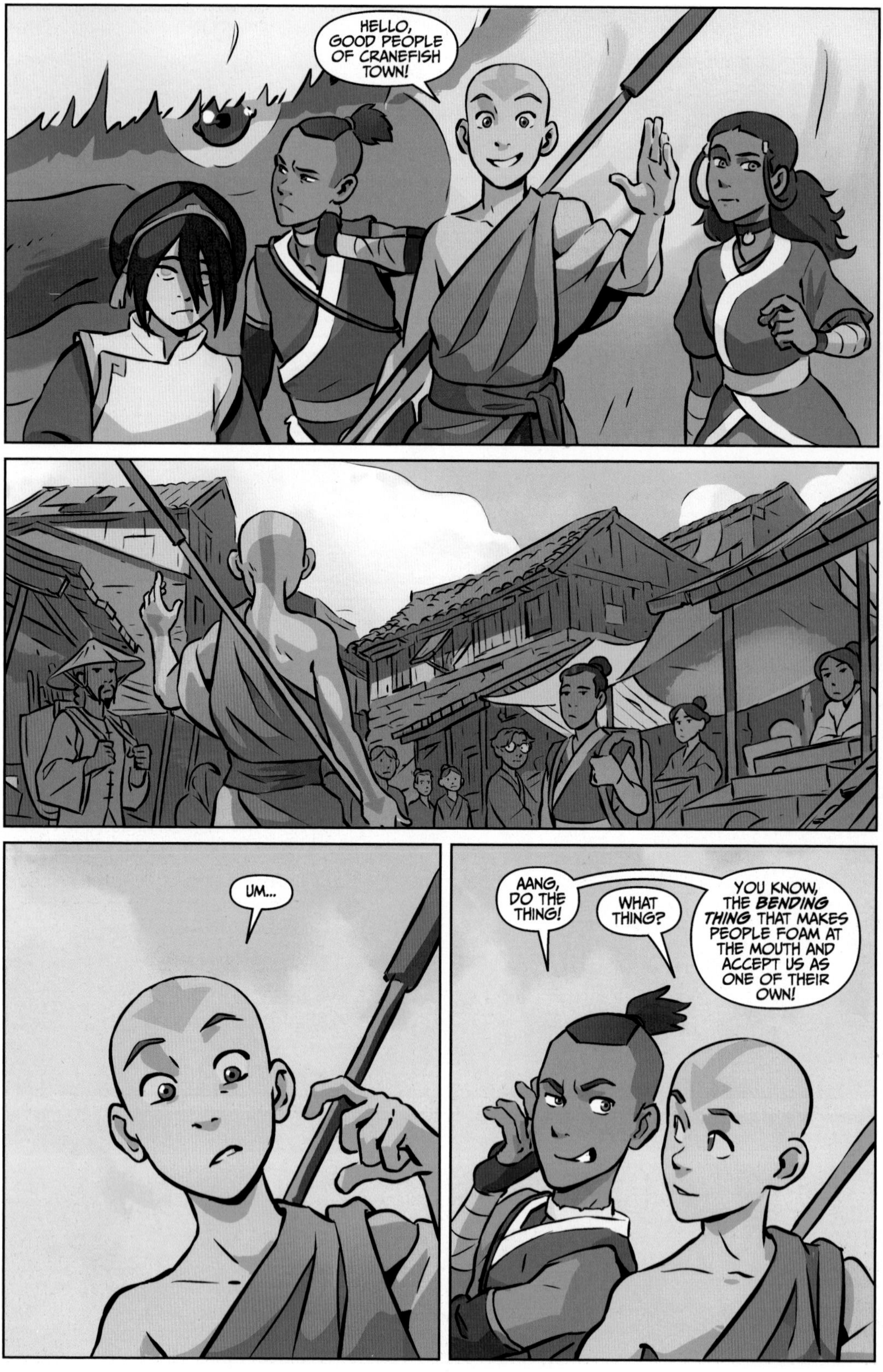
HELLO, GOOD PEOPLE OF CRANEFISH TOWN!
UM...
AANG, DO THE THING!
WHAT THING?
YOU KNOW, THE **BENDING THING** THAT MAKES PEOPLE FOAM AT THE MOUTH AND ACCEPT US AS ONE OF THEIR OWN!

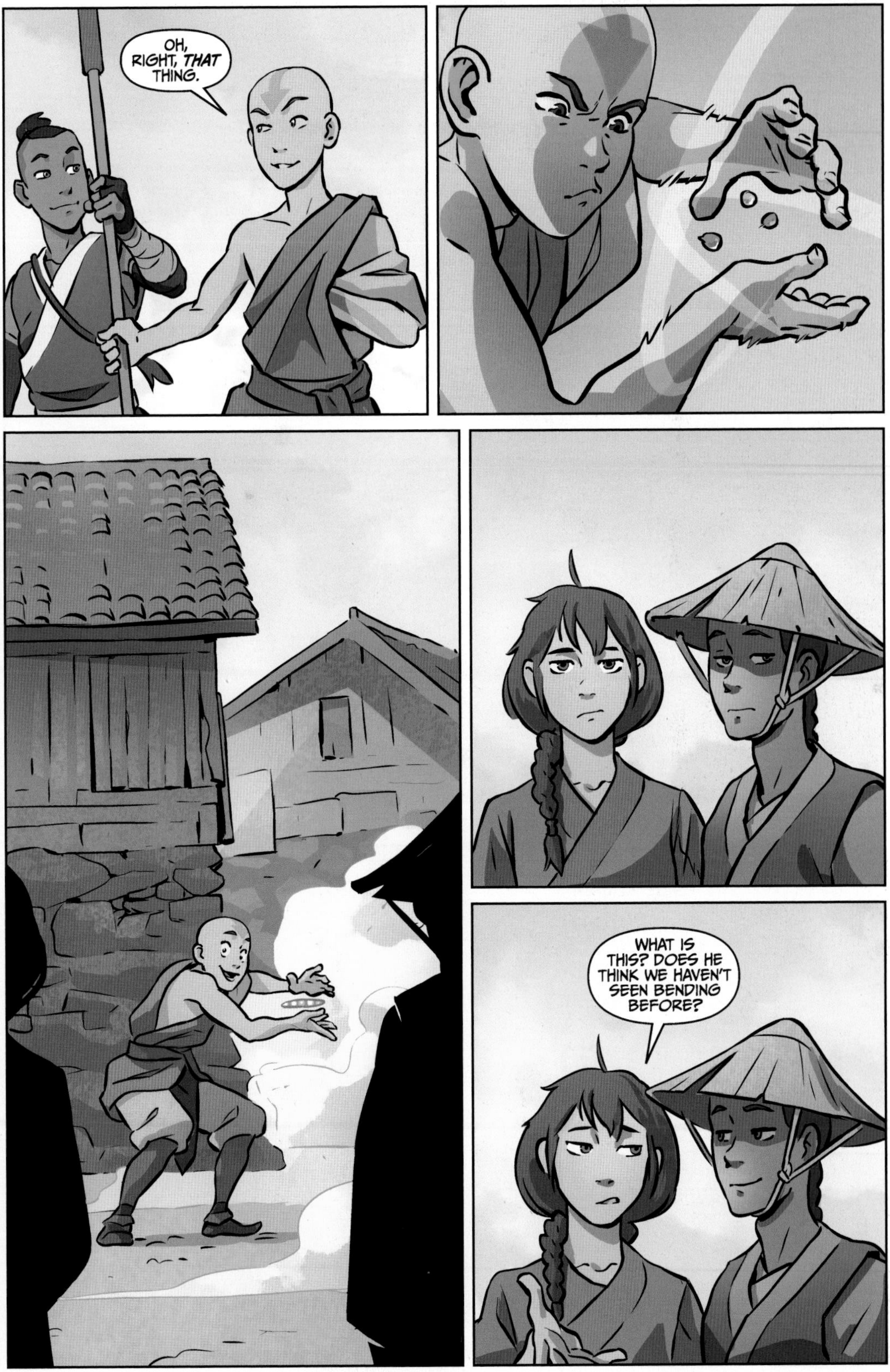
OH, RIGHT, *THAT* THING.
WHAT IS THIS? DOES HE THINK WE HAVEN'T SEEN BENDING BEFORE?

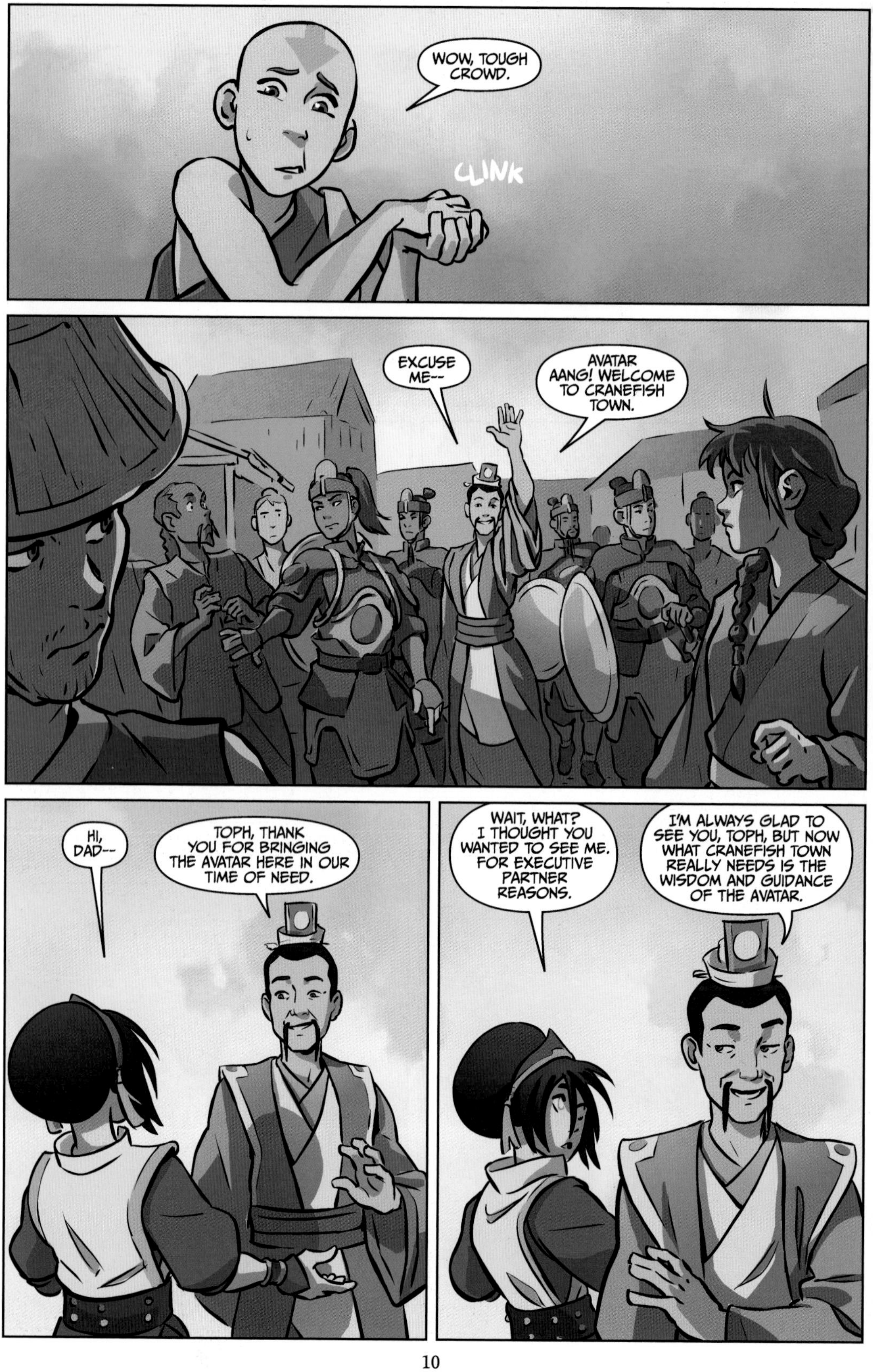
WOW, TOUGH CROWD.
CLINK
EXCUSE ME--
AVATAR AANG! WELCOME TO CRANEFISH TOWN.
HI, DAD--
TOPH, THANK YOU FOR BRINGING THE AVATAR HERE IN OUR TIME OF NEED.
WAIT, WHAT? I THOUGHT YOU WANTED TO SEE ME. FOR EXECUTIVE PARTNER REASONS.
I'M ALWAYS GLAD TO SEE YOU, TOPH, BUT NOW WHAT CRANEFISH TOWN REALLY NEEDS IS THE WISDOM AND GUIDANCE OF THE AVATAR.

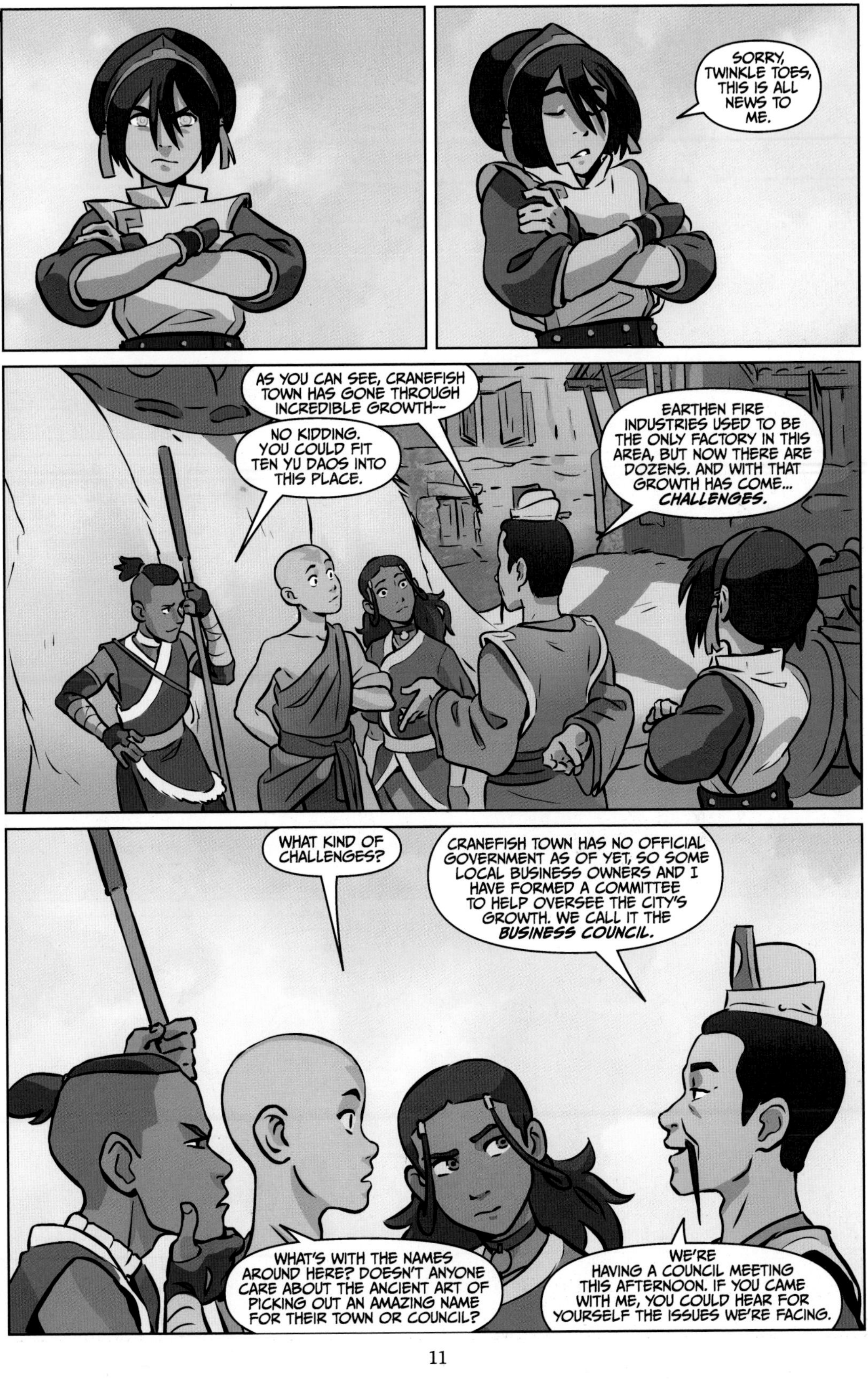
SORRY, TWINKLE TOES, THIS IS ALL NEWS TO ME.
AS YOU CAN SEE, CRANEFISH TOWN HAS GONE THROUGH INCREDIBLE GROWTH--
NO KIDDING. YOU COULD FIT TEN YU DAOS INTO THIS PLACE.
EARTHEN FIRE INDUSTRIES USED TO BE THE ONLY FACTORY IN THIS AREA, BUT NOW THERE ARE DOZENS. AND WITH THAT GROWTH HAS COME... CHALLENGES.
WHAT KIND OF CHALLENGES?
CRANEFISH TOWN HAS NO OFFICIAL GOVERNMENT AS OF YET, SO SOME LOCAL BUSINESS OWNERS AND I HAVE FORMED A COMMITTEE TO HELP OVERSEE THE CITY'S GROWTH. WE CALL IT THE BUSINESS COUNCIL.
WHAT'S WITH THE NAMES AROUND HERE? DOESN'T ANYONE CARE ABOUT THE ANCIENT ART OF PICKING OUT AN AMAZING NAME FOR THEIR TOWN OR COUNCIL?
WE'RE HAVING A COUNCIL MEETING THIS AFTERNOON. IF YOU CAME WITH ME, YOU COULD HEAR FOR YOURSELF THE ISSUES WE'RE FACING.

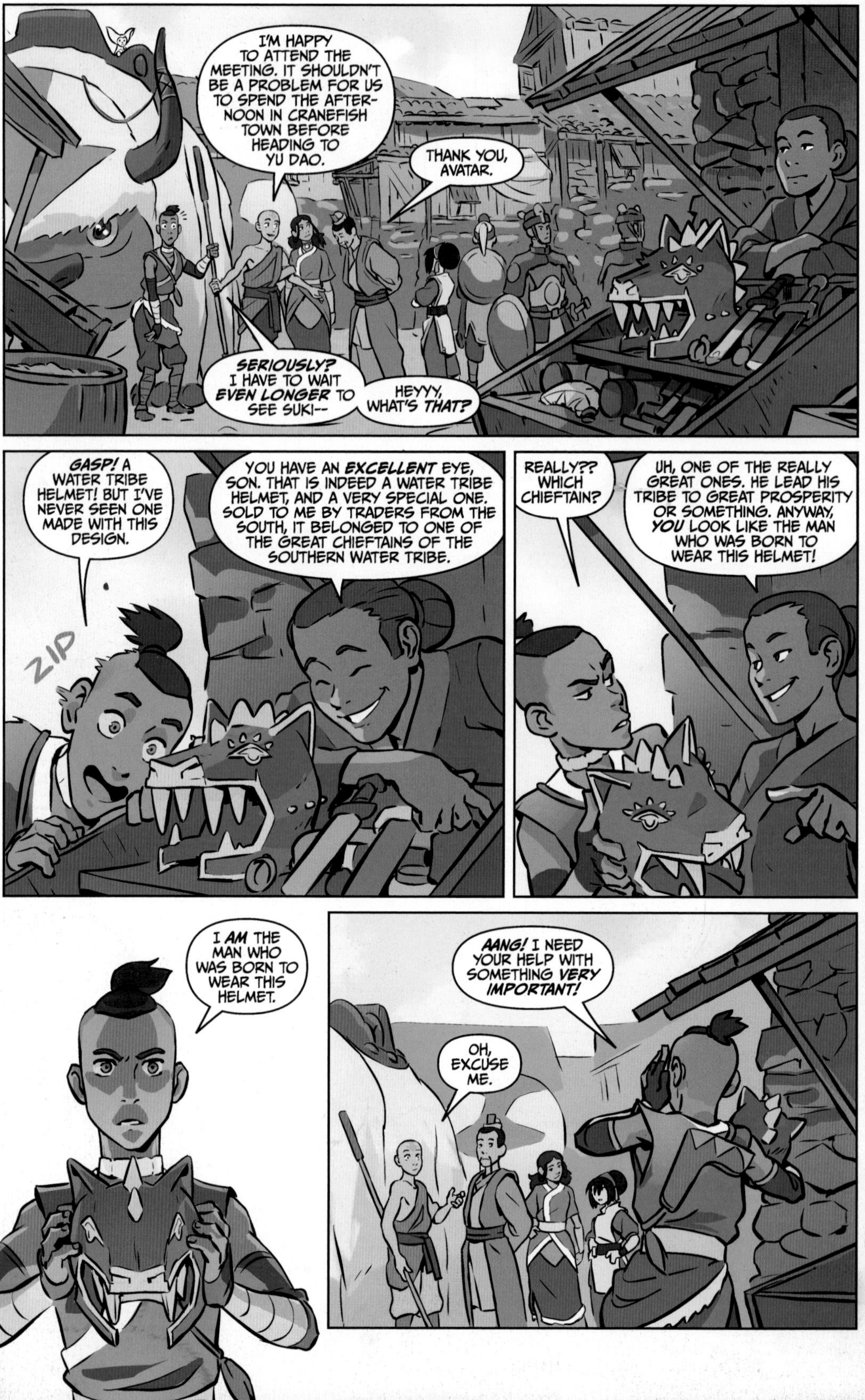
I'M HAPPY TO ATTEND THE MEETING. IT SHOULDN'T BE A PROBLEM FOR US TO SPEND THE AFTER-NOON IN CRANEFISH TOWN BEFORE HEADING TO YU DAO.
THANK YOU, AVATAR.
SERIOUSLY? I HAVE TO WAIT EVEN LONGER TO SEE SUKI--
HEYYY, WHAT'S THAT?
GASP! A WATER TRIBE HELMET! BUT I'VE NEVER SEEN ONE MADE WITH THIS DESIGN.
ZIP
YOU HAVE AN EXCELLENT EYE, SON. THAT IS INDEED A WATER TRIBE HELMET, AND A VERY SPECIAL ONE. SOLD TO ME BY TRADERS FROM THE SOUTH, IT BELONGED TO ONE OF THE GREAT CHIEFTAINS OF THE SOUTHERN WATER TRIBE.
REALLY?? WHICH CHIEFTAIN?
UH, ONE OF THE REALLY GREAT ONES. HE LEAD HIS TRIBE TO GREAT PROSPERITY OR SOMETHING. ANYWAY, YOU LOOK LIKE THE MAN WHO WAS BORN TO WEAR THIS HELMET!
I AM THE MAN WHO WAS BORN TO WEAR THIS HELMET.
AANG! I NEED YOUR HELP WITH SOMETHING VERY IMPORTANT!
OH, EXCUSE ME.

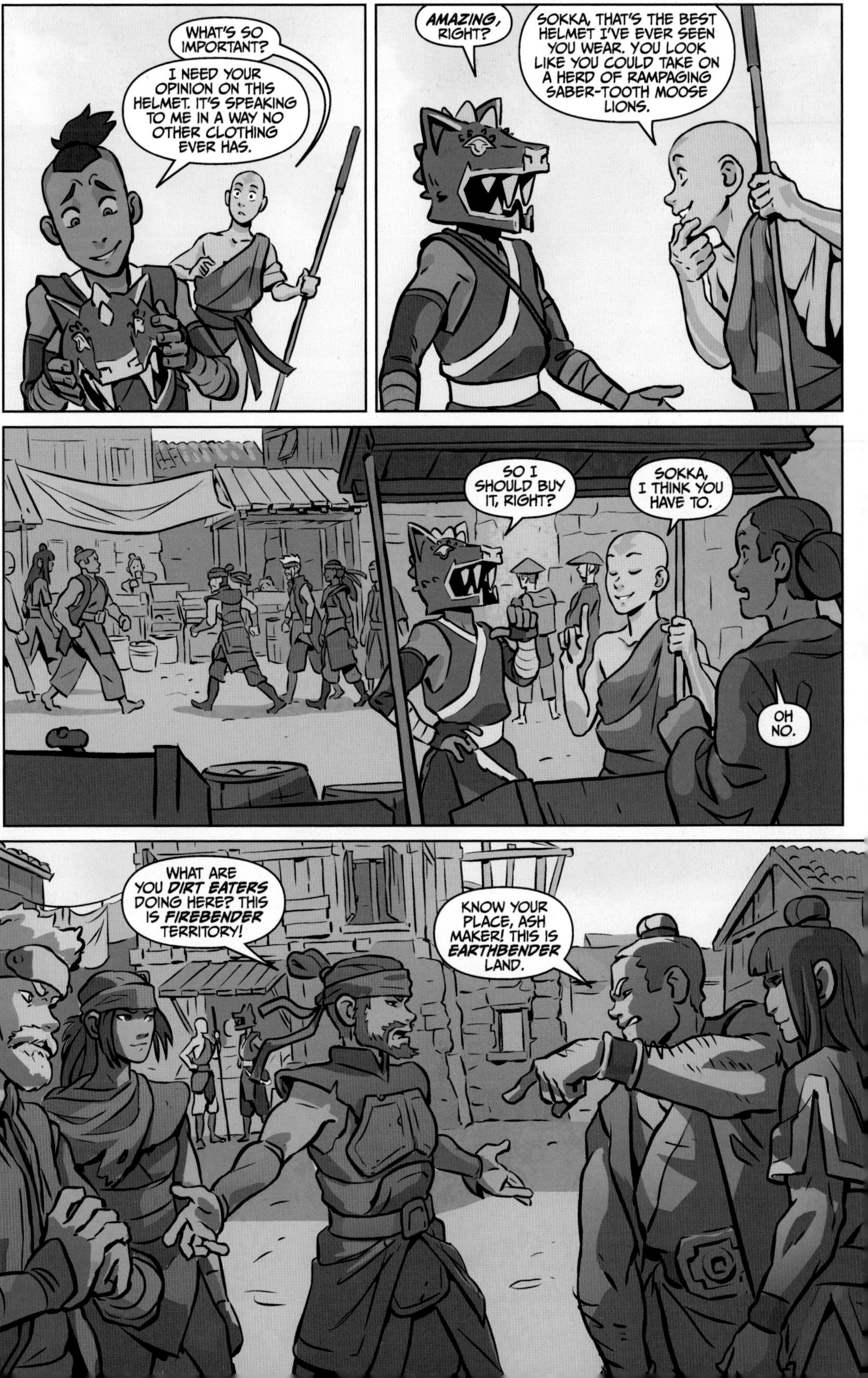
WHAT'S SO IMPORTANT?
I NEED YOUR OPINION ON THIS HELMET. IT'S SPEAKING TO ME IN A WAY NO OTHER CLOTHING EVER HAS.
AMAZING, RIGHT?
SOKKA, THAT'S THE BEST HELMET I'VE EVER SEEN YOU WEAR. YOU LOOK LIKE YOU COULD TAKE ON A HERD OF RAMPAGING SABER-TOOTH MOOSE LIONS.
SO I SHOULD BUY IT, RIGHT?
SOKKA, I THINK YOU HAVE TO.
OH NO.
WHAT ARE YOU DIRT EATERS DOING HERE? THIS IS FIREBENDER TERRITORY!
KNOW YOUR PLACE, ASH MAKER! THIS IS EARTHBENDER LAND.

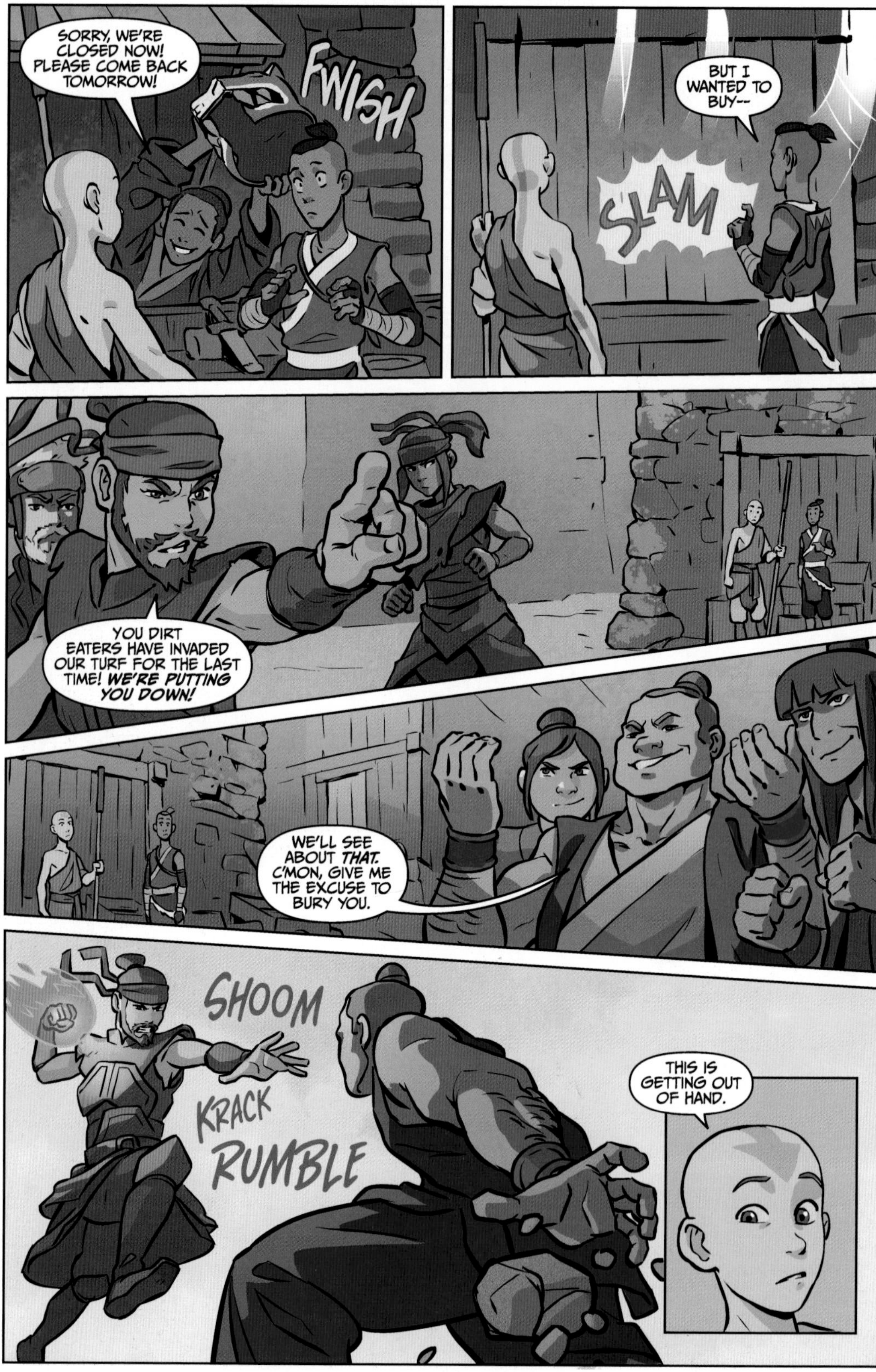
SORRY, WE'RE CLOSED NOW! PLEASE COME BACK TOMORROW!
FWISH
BUT I WANTED TO BUY--
SLAM
YOU DIRT EATERS HAVE INVADED OUR TURF FOR THE LAST TIME! *WE'RE PUTTING YOU DOWN!*
WE'LL SEE ABOUT *THAT.* C'MON, GIVE ME THE EXCUSE TO BURY YOU.
SHOOM
KRACK
RUMBLE
THIS IS GETTING OUT OF HAND.

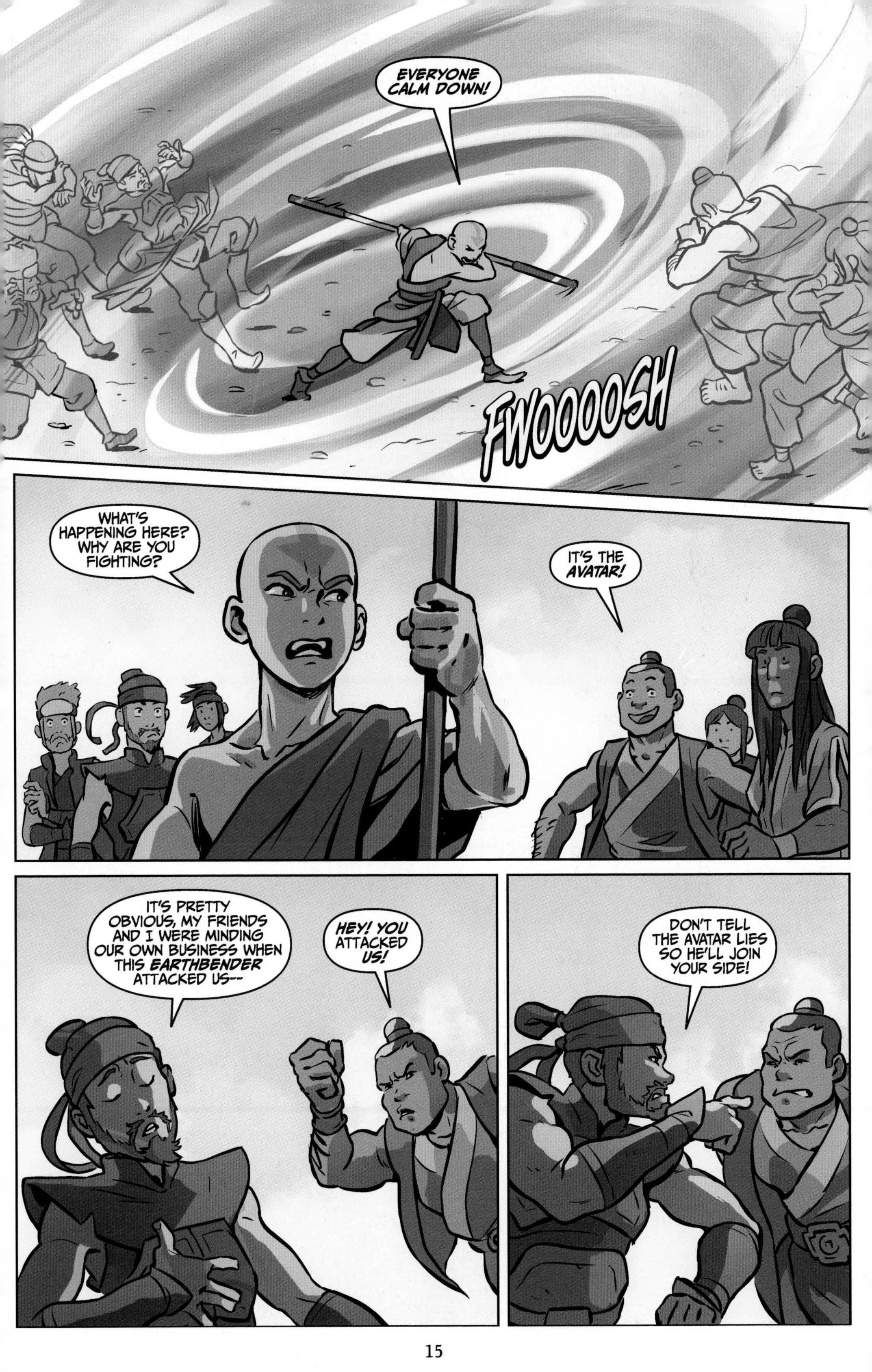
EVERYONE CALM DOWN!
FWOOOOSH
WHAT'S HAPPENING HERE? WHY ARE YOU FIGHTING?
IT'S THE AVATAR!
IT'S PRETTY OBVIOUS, MY FRIENDS AND I WERE MINDING OUR OWN BUSINESS WHEN THIS EARTHBENDER ATTACKED US--
HEY! YOU ATTACKED US!
DON'T TELL THE AVATAR LIES SO HE'LL JOIN YOUR SIDE!

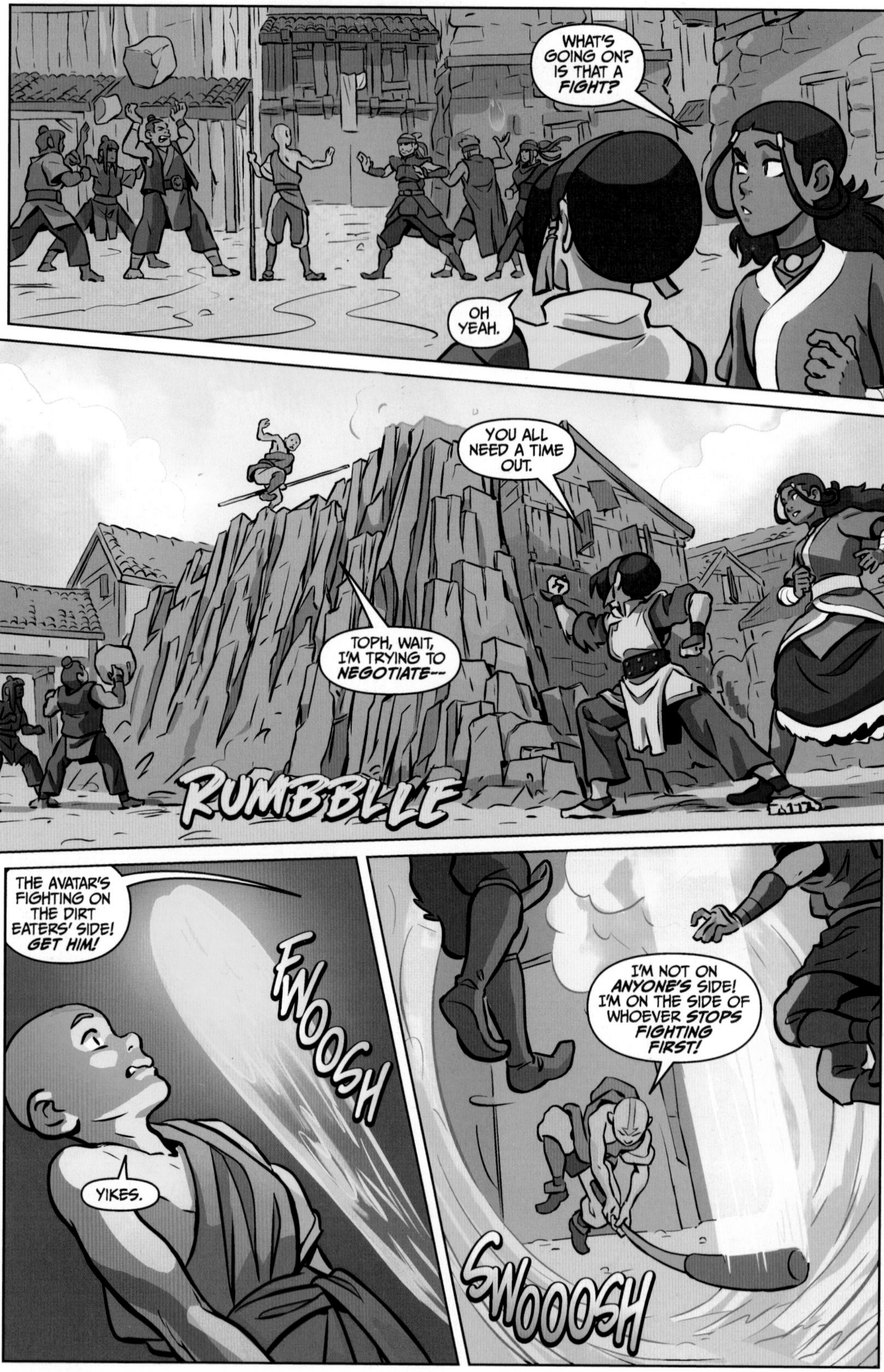
WHAT'S GOING ON? IS THAT A FIGHT?
OH YEAH.
YOU ALL NEED A TIME OUT.
TOPH, WAIT, I'M TRYING TO NEGOTIATE--
RUMBBLLE
THE AVATAR'S FIGHTING ON THE DIRT EATERS' SIDE! GET HIM!
FWOOSH
YIKES.
I'M NOT ON ANYONE'S SIDE! I'M ON THE SIDE OF WHOEVER STOPS FIGHTING FIRST!
SNOOOSH

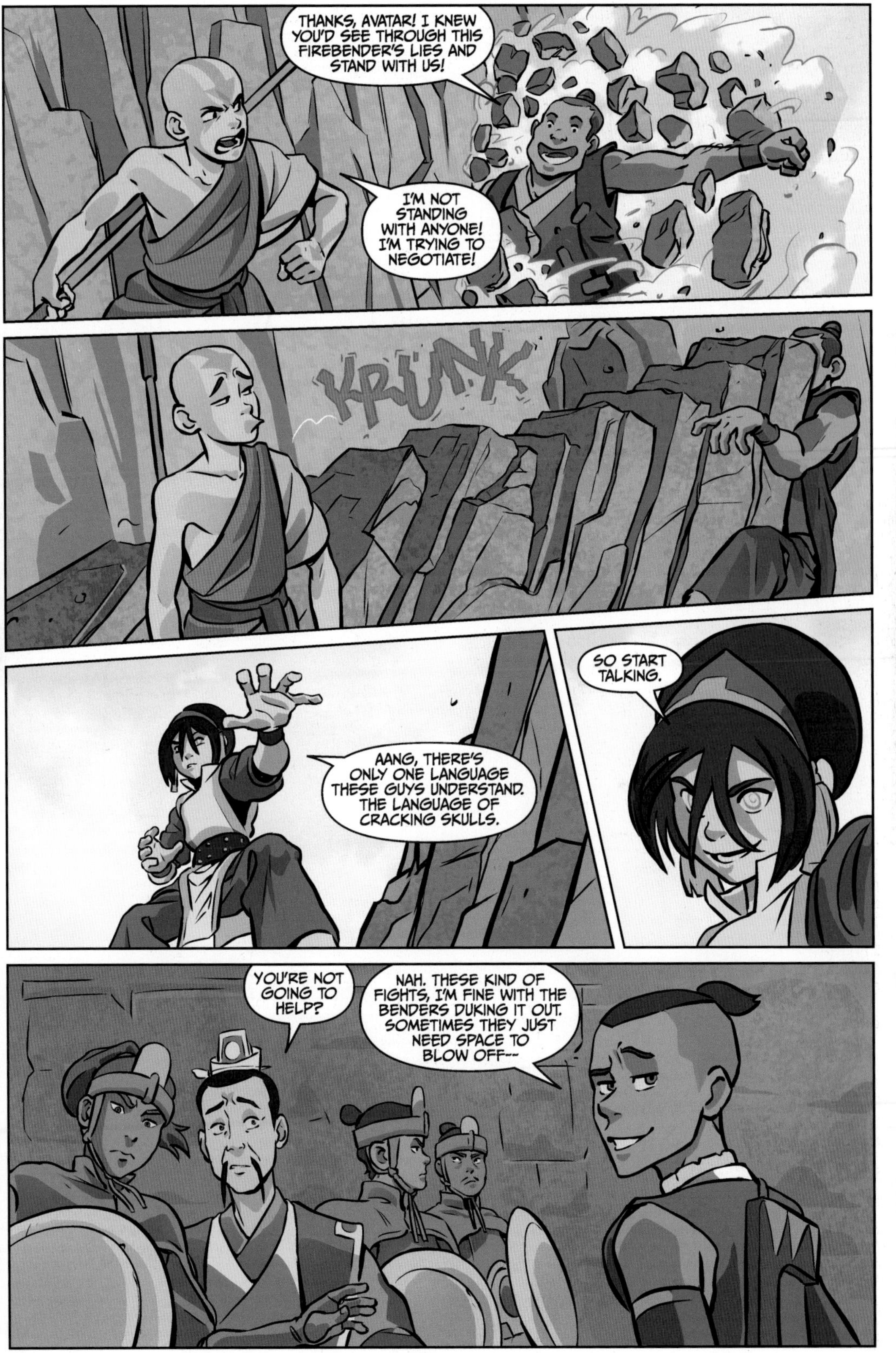
THANKS, AVATAR! I KNEW YOU'D SEE THROUGH THIS FIREBENDER'S LIES AND STAND WITH US!
I'M NOT STANDING WITH ANYONE! I'M TRYING TO NEGOTIATE!
KRUNK
AANG, THERE'S ONLY ONE LANGUAGE THESE GUYS UNDERSTAND. THE LANGUAGE OF CRACKING SKULLS.
SO START TALKING.
YOU'RE NOT GOING TO HELP?
NAH. THESE KIND OF FIGHTS, I'M FINE WITH THE BENDERS DUKING IT OUT. SOMETIMES THEY JUST NEED SPACE TO BLOW OFF--

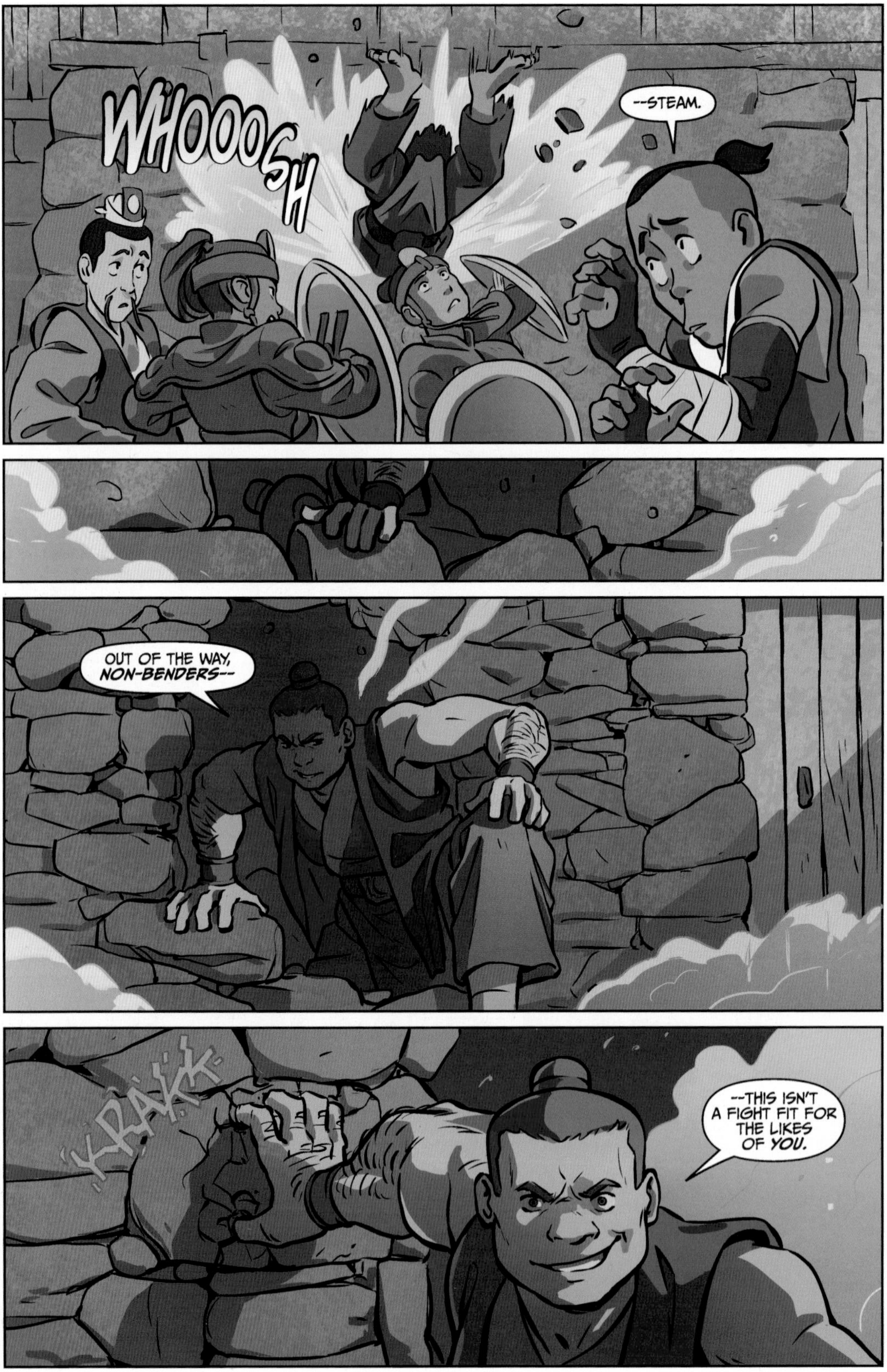
WHOOOOSH
--STEAM.
OUT OF THE WAY, NON-BENDERS--
KRAKK
--THIS ISN'T A FIGHT FIT FOR THE LIKES OF YOU.

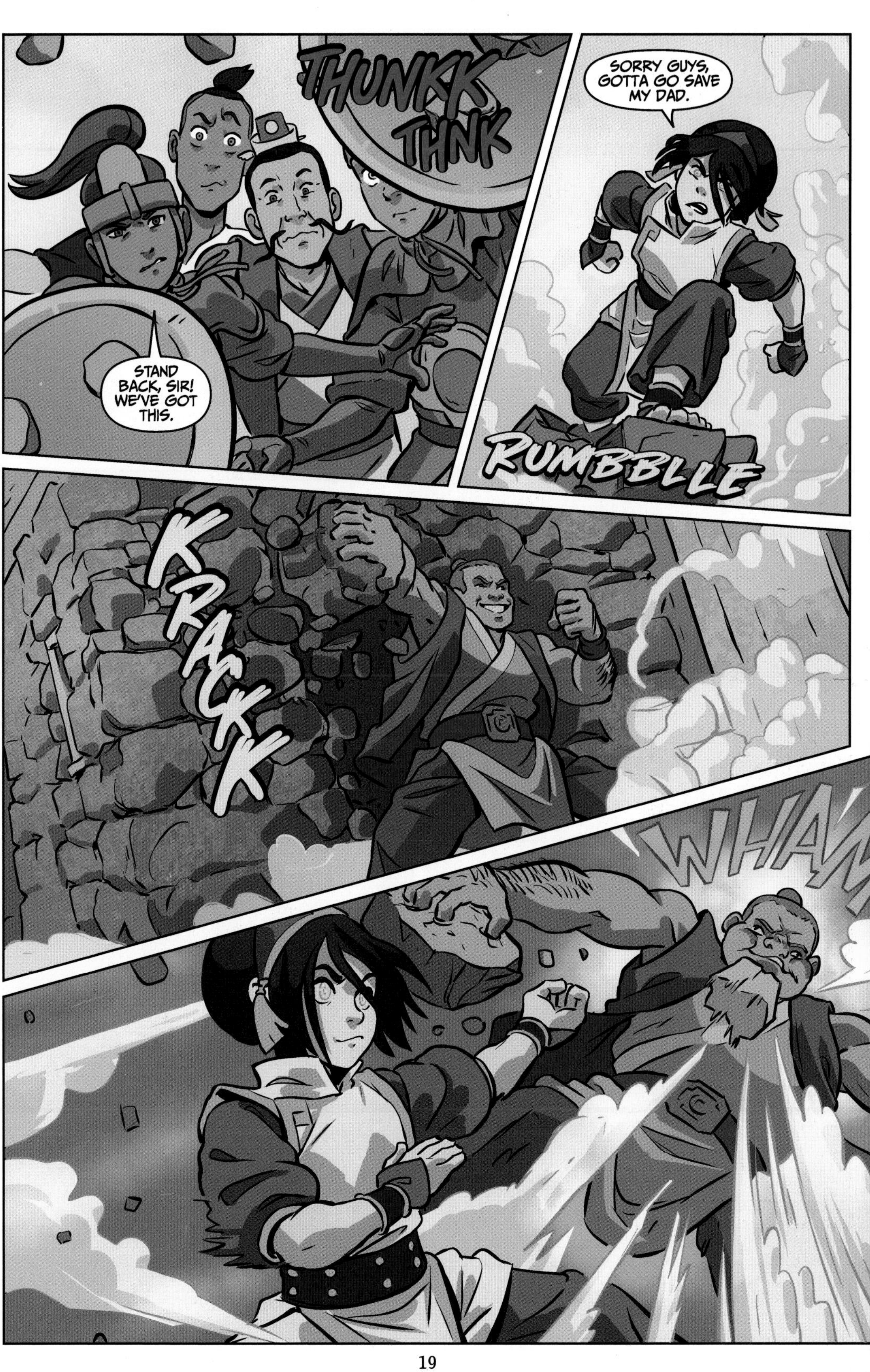
THUNKK
THNK
STAND BACK, SIR! WE'VE GOT THIS.
SORRY GUYS, GOTTA GO SAVE MY DAD.
RUMBBLLE
KRACKK
WHAM

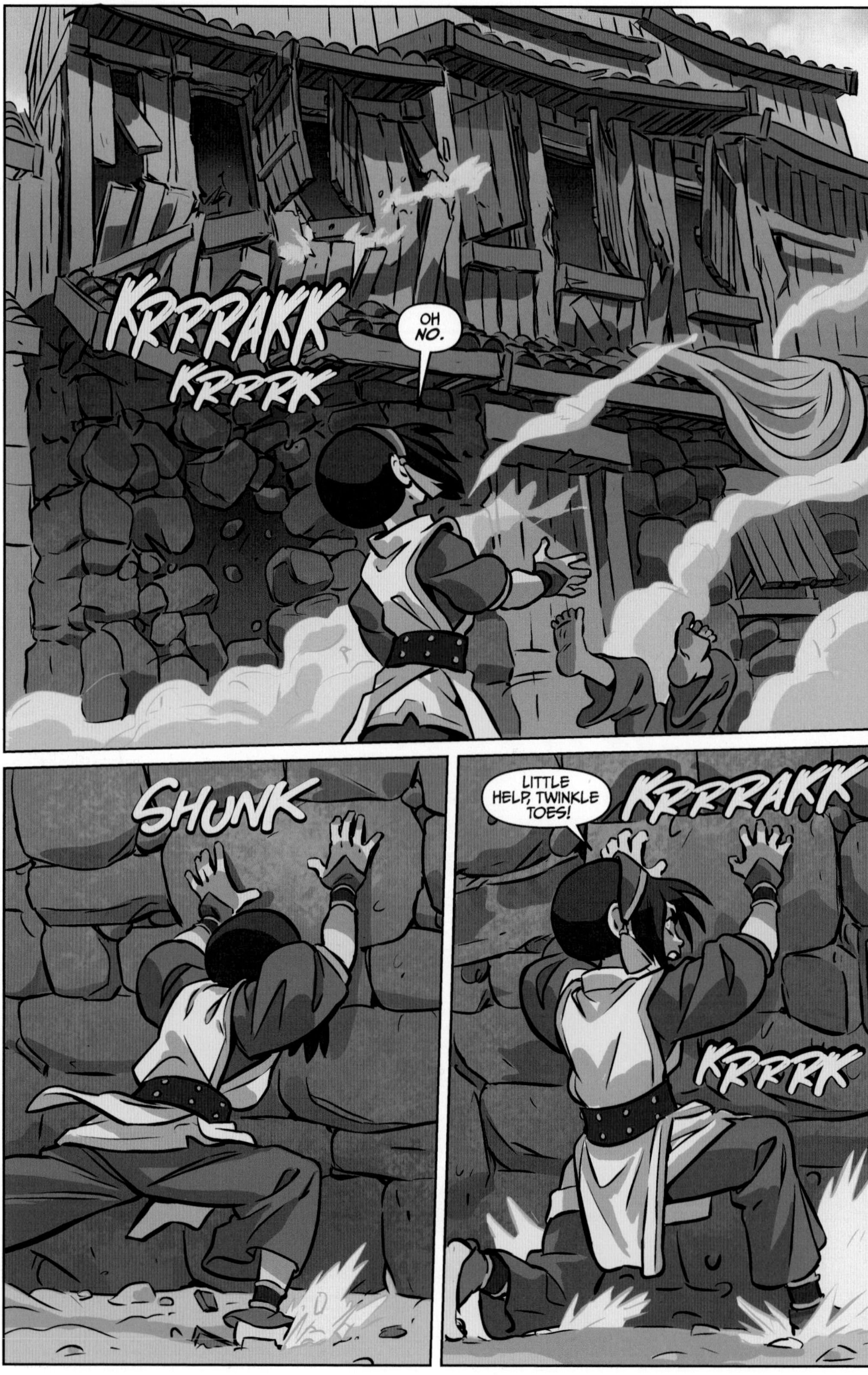
KRRRAKK
KRRRK
OH NO.
SHUNK
LITTLE HELP, TWINKLE TOES!
KRRRAKK
KRRRK

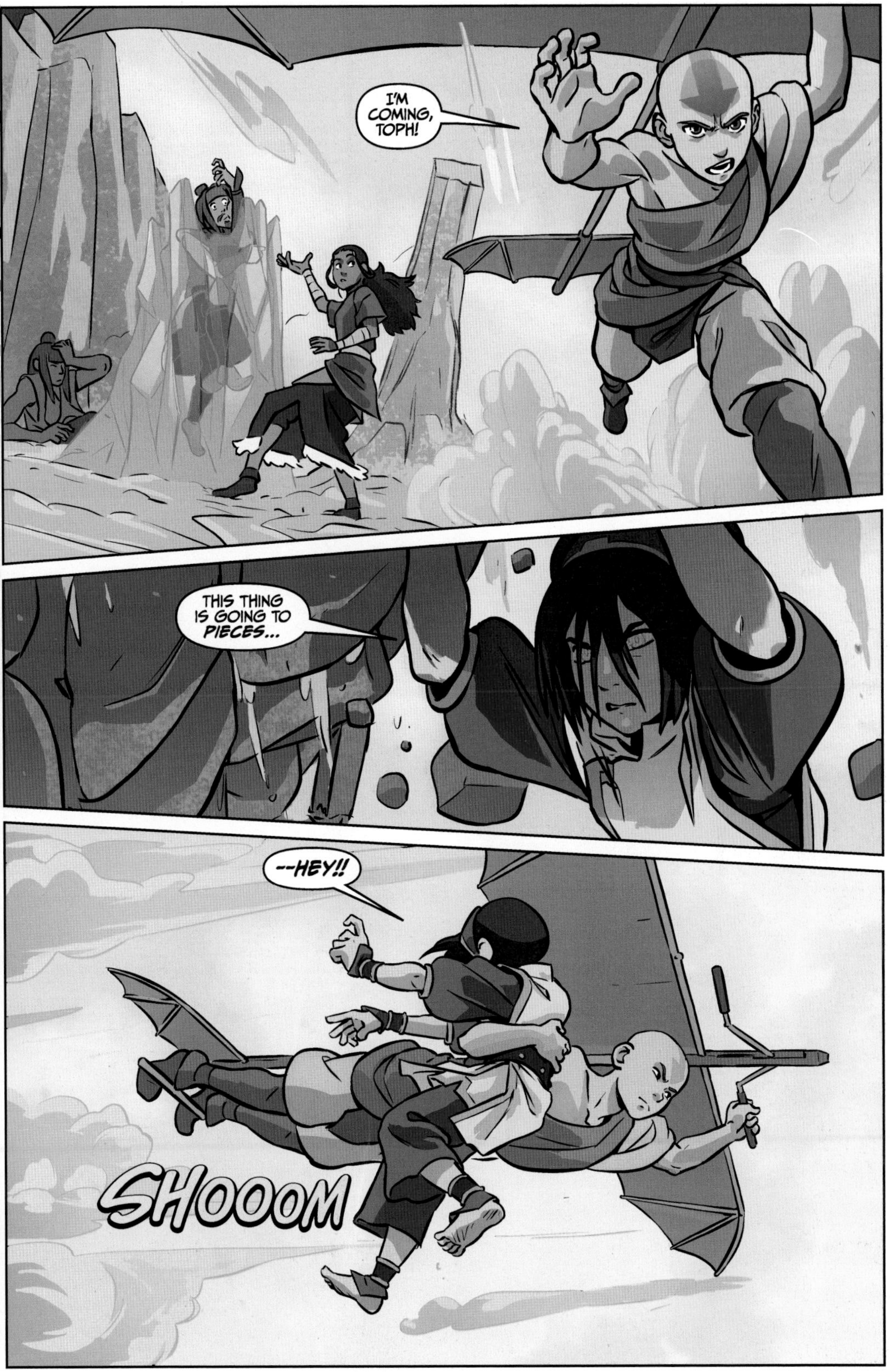
I'M COMING, TOPH!
THIS THING IS GOING TO PIECES...
--HEY!!
SHOOOM

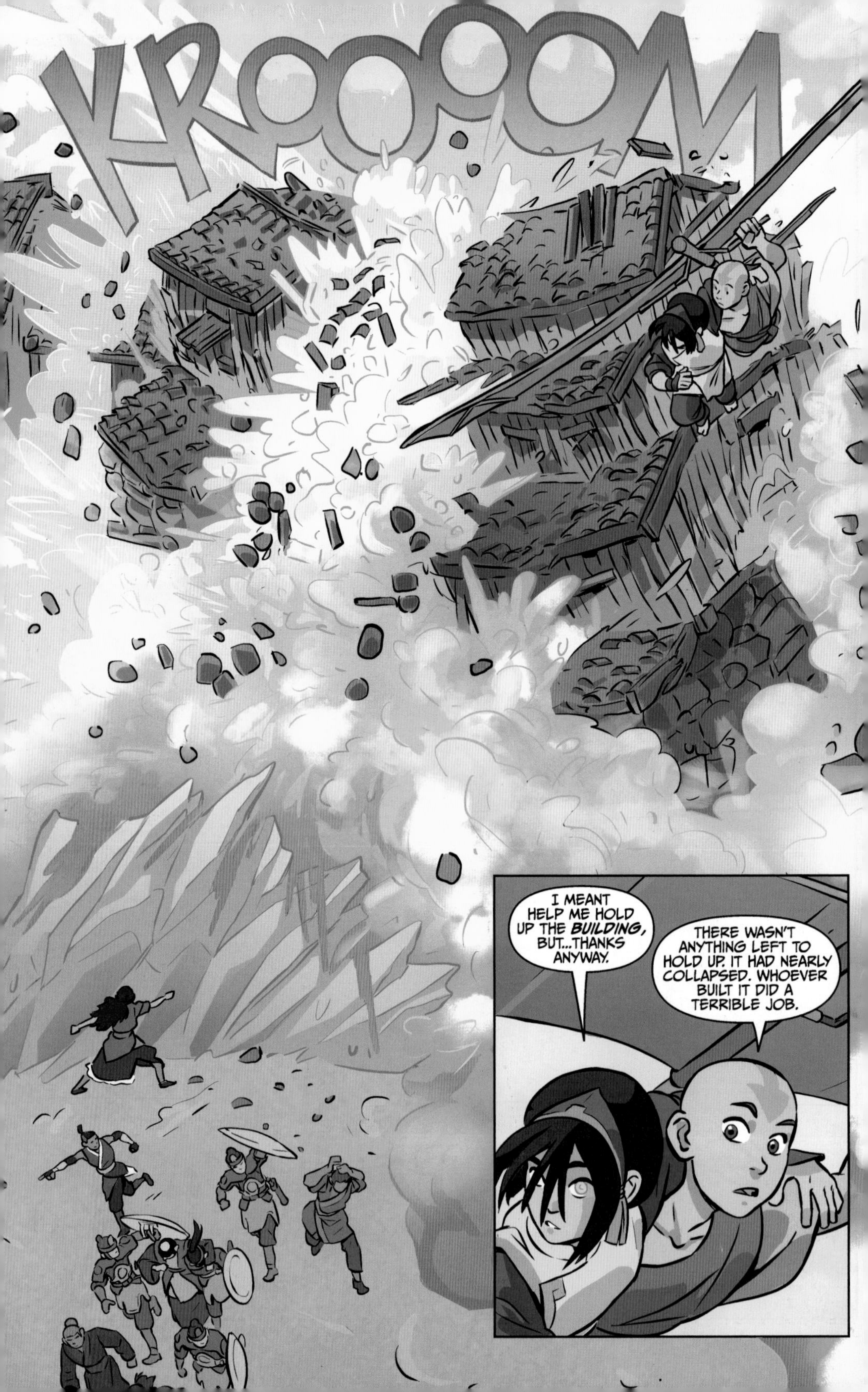
KROOOOM
I MEANT HELP ME HOLD UP THE *BUILDING*, BUT...THANKS ANYWAY.
THERE WASN'T ANYTHING LEFT TO HOLD UP. IT HAD NEARLY COLLAPSED. WHOEVER BUILT IT DID A TERRIBLE JOB.

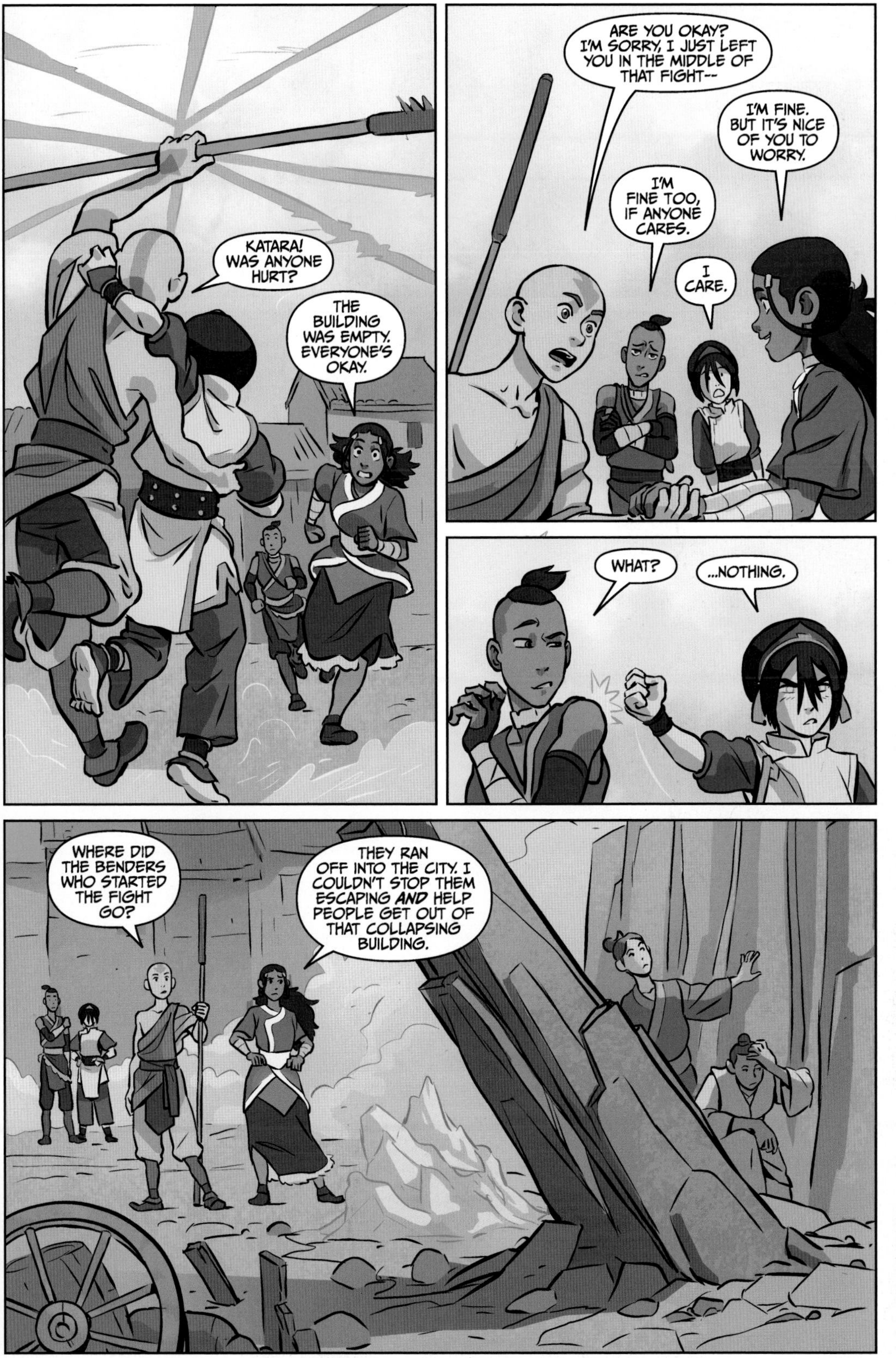
KATARA! WAS ANYONE HURT?
THE BUILDING WAS EMPTY. EVERYONE'S OKAY.
ARE YOU OKAY? I'M SORRY, I JUST LEFT YOU IN THE MIDDLE OF THAT FIGHT--
I'M FINE. BUT IT'S NICE OF YOU TO WORRY.
I'M FINE TOO, IF ANYONE CARES.
I CARE.
WHAT?
...NOTHING.
WHERE DID THE BENDERS WHO STARTED THE FIGHT GO?
THEY RAN OFF INTO THE CITY. I COULDN'T STOP THEM ESCAPING AND HELP PEOPLE GET OUT OF THAT COLLAPSING BUILDING.

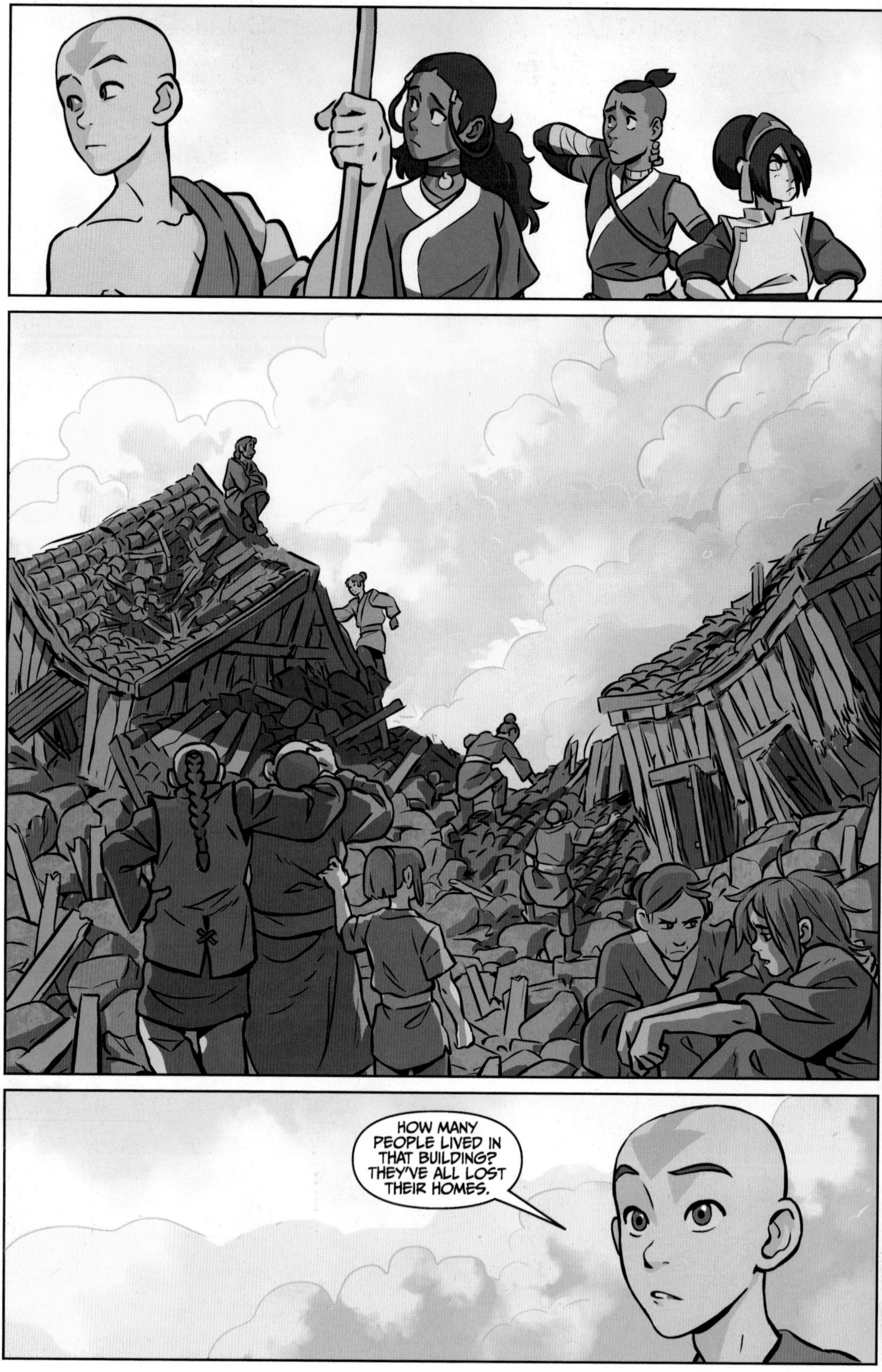
HOW MANY PEOPLE LIVED IN THAT BUILDING? THEY'VE ALL LOST THEIR HOMES.

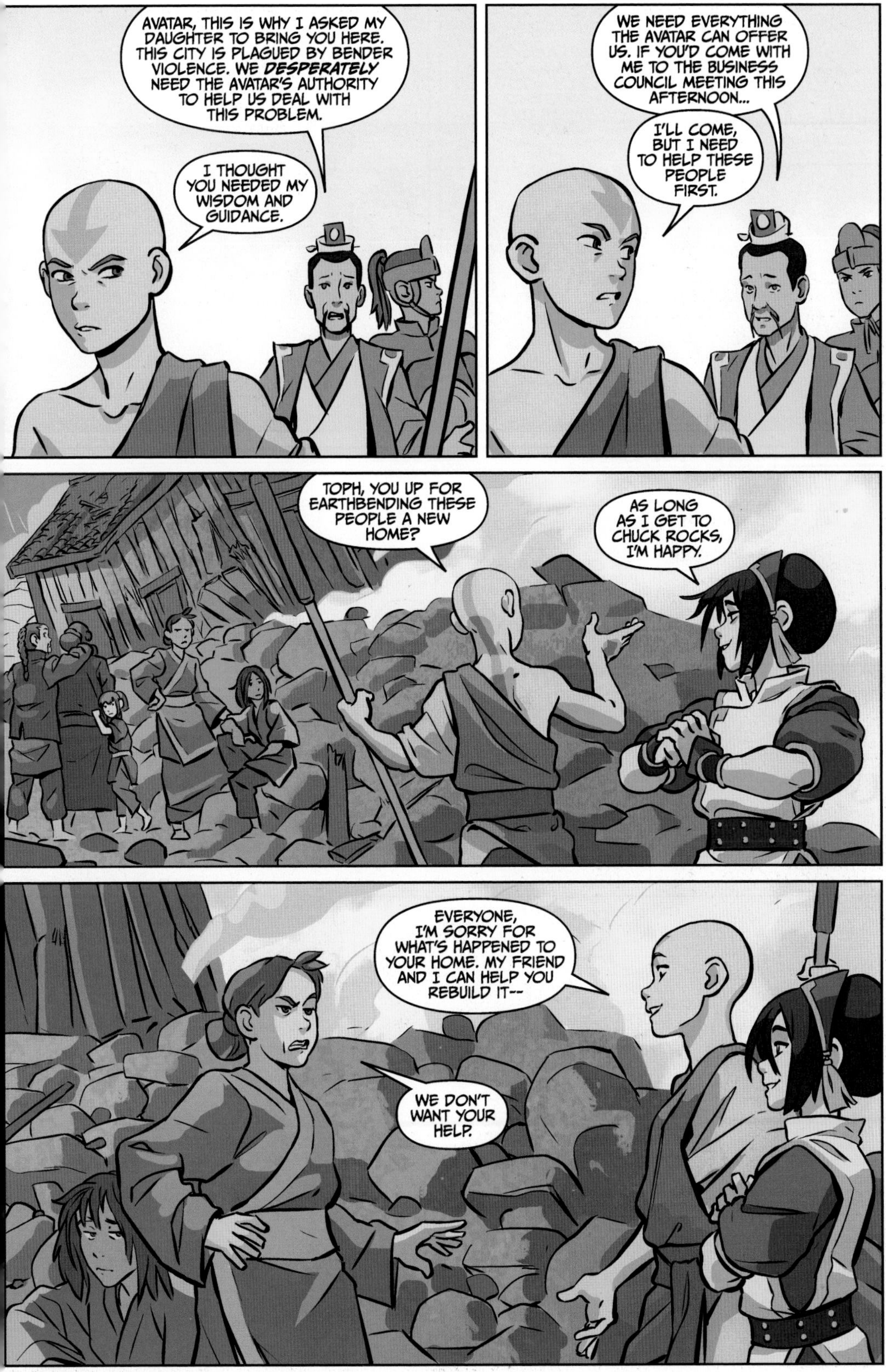
AVATAR, THIS IS WHY I ASKED MY DAUGHTER TO BRING YOU HERE. THIS CITY IS PLAGUED BY BENDER VIOLENCE. WE *DESPERATELY* NEED THE AVATAR'S AUTHORITY TO HELP US DEAL WITH THIS PROBLEM.
I THOUGHT YOU NEEDED MY WISDOM AND GUIDANCE.
WE NEED EVERYTHING THE AVATAR CAN OFFER US. IF YOU'D COME WITH ME TO THE BUSINESS COUNCIL MEETING THIS AFTERNOON...
I'LL COME, BUT I NEED TO HELP THESE PEOPLE FIRST.
TOPH, YOU UP FOR EARTHBENDING THESE PEOPLE A NEW HOME?
AS LONG AS I GET TO CHUCK ROCKS, I'M HAPPY.
EVERYONE, I'M SORRY FOR WHAT'S HAPPENED TO YOUR HOME. MY FRIEND AND I CAN HELP YOU REBUILD IT--
WE DON'T WANT YOUR HELP.

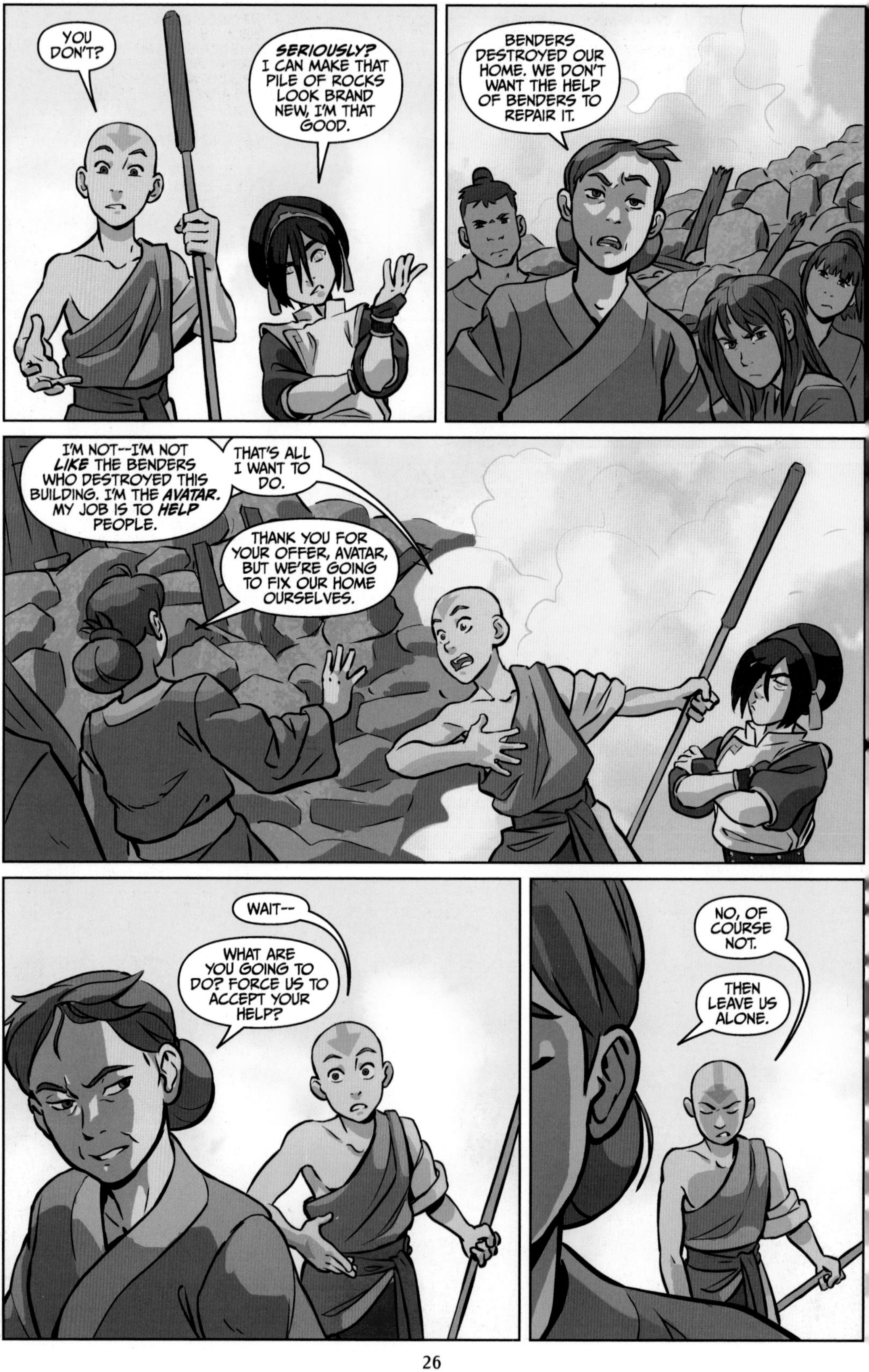
YOU DON'T?
SERIOUSLY? I CAN MAKE THAT PILE OF ROCKS LOOK BRAND NEW, I'M THAT GOOD.
BENDERS DESTROYED OUR HOME. WE DON'T WANT THE HELP OF BENDERS TO REPAIR IT.
I'M NOT--I'M NOT LIKE THE BENDERS WHO DESTROYED THIS BUILDING. I'M THE AVATAR. MY JOB IS TO HELP PEOPLE.
THAT'S ALL I WANT TO DO.
THANK YOU FOR YOUR OFFER, AVATAR, BUT WE'RE GOING TO FIX OUR HOME OURSELVES.
WAIT--
WHAT ARE YOU GOING TO DO? FORCE US TO ACCEPT YOUR HELP?
NO, OF COURSE NOT.
THEN LEAVE US ALONE.

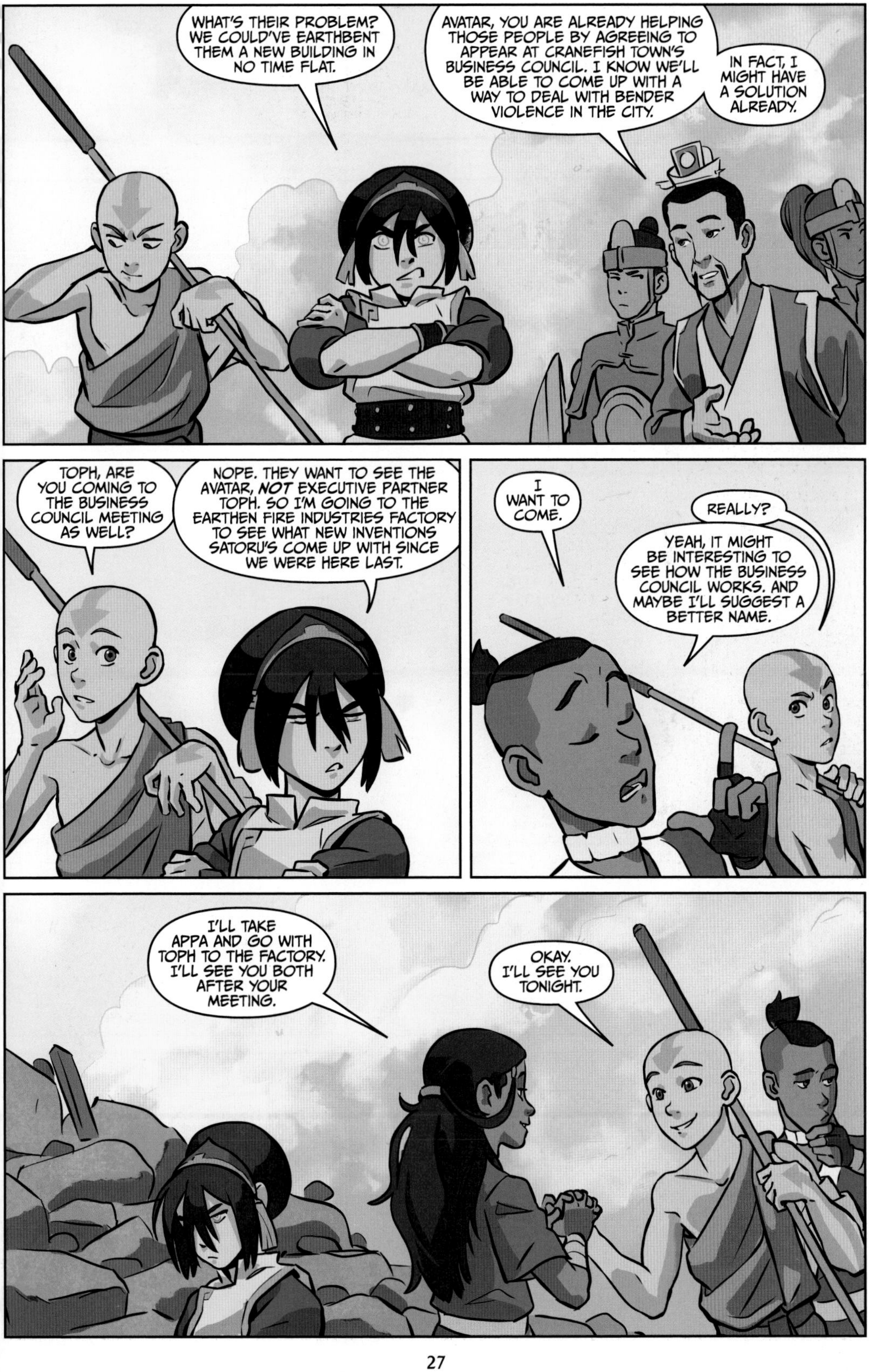

WHAT'S THEIR PROBLEM? WE COULD'VE EARTHBENT THEM A NEW BUILDING IN NO TIME FLAT.
AVATAR, YOU ARE ALREADY HELPING THOSE PEOPLE BY AGREEING TO APPEAR AT CRANEFISH TOWN'S BUSINESS COUNCIL. I KNOW WE'LL BE ABLE TO COME UP WITH A WAY TO DEAL WITH BENDER VIOLENCE IN THE CITY.
IN FACT, I MIGHT HAVE A SOLUTION ALREADY.
TOPH, ARE YOU COMING TO THE BUSINESS COUNCIL MEETING AS WELL?
NOPE. THEY WANT TO SEE THE AVATAR, *NOT* EXECUTIVE PARTNER TOPH. SO I'M GOING TO THE EARTHEN FIRE INDUSTRIES FACTORY TO SEE WHAT NEW INVENTIONS SATORU'S COME UP WITH SINCE WE WERE HERE LAST.
I WANT TO COME.
REALLY?
YEAH, IT MIGHT BE INTERESTING TO SEE HOW THE BUSINESS COUNCIL WORKS. AND MAYBE I'LL SUGGEST A BETTER NAME.
I'LL TAKE APPA AND GO WITH TOPH TO THE FACTORY. I'LL SEE YOU BOTH AFTER YOUR MEETING.
OKAY. I'LL SEE YOU TONIGHT.

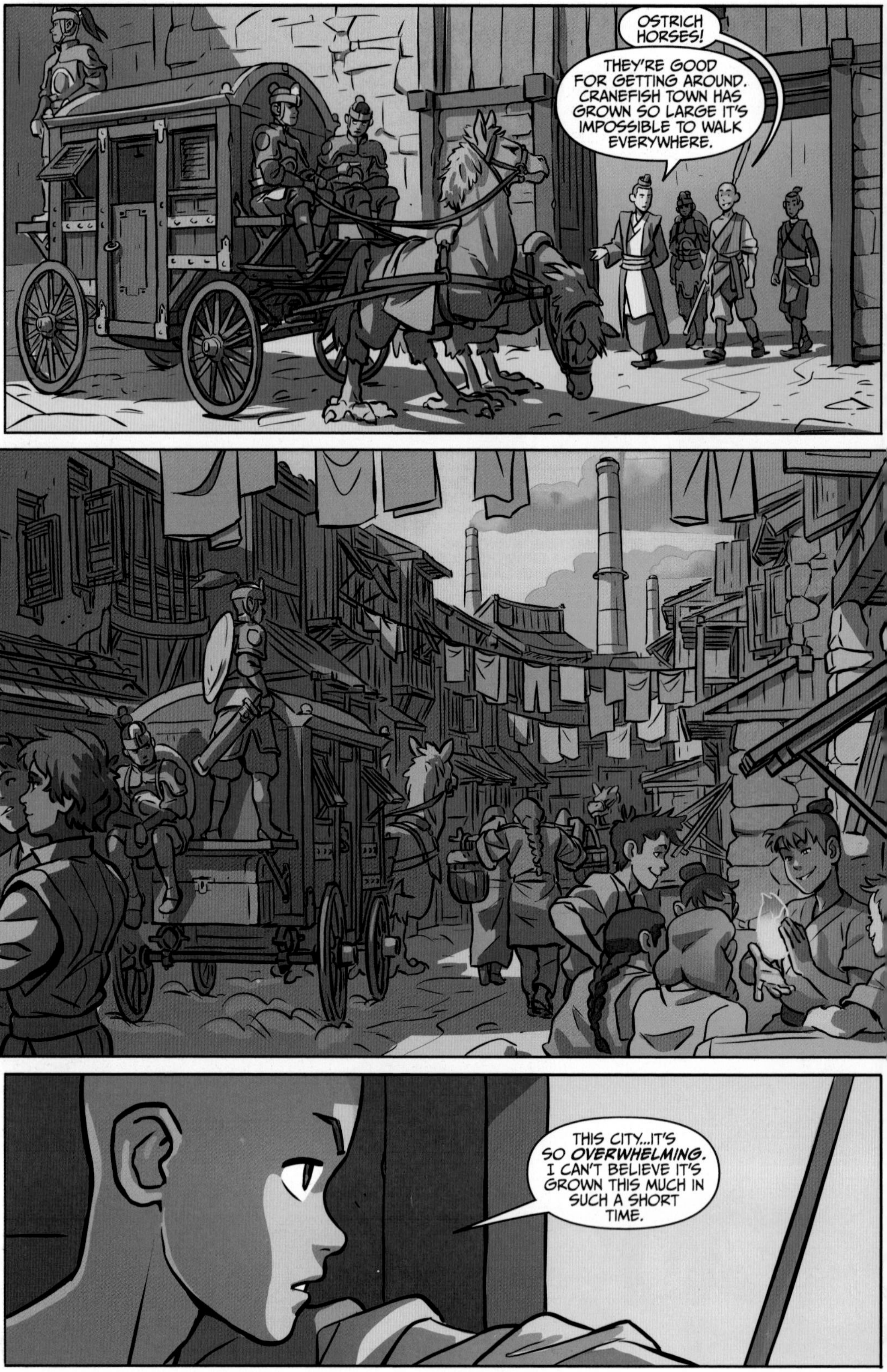
OSTRICH HORSES!
THEY'RE GOOD FOR GETTING AROUND. CRANEFISH TOWN HAS GROWN SO LARGE IT'S IMPOSSIBLE TO WALK EVERYWHERE.
THIS CITY...IT'S SO ***OVERWHELMING.*** I CAN'T BELIEVE IT'S GROWN THIS MUCH IN SUCH A SHORT TIME.

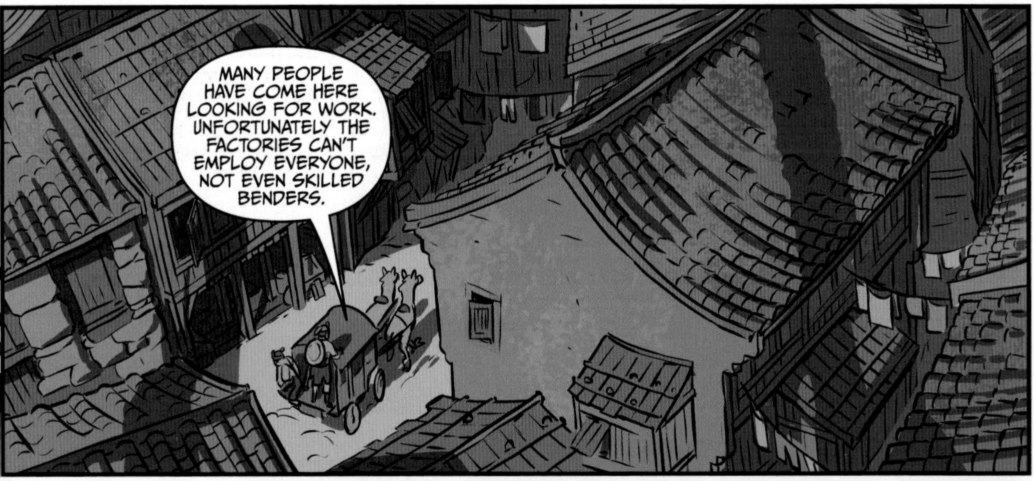
MANY PEOPLE HAVE COME HERE LOOKING FOR WORK. UNFORTUNATELY THE FACTORIES CAN'T EMPLOY EVERYONE, NOT EVEN SKILLED BENDERS.

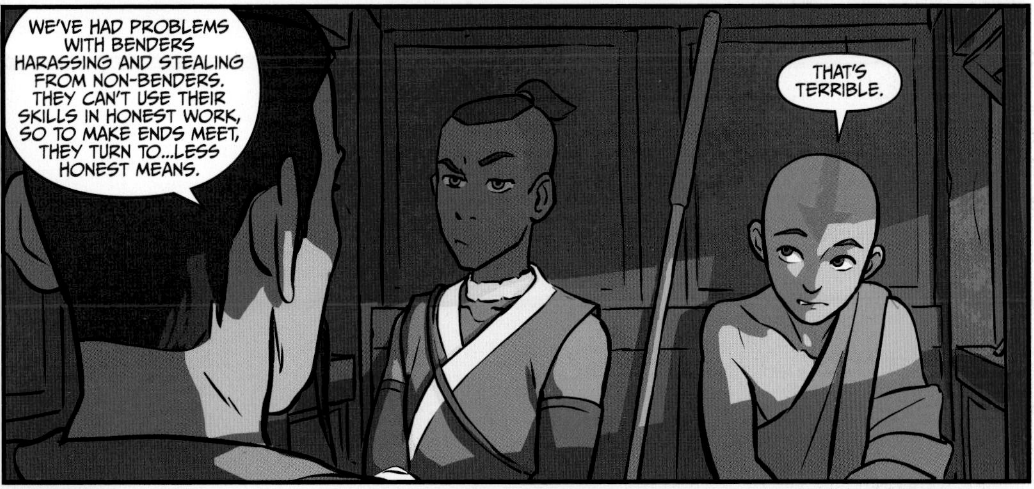
WE'VE HAD PROBLEMS WITH BENDERS HARASSING AND STEALING FROM NON-BENDERS. THEY CAN'T USE THEIR SKILLS IN HONEST WORK, SO TO MAKE ENDS MEET, THEY TURN TO...LESS HONEST MEANS.
THAT'S TERRIBLE.

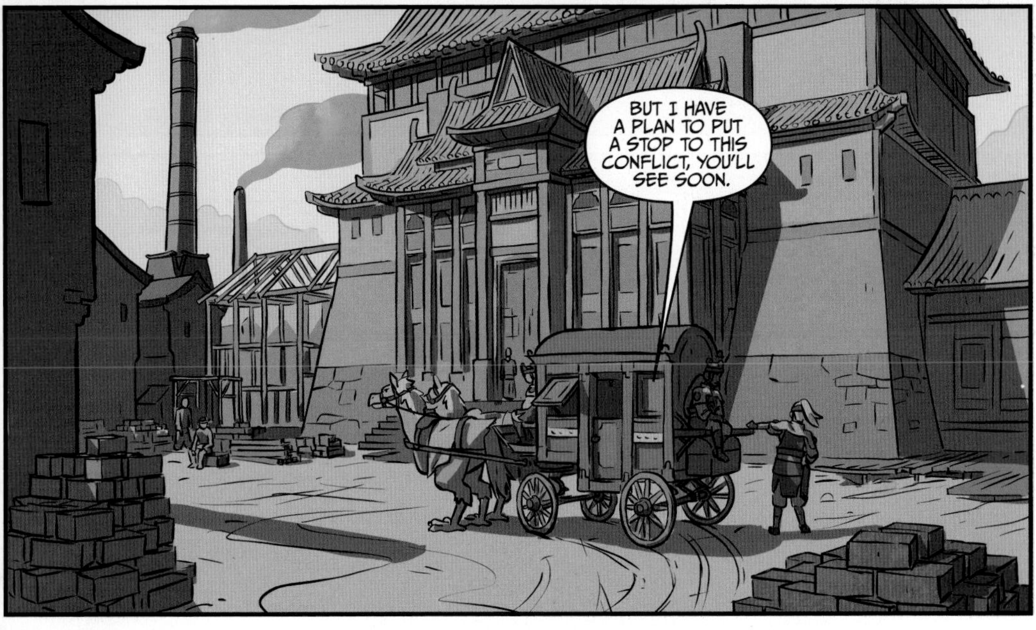
BUT I HAVE A PLAN TO PUT A STOP TO THIS CONFLICT, YOU'LL SEE SOON.

GOOD AFTERNOON, FELLOW COUNCIL MEMBERS.

WE THOUGHT YOU MIGHT NOT BE COMING. BETTER LATE THAN NEVER.

LAO, GOOD OF YOU TO JOIN US.

COUNCILMAN LAO HAS ATTENDED EVERY BUSINESS COUNCIL MEETING. THERE WAS NO REASON TO THINK HE WOULDN'T BE HERE TODAY.

YOU WERE JUST LOOKING FOR A REASON TO START WITHOUT HIM.

I WAS DELAYED, BUT I HAVE SOME GOOD NEWS.

AANG, YOU NOTICE SOMETHING ABOUT THE PEOPLE ON THIS BUSINESS COUNCIL?

NOTICE WHAT?

LOOK AT THEM.

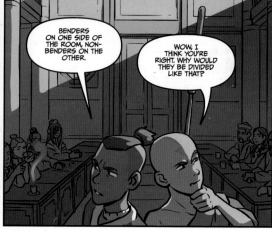

BENDERS ON ONE SIDE OF THE ROOM, NON-BENDERS ON THE OTHER.

WOW, I THINK YOU'RE RIGHT. WHY WOULD THEY BE DIVIDED LIKE THAT?

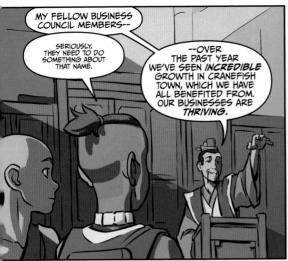

MY FELLOW BUSINESS COUNCIL MEMBERS--

SERIOUSLY, THEY NEED TO DO SOMETHING ABOUT THAT NAME.

--OVER THE PAST YEAR WE'VE SEEN *INCREDIBLE* GROWTH IN CRANEFISH TOWN, WHICH WE HAVE ALL BENEFITED FROM. OUR BUSINESSES ARE *THRIVING*.

HOWEVER, OUR CITY'S GROWTH HAS ALSO BROUGHT... *CHALLENGES.*

OUR HOME IS PLAGUED BY VIOLENCE, ESPECIALLY *BENDER* VIOLENCE. OUR FACTORY EMPLOYEES ARE AFRAID TO WALK TO WORK FOR FEAR OF BEING ATTACKED.

I WANT TO PROPOSE SOMETHING. *WE* ARE CRANEFISH TOWN'S COMMUNITY LEADERS. IT'S UP TO *US* TO FIND A WAY TO DEAL WITH THE ISSUES OUR CITY IS FACING.

I PROPOSE THAT BENDING BE *BANNED* ON PUBLIC STREETS. THIS WILL HELP PREVENT THE BENDER VIOLENCE THAT IS CAUSING SO MANY PROBLEMS.

BAN *BENDING...?*

31

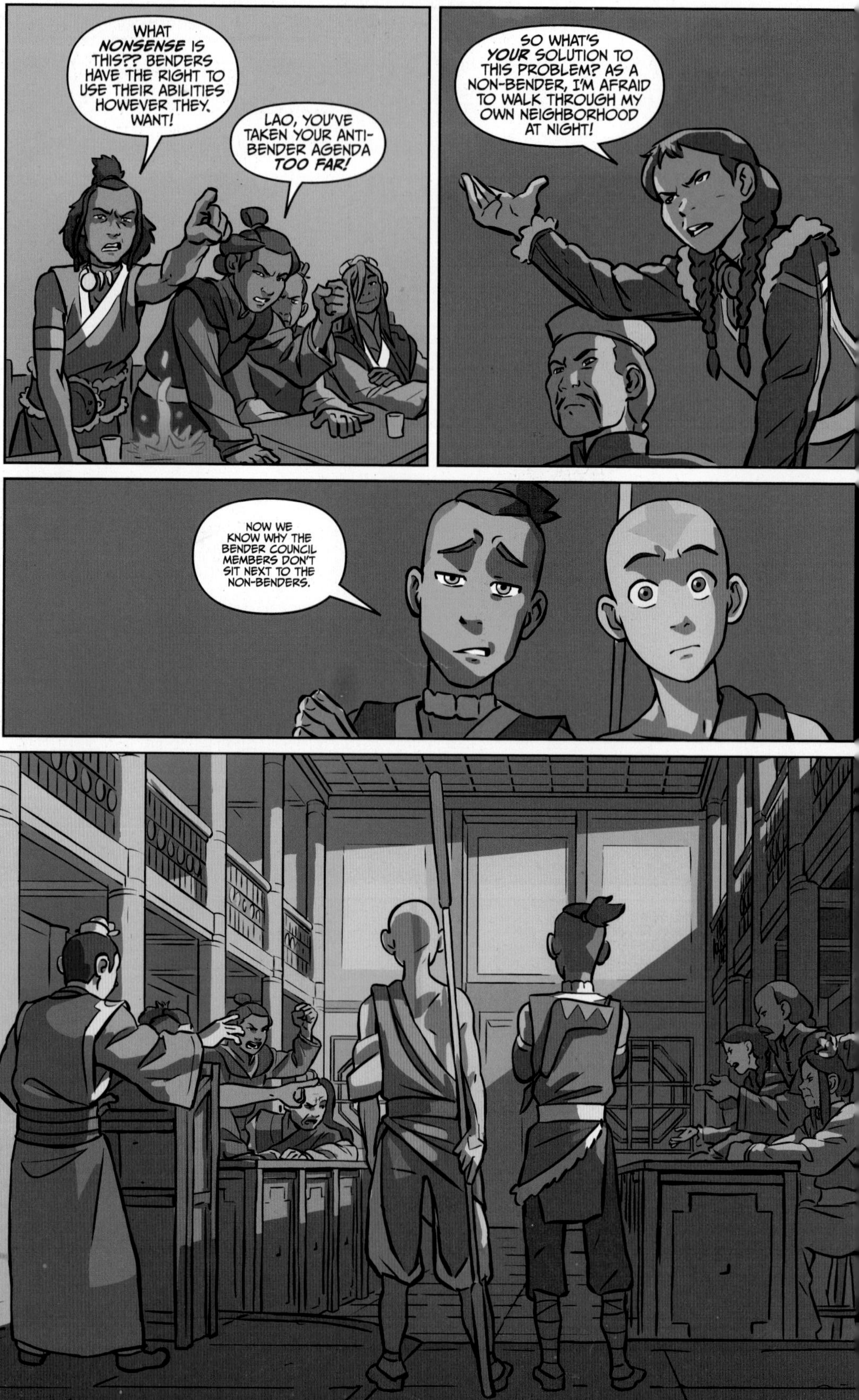
WHAT NONSENSE IS THIS?? BENDERS HAVE THE RIGHT TO USE THEIR ABILITIES HOWEVER THEY WANT!
LAO, YOU'VE TAKEN YOUR ANTI-BENDER AGENDA TOO FAR!
SO WHAT'S YOUR SOLUTION TO THIS PROBLEM? AS A NON-BENDER, I'M AFRAID TO WALK THROUGH MY OWN NEIGHBORHOOD AT NIGHT!
NOW WE KNOW WHY THE BENDER COUNCIL MEMBERS DON'T SIT NEXT TO THE NON-BENDERS.

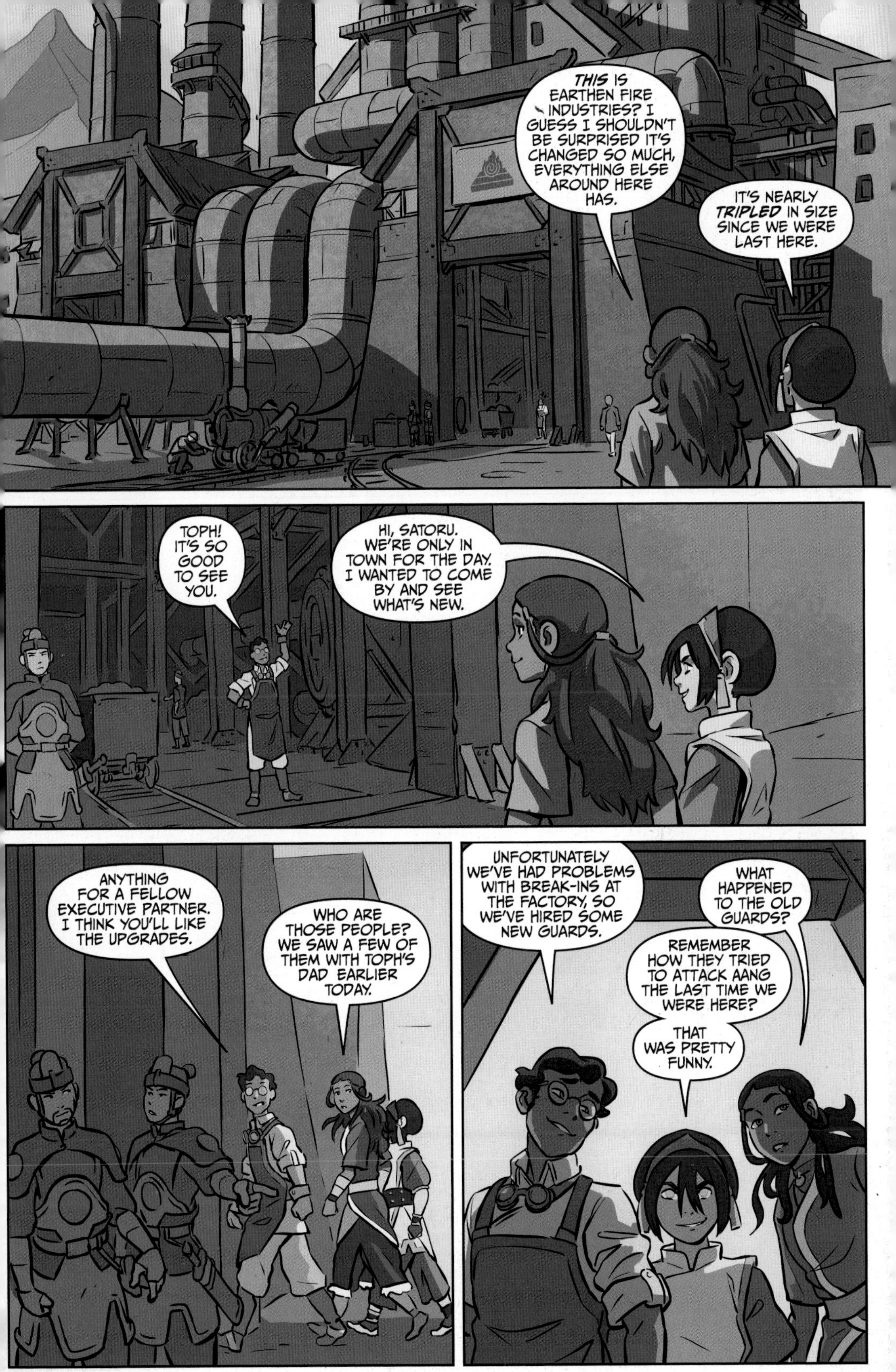
THIS IS EARTHEN FIRE INDUSTRIES? I GUESS I SHOULDN'T BE SURPRISED IT'S CHANGED SO MUCH, EVERYTHING ELSE AROUND HERE HAS.
IT'S NEARLY TRIPLED IN SIZE SINCE WE WERE LAST HERE.
TOPH! IT'S SO GOOD TO SEE YOU.
HI, SATORU. WE'RE ONLY IN TOWN FOR THE DAY. I WANTED TO COME BY AND SEE WHAT'S NEW.
ANYTHING FOR A FELLOW EXECUTIVE PARTNER. I THINK YOU'LL LIKE THE UPGRADES.
WHO ARE THOSE PEOPLE? WE SAW A FEW OF THEM WITH TOPH'S DAD EARLIER TODAY.
UNFORTUNATELY WE'VE HAD PROBLEMS WITH BREAK-INS AT THE FACTORY, SO WE'VE HIRED SOME NEW GUARDS.
WHAT HAPPENED TO THE OLD GUARDS?
REMEMBER HOW THEY TRIED TO ATTACK AANG THE LAST TIME WE WERE HERE?
THAT WAS PRETTY FUNNY.

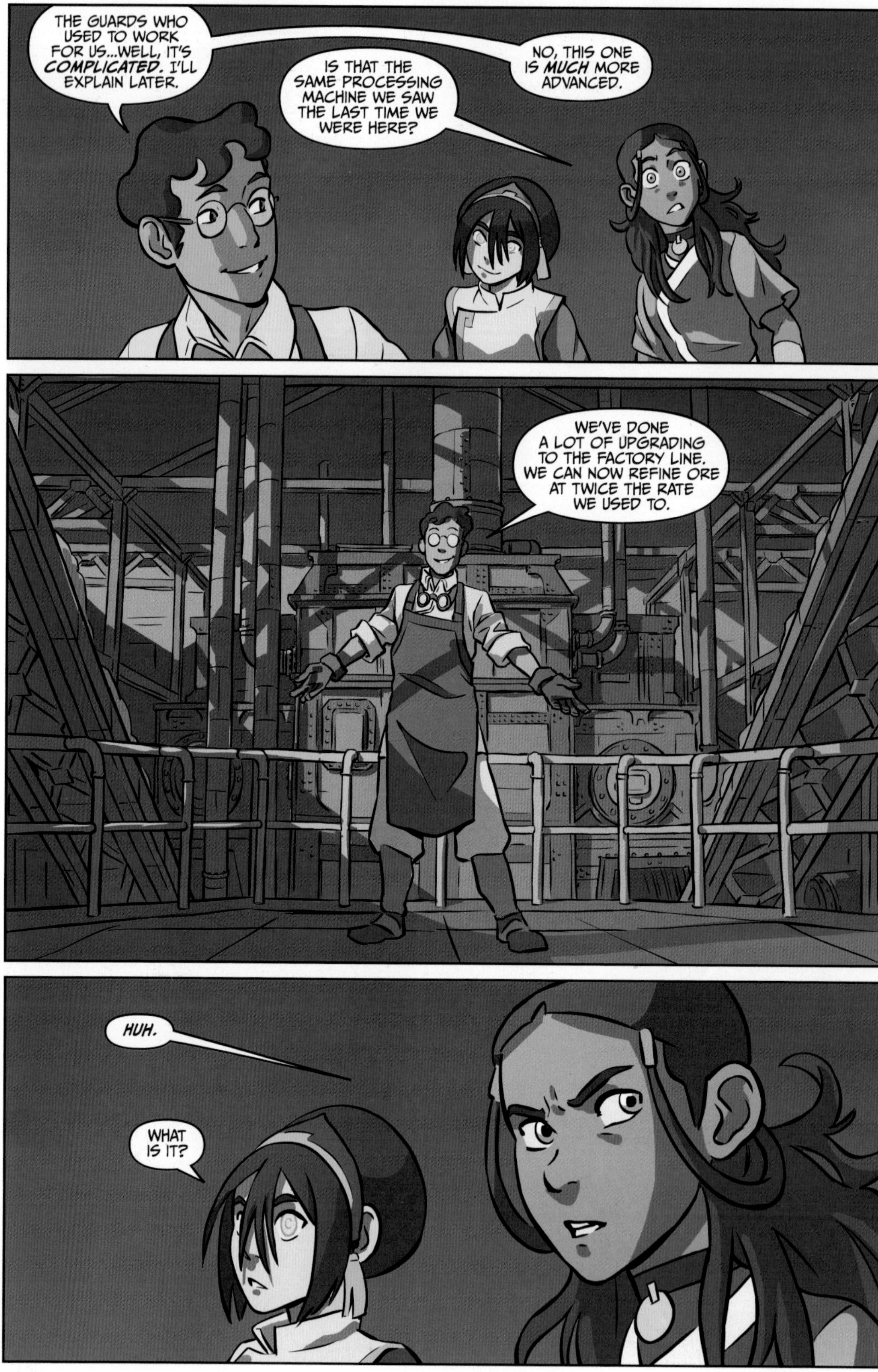
THE GUARDS WHO USED TO WORK FOR US...WELL, IT'S *COMPLICATED.* I'LL EXPLAIN LATER.
IS THAT THE SAME PROCESSING MACHINE WE SAW THE LAST TIME WE WERE HERE?
NO, THIS ONE IS *MUCH* MORE ADVANCED.
WE'VE DONE A LOT OF UPGRADING TO THE FACTORY LINE. WE CAN NOW REFINE ORE AT TWICE THE RATE WE USED TO.
HUH.
WHAT IS IT?

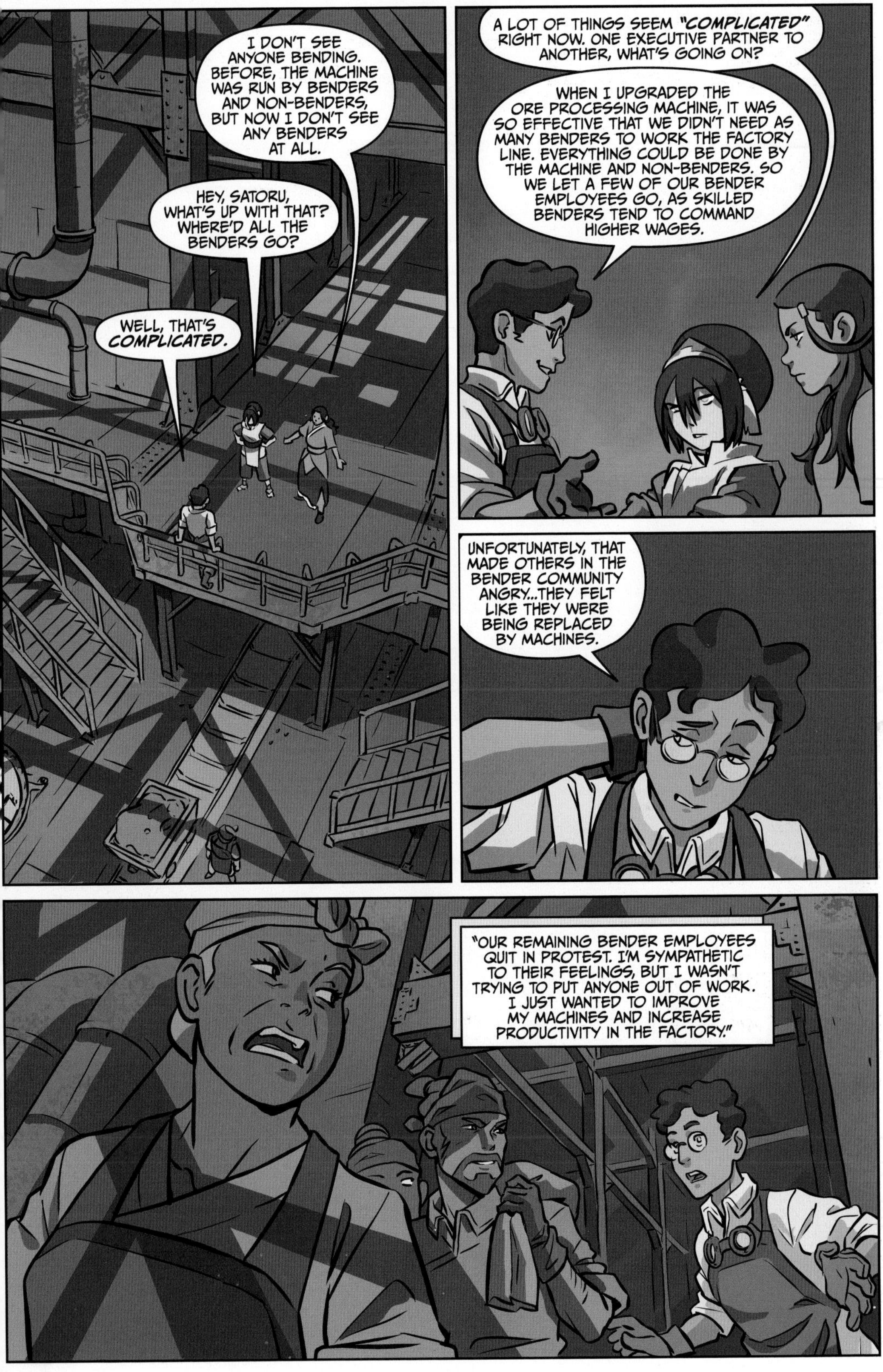
I DON'T SEE ANYONE BENDING. BEFORE, THE MACHINE WAS RUN BY BENDERS AND NON-BENDERS, BUT NOW I DON'T SEE ANY BENDERS AT ALL.
HEY, SATORU, WHAT'S UP WITH THAT? WHERE'D ALL THE BENDERS GO?
WELL, THAT'S *COMPLICATED.*
A LOT OF THINGS SEEM *"COMPLICATED"* RIGHT NOW. ONE EXECUTIVE PARTNER TO ANOTHER, WHAT'S GOING ON?
WHEN I UPGRADED THE ORE PROCESSING MACHINE, IT WAS SO EFFECTIVE THAT WE DIDN'T NEED AS MANY BENDERS TO WORK THE FACTORY LINE. EVERYTHING COULD BE DONE BY THE MACHINE AND NON-BENDERS. SO WE LET A FEW OF OUR BENDER EMPLOYEES GO, AS SKILLED BENDERS TEND TO COMMAND HIGHER WAGES.
UNFORTUNATELY, THAT MADE OTHERS IN THE BENDER COMMUNITY ANGRY...THEY FELT LIKE THEY WERE BEING REPLACED BY MACHINES.
"OUR REMAINING BENDER EMPLOYEES QUIT IN PROTEST. I'M SYMPATHETIC TO THEIR FEELINGS, BUT I WASN'T TRYING TO PUT ANYONE OUT OF WORK. I JUST WANTED TO IMPROVE MY MACHINES AND INCREASE PRODUCTIVITY IN THE FACTORY."

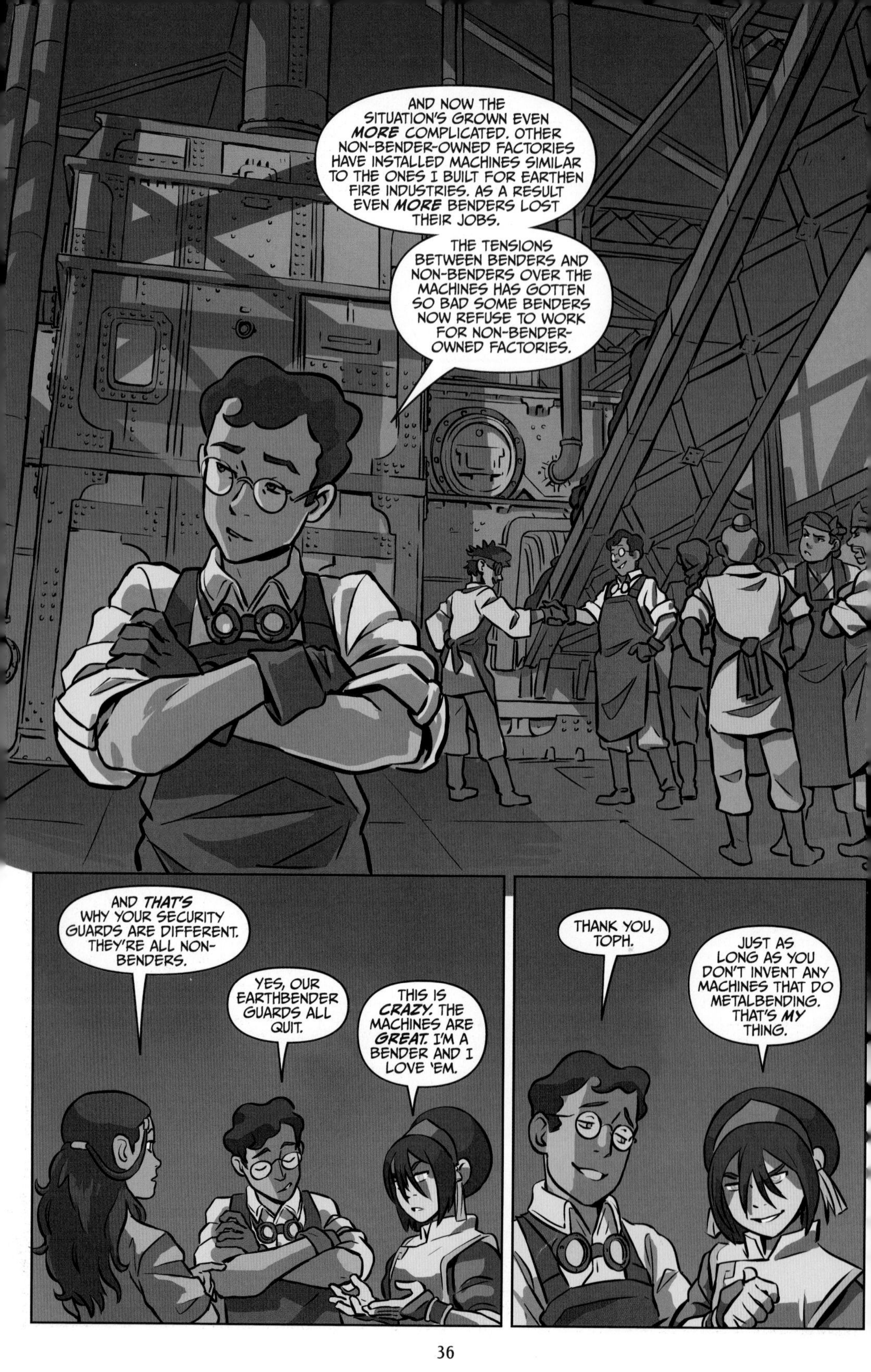
AND NOW THE SITUATION'S GROWN EVEN MORE COMPLICATED. OTHER NON-BENDER-OWNED FACTORIES HAVE INSTALLED MACHINES SIMILAR TO THE ONES I BUILT FOR EARTHEN FIRE INDUSTRIES. AS A RESULT EVEN MORE BENDERS LOST THEIR JOBS.
THE TENSIONS BETWEEN BENDERS AND NON-BENDERS OVER THE MACHINES HAS GOTTEN SO BAD SOME BENDERS NOW REFUSE TO WORK FOR NON-BENDER-OWNED FACTORIES.
AND THAT'S WHY YOUR SECURITY GUARDS ARE DIFFERENT. THEY'RE ALL NON-BENDERS.
YES, OUR EARTHBENDER GUARDS ALL QUIT.
THIS IS CRAZY. THE MACHINES ARE GREAT. I'M A BENDER AND I LOVE 'EM.
THANK YOU, TOPH.
JUST AS LONG AS YOU DON'T INVENT ANY MACHINES THAT DO METALBENDING. THAT'S MY THING.

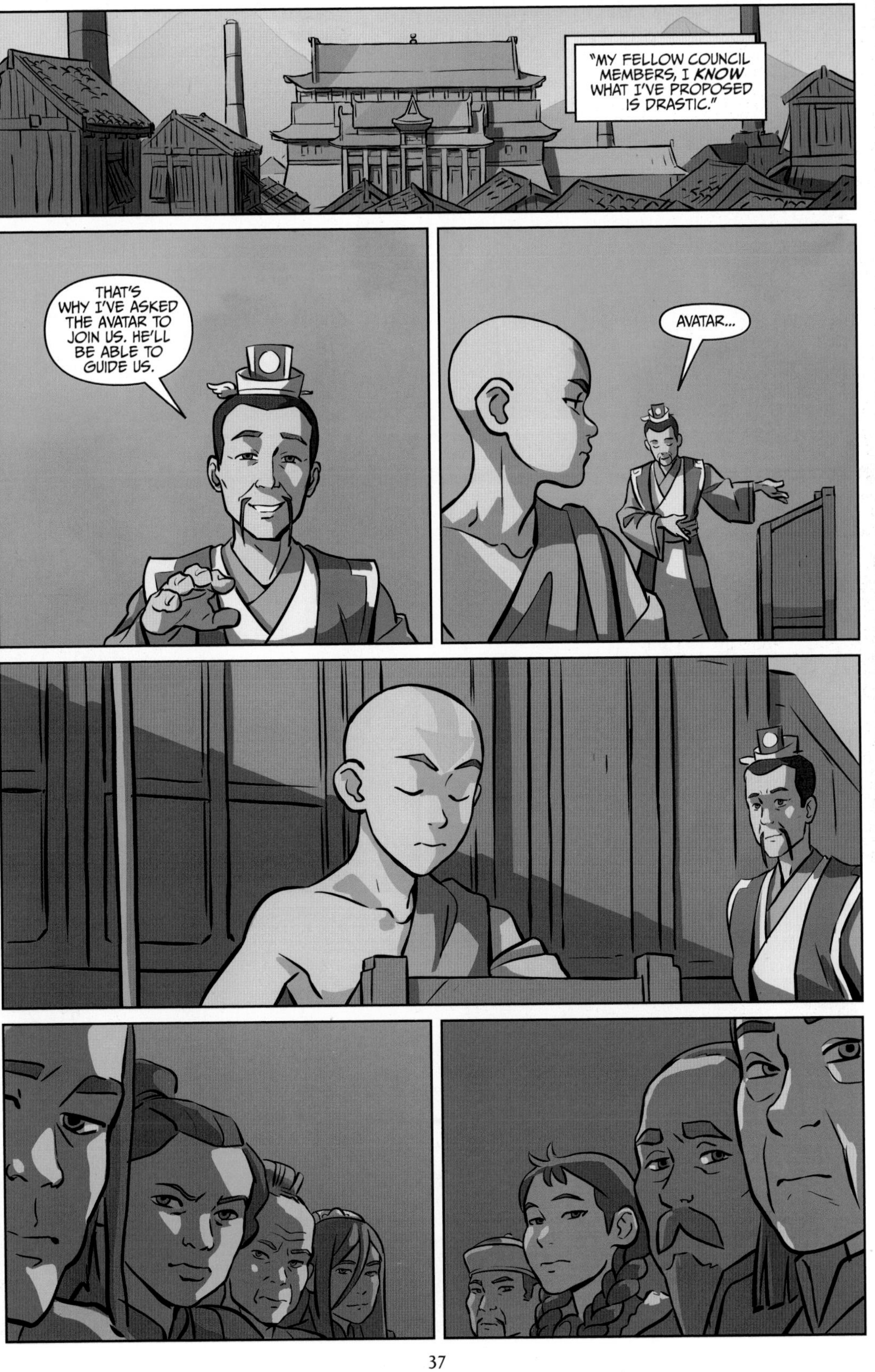
"MY FELLOW COUNCIL MEMBERS, I KNOW WHAT I'VE PROPOSED IS DRASTIC."
THAT'S WHY I'VE ASKED THE AVATAR TO JOIN US. HE'LL BE ABLE TO GUIDE US.
AVATAR...

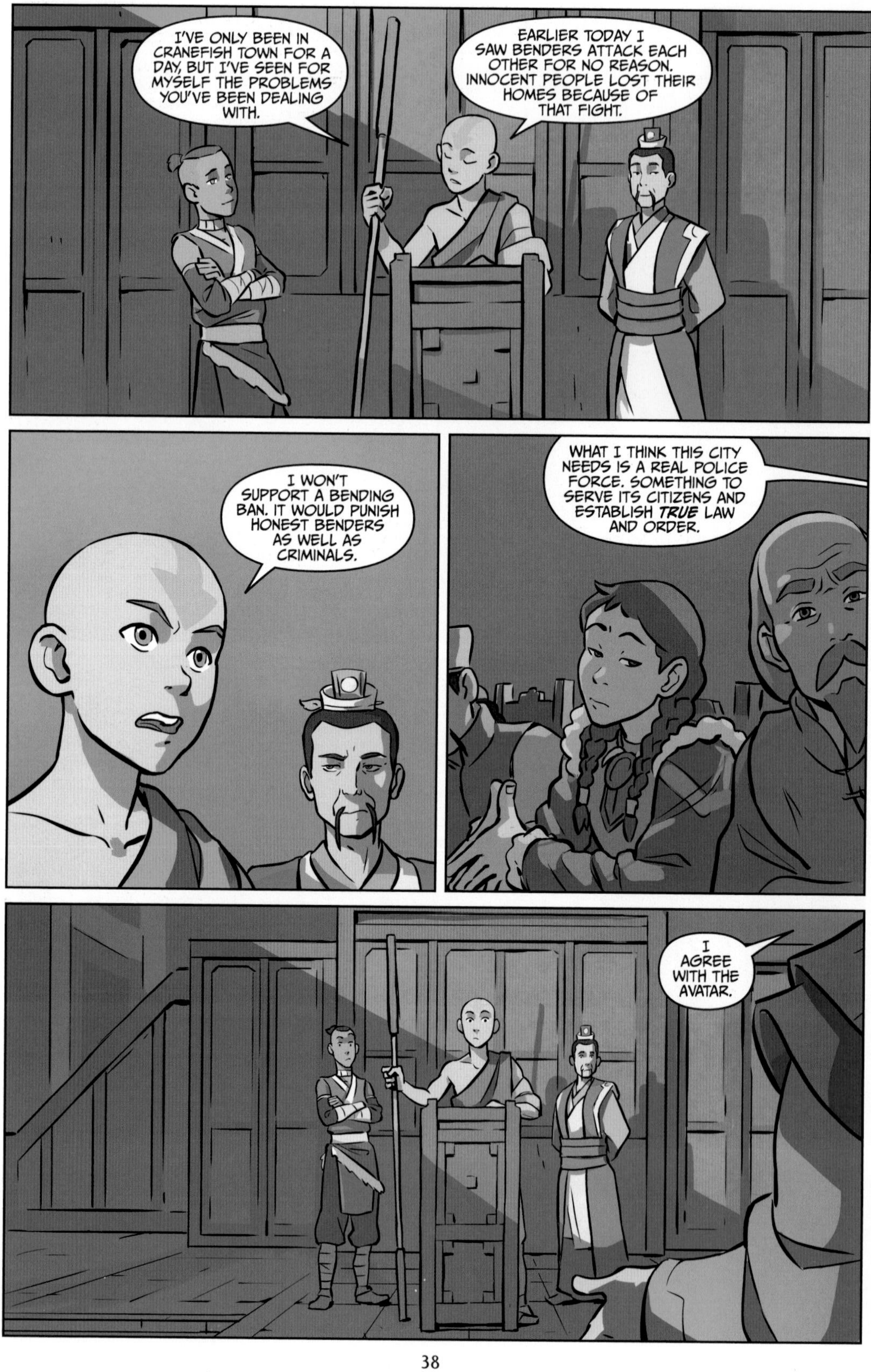
I'VE ONLY BEEN IN CRANEFISH TOWN FOR A DAY, BUT I'VE SEEN FOR MYSELF THE PROBLEMS YOU'VE BEEN DEALING WITH.
EARLIER TODAY I SAW BENDERS ATTACK EACH OTHER FOR NO REASON. INNOCENT PEOPLE LOST THEIR HOMES BECAUSE OF THAT FIGHT.
I WON'T SUPPORT A BENDING BAN. IT WOULD PUNISH HONEST BENDERS AS WELL AS CRIMINALS.
WHAT I THINK THIS CITY NEEDS IS A REAL POLICE FORCE. SOMETHING TO SERVE ITS CITIZENS AND ESTABLISH *TRUE* LAW AND ORDER.
I AGREE WITH THE AVATAR.

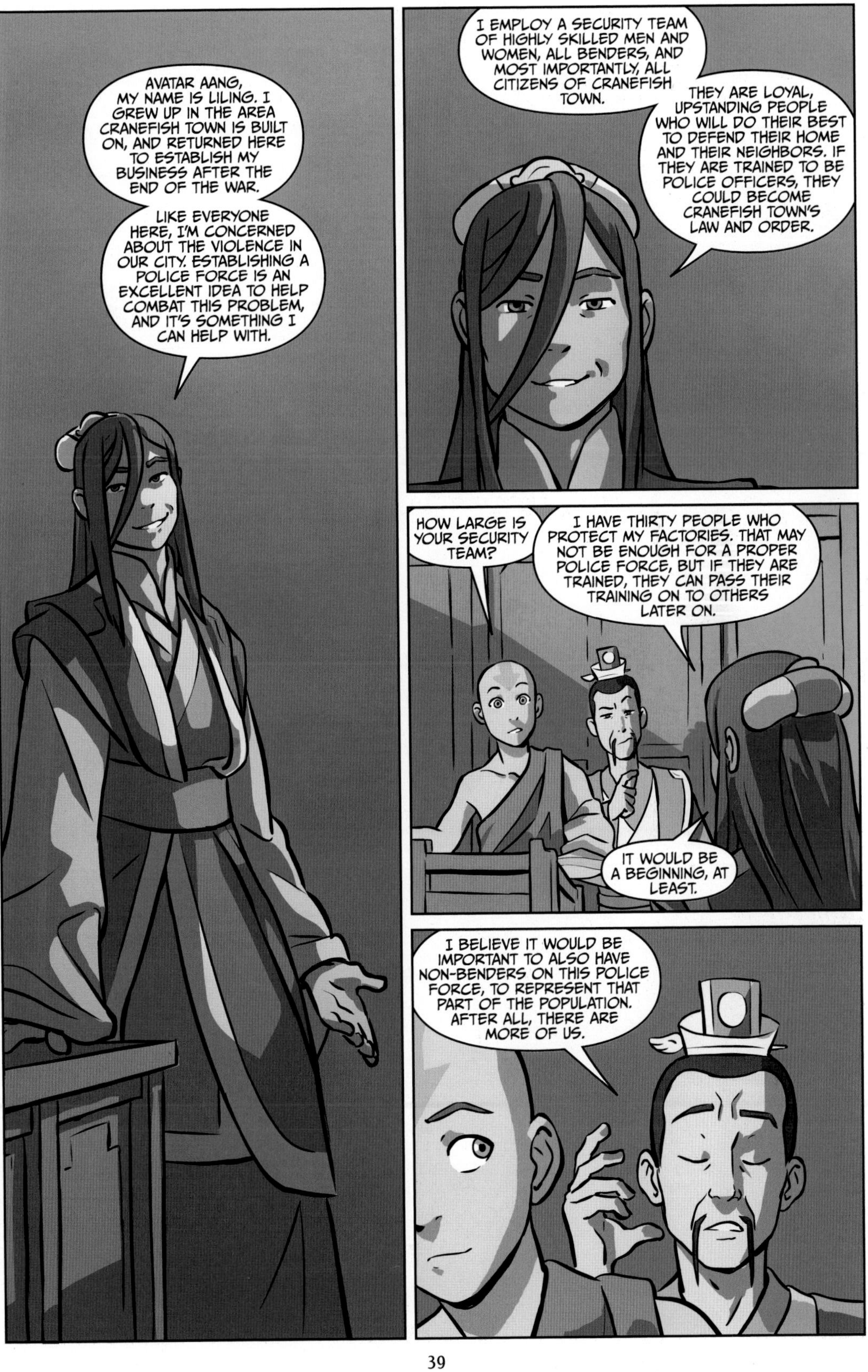
AVATAR AANG, MY NAME IS LILING. I GREW UP IN THE AREA CRANEFISH TOWN IS BUILT ON, AND RETURNED HERE TO ESTABLISH MY BUSINESS AFTER THE END OF THE WAR.
LIKE EVERYONE HERE, I'M CONCERNED ABOUT THE VIOLENCE IN OUR CITY. ESTABLISHING A POLICE FORCE IS AN EXCELLENT IDEA TO HELP COMBAT THIS PROBLEM, AND IT'S SOMETHING I CAN HELP WITH.
I EMPLOY A SECURITY TEAM OF HIGHLY SKILLED MEN AND WOMEN, ALL BENDERS, AND MOST IMPORTANTLY, ALL CITIZENS OF CRANEFISH TOWN.
THEY ARE LOYAL, UPSTANDING PEOPLE WHO WILL DO THEIR BEST TO DEFEND THEIR HOME AND THEIR NEIGHBORS. IF THEY ARE TRAINED TO BE POLICE OFFICERS, THEY COULD BECOME CRANEFISH TOWN'S LAW AND ORDER.
HOW LARGE IS YOUR SECURITY TEAM?
I HAVE THIRTY PEOPLE WHO PROTECT MY FACTORIES. THAT MAY NOT BE ENOUGH FOR A PROPER POLICE FORCE, BUT IF THEY ARE TRAINED, THEY CAN PASS THEIR TRAINING ON TO OTHERS LATER ON.
IT WOULD BE A BEGINNING, AT LEAST.
I BELIEVE IT WOULD BE IMPORTANT TO ALSO HAVE NON-BENDERS ON THIS POLICE FORCE, TO REPRESENT THAT PART OF THE POPULATION. AFTER ALL, THERE ARE MORE OF US.

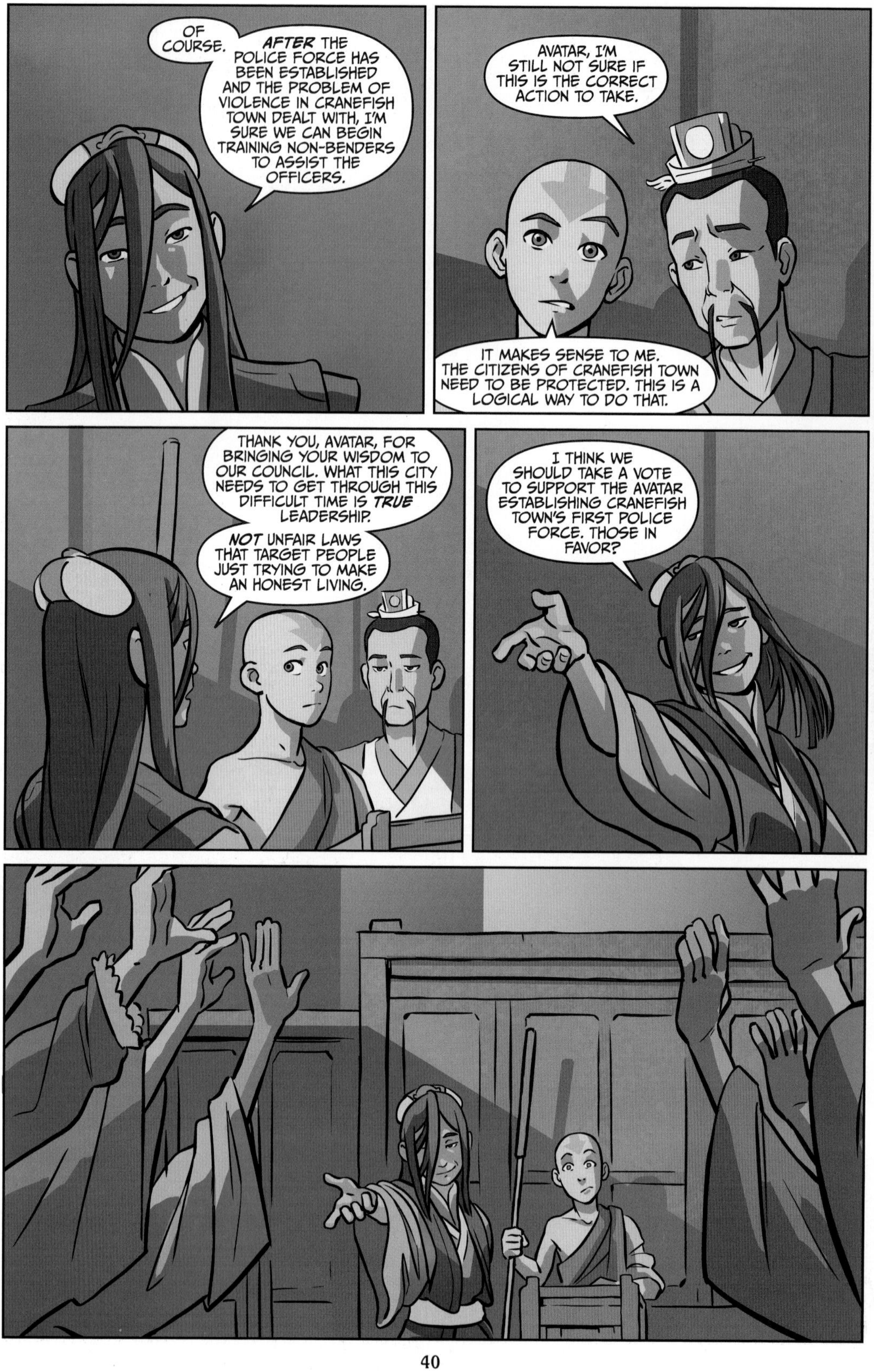
OF COURSE.
AFTER THE POLICE FORCE HAS BEEN ESTABLISHED AND THE PROBLEM OF VIOLENCE IN CRANEFISH TOWN DEALT WITH, I'M SURE WE CAN BEGIN TRAINING NON-BENDERS TO ASSIST THE OFFICERS.
AVATAR, I'M STILL NOT SURE IF THIS IS THE CORRECT ACTION TO TAKE.
IT MAKES SENSE TO ME. THE CITIZENS OF CRANEFISH TOWN NEED TO BE PROTECTED. THIS IS A LOGICAL WAY TO DO THAT.
THANK YOU, AVATAR, FOR BRINGING YOUR WISDOM TO OUR COUNCIL. WHAT THIS CITY NEEDS TO GET THROUGH THIS DIFFICULT TIME IS TRUE LEADERSHIP.
NOT UNFAIR LAWS THAT TARGET PEOPLE JUST TRYING TO MAKE AN HONEST LIVING.
I THINK WE SHOULD TAKE A VOTE TO SUPPORT THE AVATAR ESTABLISHING CRANEFISH TOWN'S FIRST POLICE FORCE. THOSE IN FAVOR?

WE *BELIEVE* IN YOU, AVATAR.

THAT COUNCIL LADY SEEMED ALL RIGHT, VOLUNTEERING HER OWN SECURITY TEAM TO HELP CLEAN UP CRANEFISH TOWN'S STREETS.

YES, EVERYONE WANTED TO HELP.

WE'RE DEFINITELY SPENDING LONGER THAN JUST A DAY HERE, HUH?

LOOKS LIKE. I DON'T THINK WE'LL BE GETTING TO YU DAO ANYTIME SOON.

IN THAT CASE, I'M GONNA SEND A MESSENGER HAWK TO SUKI AND TELL HER TO JOIN US HERE.

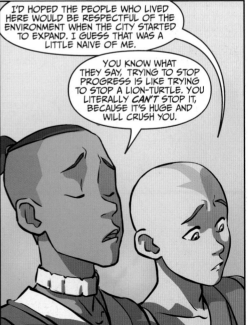

I'D HOPED THE PEOPLE WHO LIVED HERE WOULD BE RESPECTFUL OF THE ENVIRONMENT WHEN THE CITY STARTED TO EXPAND. I GUESS THAT WAS A LITTLE NAIVE OF ME.

YOU KNOW WHAT THEY SAY, TRYING TO STOP PROGRESS IS LIKE TRYING TO STOP A LION-TURTLE. YOU LITERALLY *CAN'T* STOP IT, BECAUSE IT'S HUGE AND WILL CRUSH YOU.

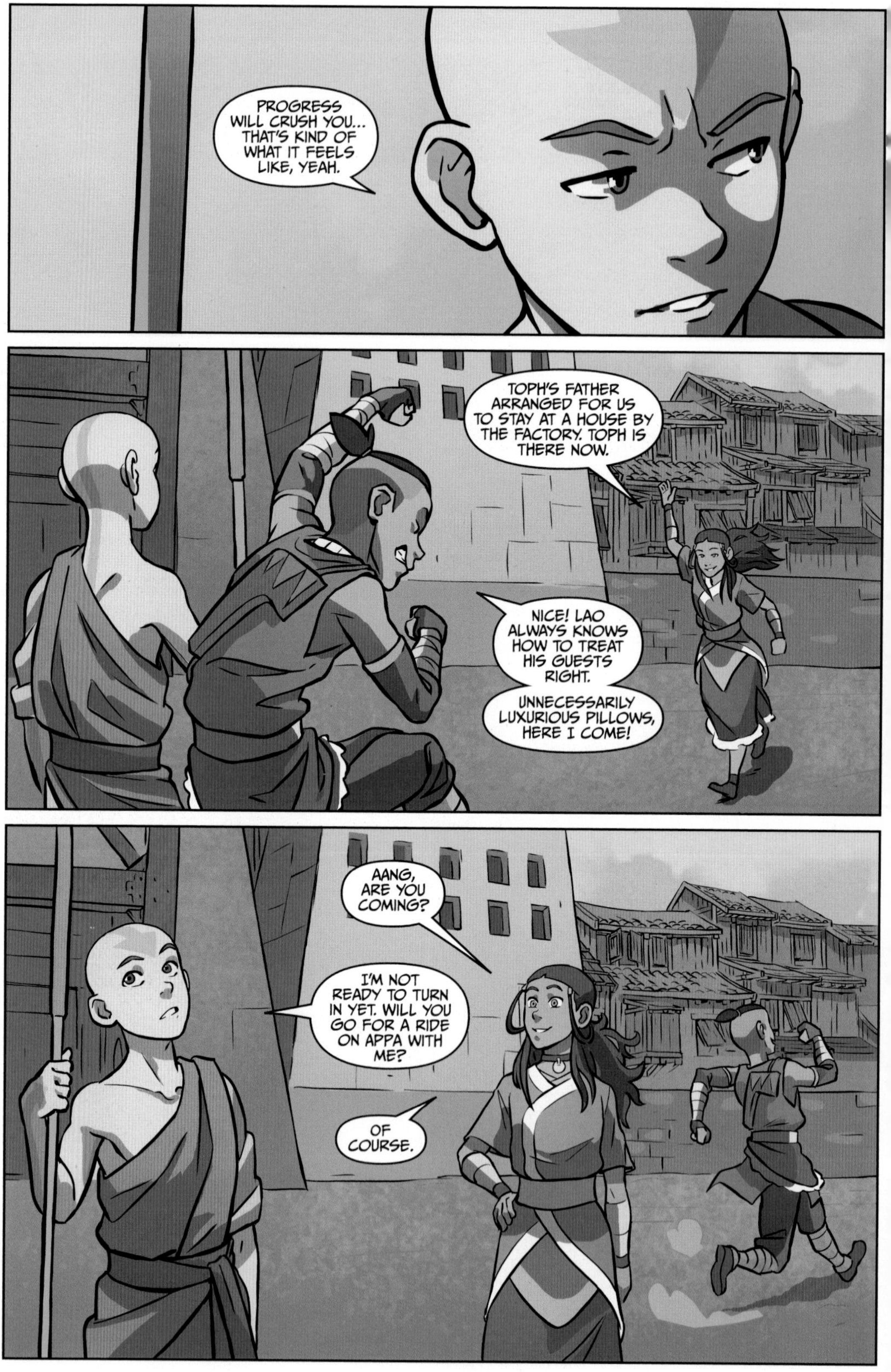
PROGRESS WILL CRUSH YOU... THAT'S KIND OF WHAT IT FEELS LIKE, YEAH.
TOPH'S FATHER ARRANGED FOR US TO STAY AT A HOUSE BY THE FACTORY. TOPH IS THERE NOW.
NICE! LAO ALWAYS KNOWS HOW TO TREAT HIS GUESTS RIGHT.
UNNECESSARILY LUXURIOUS PILLOWS, HERE I COME!
AANG, ARE YOU COMING?
I'M NOT READY TO TURN IN YET. WILL YOU GO FOR A RIDE ON APPA WITH ME?
OF COURSE.

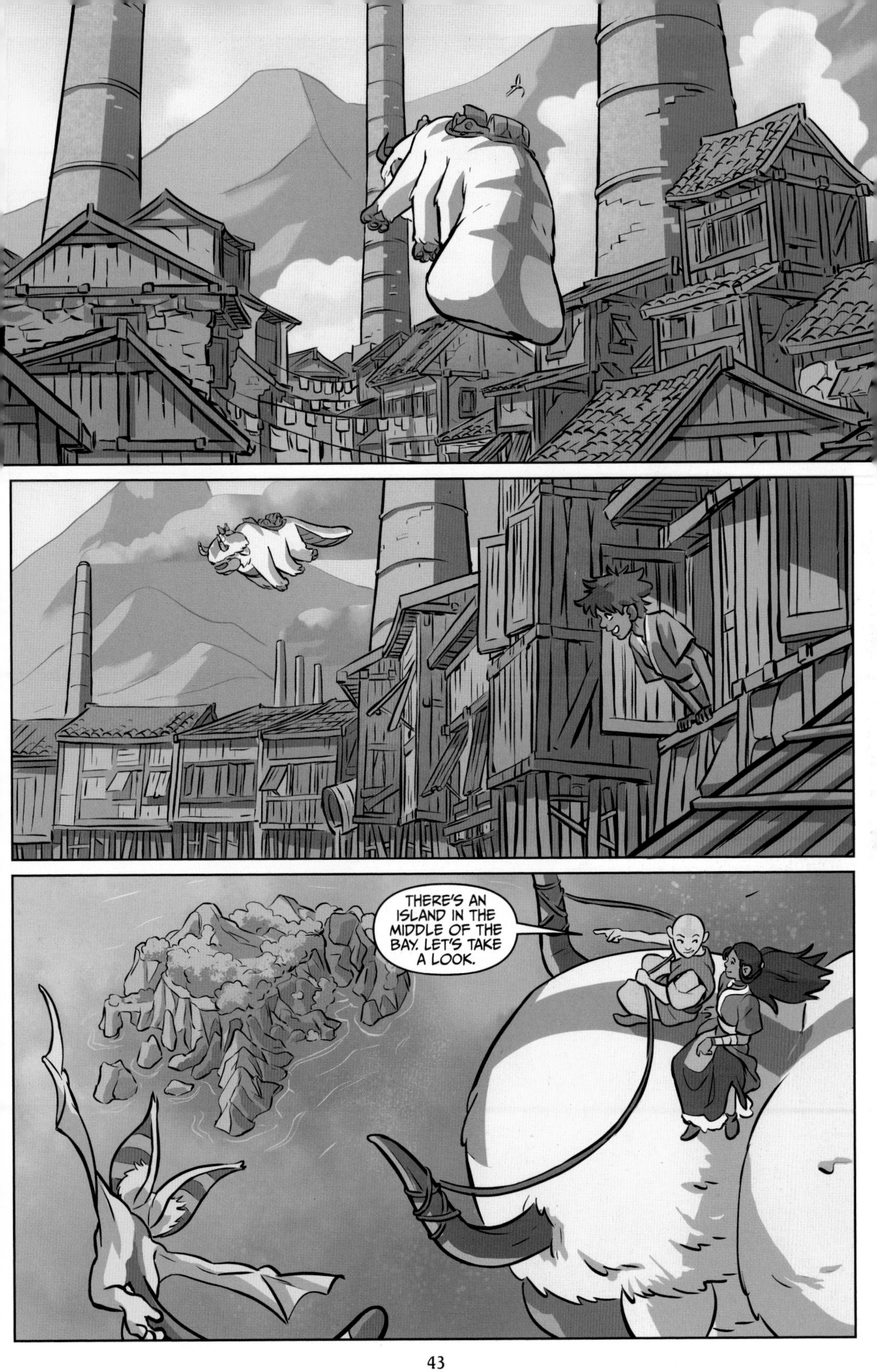
THERE'S AN ISLAND IN THE MIDDLE OF THE BAY. LET'S TAKE A LOOK.

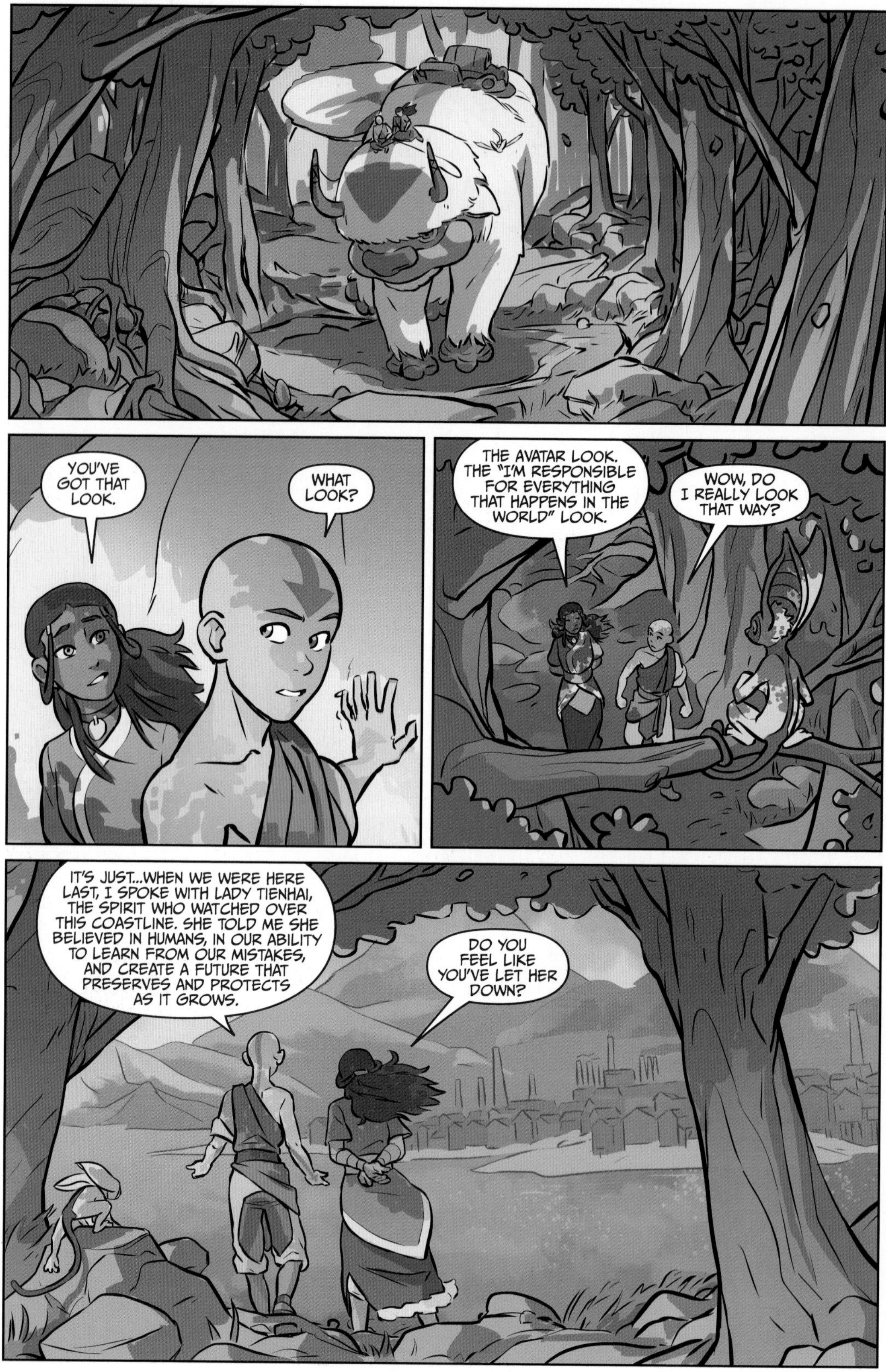

YOU'VE GOT THAT LOOK.
WHAT LOOK?
THE AVATAR LOOK. THE "I'M RESPONSIBLE FOR EVERYTHING THAT HAPPENS IN THE WORLD" LOOK.
WOW, DO I REALLY LOOK THAT WAY?
IT'S JUST...WHEN WE WERE HERE LAST, I SPOKE WITH LADY TIENHAI, THE SPIRIT WHO WATCHED OVER THIS COASTLINE. SHE TOLD ME SHE BELIEVED IN HUMANS, IN OUR ABILITY TO LEARN FROM OUR MISTAKES, AND CREATE A FUTURE THAT PRESERVES AND PROTECTS AS IT GROWS.
DO YOU FEEL LIKE YOU'VE LET HER DOWN?

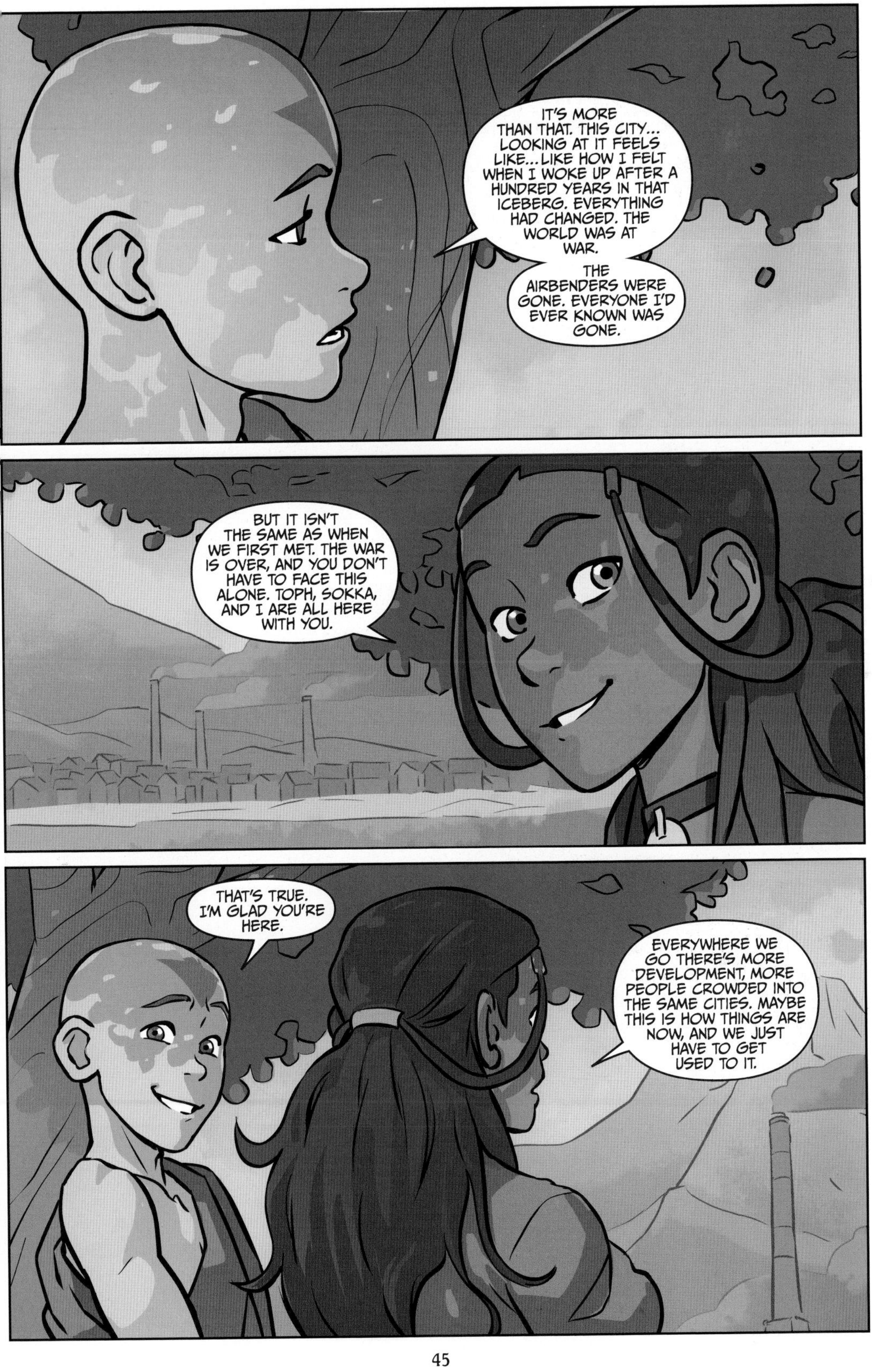
IT'S MORE THAN THAT. THIS CITY... LOOKING AT IT FEELS LIKE... LIKE HOW I FELT WHEN I WOKE UP AFTER A HUNDRED YEARS IN THAT ICEBERG. EVERYTHING HAD CHANGED. THE WORLD WAS AT WAR.
THE AIRBENDERS WERE GONE. EVERYONE I'D EVER KNOWN WAS GONE.
BUT IT ISN'T THE SAME AS WHEN WE FIRST MET. THE WAR IS OVER, AND YOU DON'T HAVE TO FACE THIS ALONE. TOPH, SOKKA, AND I ARE ALL HERE WITH YOU.
THAT'S TRUE. I'M GLAD YOU'RE HERE.
EVERYWHERE WE GO THERE'S MORE DEVELOPMENT, MORE PEOPLE CROWDED INTO THE SAME CITIES. MAYBE THIS IS HOW THINGS ARE NOW, AND WE JUST HAVE TO GET USED TO IT.

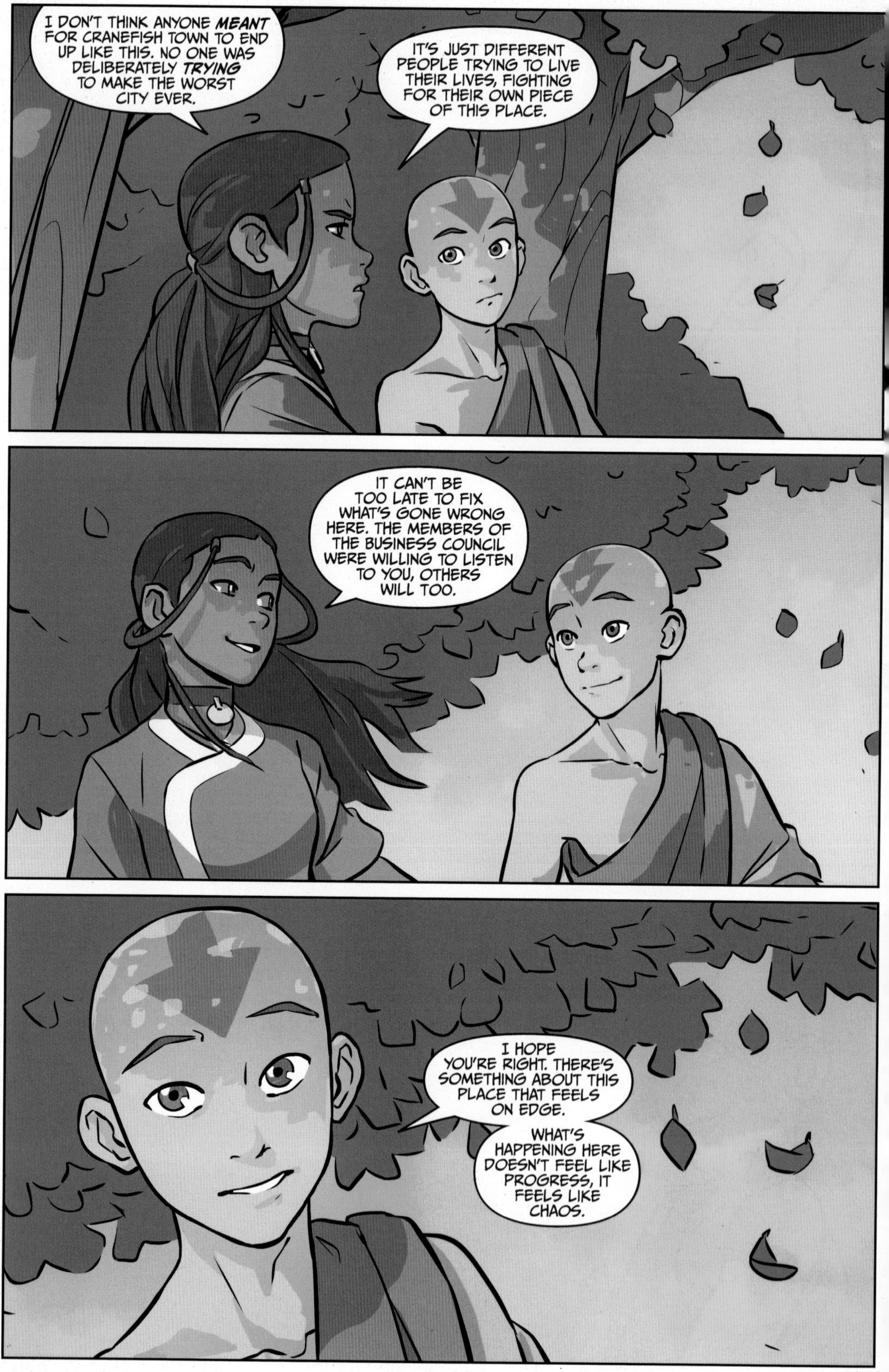
I DON'T THINK ANYONE **MEANT** FOR CRANEFISH TOWN TO END UP LIKE THIS. NO ONE WAS DELIBERATELY **TRYING** TO MAKE THE WORST CITY EVER.
IT'S JUST DIFFERENT PEOPLE TRYING TO LIVE THEIR LIVES, FIGHTING FOR THEIR OWN PIECE OF THIS PLACE.
IT CAN'T BE TOO LATE TO FIX WHAT'S GONE WRONG HERE. THE MEMBERS OF THE BUSINESS COUNCIL WERE WILLING TO LISTEN TO YOU, OTHERS WILL TOO.
I HOPE YOU'RE RIGHT. THERE'S SOMETHING ABOUT THIS PLACE THAT FEELS ON EDGE.
WHAT'S HAPPENING HERE DOESN'T FEEL LIKE PROGRESS, IT FEELS LIKE CHAOS.

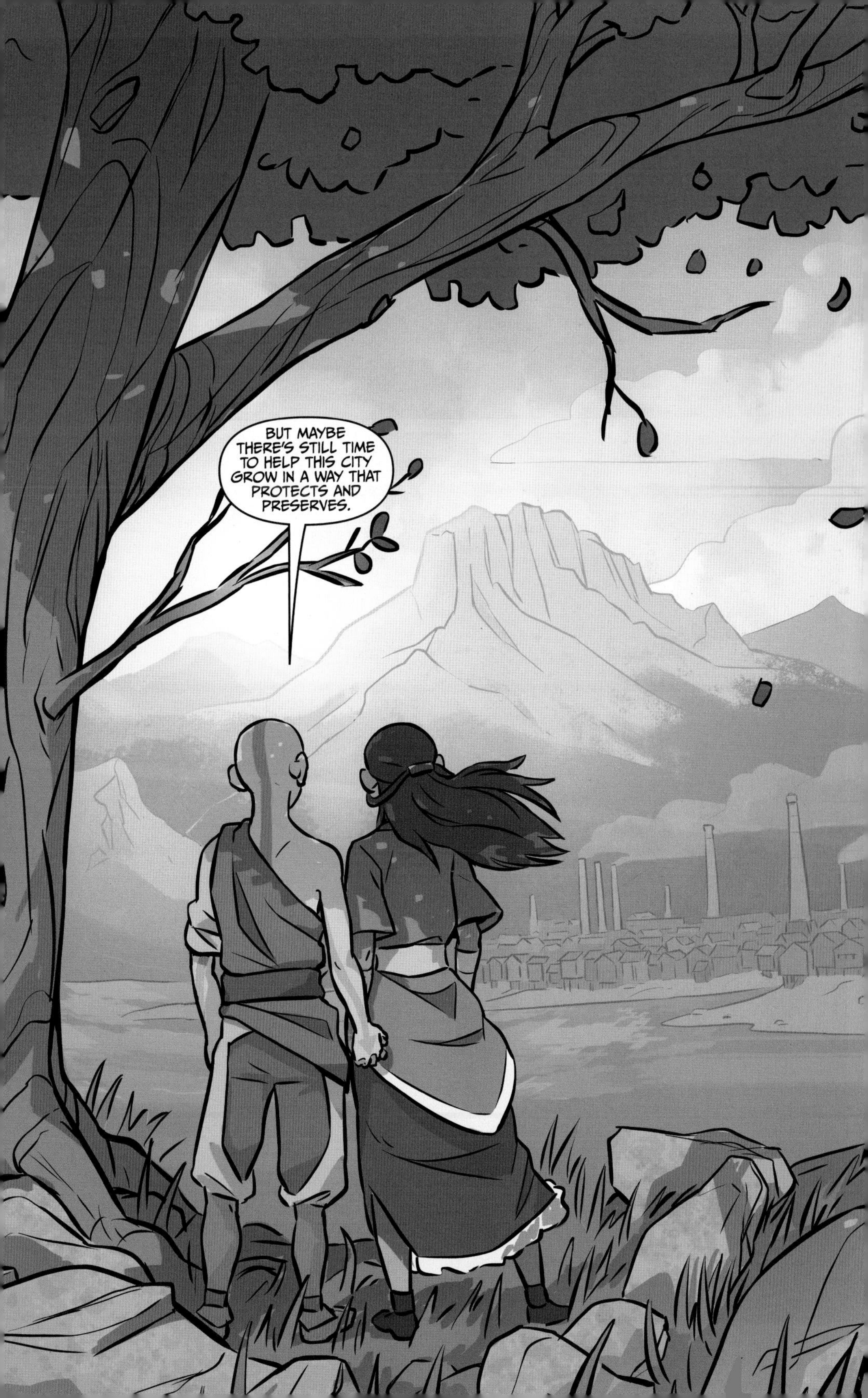
BUT MAYBE THERE'S STILL TIME TO HELP THIS CITY GROW IN A WAY THAT PROTECTS AND PRESERVES.

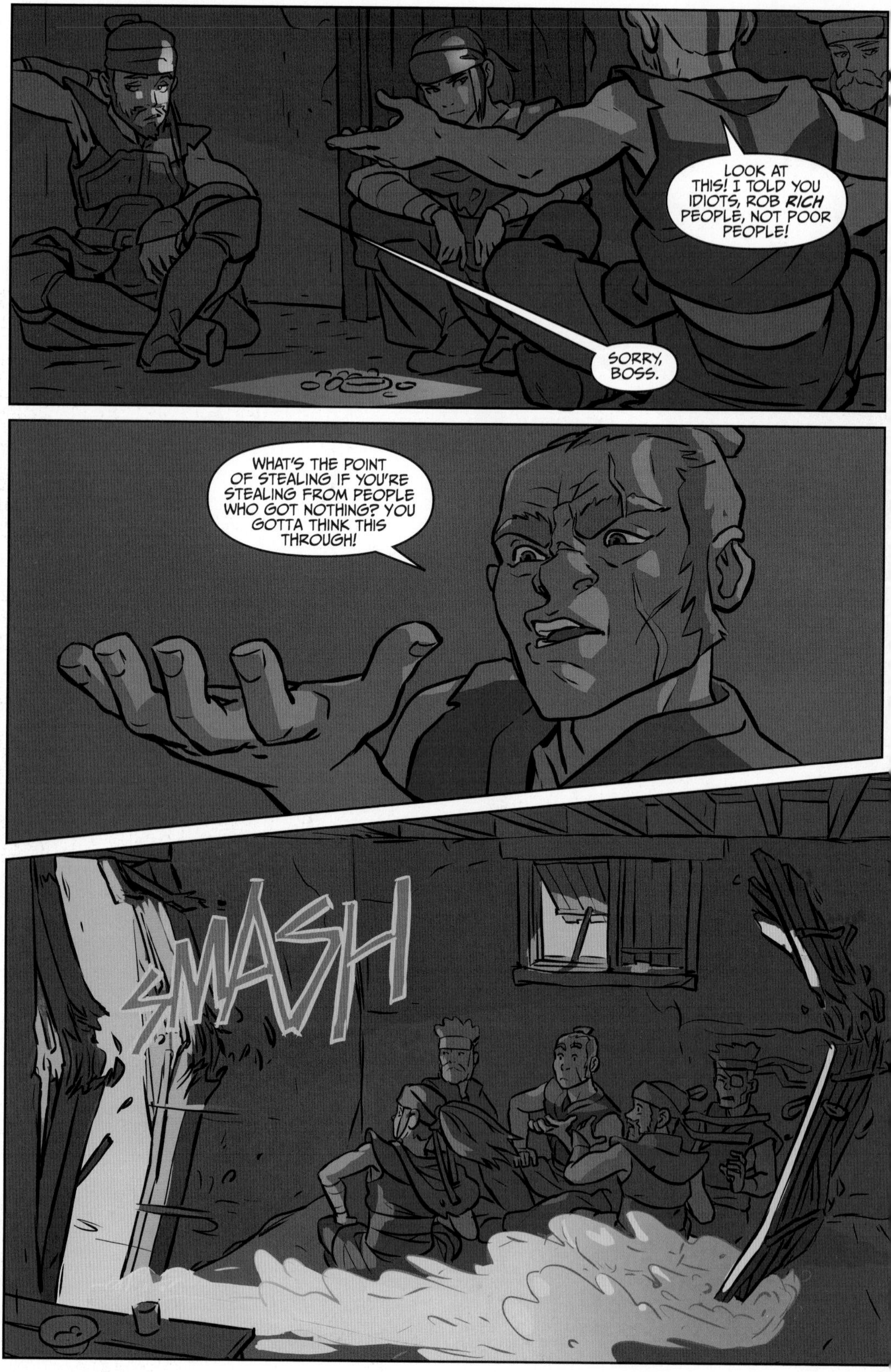
LOOK AT THIS! I TOLD YOU IDIOTS, ROB RICH PEOPLE, NOT POOR PEOPLE!
SORRY, BOSS.
WHAT'S THE POINT OF STEALING IF YOU'RE STEALING FROM PEOPLE WHO GOT NOTHING? YOU GOTTA THINK THIS THROUGH!
SMASH

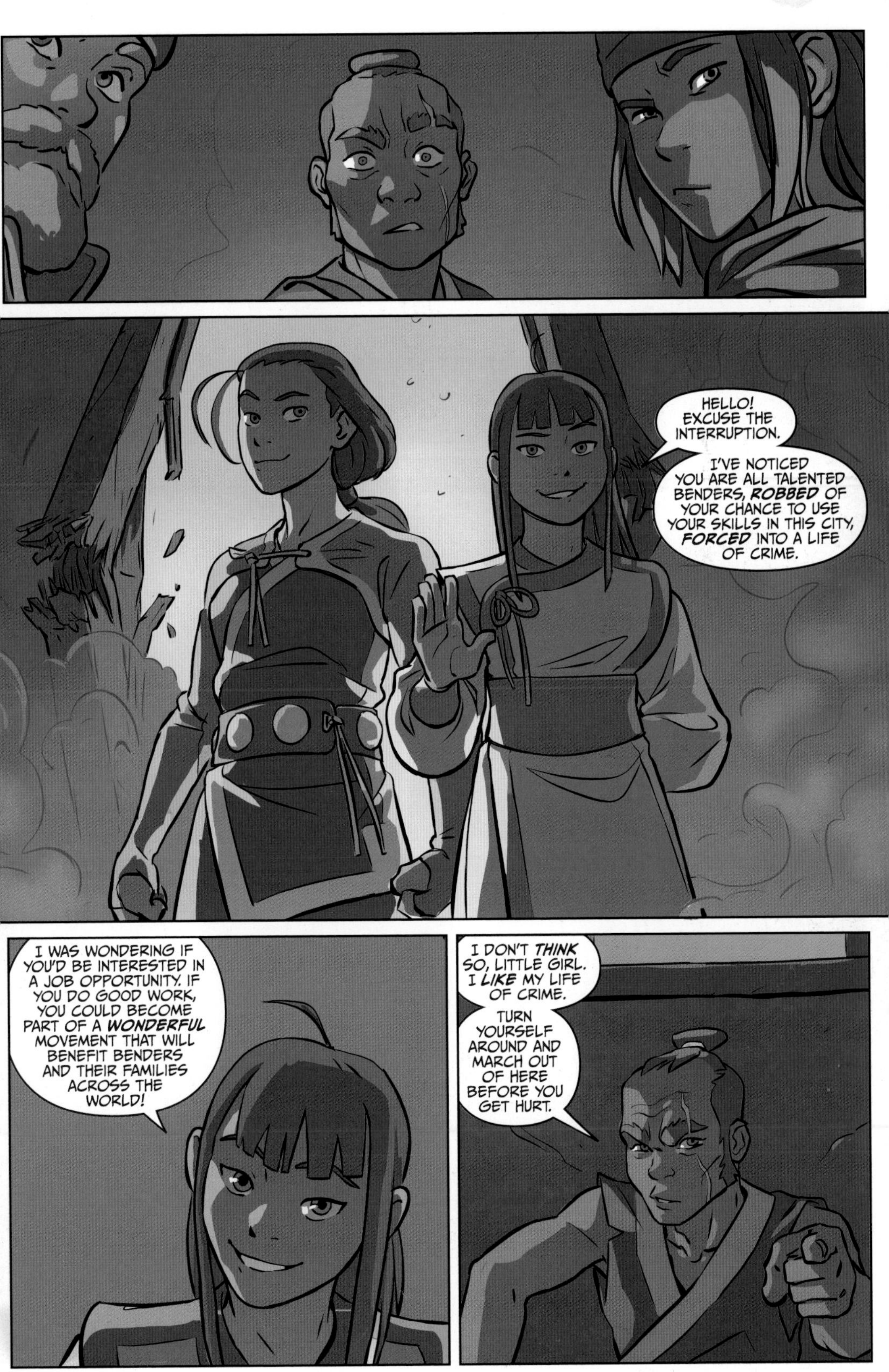
HELLO! EXCUSE THE INTERRUPTION.
I'VE NOTICED YOU ARE ALL TALENTED BENDERS, ROBBED OF YOUR CHANCE TO USE YOUR SKILLS IN THIS CITY, FORCED INTO A LIFE OF CRIME.
I WAS WONDERING IF YOU'D BE INTERESTED IN A JOB OPPORTUNITY. IF YOU DO GOOD WORK, YOU COULD BECOME PART OF A WONDERFUL MOVEMENT THAT WILL BENEFIT BENDERS AND THEIR FAMILIES ACROSS THE WORLD!
I DON'T THINK SO, LITTLE GIRL. I LIKE MY LIFE OF CRIME.
TURN YOURSELF AROUND AND MARCH OUT OF HERE BEFORE YOU GET HURT.

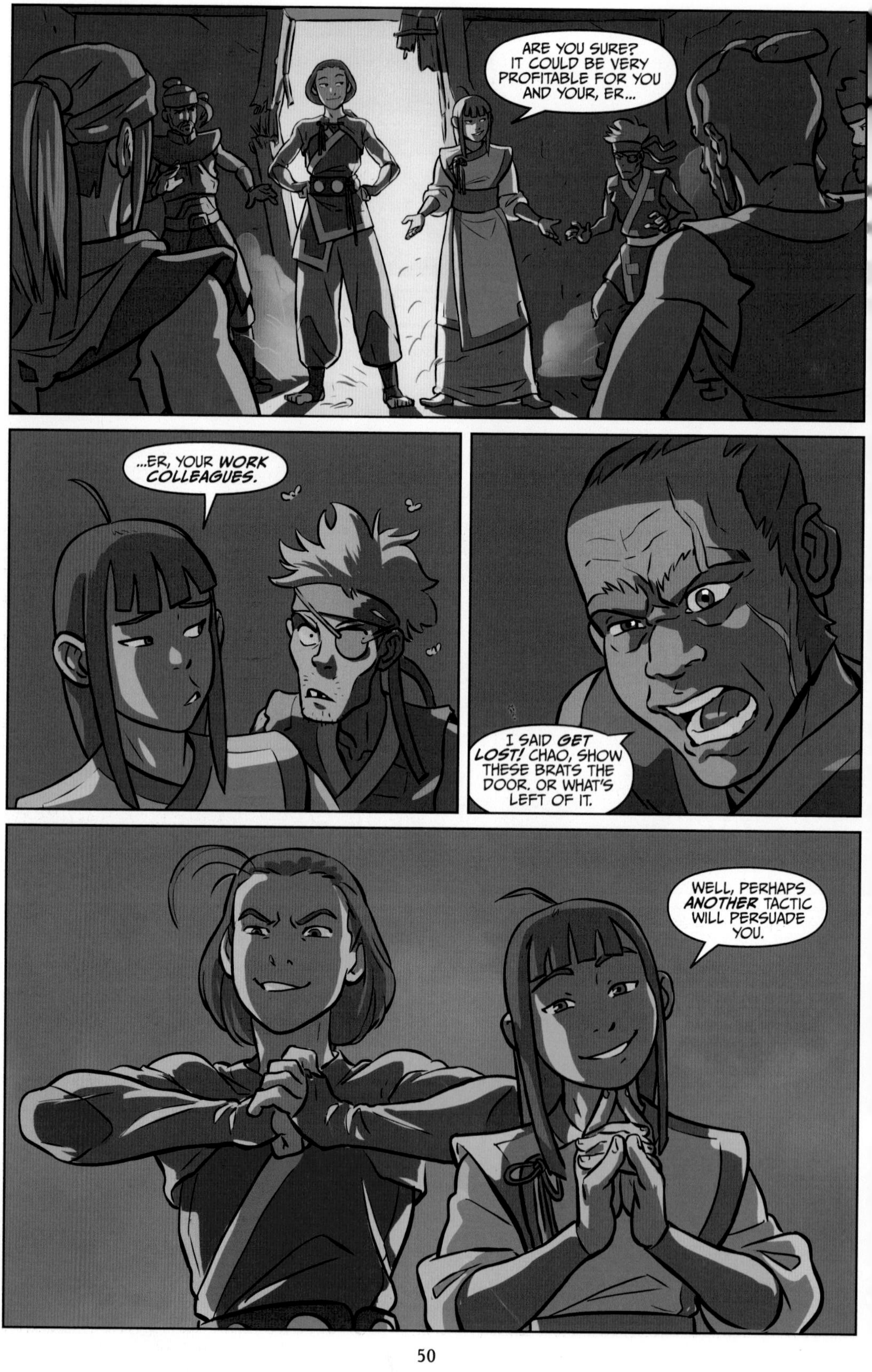
ARE YOU SURE? IT COULD BE VERY PROFITABLE FOR YOU AND YOUR, ER...
...ER, YOUR WORK COLLEAGUES.
I SAID GET LOST! CHAO, SHOW THESE BRATS THE DOOR. OR WHAT'S LEFT OF IT.
WELL, PERHAPS ANOTHER TACTIC WILL PERSUADE YOU.

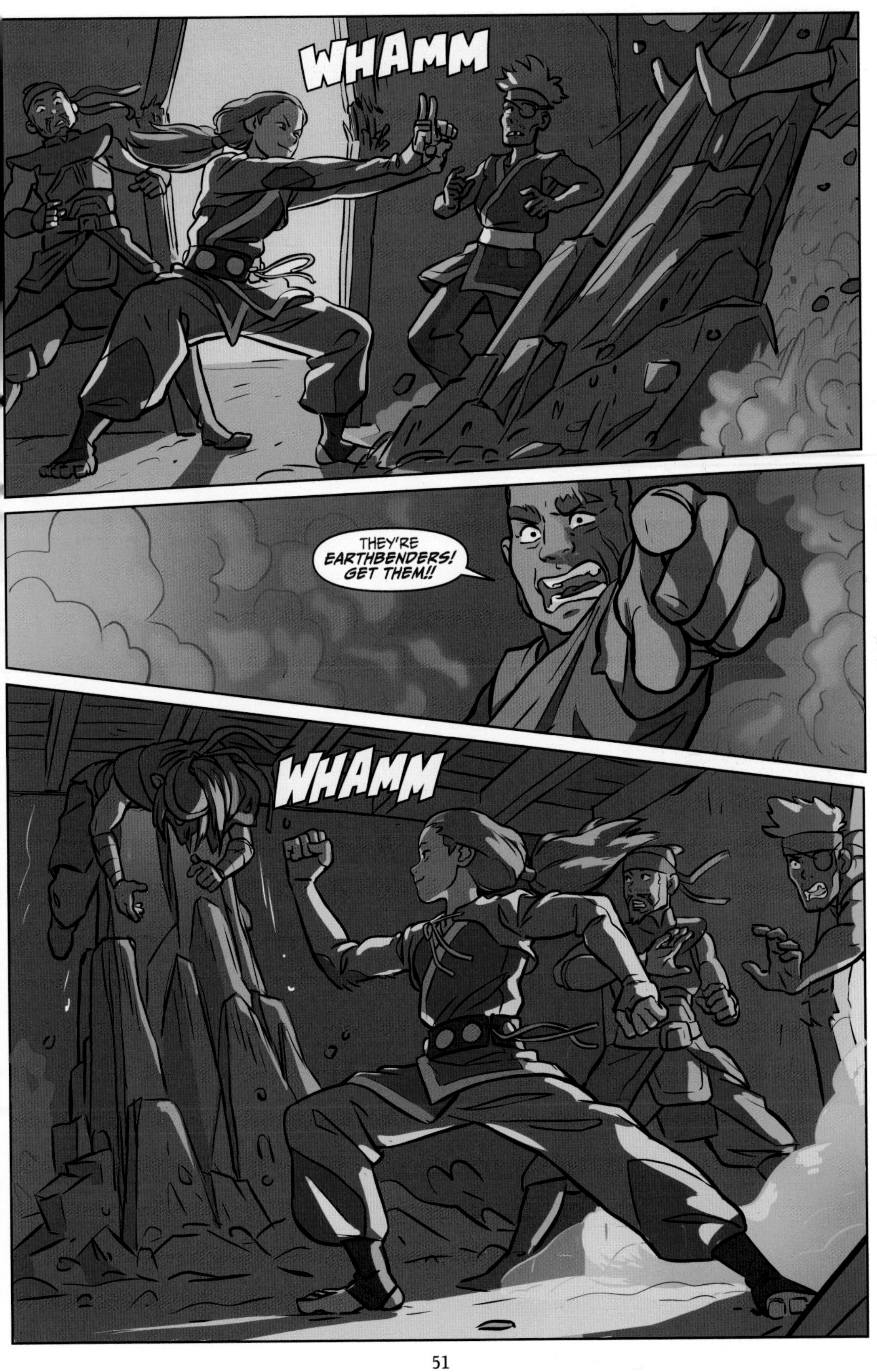
WHAMM
THEY'RE EARTHBENDERS! GET THEM!!
WHAMM

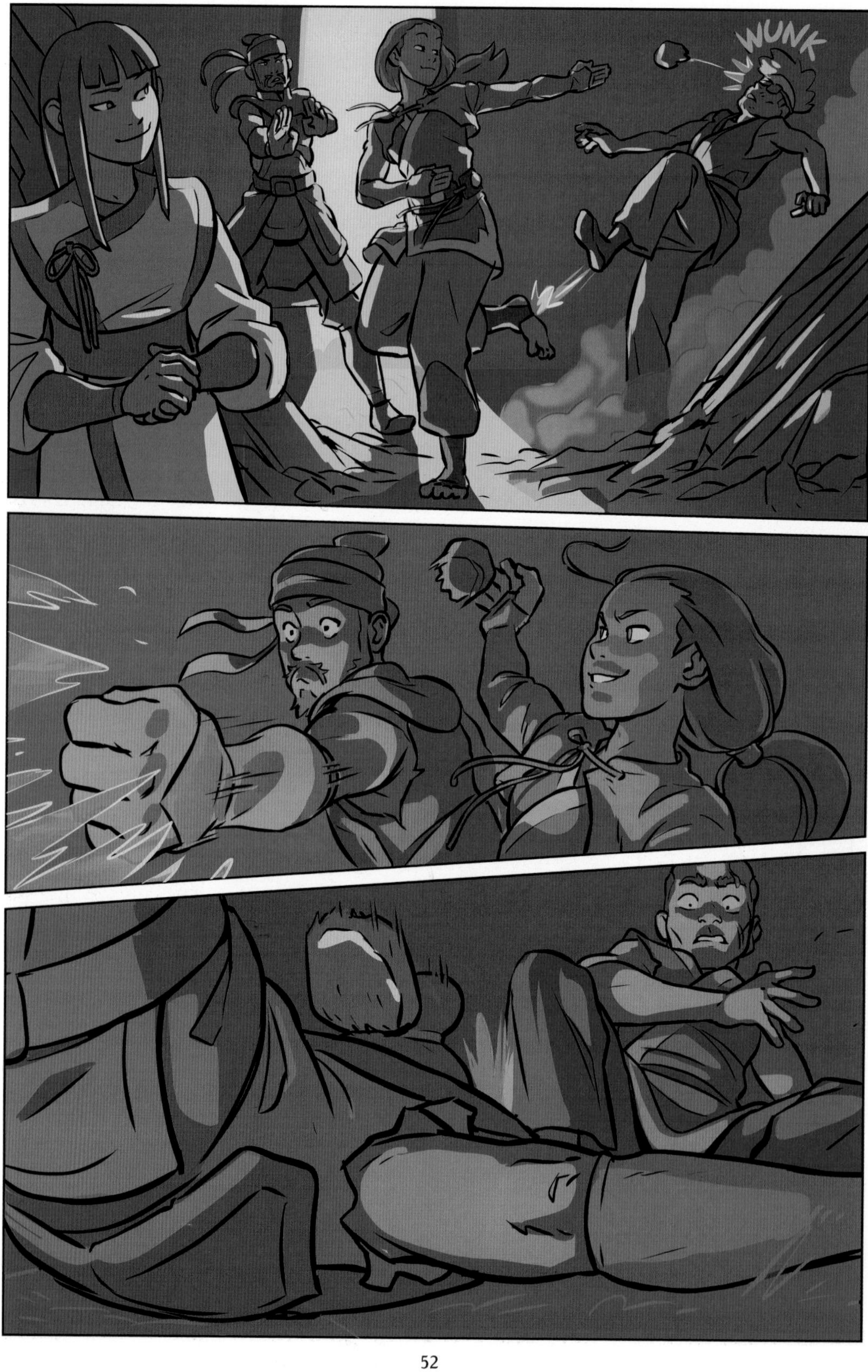
WUNK

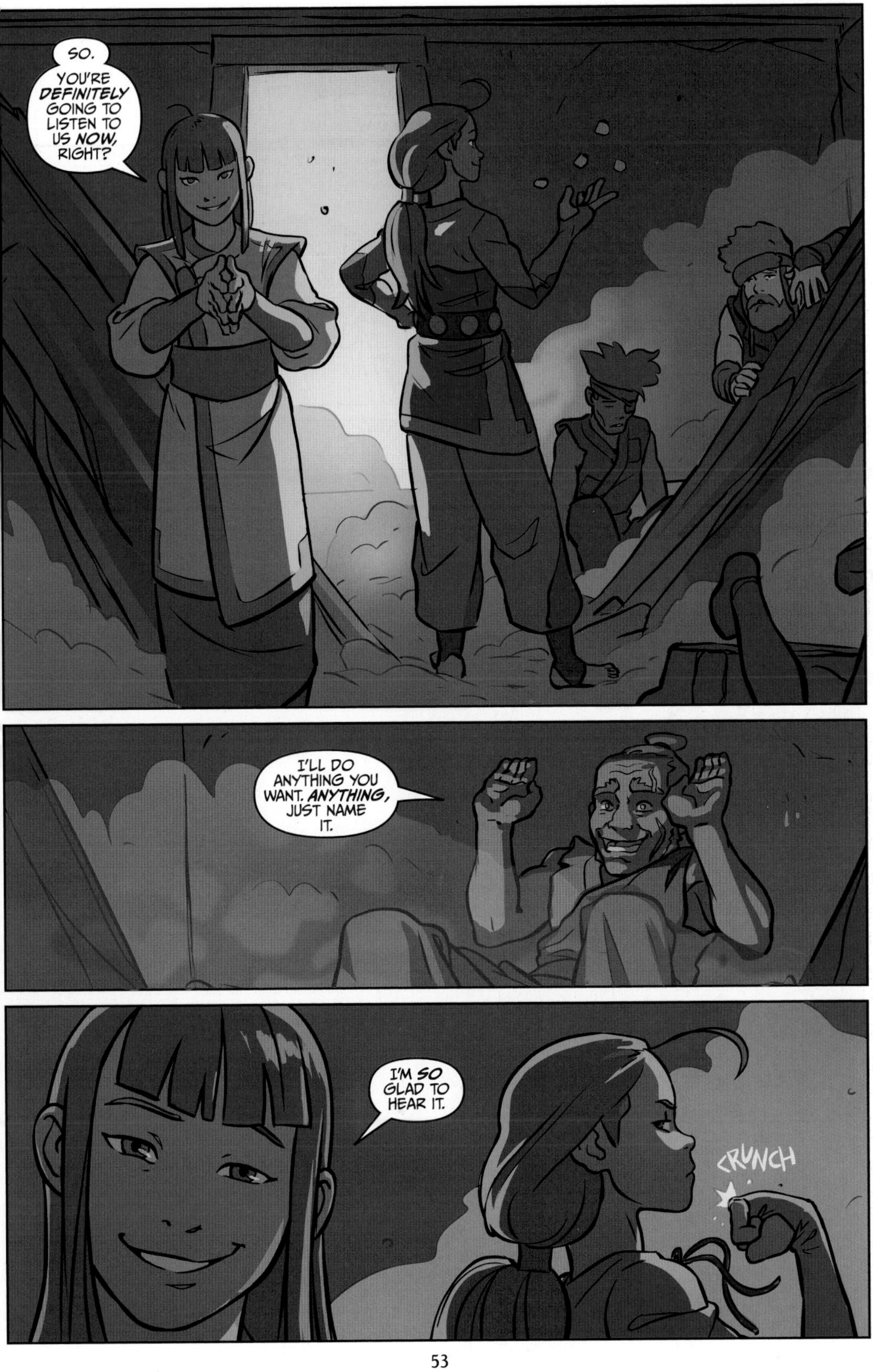
SO.
YOU'RE DEFINITELY GOING TO LISTEN TO US NOW, RIGHT?
I'LL DO ANYTHING YOU WANT. ANYTHING, JUST NAME IT.
I'M SO GLAD TO HEAR IT.
CRUNCH

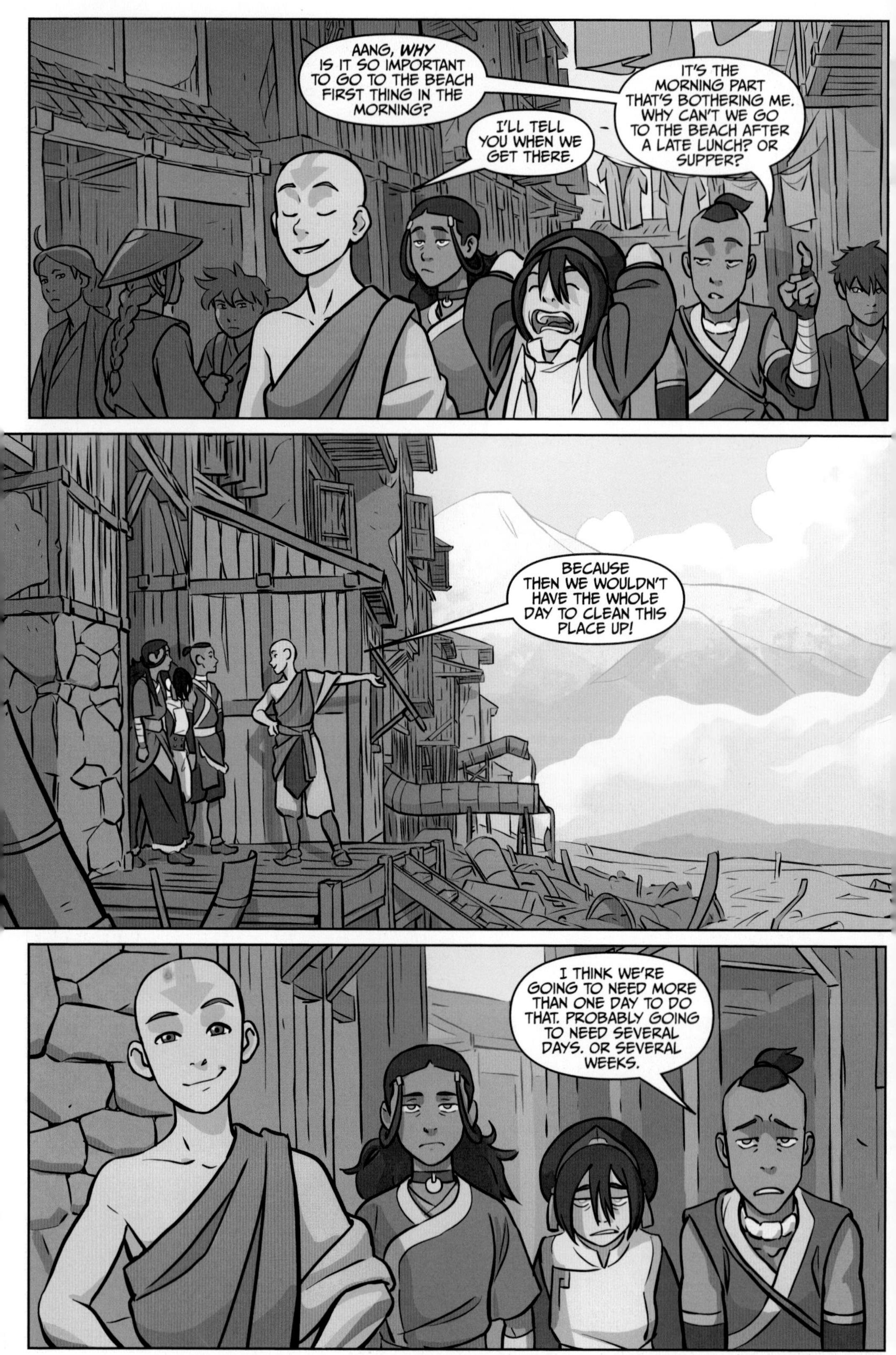
AANG, *WHY* IS IT SO IMPORTANT TO GO TO THE BEACH FIRST THING IN THE MORNING?
I'LL TELL YOU WHEN WE GET THERE.
IT'S THE MORNING PART THAT'S BOTHERING ME. WHY CAN'T WE GO TO THE BEACH AFTER A LATE LUNCH? OR SUPPER?
BECAUSE THEN WE WOULDN'T HAVE THE WHOLE DAY TO CLEAN THIS PLACE UP!
I THINK WE'RE GOING TO NEED MORE THAN ONE DAY TO DO THAT. PROBABLY GOING TO NEED SEVERAL DAYS. OR SEVERAL WEEKS.

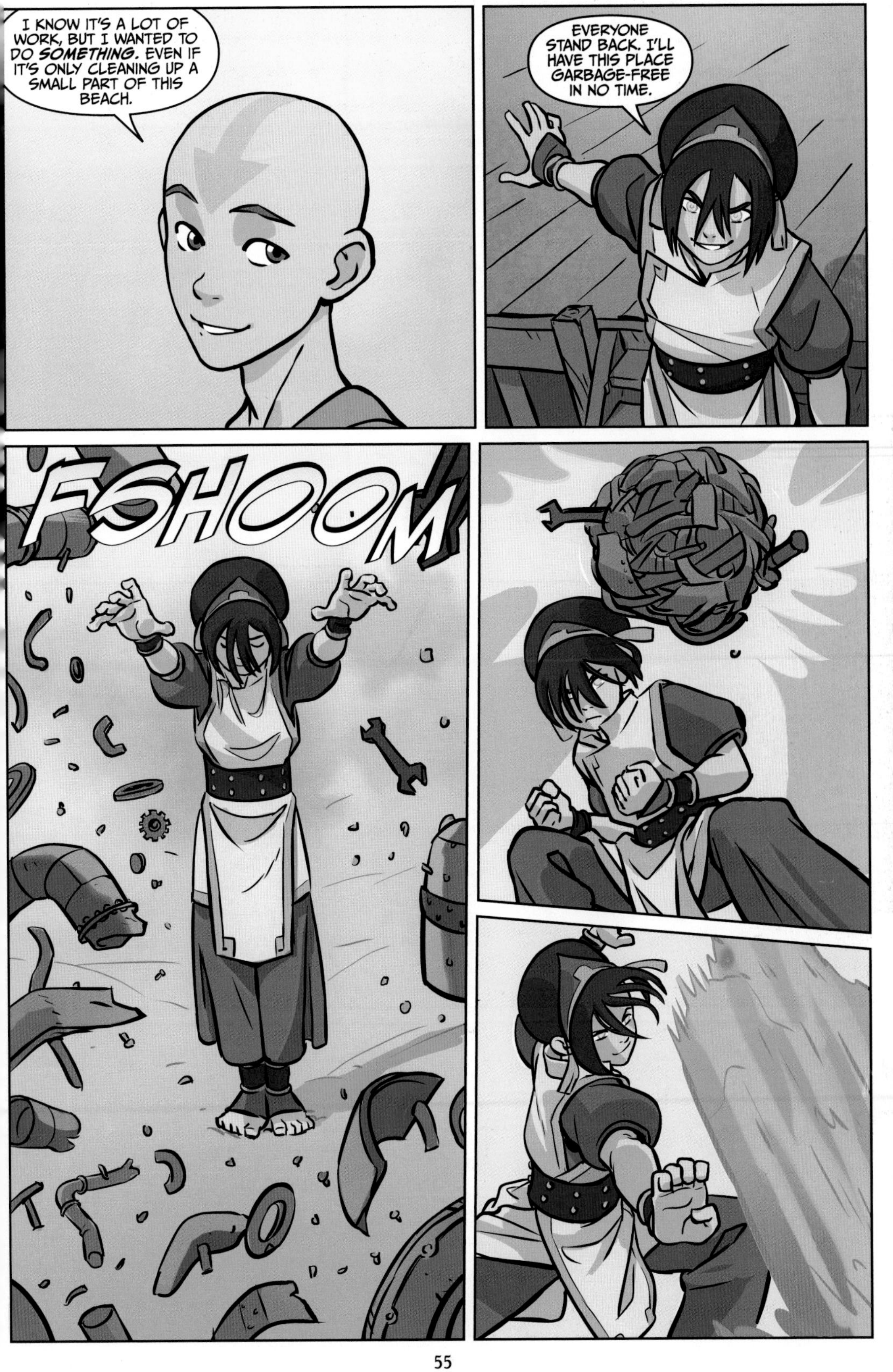
I KNOW IT'S A LOT OF WORK, BUT I WANTED TO DO **SOMETHING**. EVEN IF IT'S ONLY CLEANING UP A SMALL PART OF THIS BEACH.
EVERYONE STAND BACK. I'LL HAVE THIS PLACE GARBAGE-FREE IN NO TIME.
FSHOOM

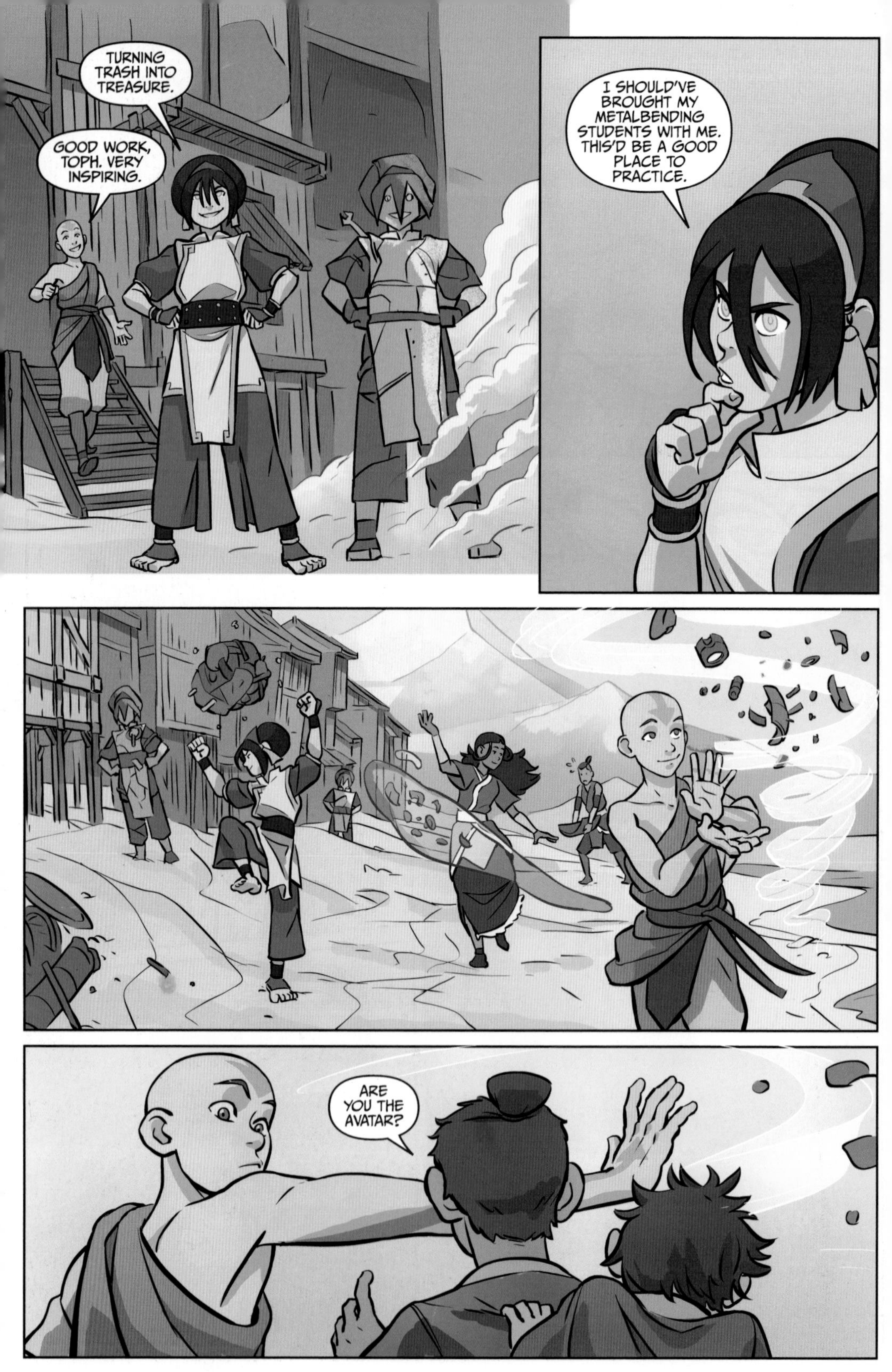
TURNING TRASH INTO TREASURE.
GOOD WORK, TOPH. VERY INSPIRING.
I SHOULD'VE BROUGHT MY METALBENDING STUDENTS WITH ME. THIS'D BE A GOOD PLACE TO PRACTICE.
ARE YOU THE AVATAR?

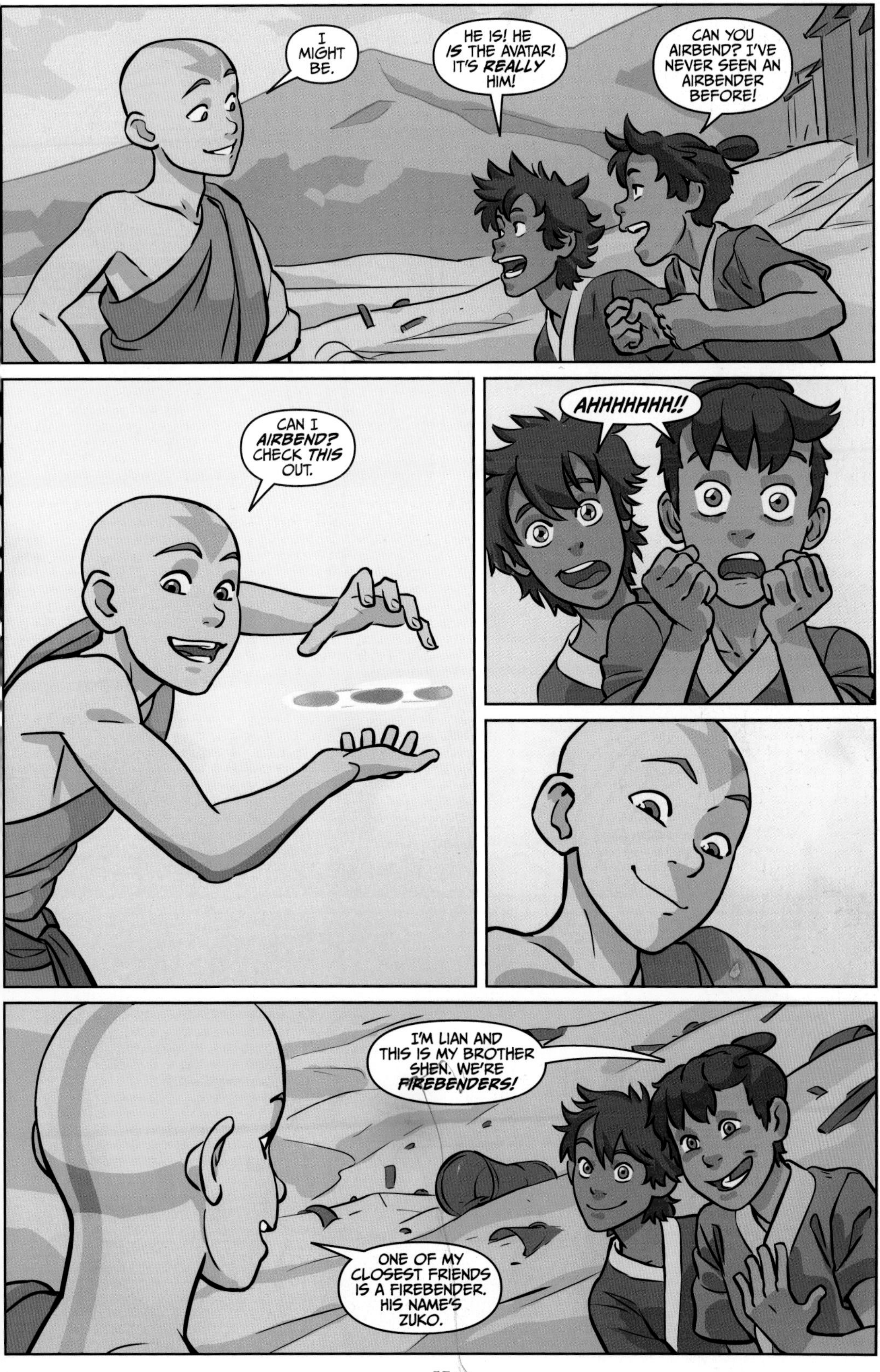
I MIGHT BE.
HE IS! HE *IS* THE AVATAR! IT'S *REALLY* HIM!
CAN YOU AIRBEND? I'VE NEVER SEEN AN AIRBENDER BEFORE!
CAN I *AIRBEND?* CHECK *THIS* OUT.
AHHHHHHH!!
I'M LIAN AND THIS IS MY BROTHER SHEN. WE'RE *FIREBENDERS!*
ONE OF MY CLOSEST FRIENDS IS A FIREBENDER. HIS NAME'S ZUKO.

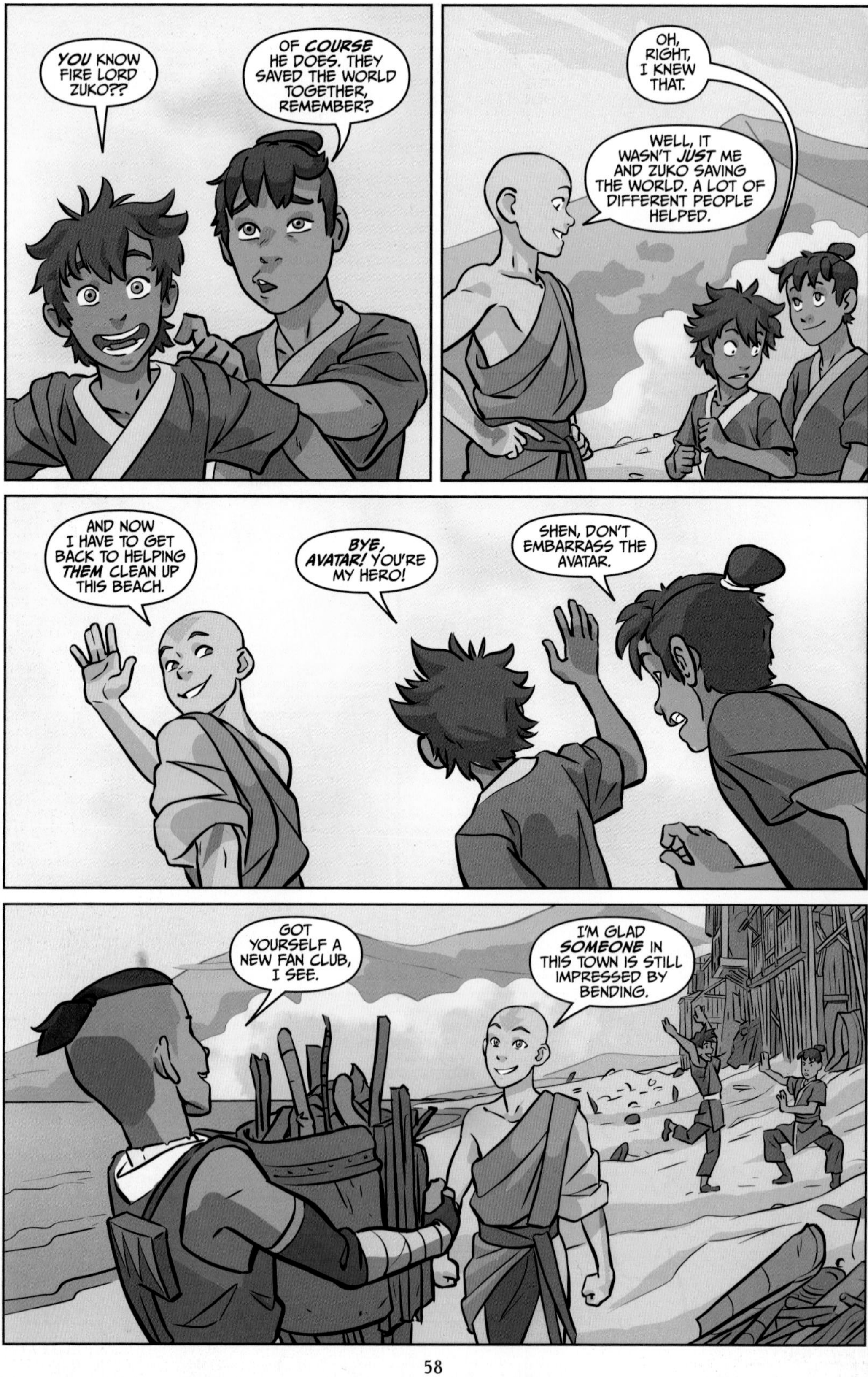
YOU KNOW FIRE LORD ZUKO??
OF COURSE HE DOES. THEY SAVED THE WORLD TOGETHER, REMEMBER?
OH, RIGHT, I KNEW THAT.
WELL, IT WASN'T JUST ME AND ZUKO SAVING THE WORLD. A LOT OF DIFFERENT PEOPLE HELPED.
AND NOW I HAVE TO GET BACK TO HELPING THEM CLEAN UP THIS BEACH.
BYE, AVATAR! YOU'RE MY HERO!
SHEN, DON'T EMBARRASS THE AVATAR.
GOT YOURSELF A NEW FAN CLUB, I SEE.
I'M GLAD SOMEONE IN THIS TOWN IS STILL IMPRESSED BY BENDING.

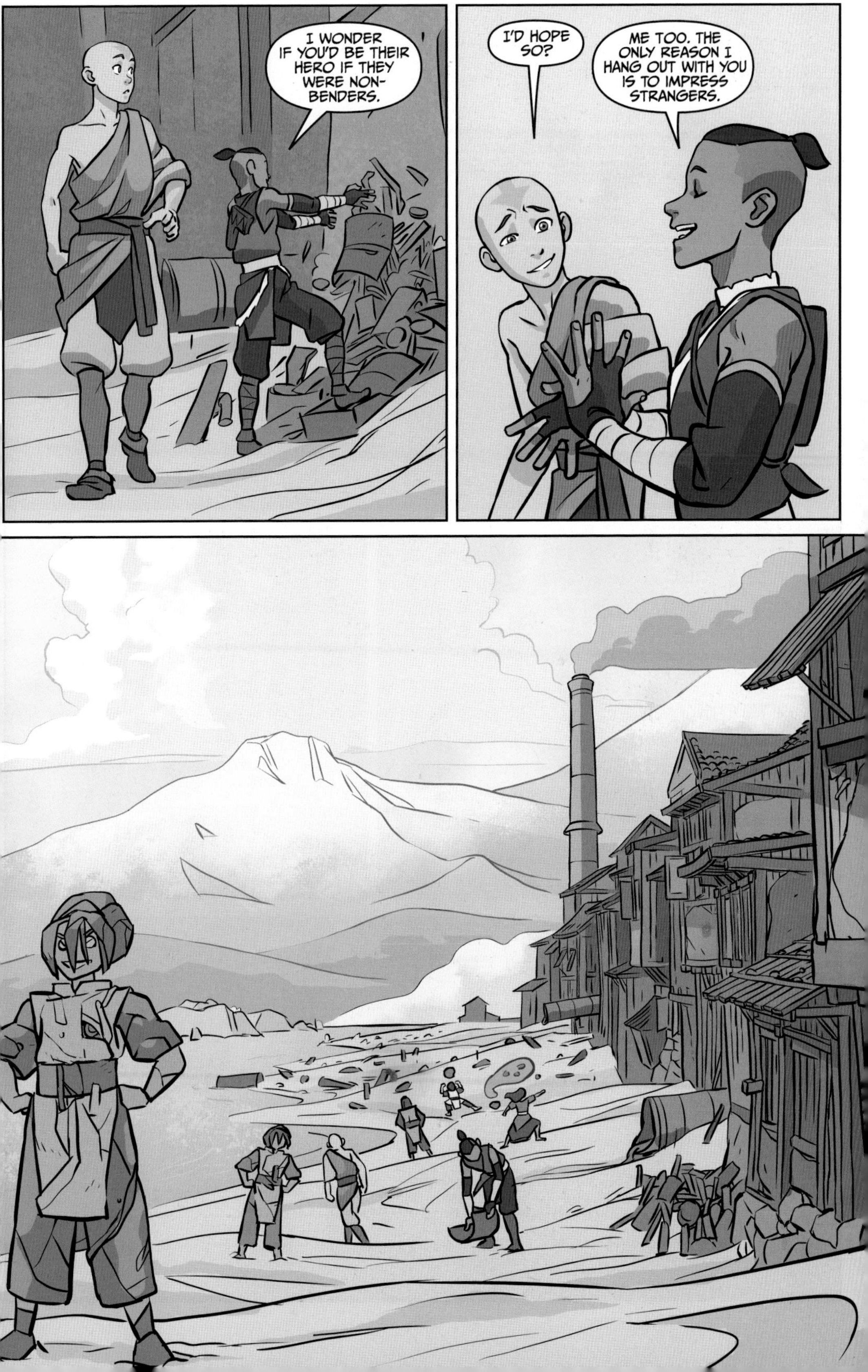
I WONDER IF YOU'D BE THEIR HERO IF THEY WERE NON-BENDERS.
I'D HOPE SO?
ME TOO. THE ONLY REASON I HANG OUT WITH YOU IS TO IMPRESS STRANGERS.

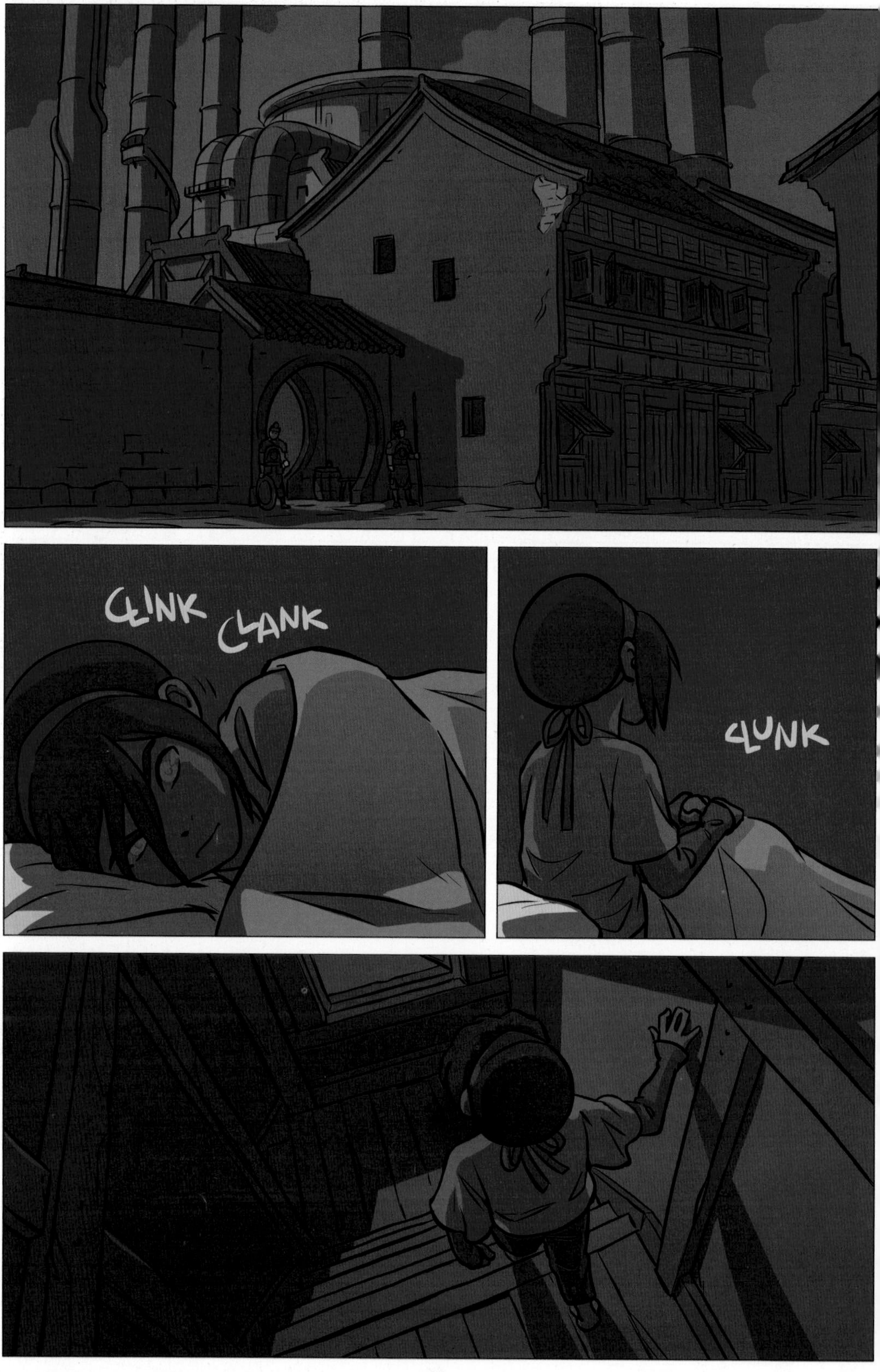
CLINK CLANK
CLUNK

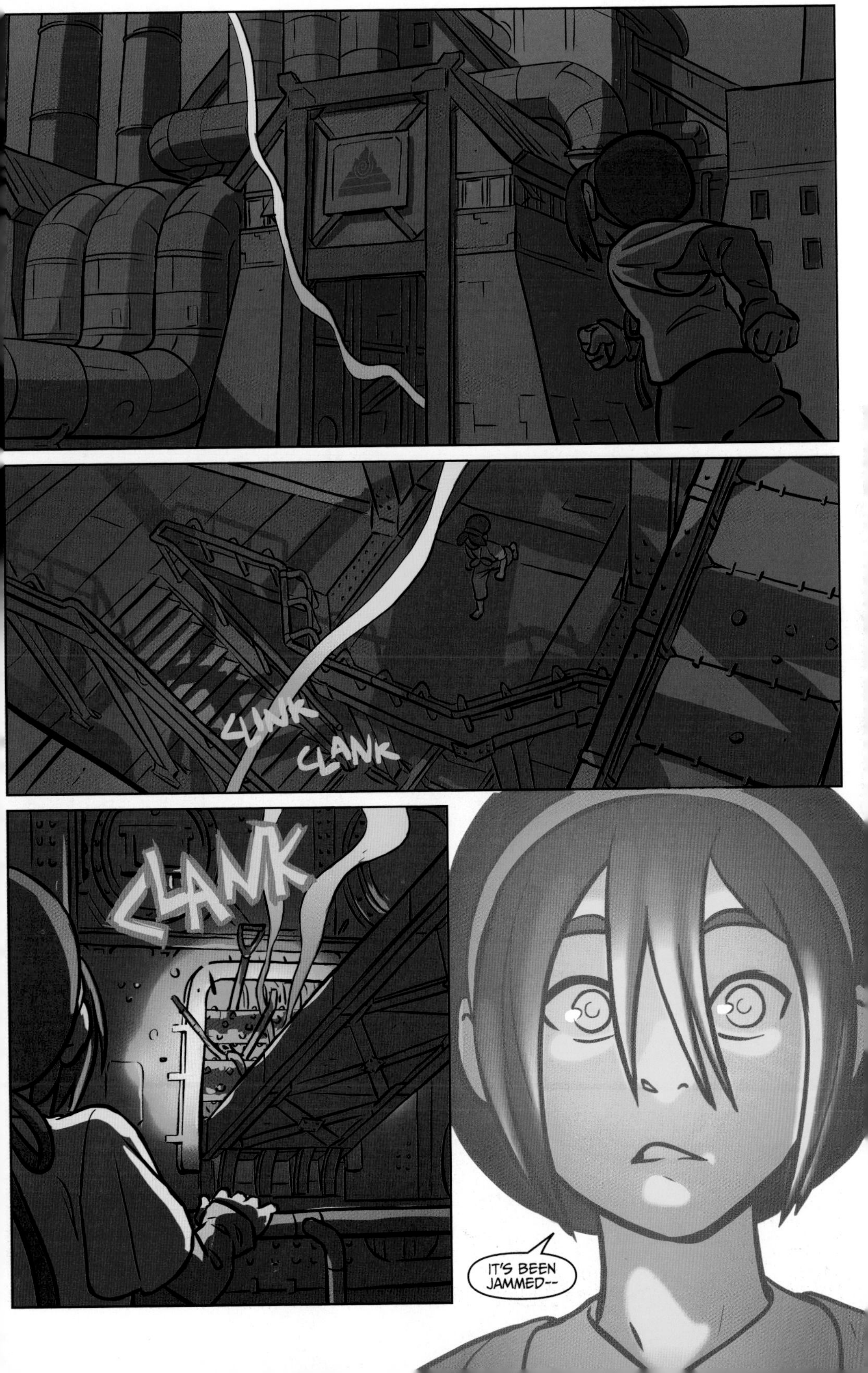
CLINK
CLANK
CLANK
IT'S BEEN JAMMED--

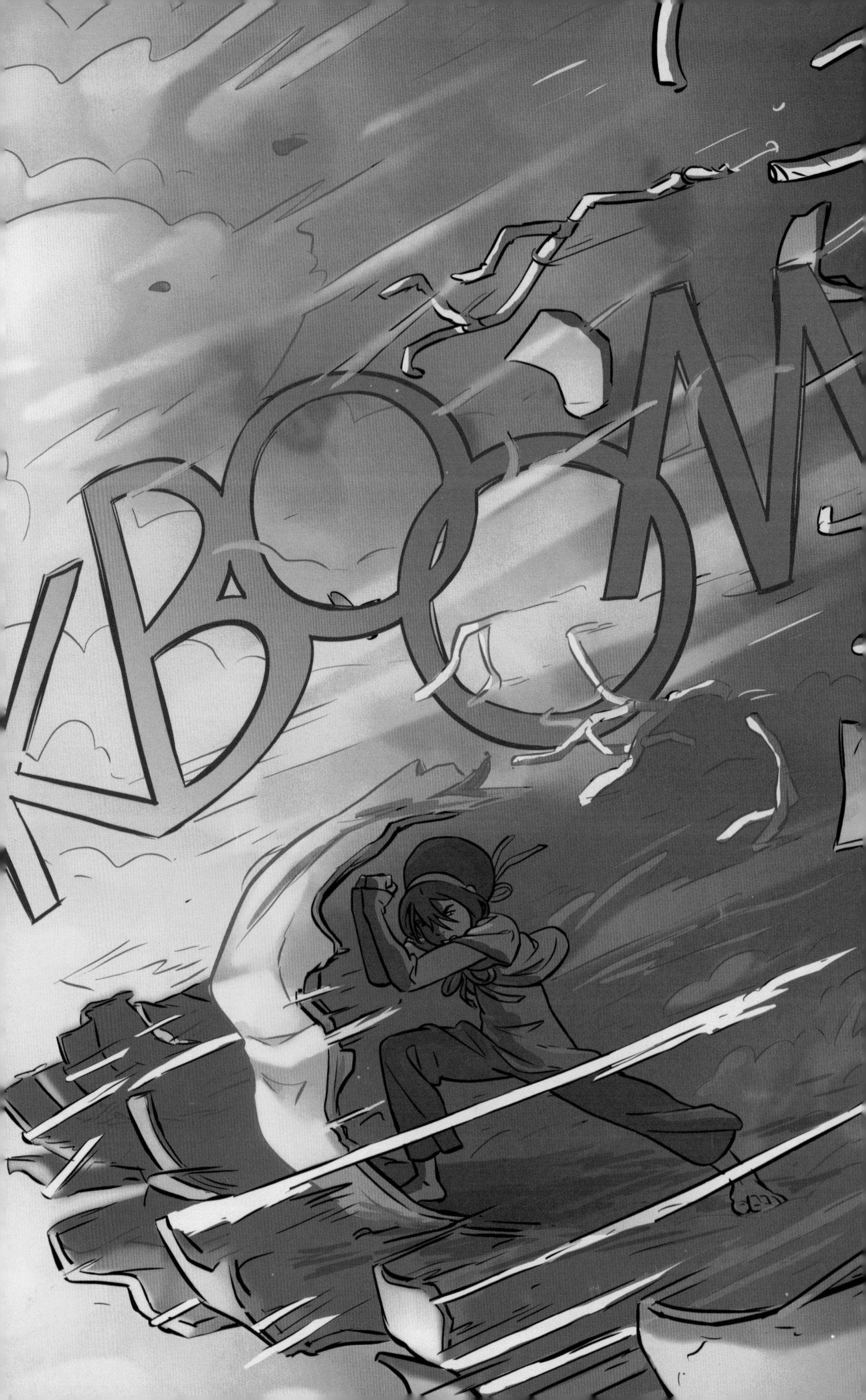
BOOM

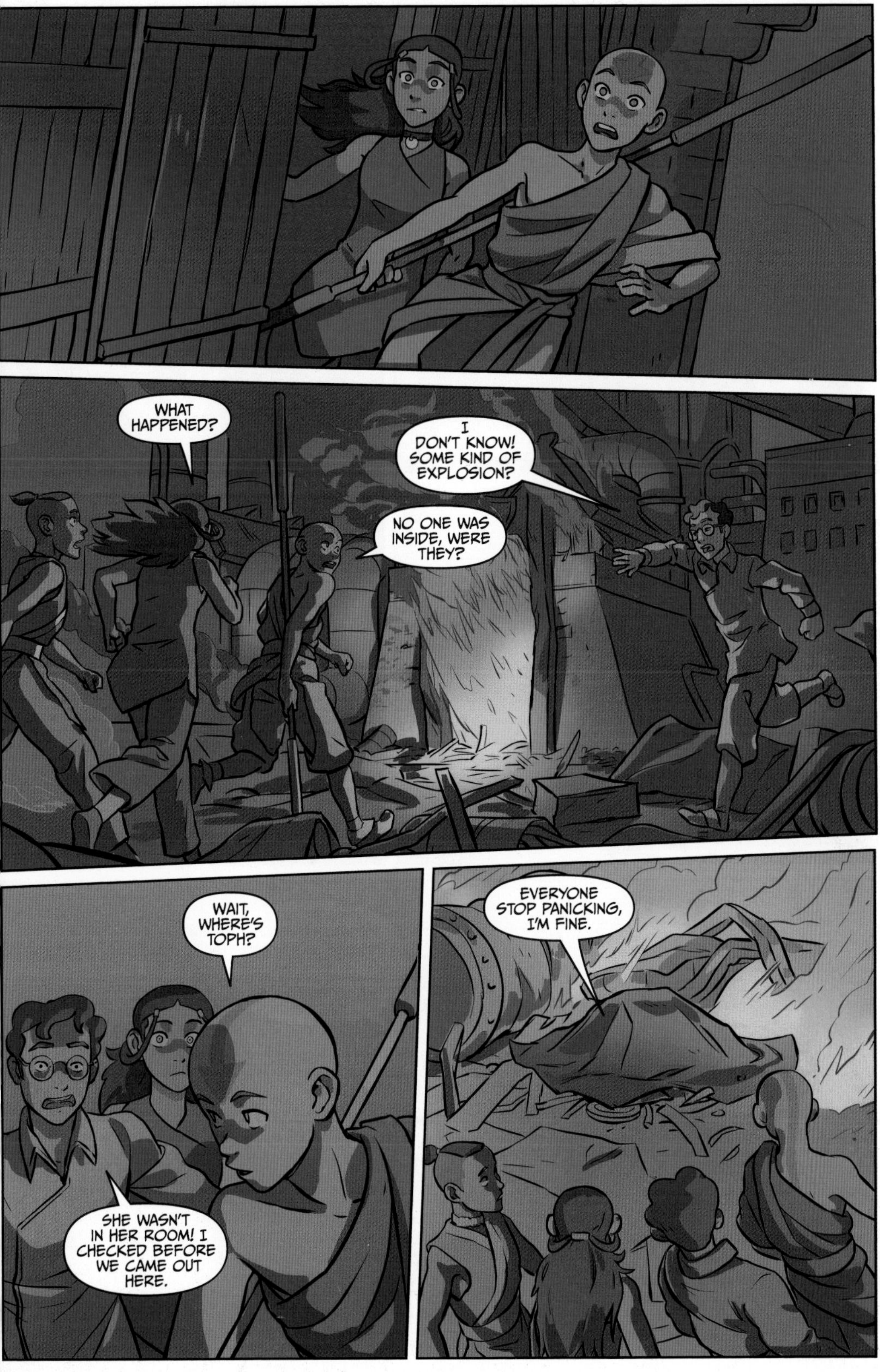
WHAT HAPPENED?
I DON'T KNOW! SOME KIND OF EXPLOSION?
NO ONE WAS INSIDE, WERE THEY?
WAIT, WHERE'S TOPH?
SHE WASN'T IN HER ROOM! I CHECKED BEFORE WE CAME OUT HERE.
EVERYONE STOP PANICKING, I'M FINE.

IT'LL TAKE A LOT MORE THAN AN EXPLODING FACTORY TO TAKE ME OUT.

GLAD YOU'RE OKAY--

DON'T DISTRACT ME, TWINKLE TOES. I NEED TO LISTEN.

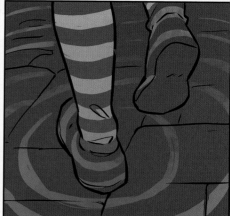

THERE! TWO PEOPLE RUNNING DOWN THAT ALLEYWAY! PROBABLY THE SAME PEOPLE WHO SABOTAGED THE MACHINE.

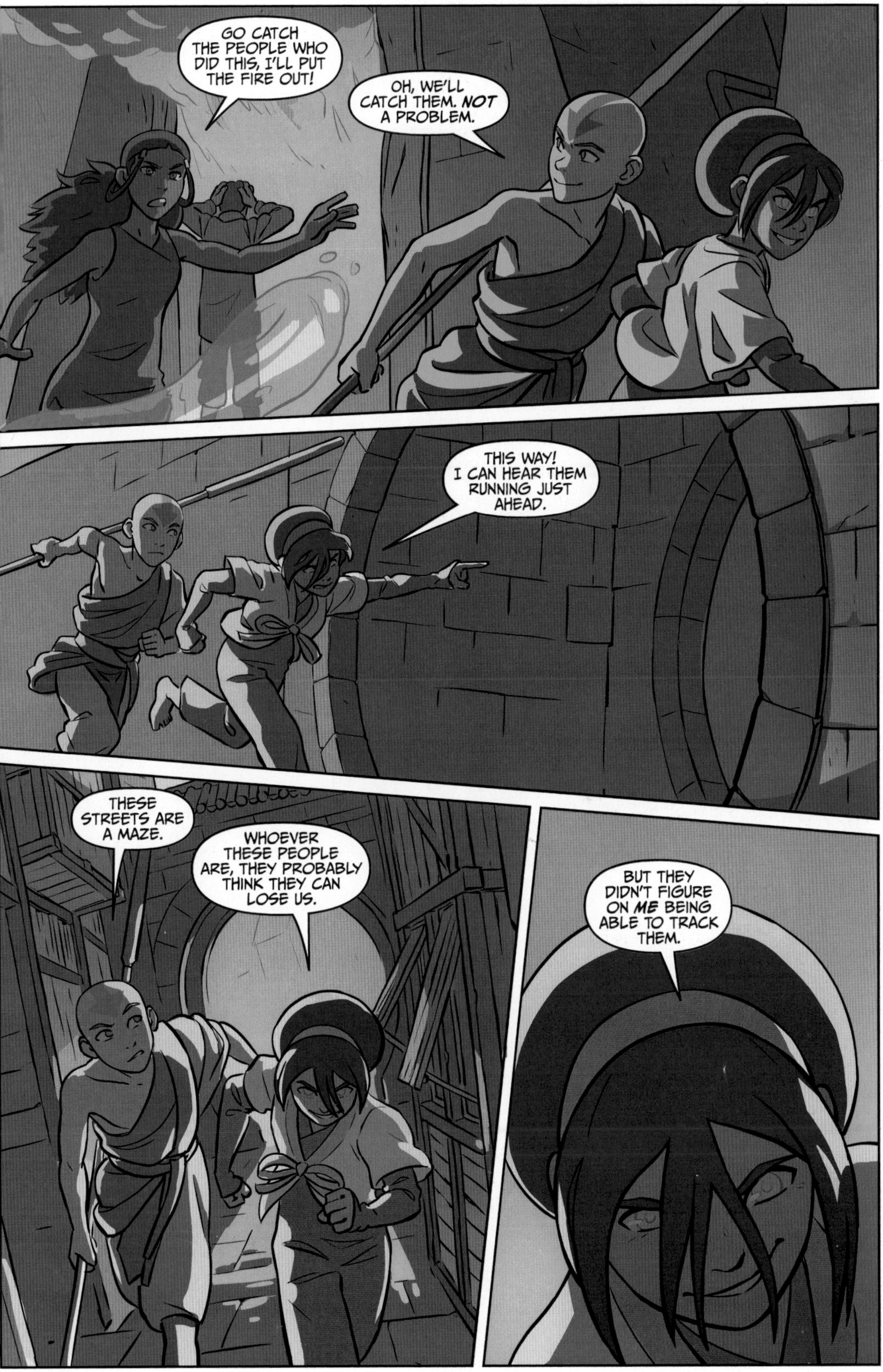
GO CATCH THE PEOPLE WHO DID THIS, I'LL PUT THE FIRE OUT!
OH, WE'LL CATCH THEM. NOT A PROBLEM.
THIS WAY! I CAN HEAR THEM RUNNING JUST AHEAD.
THESE STREETS ARE A MAZE.
WHOEVER THESE PEOPLE ARE, THEY PROBABLY THINK THEY CAN LOSE US.
BUT THEY DIDN'T FIGURE ON ME BEING ABLE TO TRACK THEM.

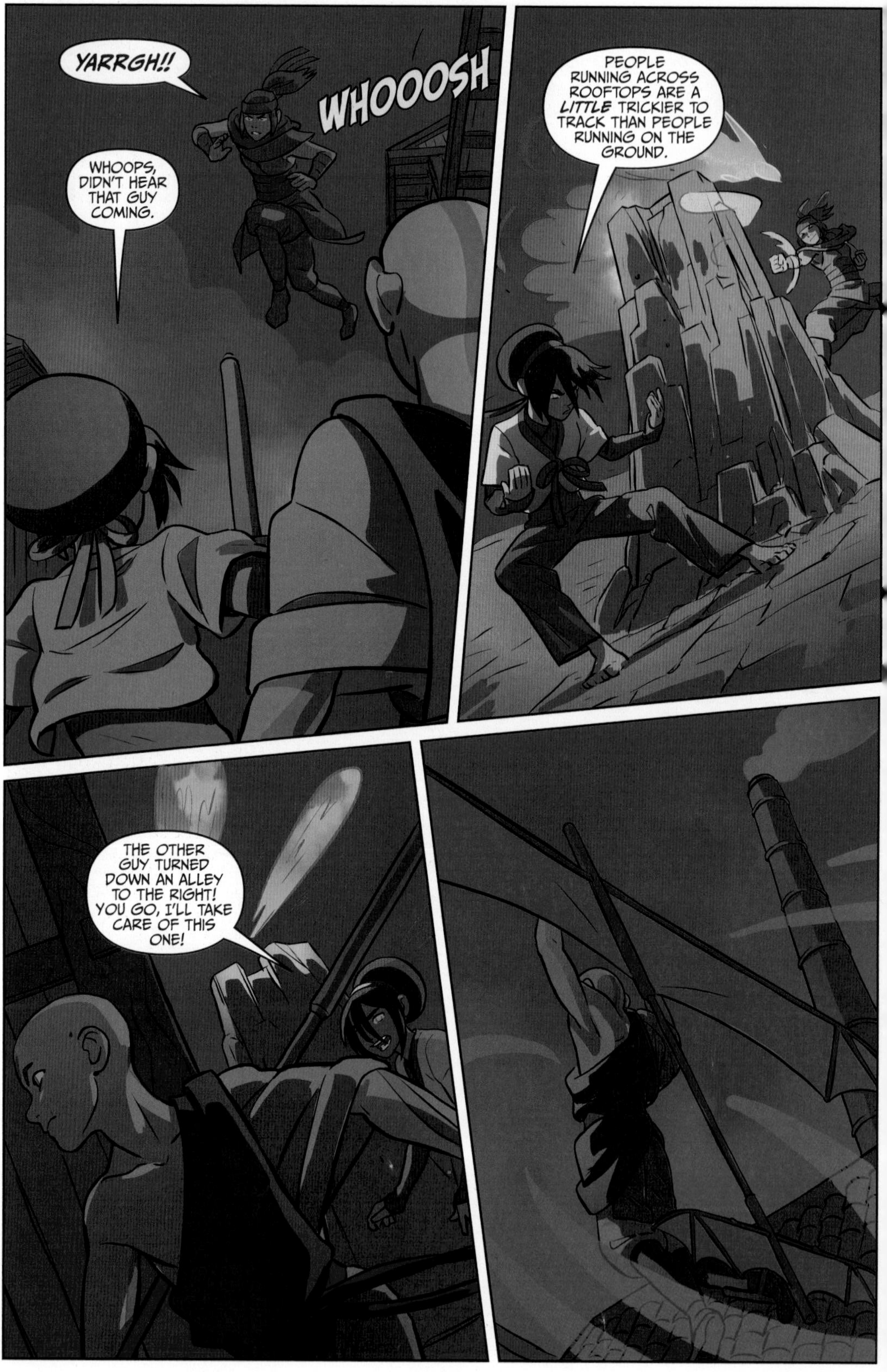
YARRGH!!
WHOOOSH
WHOOPS, DIDN'T HEAR THAT GUY COMING.
PEOPLE RUNNING ACROSS ROOFTOPS ARE A *LITTLE* TRICKIER TO TRACK THAN PEOPLE RUNNING ON THE GROUND.
THE OTHER GUY TURNED DOWN AN ALLEY TO THE RIGHT! YOU GO, I'LL TAKE CARE OF THIS ONE!

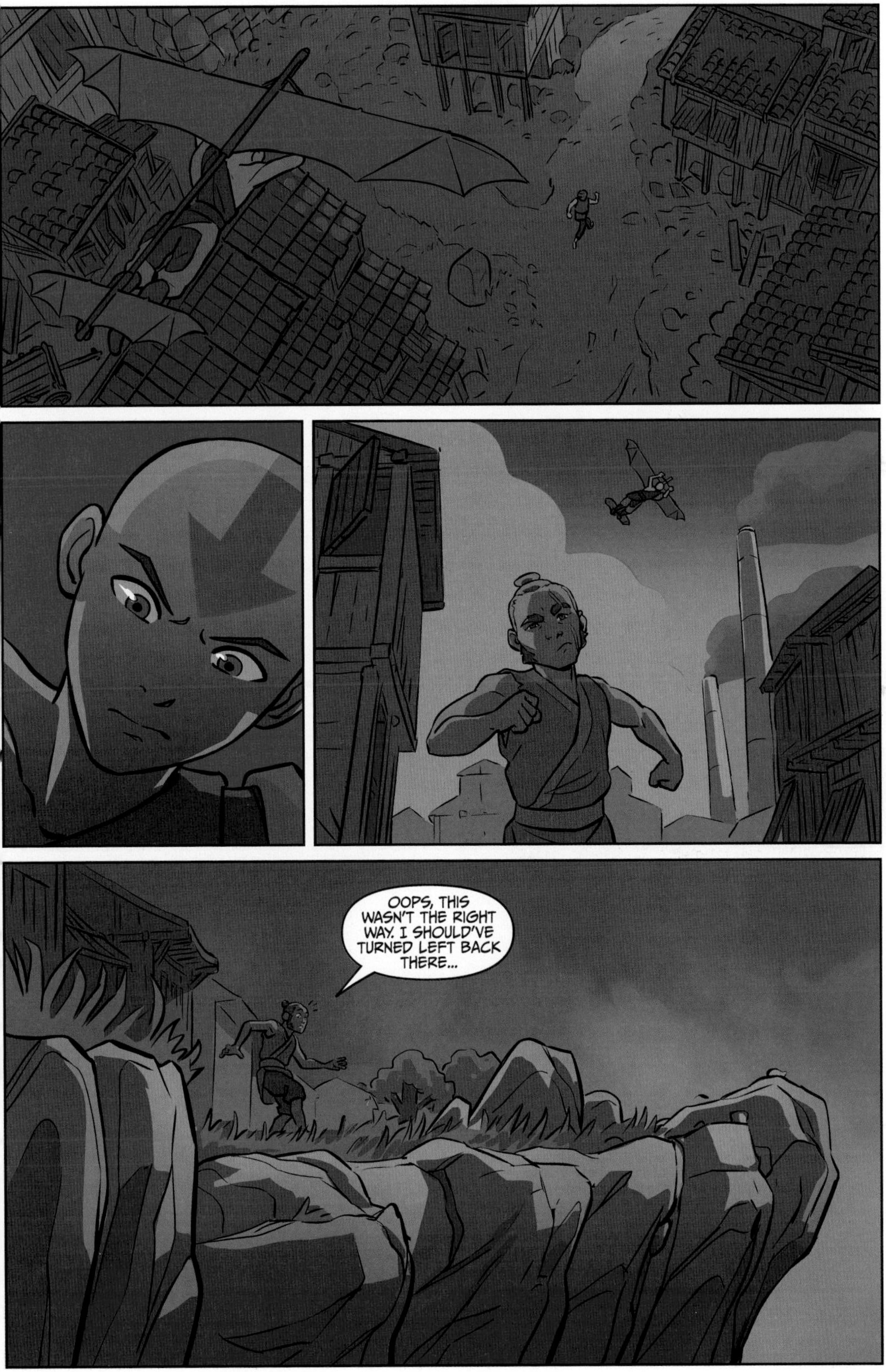
OOPS, THIS WASN'T THE RIGHT WAY. I SHOULD'VE TURNED LEFT BACK THERE...

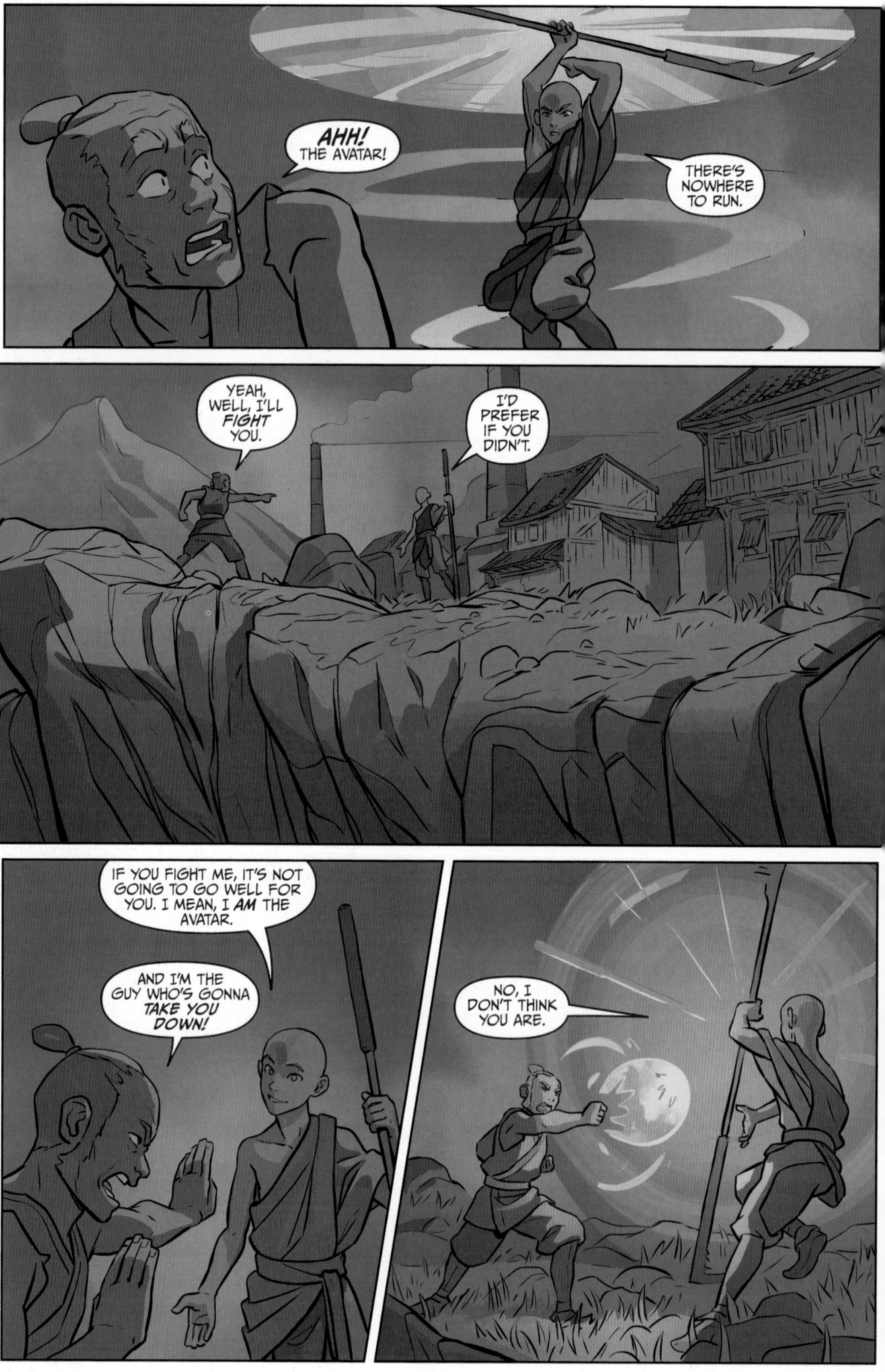
AHH! THE AVATAR!
THERE'S NOWHERE TO RUN.
YEAH, WELL, I'LL FIGHT YOU.
I'D PREFER IF YOU DIDN'T.
IF YOU FIGHT ME, IT'S NOT GOING TO GO WELL FOR YOU. I MEAN, I AM THE AVATAR.
AND I'M THE GUY WHO'S GONNA TAKE YOU DOWN!
NO, I DON'T THINK YOU ARE.

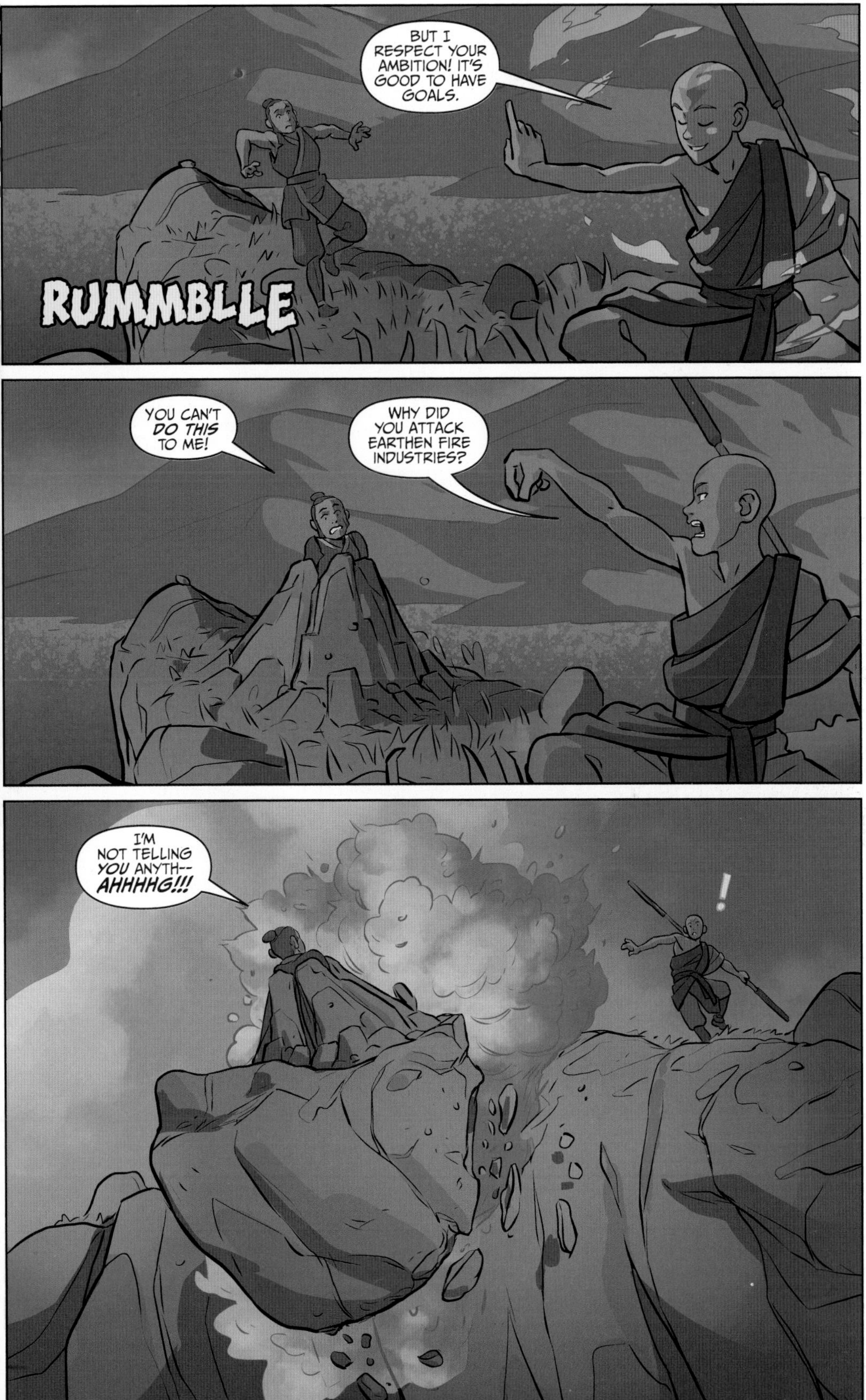
BUT I RESPECT YOUR AMBITION! IT'S GOOD TO HAVE GOALS.
RUMMBLLE
YOU CAN'T DO THIS TO ME!
WHY DID YOU ATTACK EARTHEN FIRE INDUSTRIES?
I'M NOT TELLING YOU ANYTH-- AHHHHG!!!
!

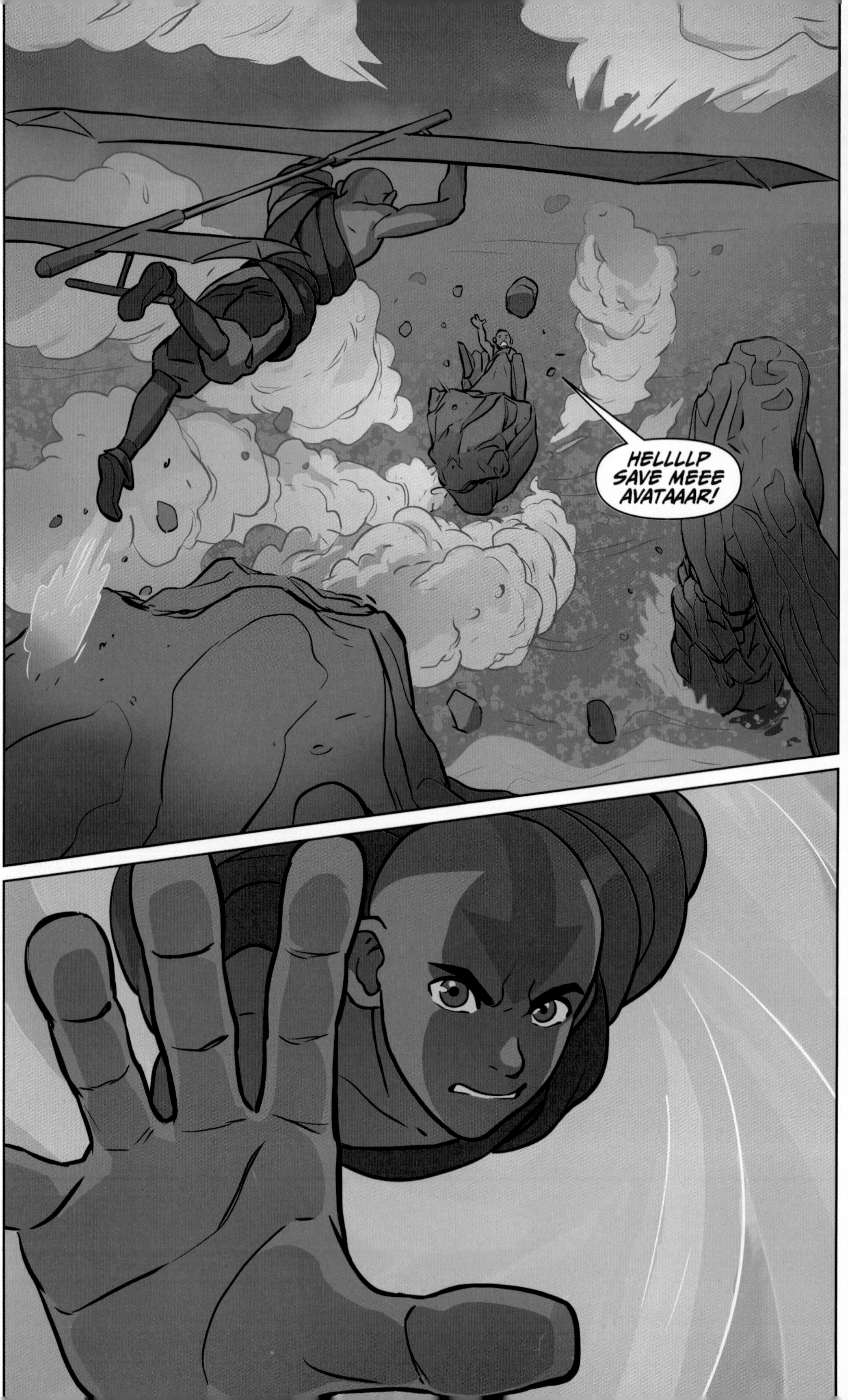
HELLLLP SAVE MEEE AVATAAAR!

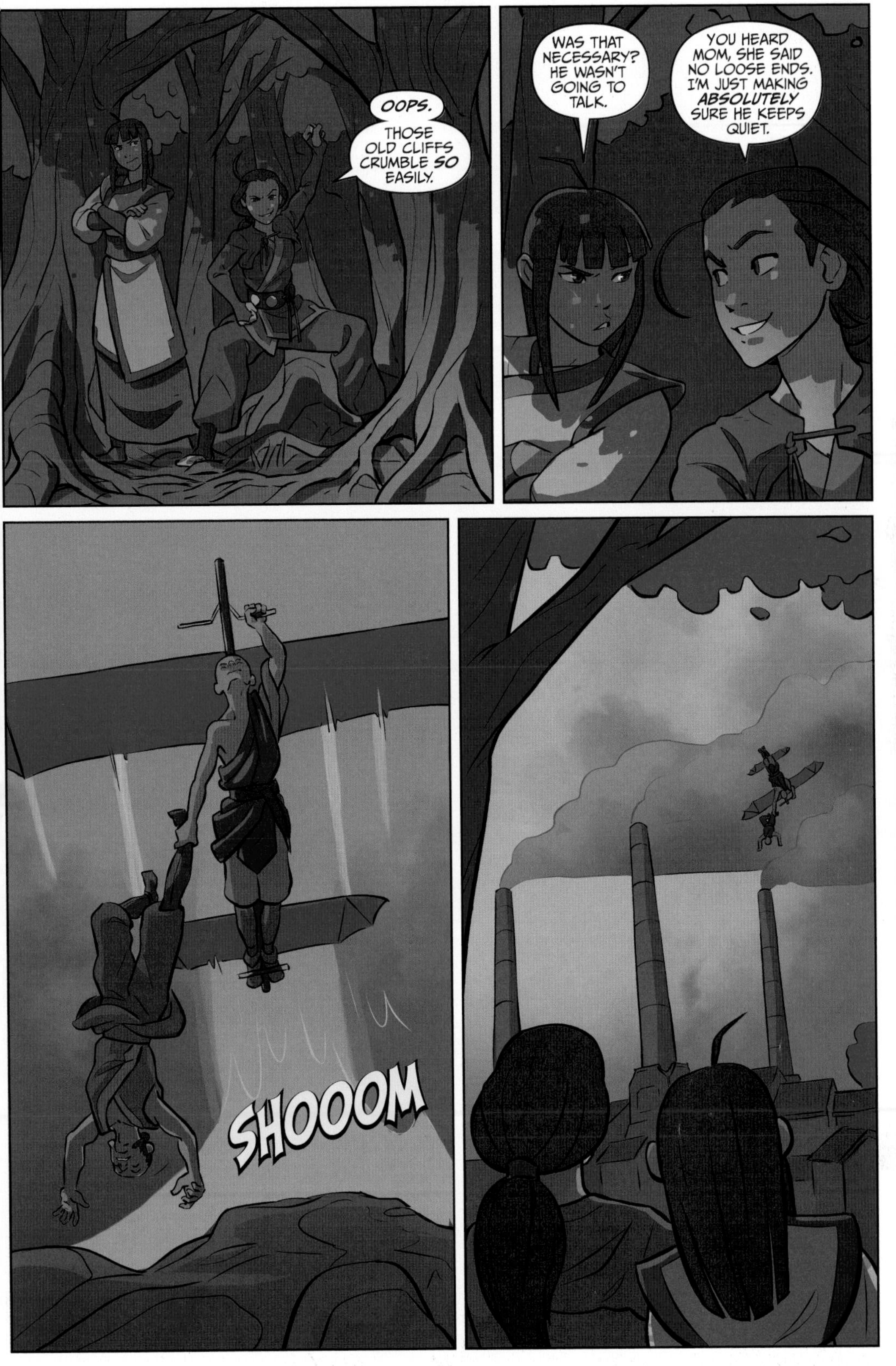

OOPS.
THOSE OLD CLIFFS CRUMBLE SO EASILY.
WAS THAT NECESSARY? HE WASN'T GOING TO TALK.
YOU HEARD MOM, SHE SAID NO LOOSE ENDS. I'M JUST MAKING ABSOLUTELY SURE HE KEEPS QUIET.
SHOOOM

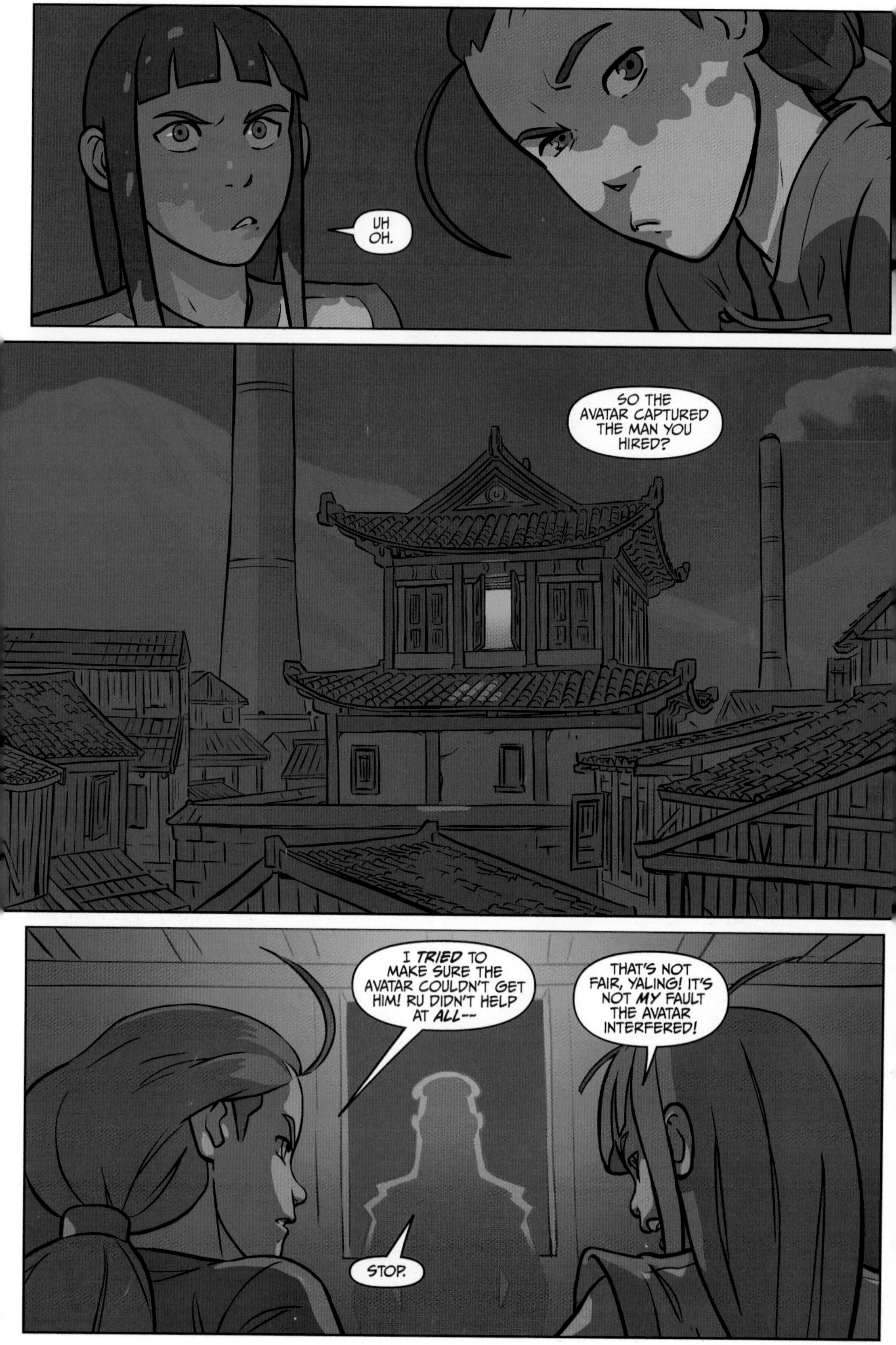
UH OH.
SO THE AVATAR CAPTURED THE MAN YOU HIRED?
I *TRIED* TO MAKE SURE THE AVATAR COULDN'T GET HIM! RU DIDN'T HELP AT *ALL*--
THAT'S NOT FAIR, YALING! IT'S NOT *MY* FAULT THE AVATAR INTERFERED!
STOP.

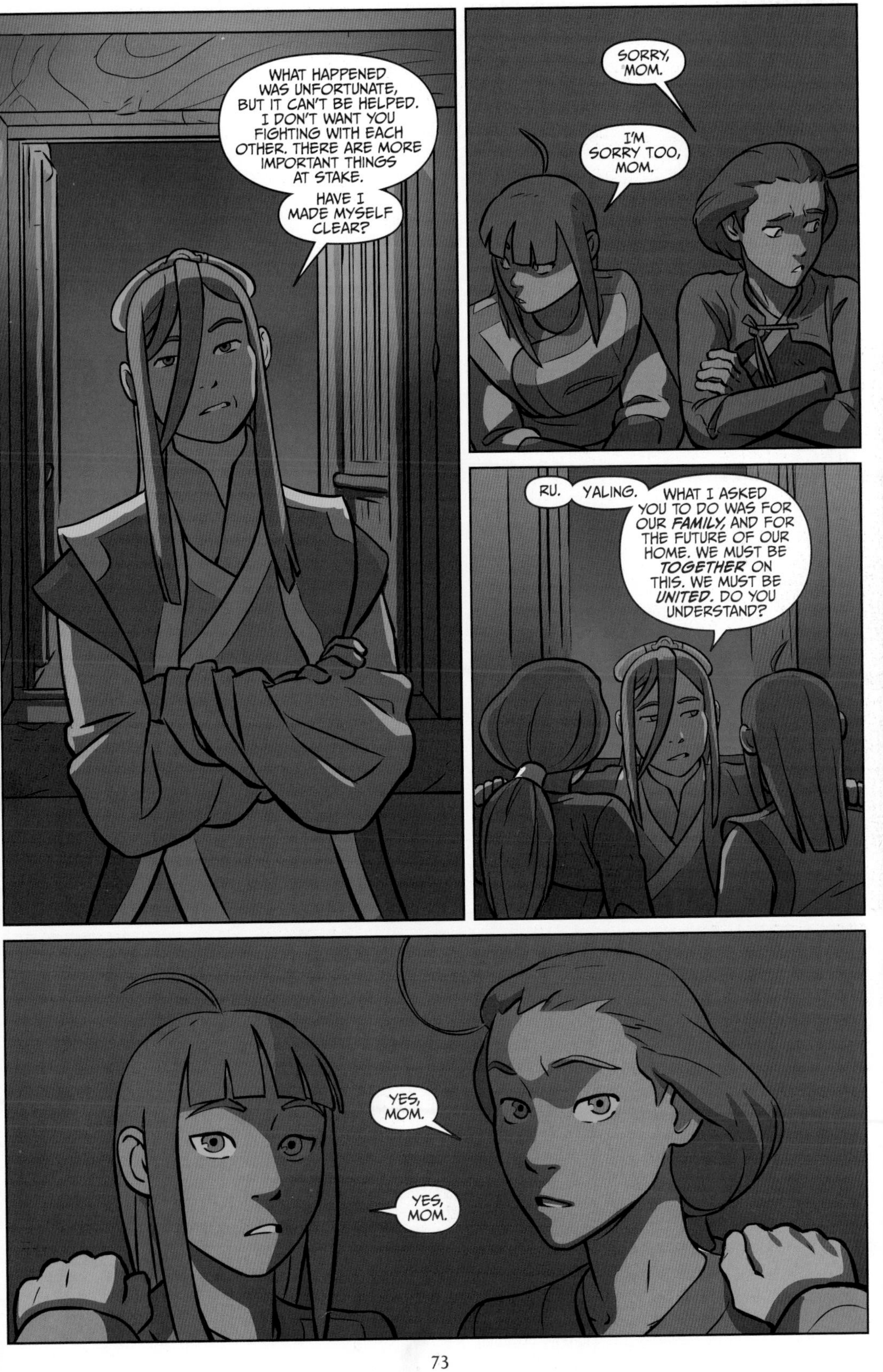
WHAT HAPPENED WAS UNFORTUNATE, BUT IT CAN'T BE HELPED. I DON'T WANT YOU FIGHTING WITH EACH OTHER. THERE ARE MORE IMPORTANT THINGS AT STAKE.
HAVE I MADE MYSELF CLEAR?
SORRY, MOM.
I'M SORRY TOO, MOM.
RU.
YALING.
WHAT I ASKED YOU TO DO WAS FOR OUR *FAMILY,* AND FOR THE FUTURE OF OUR HOME. WE MUST BE *TOGETHER* ON THIS. WE MUST BE *UNITED.* DO YOU UNDERSTAND?
YES, MOM.
YES, MOM.

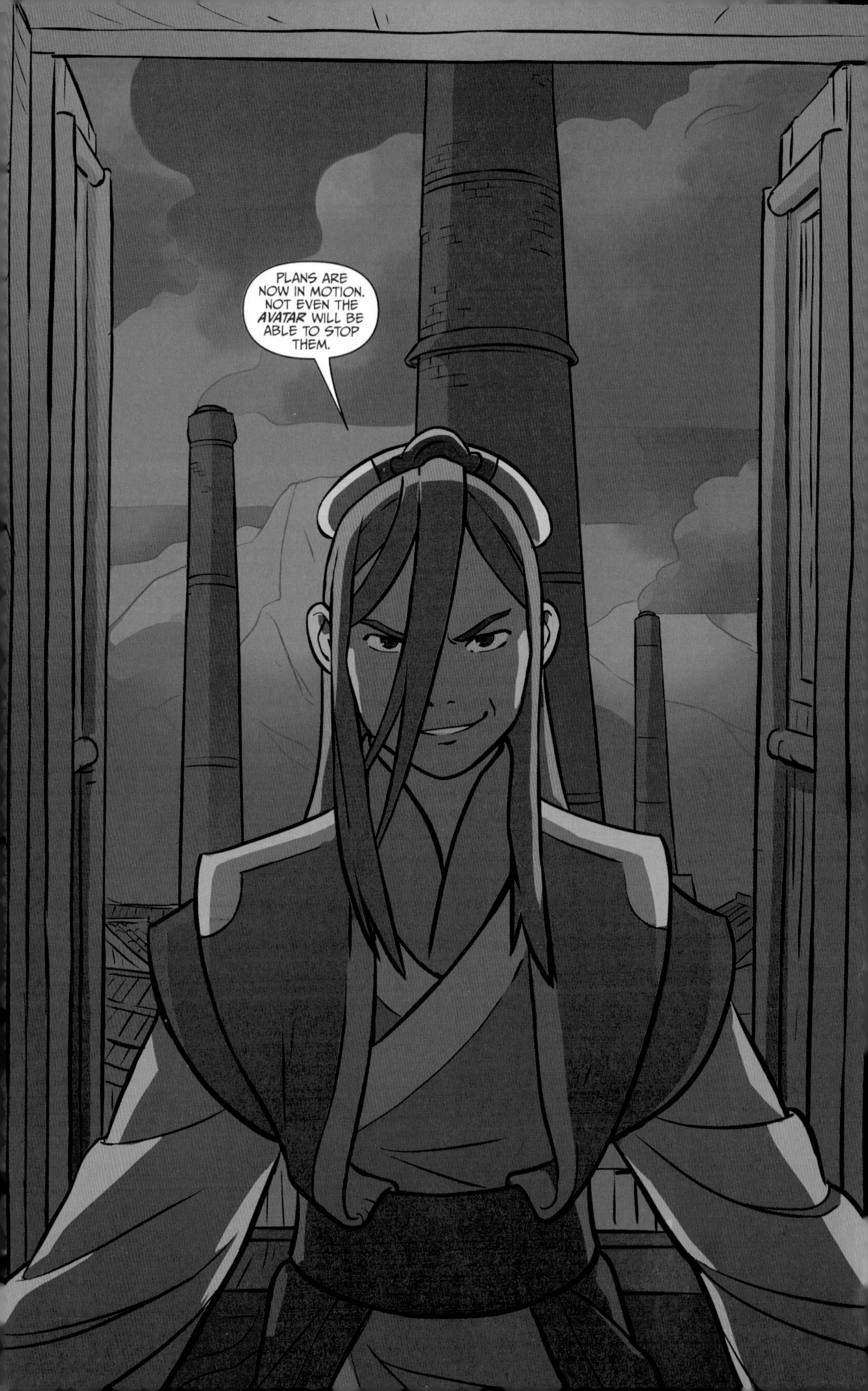
PLANS ARE NOW IN MOTION. NOT EVEN THE *AVATAR* WILL BE ABLE TO STOP THEM.

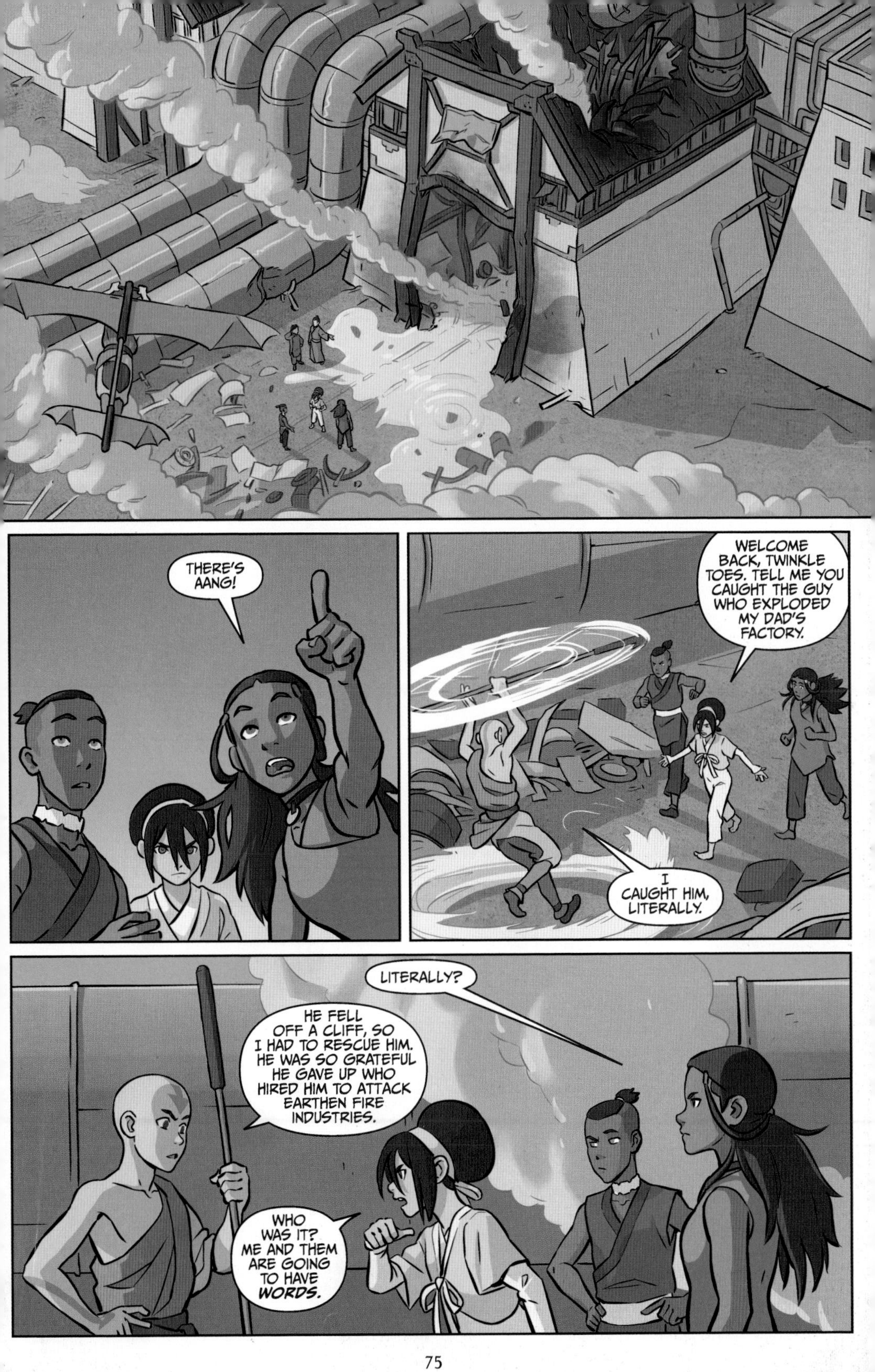
THERE'S AANG!
WELCOME BACK, TWINKLE TOES. TELL ME YOU CAUGHT THE GUY WHO EXPLODED MY DAD'S FACTORY.
I CAUGHT HIM, LITERALLY.
LITERALLY?
HE FELL OFF A CLIFF, SO I HAD TO RESCUE HIM. HE WAS SO GRATEFUL HE GAVE UP WHO HIRED HIM TO ATTACK EARTHEN FIRE INDUSTRIES.
WHO WAS IT? ME AND THEM ARE GOING TO HAVE *WORDS*.

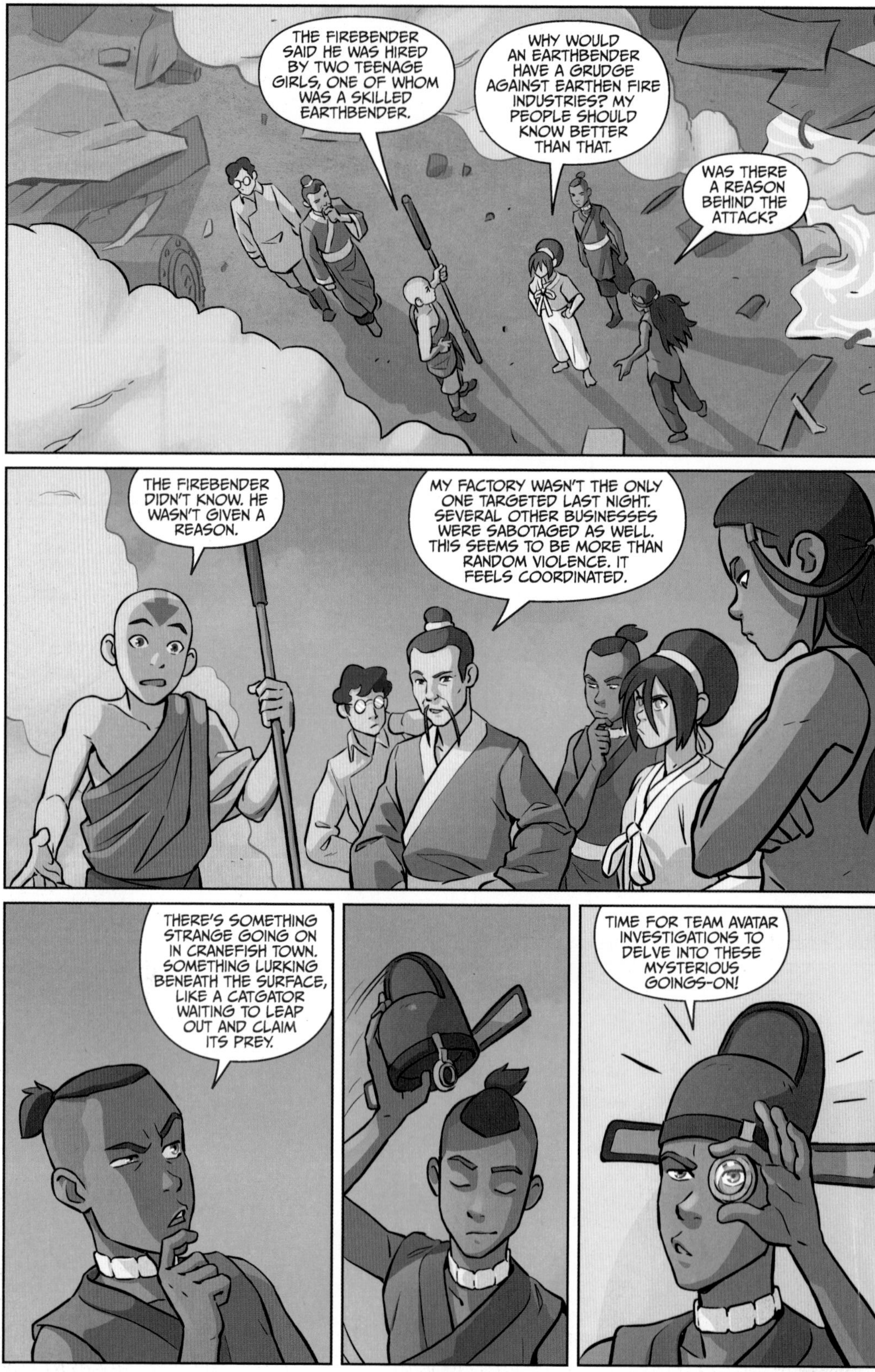
THE FIREBENDER SAID HE WAS HIRED BY TWO TEENAGE GIRLS, ONE OF WHOM WAS A SKILLED EARTHBENDER.
WHY WOULD AN EARTHBENDER HAVE A GRUDGE AGAINST EARTHEN FIRE INDUSTRIES? MY PEOPLE SHOULD KNOW BETTER THAN THAT.
WAS THERE A REASON BEHIND THE ATTACK?
THE FIREBENDER DIDN'T KNOW. HE WASN'T GIVEN A REASON.
MY FACTORY WASN'T THE ONLY ONE TARGETED LAST NIGHT. SEVERAL OTHER BUSINESSES WERE SABOTAGED AS WELL. THIS SEEMS TO BE MORE THAN RANDOM VIOLENCE. IT FEELS COORDINATED.
THERE'S SOMETHING STRANGE GOING ON IN CRANEFISH TOWN. SOMETHING LURKING BENEATH THE SURFACE, LIKE A CATGATOR WAITING TO LEAP OUT AND CLAIM ITS PREY.
TIME FOR TEAM AVATAR INVESTIGATIONS TO DELVE INTO THESE MYSTERIOUS GOINGS-ON!

I CAN'T BELIEVE YOU STILL HAVE THAT HAT.

I CAN'T BELIEVE YOU EVER THOUGHT I'D GET RID OF THIS AMAZING HAT. DO YOU KNOW ME AT ALL?

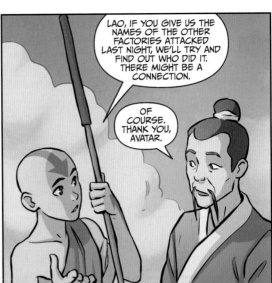

LAO, IF YOU GIVE US THE NAMES OF THE OTHER FACTORIES ATTACKED LAST NIGHT, WE'LL TRY AND FIND OUT WHO DID IT. THERE MIGHT BE A CONNECTION.

OF COURSE. THANK YOU, AVATAR.

DON'T LOOK SO DOWN, SIS. IT'S JUST A HAT.

IT'S NOT THE HAT. IT'S WHAT YOU JUST SAID. THERE'S SOMETHING GOING ON BENEATH THE SURFACE OF CRANEFISH TOWN, BUT WE HAVEN'T SEEN IT YET.

HAD ENOUGH OF HANGING OUT WITH APPA, MOMO? LET'S GO FOR A WALK IN THE CITY.

WHATEVER'S HAPPENING HERE, WE'LL BE ABLE TO HANDLE IT. WE'RE TEAM AVATAR INVESTIGATIONS.

I HOPE SO.

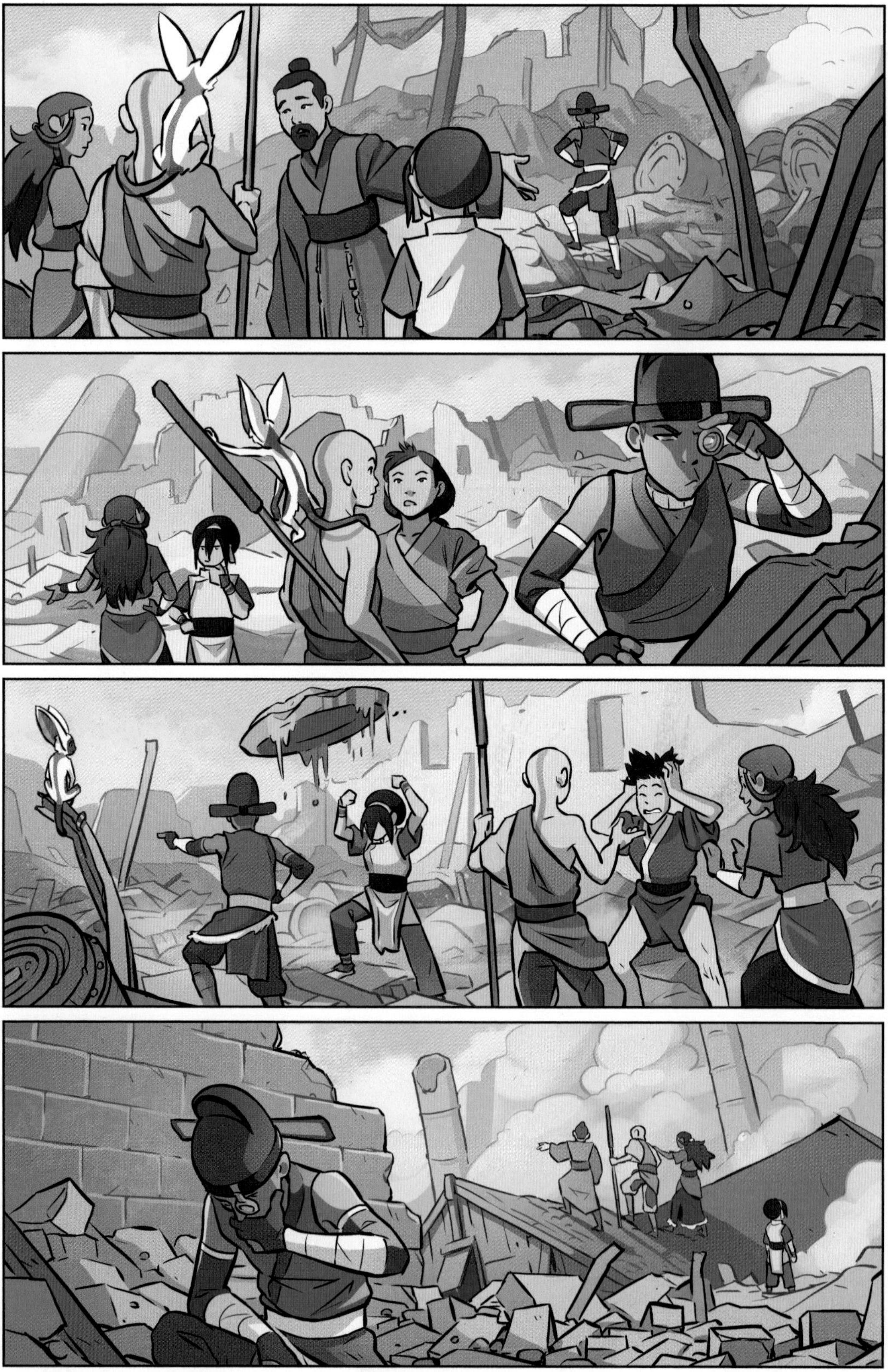

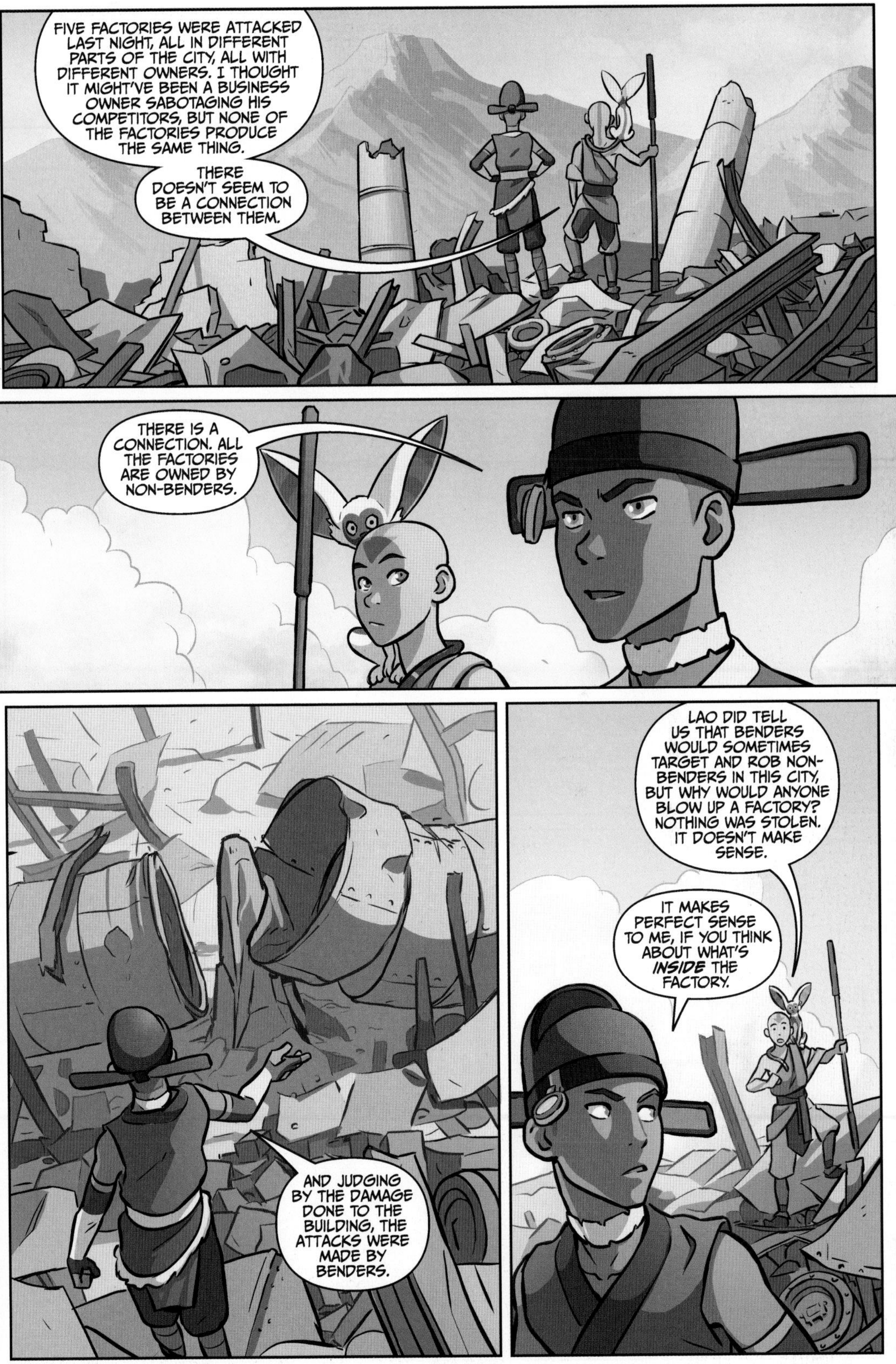
FIVE FACTORIES WERE ATTACKED LAST NIGHT, ALL IN DIFFERENT PARTS OF THE CITY, ALL WITH DIFFERENT OWNERS. I THOUGHT IT MIGHT'VE BEEN A BUSINESS OWNER SABOTAGING HIS COMPETITORS, BUT NONE OF THE FACTORIES PRODUCE THE SAME THING.
THERE DOESN'T SEEM TO BE A CONNECTION BETWEEN THEM.
THERE IS A CONNECTION. ALL THE FACTORIES ARE OWNED BY NON-BENDERS.
AND JUDGING BY THE DAMAGE DONE TO THE BUILDING, THE ATTACKS WERE MADE BY BENDERS.
LAO DID TELL US THAT BENDERS WOULD SOMETIMES TARGET AND ROB NON-BENDERS IN THIS CITY, BUT WHY WOULD ANYONE BLOW UP A FACTORY? NOTHING WAS STOLEN. IT DOESN'T MAKE SENSE.
IT MAKES PERFECT SENSE TO ME, IF YOU THINK ABOUT WHAT'S *INSIDE* THE FACTORY.

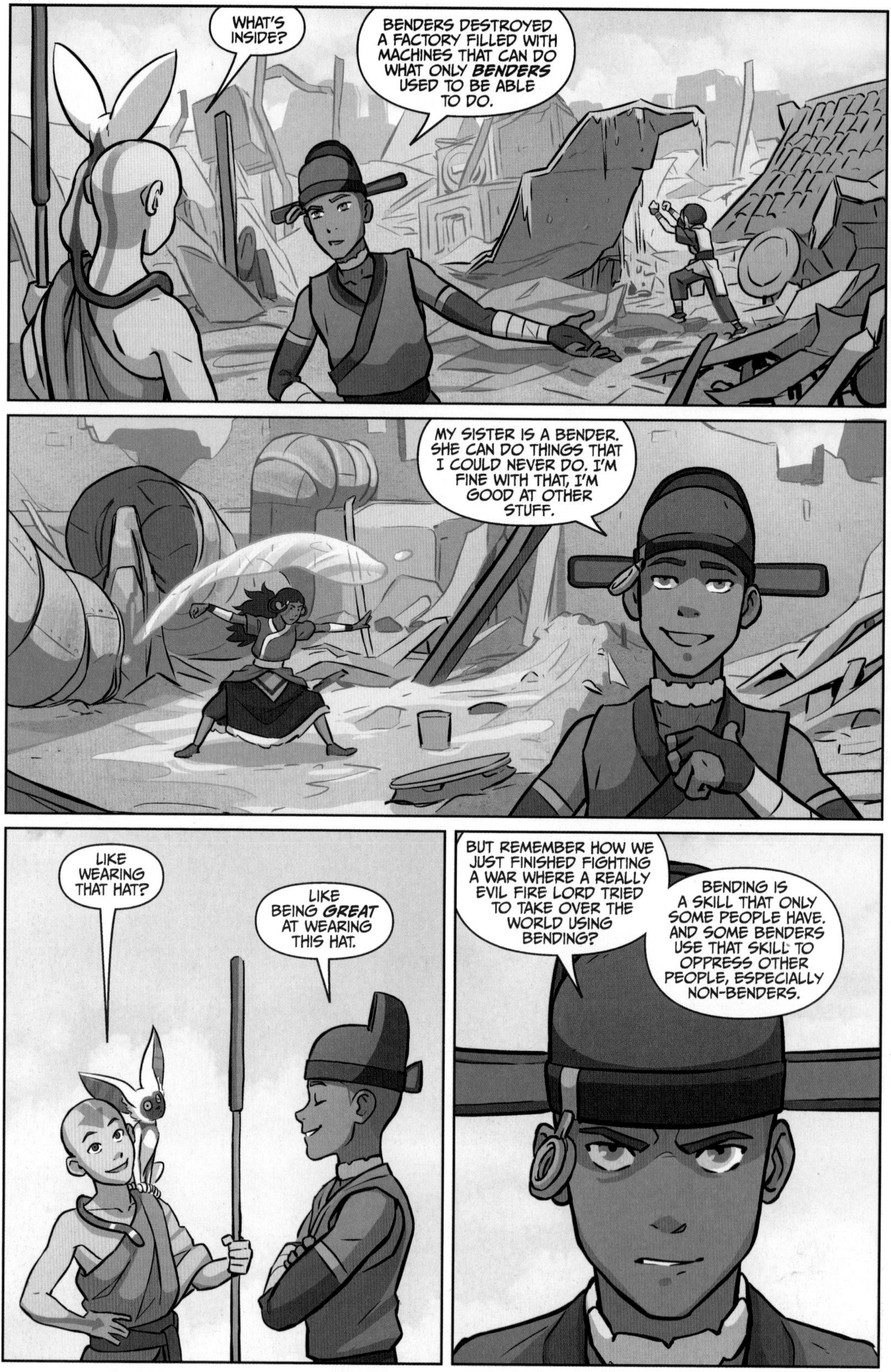
WHAT'S INSIDE?
BENDERS DESTROYED A FACTORY FILLED WITH MACHINES THAT CAN DO WHAT ONLY *BENDERS* USED TO BE ABLE TO DO.
MY SISTER IS A BENDER. SHE CAN DO THINGS THAT I COULD NEVER DO. I'M FINE WITH THAT, I'M GOOD AT OTHER STUFF.
LIKE WEARING THAT HAT?
LIKE BEING *GREAT* AT WEARING THIS HAT.
BUT REMEMBER HOW WE JUST FINISHED FIGHTING A WAR WHERE A REALLY EVIL FIRE LORD TRIED TO TAKE OVER THE WORLD USING BENDING?
BENDING IS A SKILL THAT ONLY SOME PEOPLE HAVE. AND SOME BENDERS USE THAT SKILL TO OPPRESS OTHER PEOPLE, ESPECIALLY NON-BENDERS.

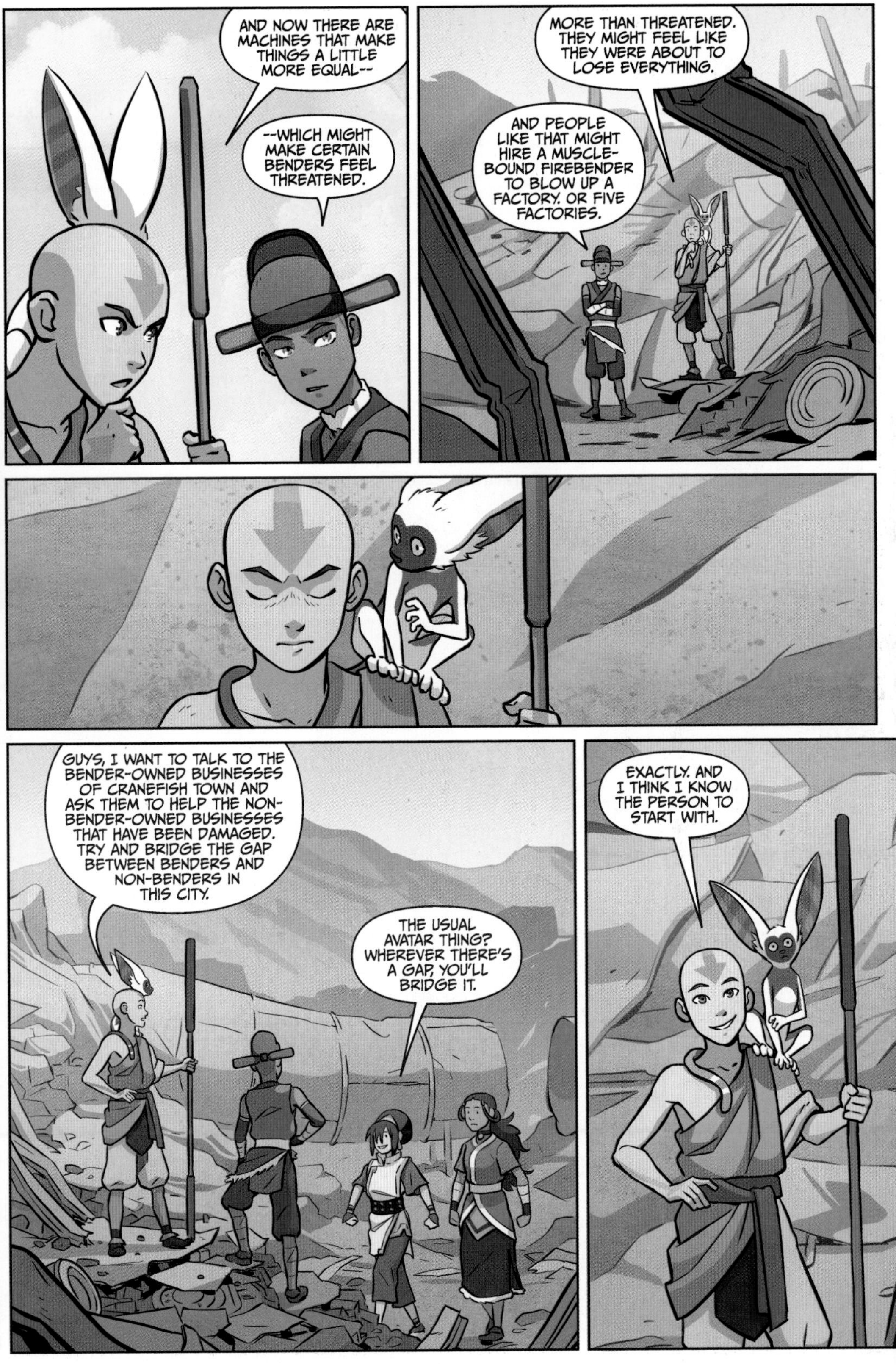
AND NOW THERE ARE MACHINES THAT MAKE THINGS A LITTLE MORE EQUAL--
--WHICH MIGHT MAKE CERTAIN BENDERS FEEL THREATENED.
MORE THAN THREATENED. THEY MIGHT FEEL LIKE THEY WERE ABOUT TO LOSE EVERYTHING.
AND PEOPLE LIKE THAT MIGHT HIRE A MUSCLE-BOUND FIREBENDER TO BLOW UP A FACTORY. OR FIVE FACTORIES.
GUYS, I WANT TO TALK TO THE BENDER-OWNED BUSINESSES OF CRANEFISH TOWN AND ASK THEM TO HELP THE NON-BENDER-OWNED BUSINESSES THAT HAVE BEEN DAMAGED. TRY AND BRIDGE THE GAP BETWEEN BENDERS AND NON-BENDERS IN THIS CITY.
THE USUAL AVATAR THING? WHEREVER THERE'S A GAP, YOU'LL BRIDGE IT.
EXACTLY. AND I THINK I KNOW THE PERSON TO START WITH.

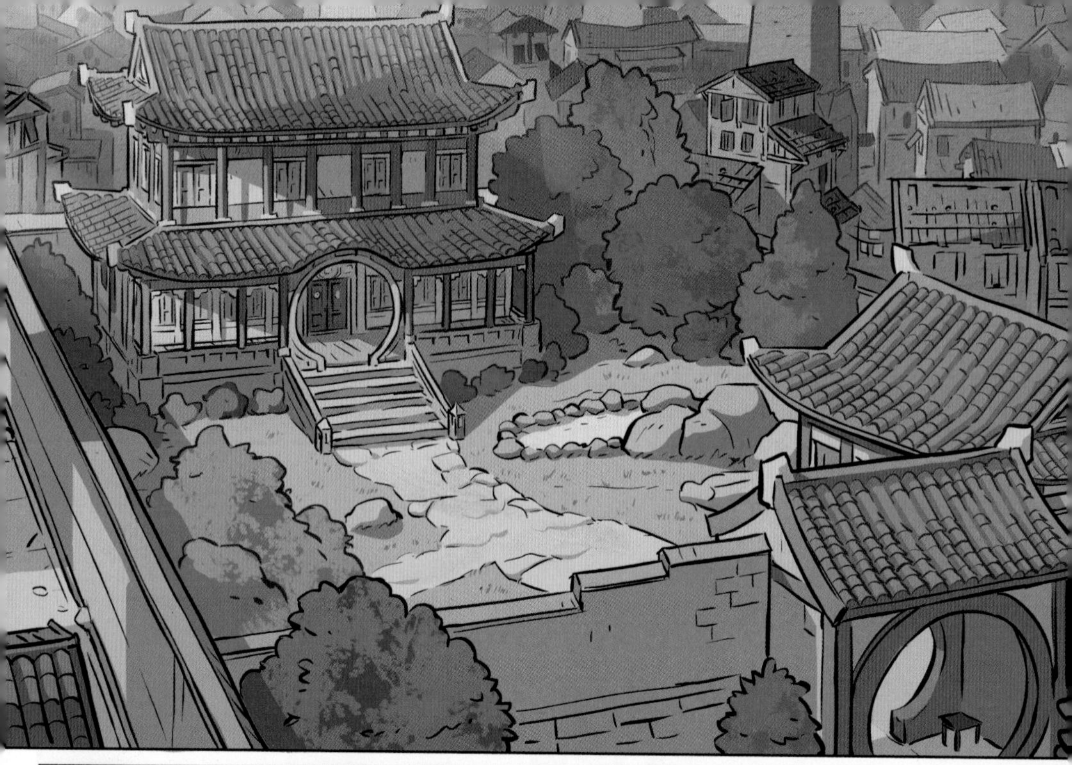

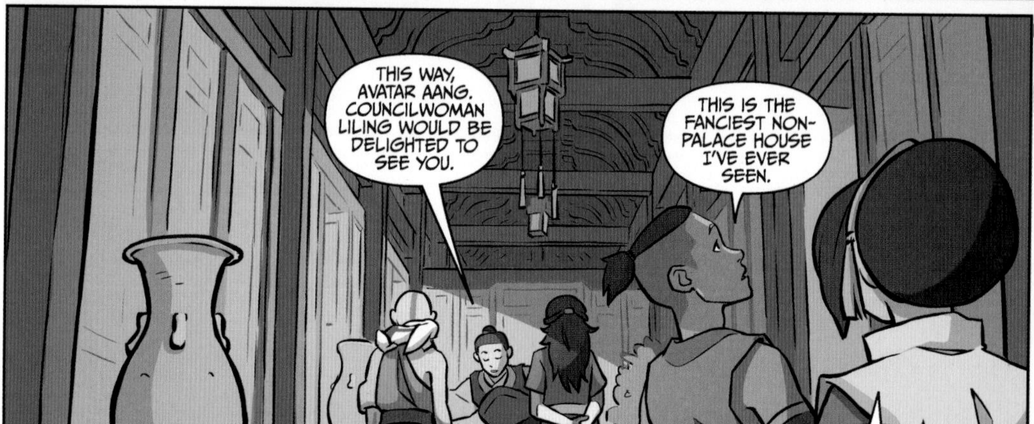
THIS WAY, AVATAR AANG. COUNCILWOMAN LILING WOULD BE DELIGHTED TO SEE YOU.
THIS IS THE FANCIEST NON-PALACE HOUSE I'VE EVER SEEN.
EH, I'VE LIVED IN FANCIER.

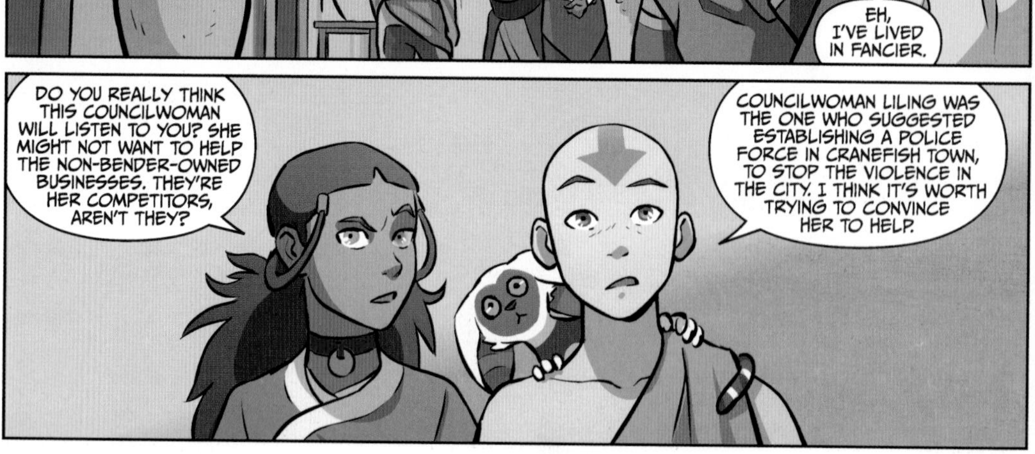
DO YOU REALLY THINK THIS COUNCILWOMAN WILL LISTEN TO YOU? SHE MIGHT NOT WANT TO HELP THE NON-BENDER-OWNED BUSINESSES. THEY'RE HER COMPETITORS, AREN'T THEY?
COUNCILWOMAN LILING WAS THE ONE WHO SUGGESTED ESTABLISHING A POLICE FORCE IN CRANEFISH TOWN, TO STOP THE VIOLENCE IN THE CITY. I THINK IT'S WORTH TRYING TO CONVINCE HER TO HELP.

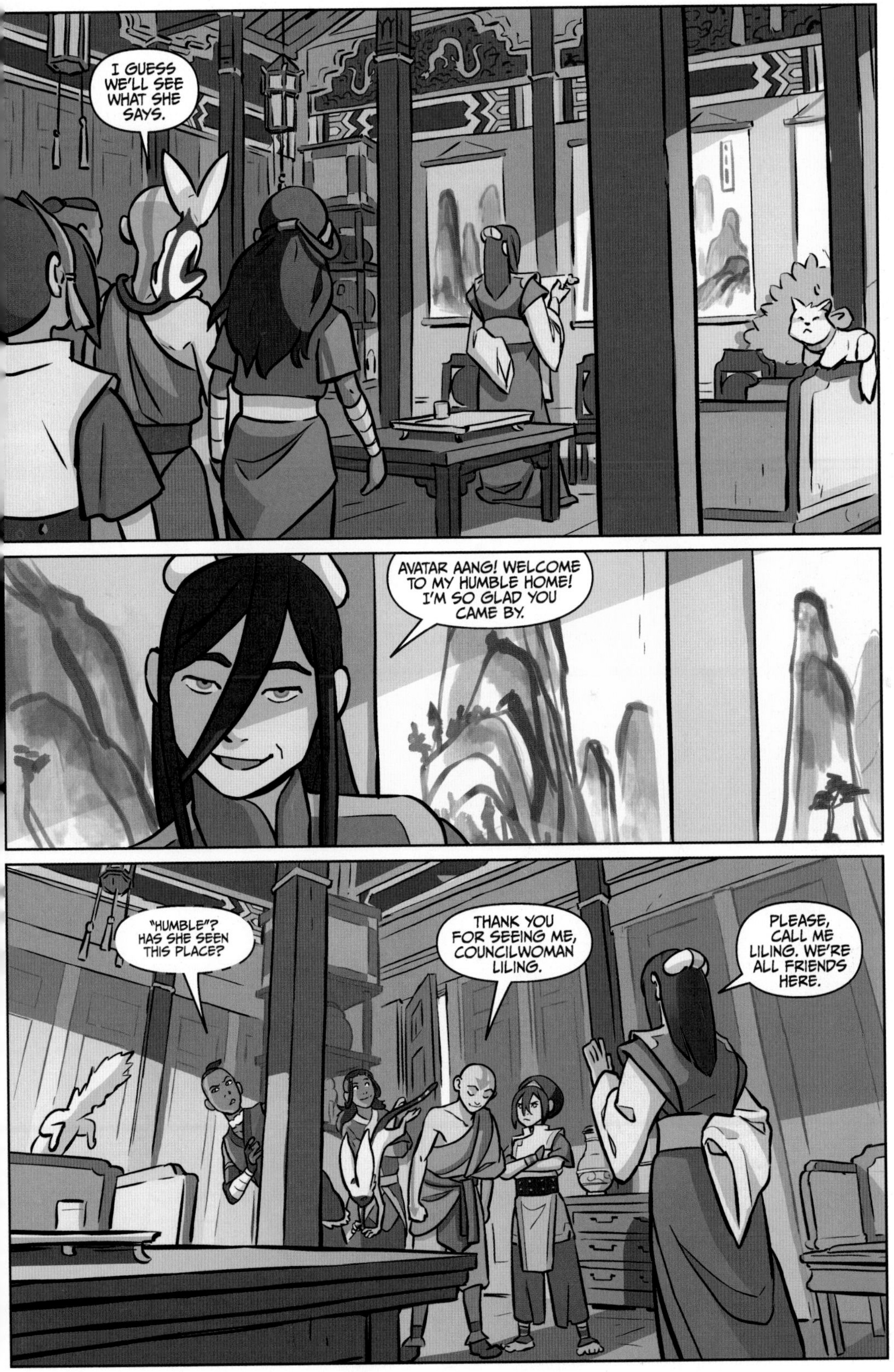
I GUESS WE'LL SEE WHAT SHE SAYS.
AVATAR AANG! WELCOME TO MY HUMBLE HOME! I'M SO GLAD YOU CAME BY.
"HUMBLE"? HAS SHE SEEN THIS PLACE?
THANK YOU FOR SEEING ME, COUNCILWOMAN LILING.
PLEASE, CALL ME LILING. WE'RE ALL FRIENDS HERE.

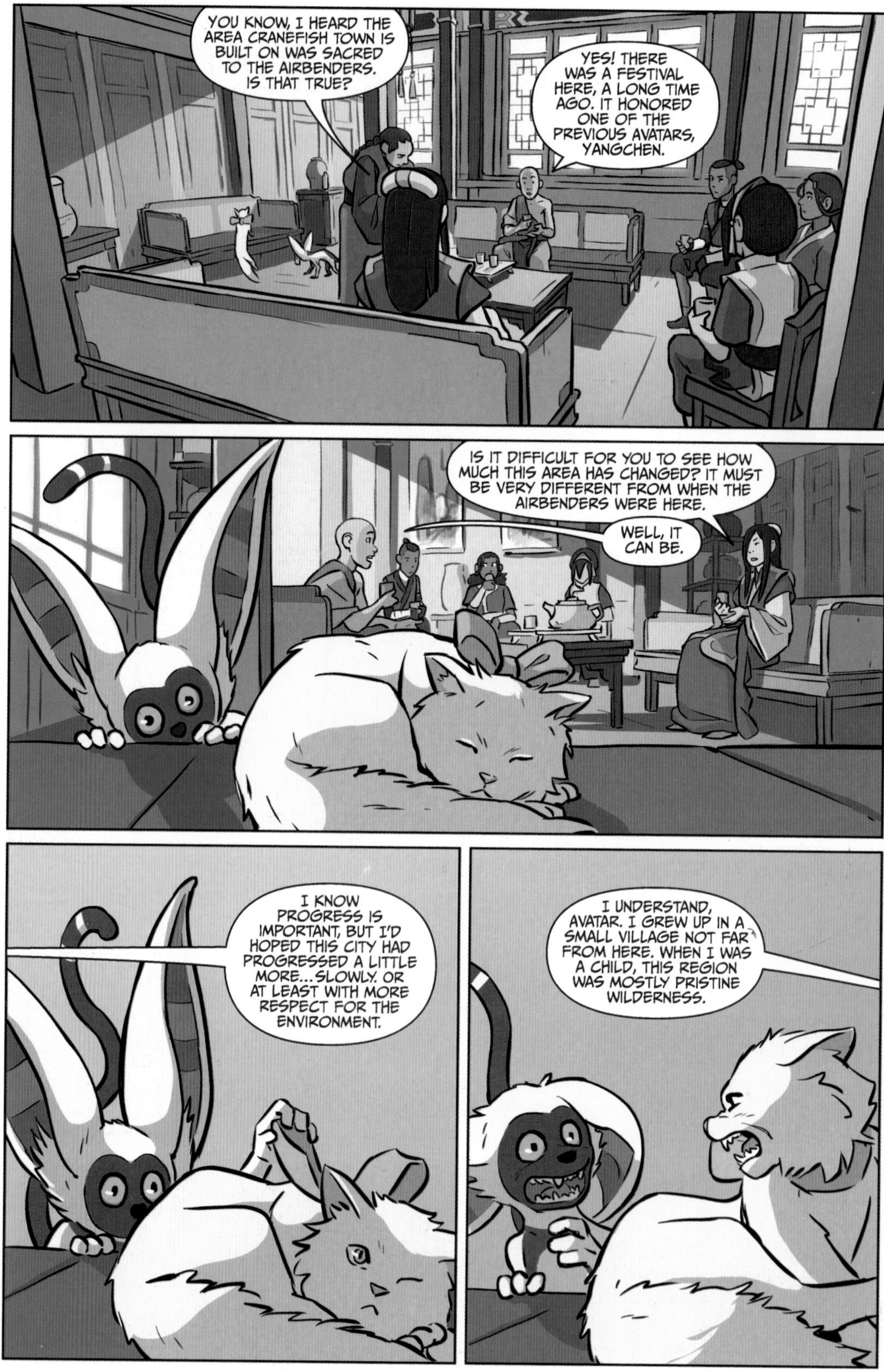
YOU KNOW, I HEARD THE AREA CRANEFISH TOWN IS BUILT ON WAS SACRED TO THE AIRBENDERS. IS THAT TRUE?
YES! THERE WAS A FESTIVAL HERE, A LONG TIME AGO. IT HONORED ONE OF THE PREVIOUS AVATARS, YANGCHEN.
IS IT DIFFICULT FOR YOU TO SEE HOW MUCH THIS AREA HAS CHANGED? IT MUST BE VERY DIFFERENT FROM WHEN THE AIRBENDERS WERE HERE.
WELL, IT CAN BE.
I KNOW PROGRESS IS IMPORTANT, BUT I'D HOPED THIS CITY HAD PROGRESSED A LITTLE MORE... SLOWLY. OR AT LEAST WITH MORE RESPECT FOR THE ENVIRONMENT.
I UNDERSTAND, AVATAR. I GREW UP IN A SMALL VILLAGE NOT FAR FROM HERE. WHEN I WAS A CHILD, THIS REGION WAS MOSTLY PRISTINE WILDERNESS.

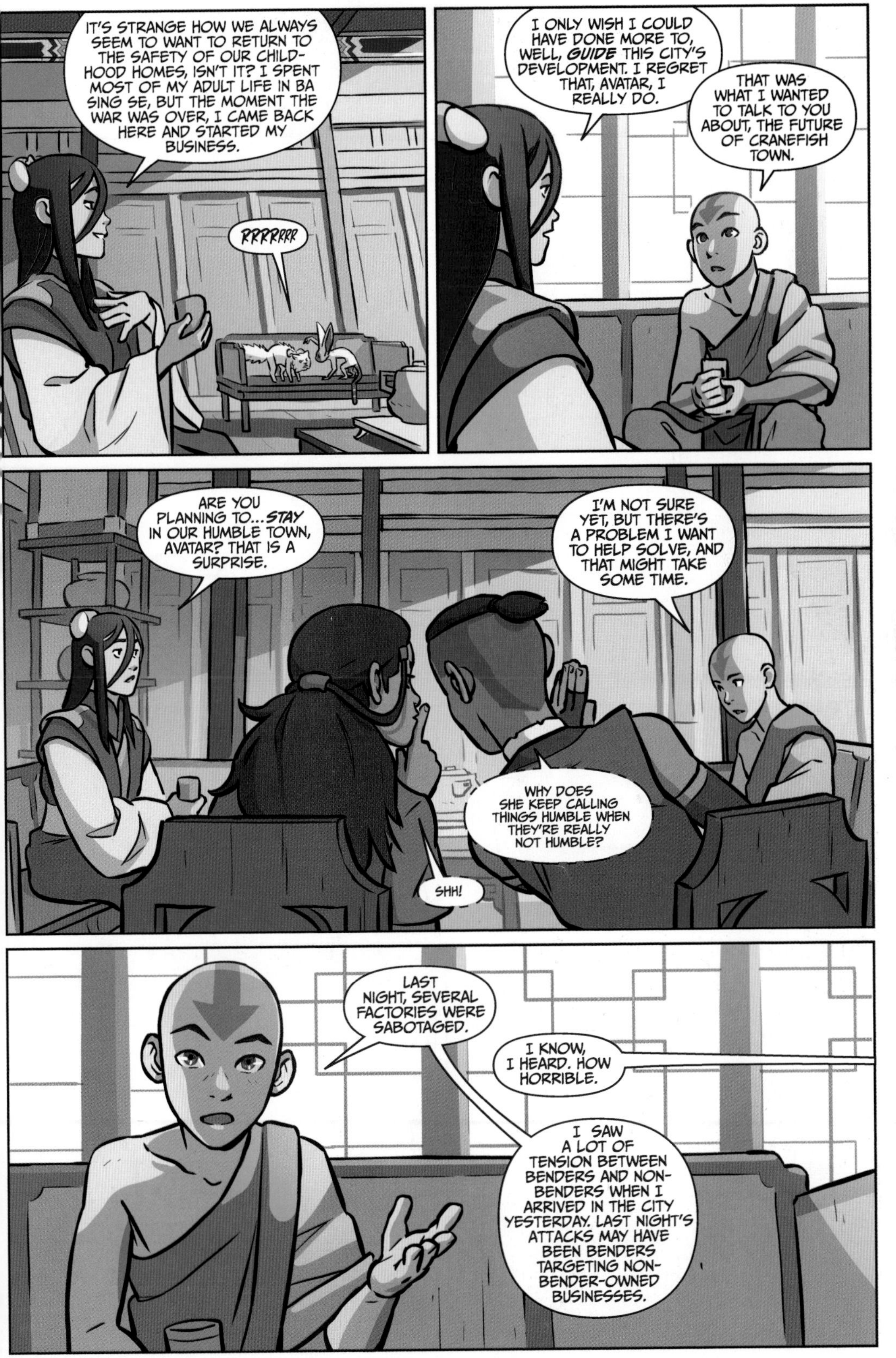
IT'S STRANGE HOW WE ALWAYS SEEM TO WANT TO RETURN TO THE SAFETY OF OUR CHILD-HOOD HOMES, ISN'T IT? I SPENT MOST OF MY ADULT LIFE IN BA SING SE, BUT THE MOMENT THE WAR WAS OVER, I CAME BACK HERE AND STARTED MY BUSINESS.
RRRRRRR
I ONLY WISH I COULD HAVE DONE MORE TO, WELL, GUIDE THIS CITY'S DEVELOPMENT. I REGRET THAT, AVATAR, I REALLY DO.
THAT WAS WHAT I WANTED TO TALK TO YOU ABOUT, THE FUTURE OF CRANEFISH TOWN.
ARE YOU PLANNING TO...STAY IN OUR HUMBLE TOWN, AVATAR? THAT IS A SURPRISE.
I'M NOT SURE YET, BUT THERE'S A PROBLEM I WANT TO HELP SOLVE, AND THAT MIGHT TAKE SOME TIME.
WHY DOES SHE KEEP CALLING THINGS HUMBLE WHEN THEY'RE REALLY NOT HUMBLE?
SHH!
LAST NIGHT, SEVERAL FACTORIES WERE SABOTAGED.
I KNOW, I HEARD. HOW HORRIBLE.
I SAW A LOT OF TENSION BETWEEN BENDERS AND NON-BENDERS WHEN I ARRIVED IN THE CITY YESTERDAY. LAST NIGHT'S ATTACKS MAY HAVE BEEN BENDERS TARGETING NON-BENDER-OWNED BUSINESSES.

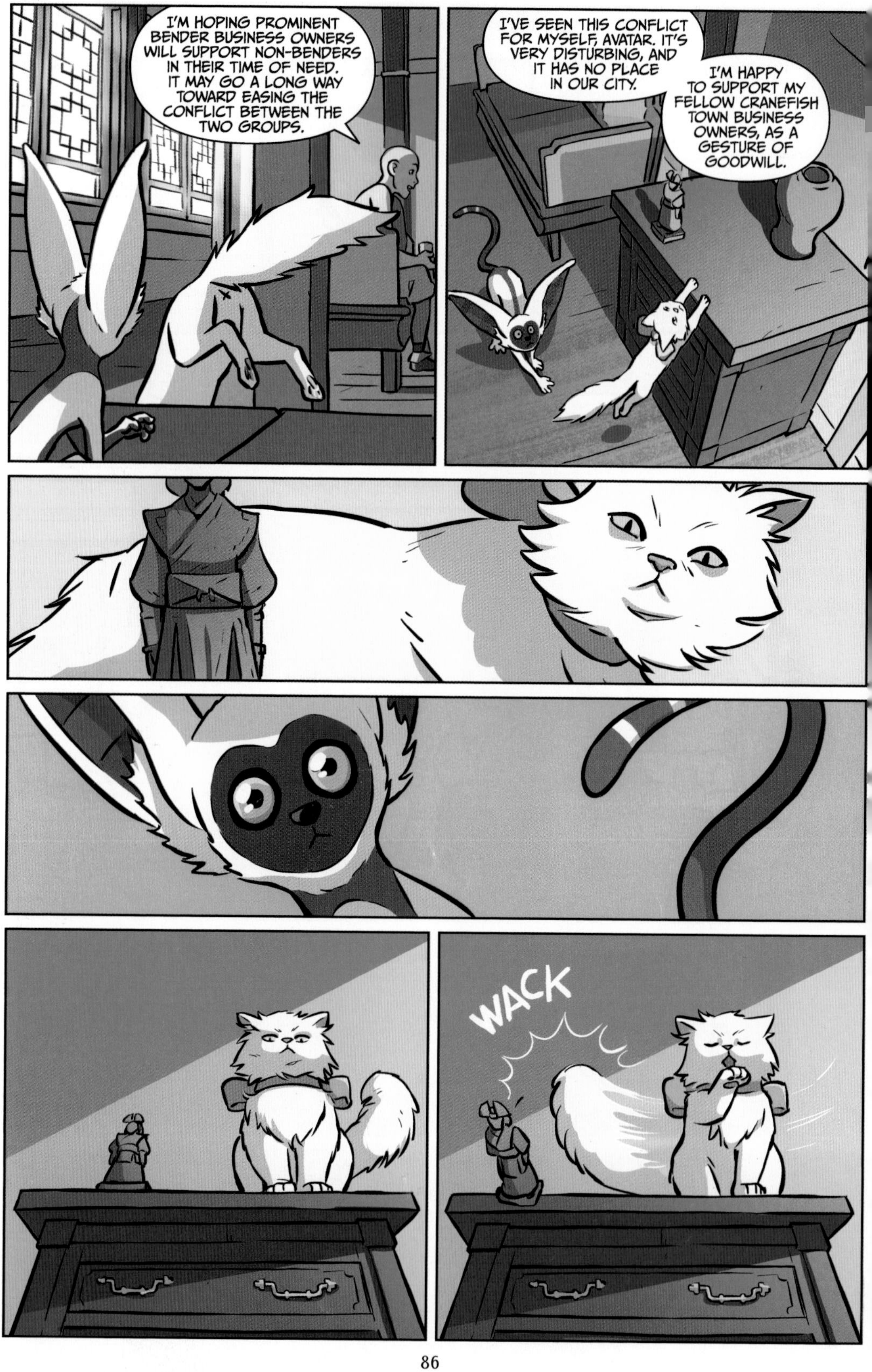
I'M HOPING PROMINENT BENDER BUSINESS OWNERS WILL SUPPORT NON-BENDERS IN THEIR TIME OF NEED. IT MAY GO A LONG WAY TOWARD EASING THE CONFLICT BETWEEN THE TWO GROUPS.
I'VE SEEN THIS CONFLICT FOR MYSELF, AVATAR. IT'S VERY DISTURBING, AND IT HAS NO PLACE IN OUR CITY.
I'M HAPPY TO SUPPORT MY FELLOW CRANEFISH TOWN BUSINESS OWNERS, AS A GESTURE OF GOODWILL.
WACK

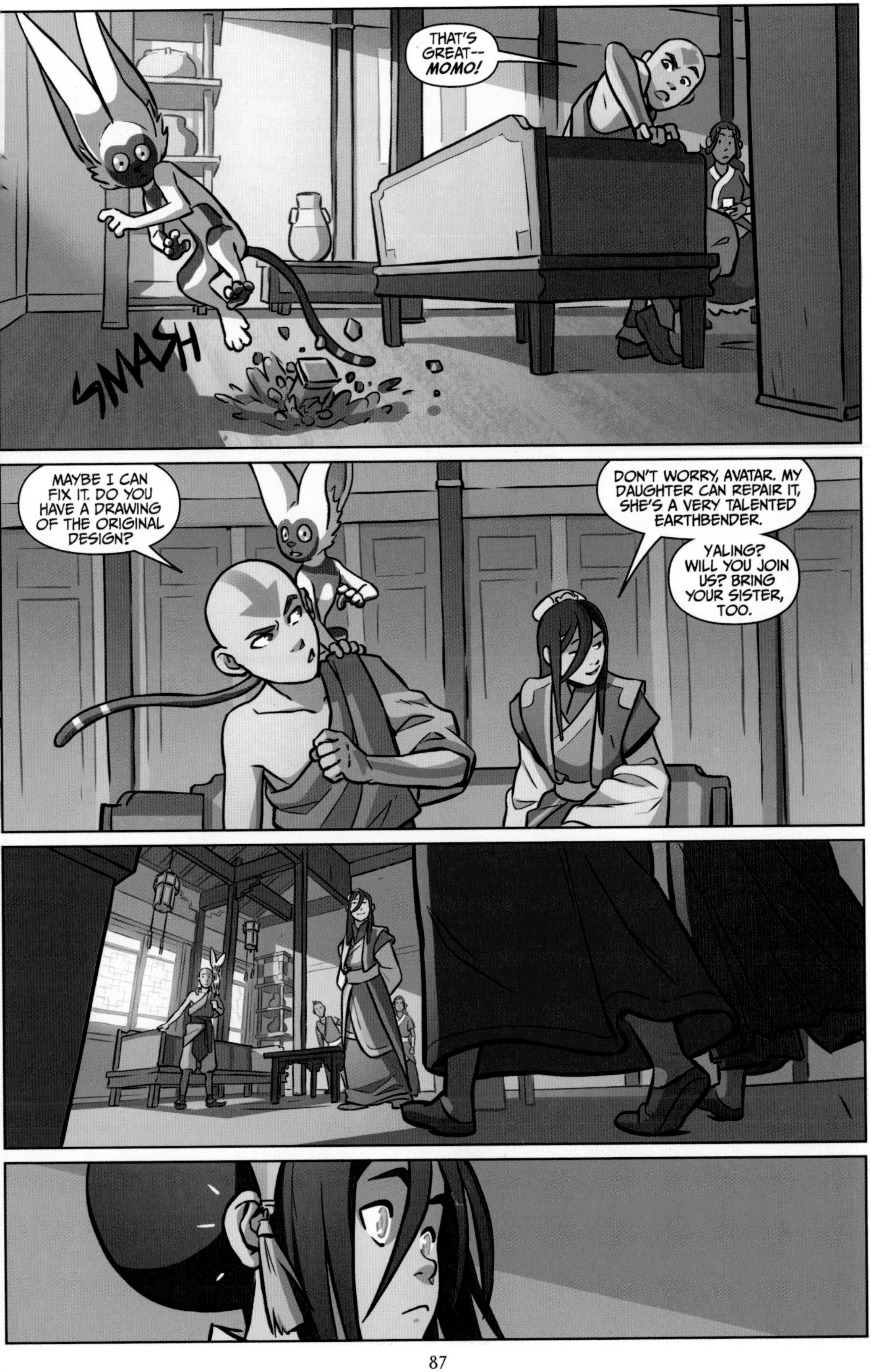
THAT'S GREAT-- MOMO!
SMASH
MAYBE I CAN FIX IT. DO YOU HAVE A DRAWING OF THE ORIGINAL DESIGN?
DON'T WORRY, AVATAR. MY DAUGHTER CAN REPAIR IT, SHE'S A VERY TALENTED EARTHBENDER.
YALING? WILL YOU JOIN US? BRING YOUR SISTER, TOO.

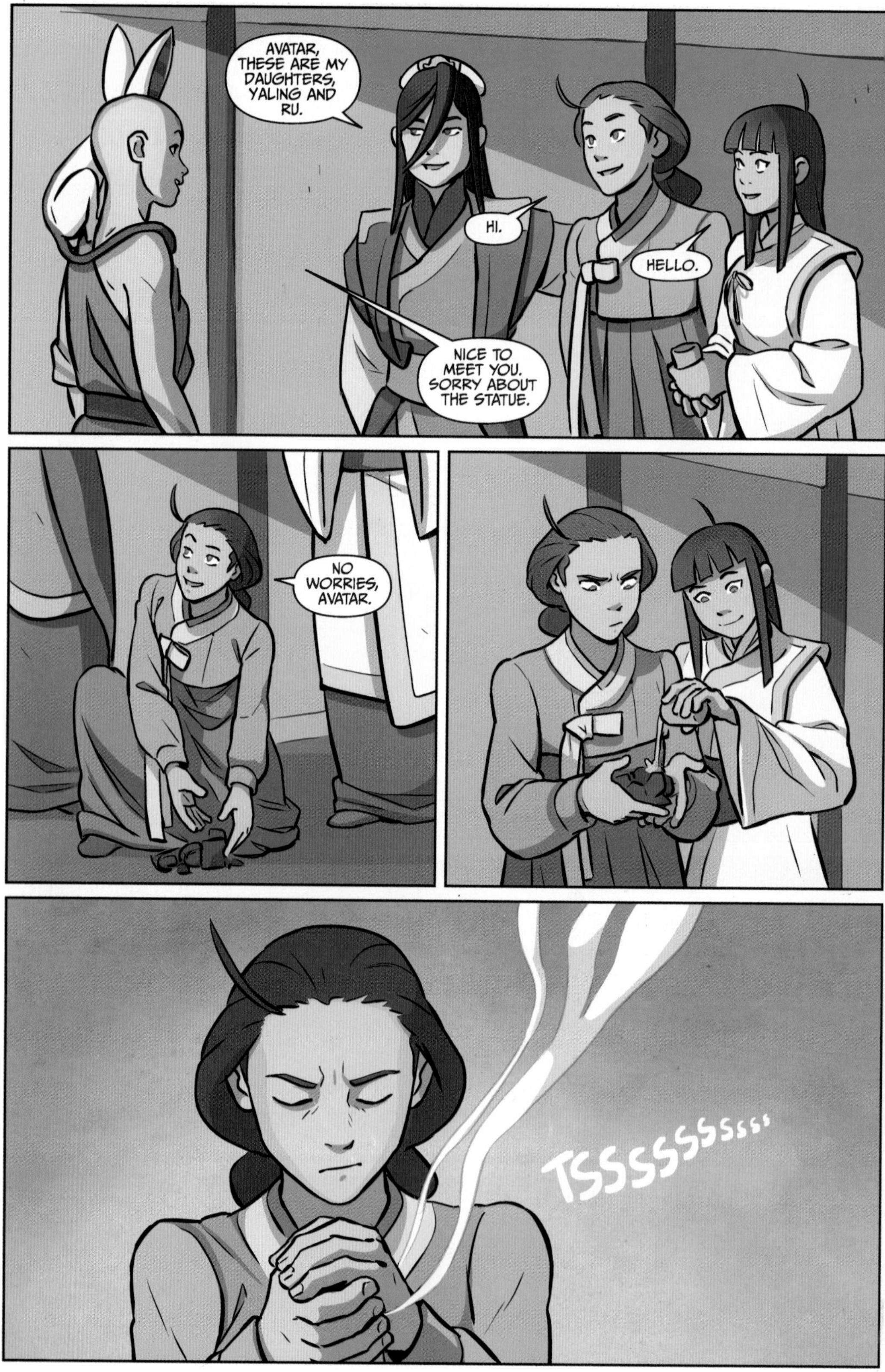
AVATAR, THESE ARE MY DAUGHTERS, YALING AND RU.
HI.
HELLO.
NICE TO MEET YOU. SORRY ABOUT THE STATUE.
NO WORRIES, AVATAR.
TSSSSSSsss

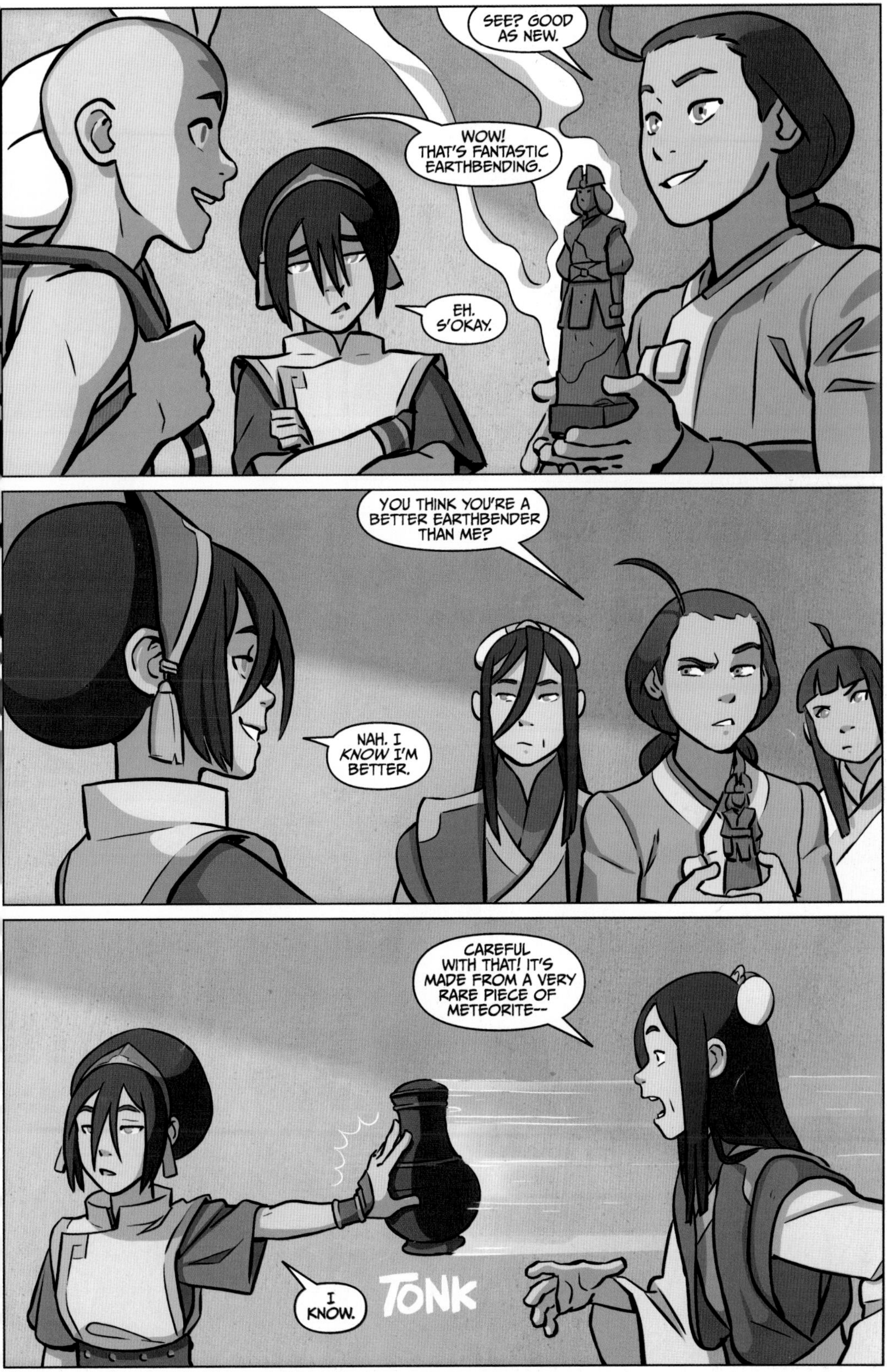
SEE? GOOD AS NEW.
WOW! THAT'S FANTASTIC EARTHBENDING.
EH. S'OKAY.
YOU THINK YOU'RE A BETTER EARTHBENDER THAN ME?
NAH. I *KNOW* I'M BETTER.
CAREFUL WITH THAT! IT'S MADE FROM A VERY RARE PIECE OF METEORITE--
I KNOW.
TONK

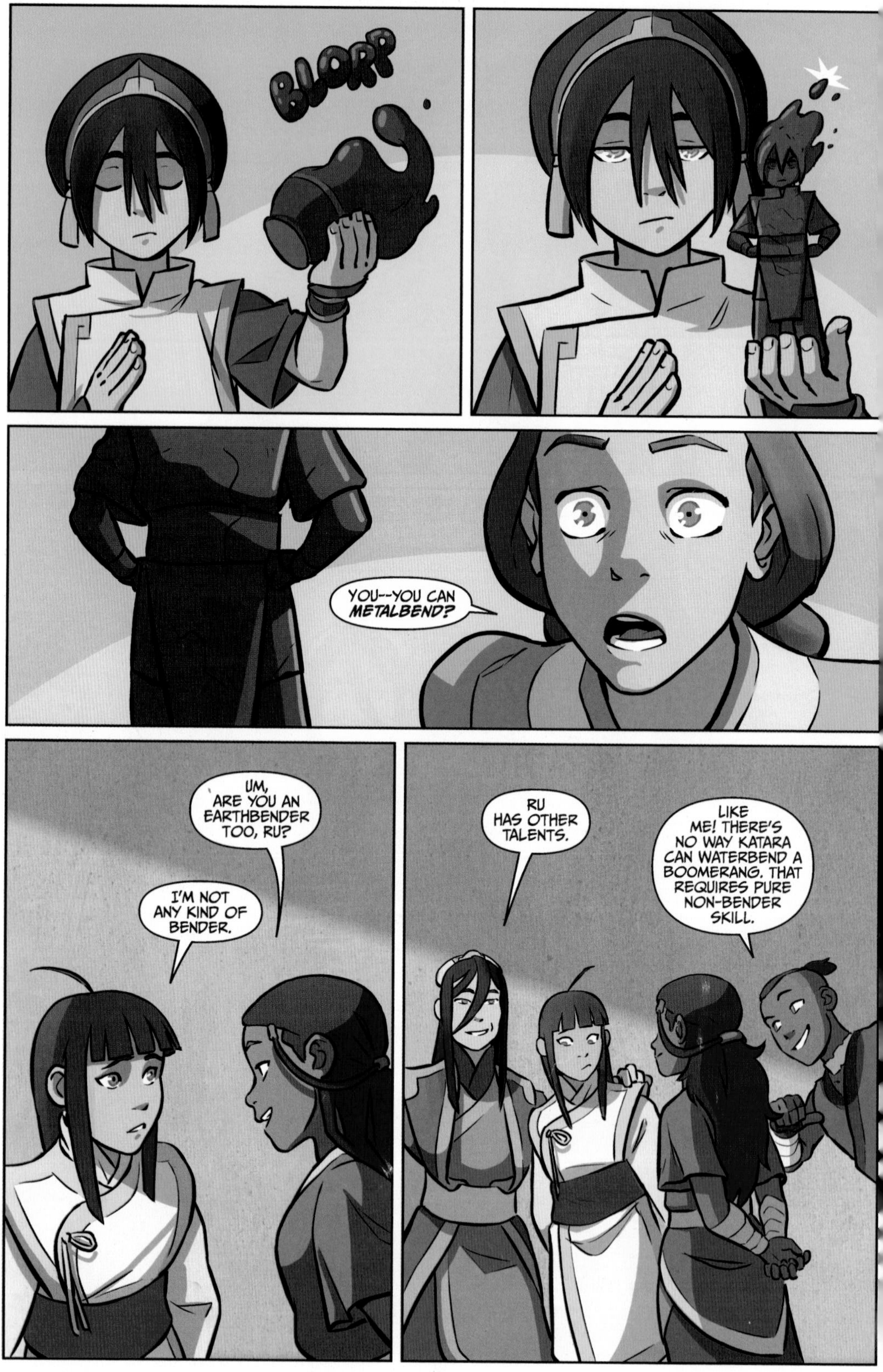
BLORP
YOU--YOU CAN METALBEND?
UM, ARE YOU AN EARTHBENDER TOO, RU?
I'M NOT ANY KIND OF BENDER.
RU HAS OTHER TALENTS.
LIKE ME! THERE'S NO WAY KATARA CAN WATERBEND A BOOMERANG. THAT REQUIRES PURE NON-BENDER SKILL.

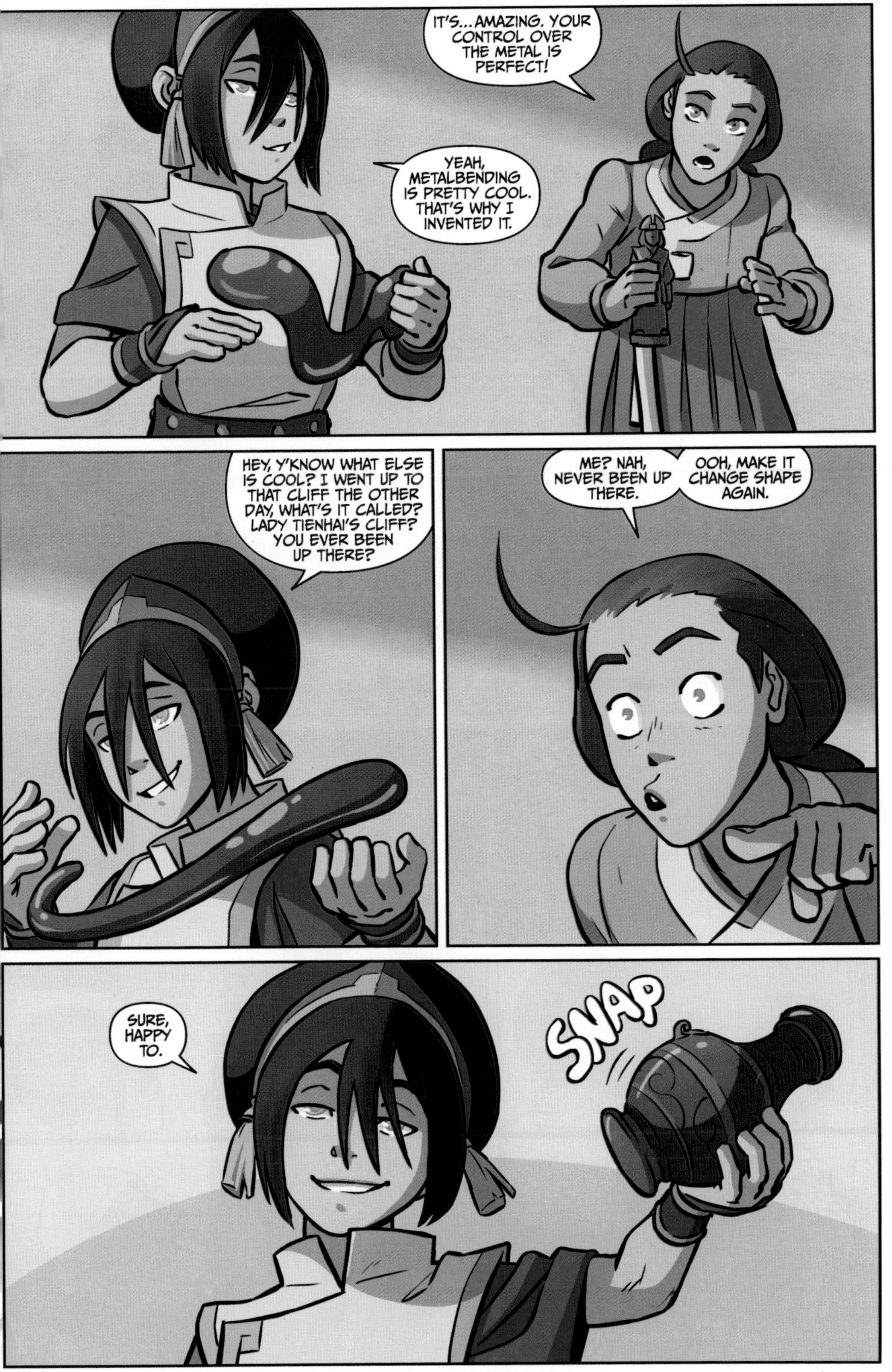
IT'S...AMAZING. YOUR CONTROL OVER THE METAL IS PERFECT!
YEAH, METALBENDING IS PRETTY COOL. THAT'S WHY I INVENTED IT.
HEY, Y'KNOW WHAT ELSE IS COOL? I WENT UP TO THAT CLIFF THE OTHER DAY, WHAT'S IT CALLED? LADY TIENHAI'S CLIFF? YOU EVER BEEN UP THERE?
ME? NAH, NEVER BEEN UP THERE.
OOH, MAKE IT CHANGE SHAPE AGAIN.
SURE, HAPPY TO.
SNAP

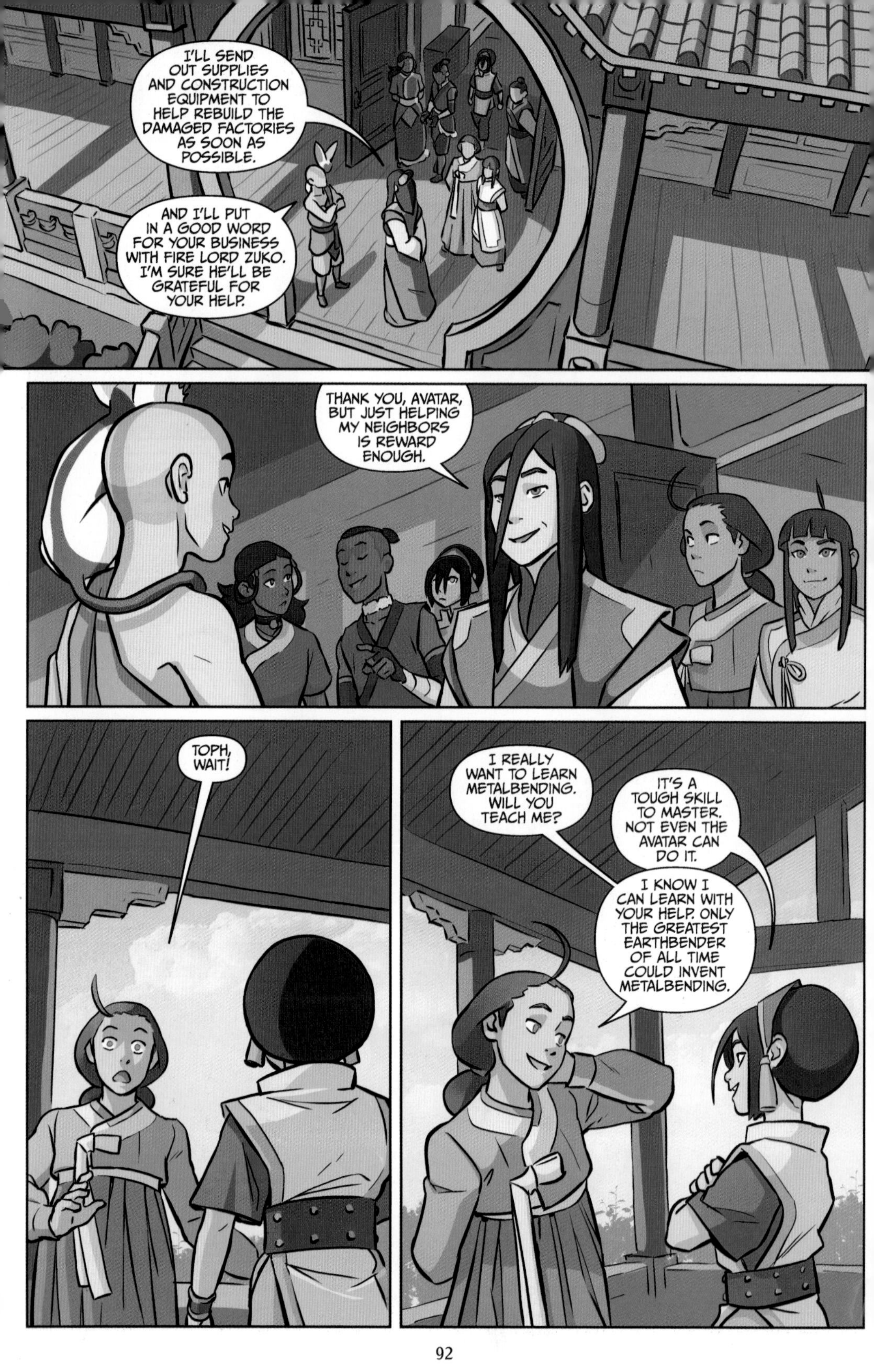
I'LL SEND OUT SUPPLIES AND CONSTRUCTION EQUIPMENT TO HELP REBUILD THE DAMAGED FACTORIES AS SOON AS POSSIBLE.
AND I'LL PUT IN A GOOD WORD FOR YOUR BUSINESS WITH FIRE LORD ZUKO. I'M SURE HE'LL BE GRATEFUL FOR YOUR HELP.
THANK YOU, AVATAR, BUT JUST HELPING MY NEIGHBORS IS REWARD ENOUGH.
TOPH, WAIT!
I REALLY WANT TO LEARN METALBENDING. WILL YOU TEACH ME?
IT'S A TOUGH SKILL TO MASTER. NOT EVEN THE AVATAR CAN DO IT.
I KNOW I CAN LEARN WITH YOUR HELP. ONLY THE GREATEST EARTHBENDER OF ALL TIME COULD INVENT METALBENDING.

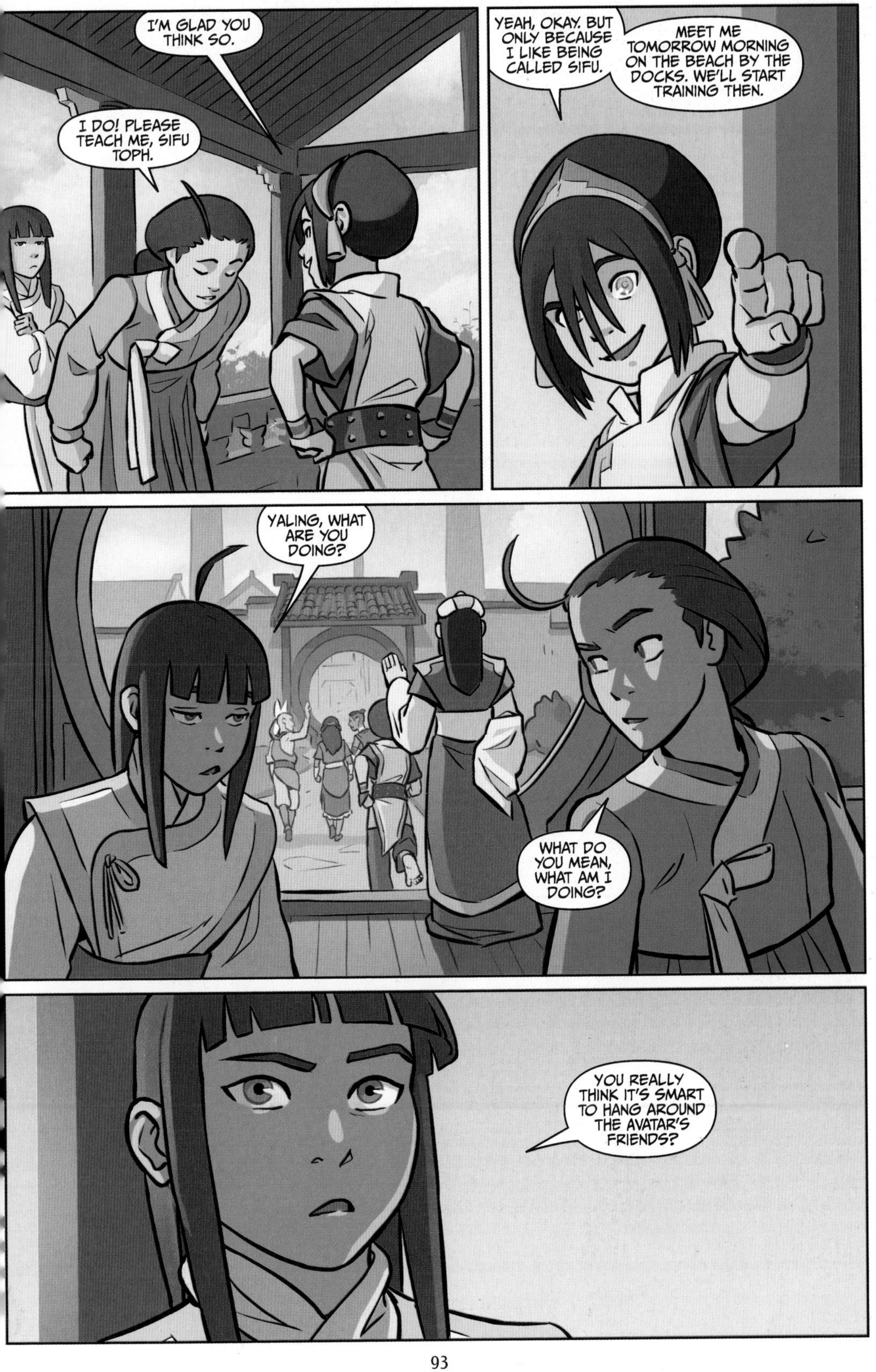

I'M GLAD YOU THINK SO.
I DO! PLEASE TEACH ME, SIFU TOPH.
YEAH, OKAY. BUT ONLY BECAUSE I LIKE BEING CALLED SIFU.
MEET ME TOMORROW MORNING ON THE BEACH BY THE DOCKS. WE'LL START TRAINING THEN.
YALING, WHAT ARE YOU DOING?
WHAT DO YOU MEAN, WHAT AM I DOING?
YOU REALLY THINK IT'S SMART TO HANG AROUND THE AVATAR'S FRIENDS?

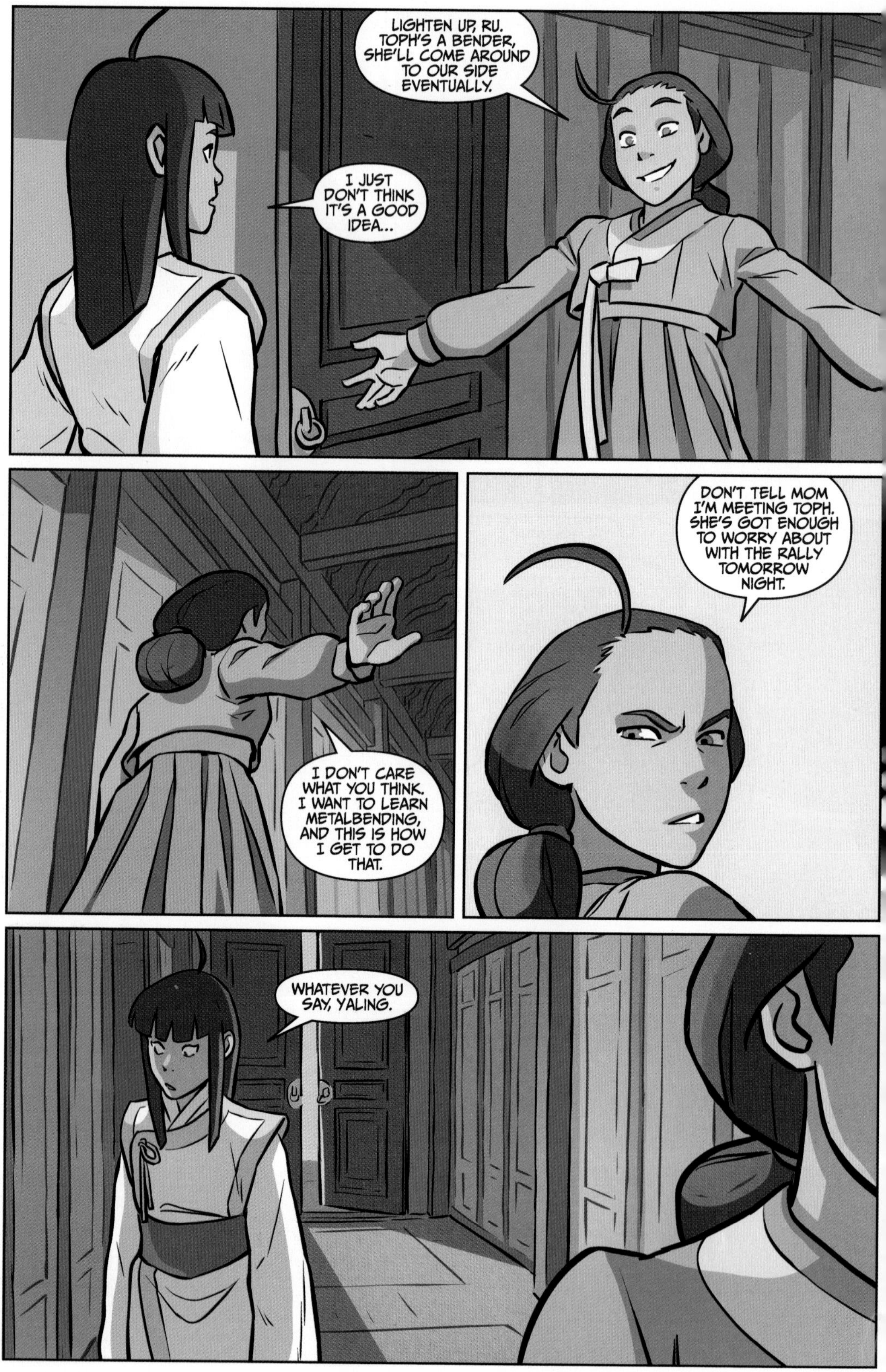
LIGHTEN UP, RU. TOPH'S A BENDER, SHE'LL COME AROUND TO OUR SIDE EVENTUALLY.
I JUST DON'T THINK IT'S A GOOD IDEA...
I DON'T CARE WHAT YOU THINK. I WANT TO LEARN METALBENDING, AND THIS IS HOW I GET TO DO THAT.
DON'T TELL MOM I'M MEETING TOPH. SHE'S GOT ENOUGH TO WORRY ABOUT WITH THE RALLY TOMORROW NIGHT.
WHATEVER YOU SAY, YALING.

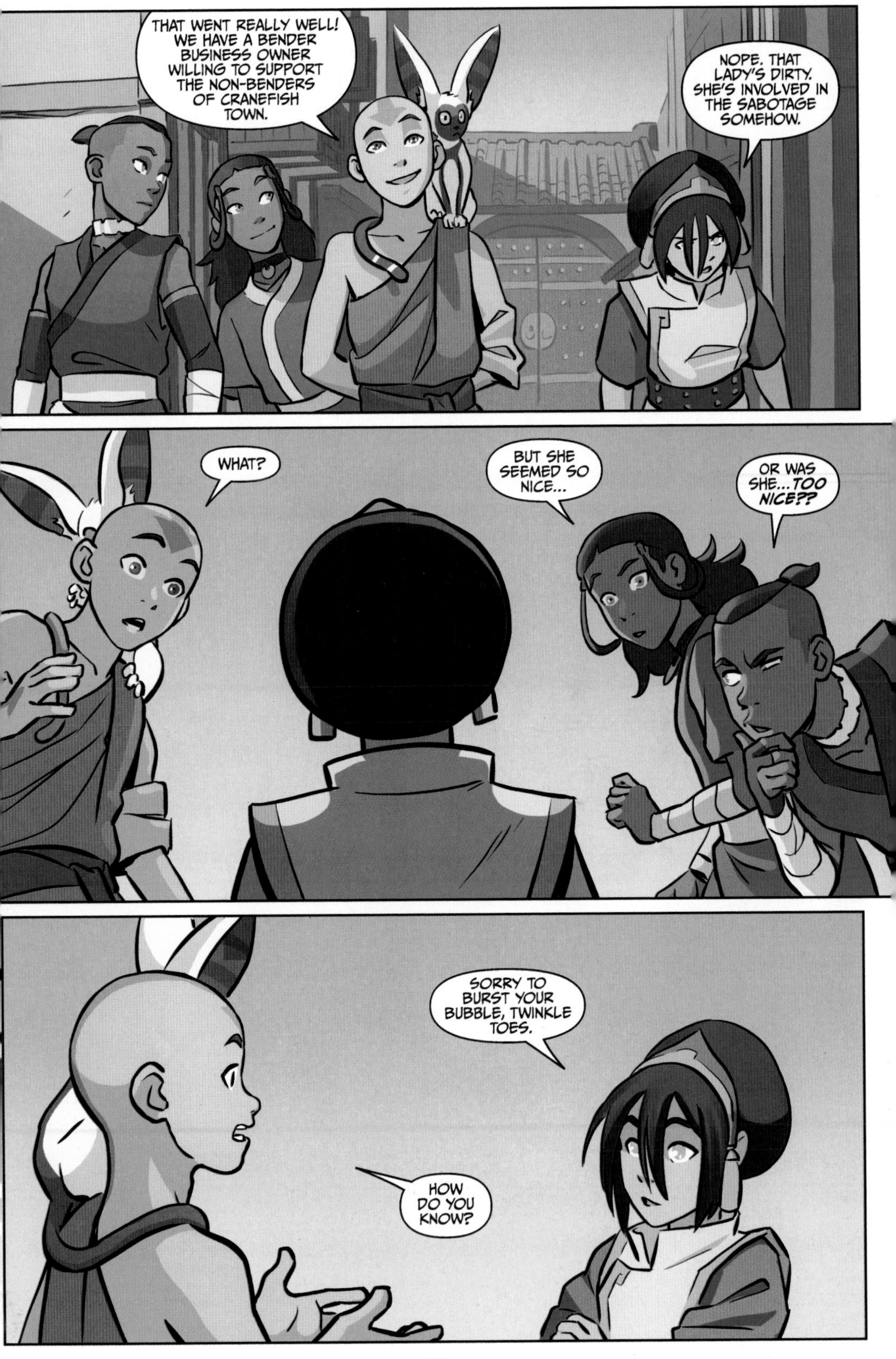
THAT WENT REALLY WELL! WE HAVE A BENDER BUSINESS OWNER WILLING TO SUPPORT THE NON-BENDERS OF CRANEFISH TOWN.
NOPE. THAT LADY'S DIRTY. SHE'S INVOLVED IN THE SABOTAGE SOMEHOW.
WHAT?
BUT SHE SEEMED SO NICE...
OR WAS SHE...*TOO NICE??*
SORRY TO BURST YOUR BUBBLE, TWINKLE TOES.
HOW DO YOU KNOW?

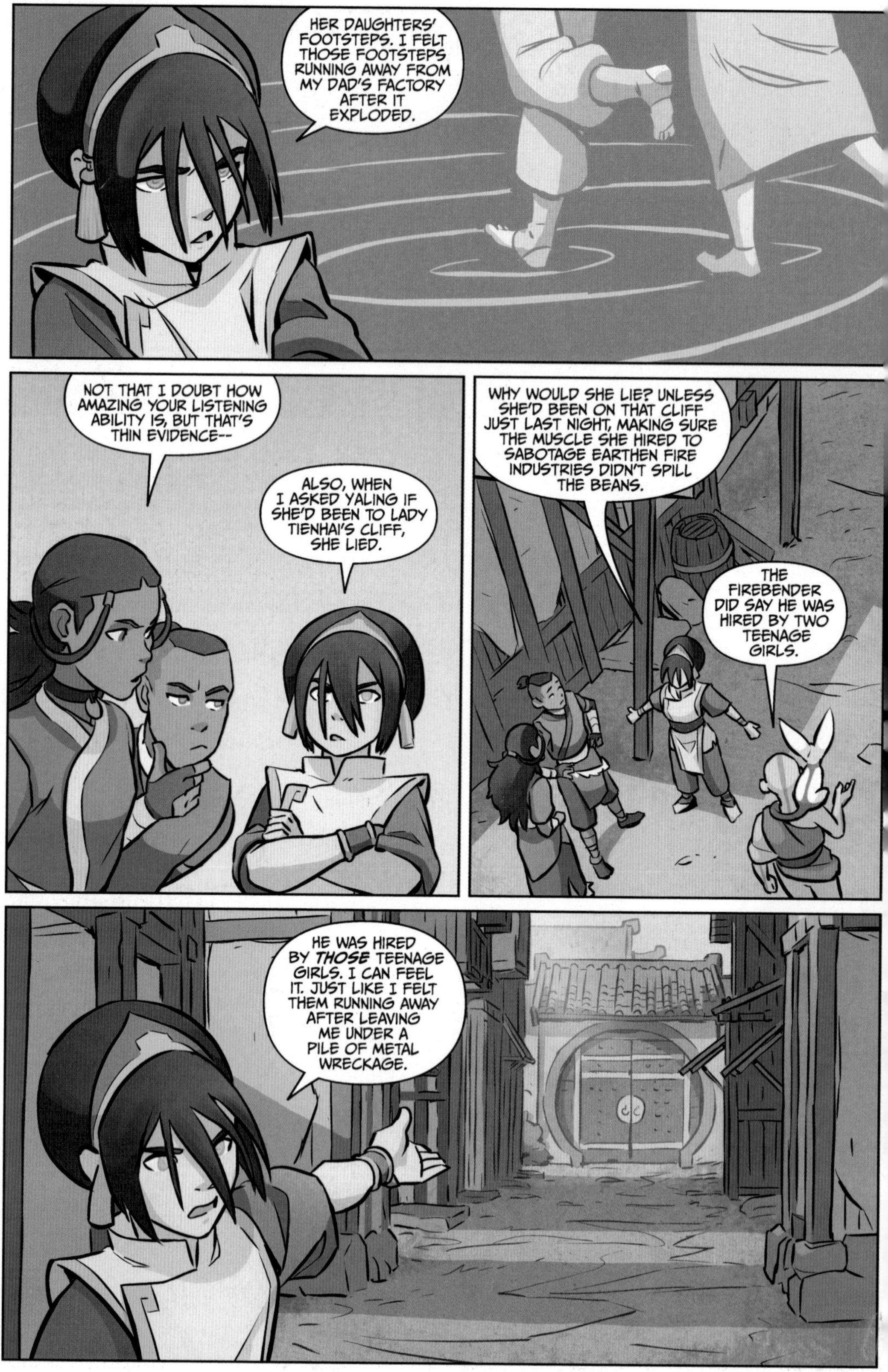
HER DAUGHTERS' FOOTSTEPS. I FELT THOSE FOOTSTEPS RUNNING AWAY FROM MY DAD'S FACTORY AFTER IT EXPLODED.
NOT THAT I DOUBT HOW AMAZING YOUR LISTENING ABILITY IS, BUT THAT'S THIN EVIDENCE--
ALSO, WHEN I ASKED YALING IF SHE'D BEEN TO LADY TIENHAI'S CLIFF, SHE LIED.
WHY WOULD SHE LIE? UNLESS SHE'D BEEN ON THAT CLIFF JUST LAST NIGHT, MAKING SURE THE MUSCLE SHE HIRED TO SABOTAGE EARTHEN FIRE INDUSTRIES DIDN'T SPILL THE BEANS.
THE FIREBENDER DID SAY HE WAS HIRED BY TWO TEENAGE GIRLS.
HE WAS HIRED BY *THOSE* TEENAGE GIRLS. I CAN FEEL IT. JUST LIKE I FELT THEM RUNNING AWAY AFTER LEAVING ME UNDER A PILE OF METAL WRECKAGE.

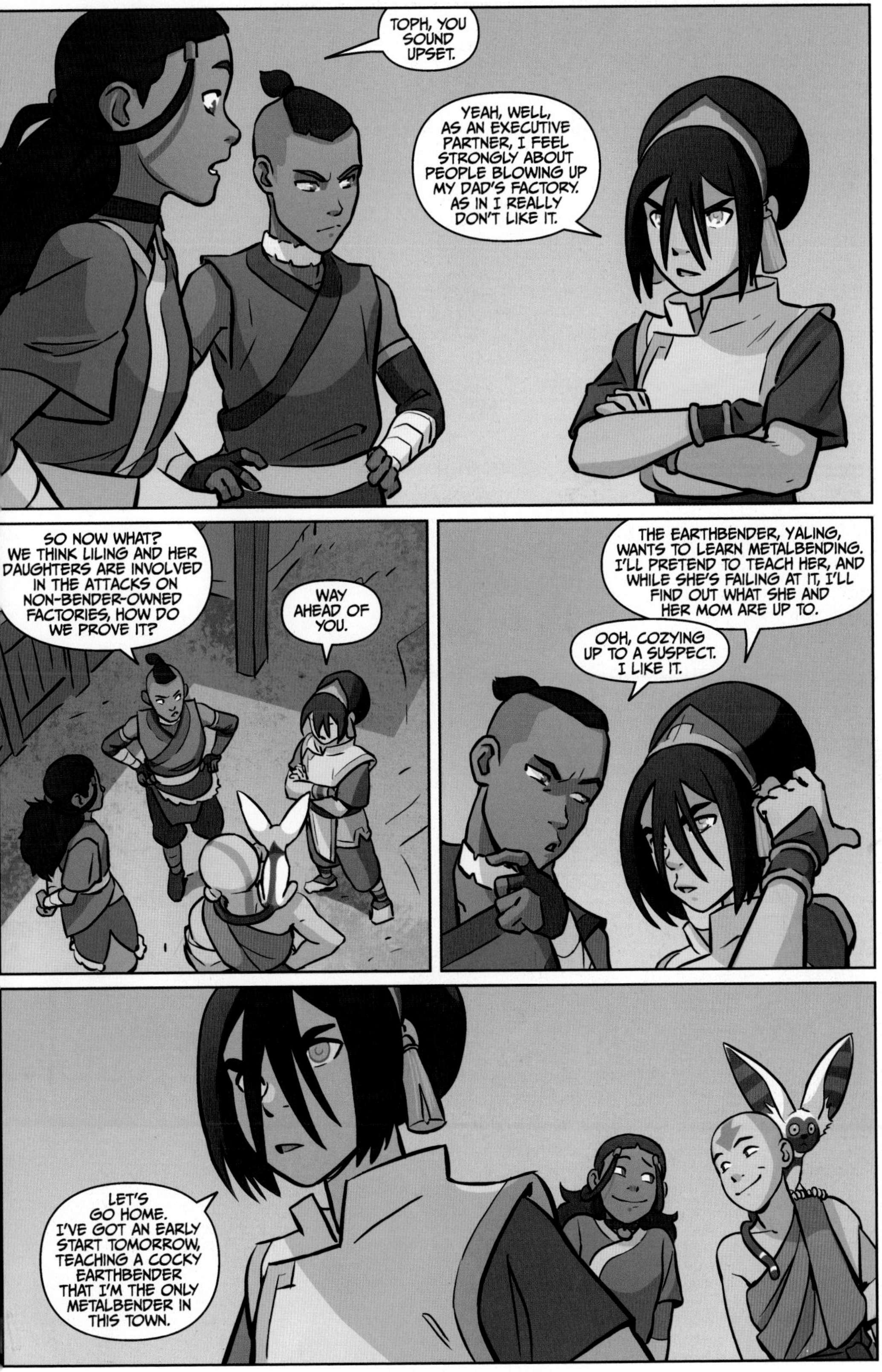
TOPH, YOU SOUND UPSET.
YEAH, WELL, AS AN EXECUTIVE PARTNER, I FEEL STRONGLY ABOUT PEOPLE BLOWING UP MY DAD'S FACTORY. AS IN I REALLY DON'T LIKE IT.
SO NOW WHAT? WE THINK LILING AND HER DAUGHTERS ARE INVOLVED IN THE ATTACKS ON NON-BENDER-OWNED FACTORIES, HOW DO WE PROVE IT?
WAY AHEAD OF YOU.
THE EARTHBENDER, YALING, WANTS TO LEARN METALBENDING. I'LL PRETEND TO TEACH HER, AND WHILE SHE'S FAILING AT IT, I'LL FIND OUT WHAT SHE AND HER MOM ARE UP TO.
OOH, COZYING UP TO A SUSPECT. I LIKE IT.
LET'S GO HOME. I'VE GOT AN EARLY START TOMORROW, TEACHING A COCKY EARTHBENDER THAT I'M THE ONLY METALBENDER IN THIS TOWN.

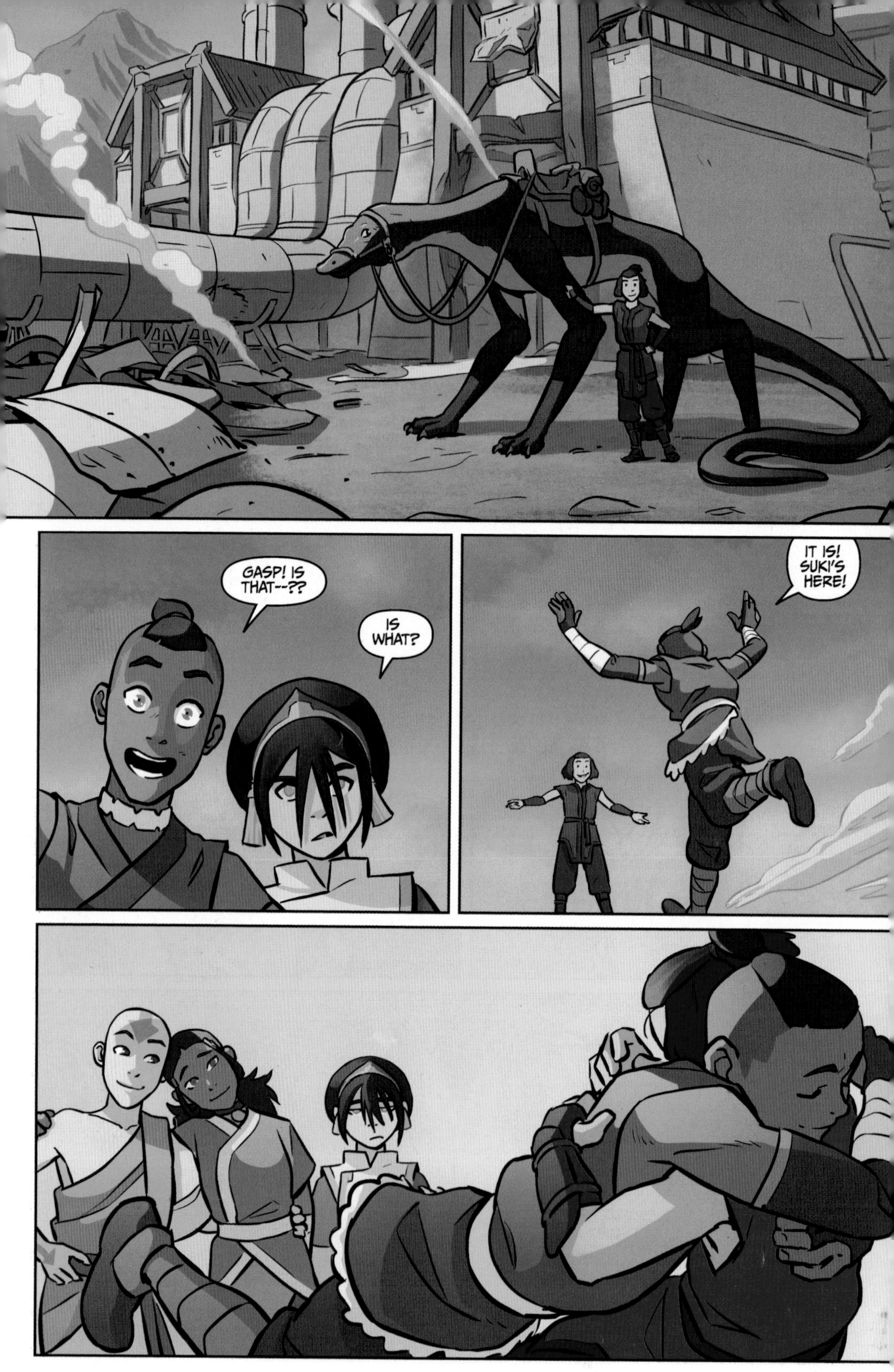
GASP! IS THAT--??
IS WHAT?
IT IS! SUKI'S HERE!

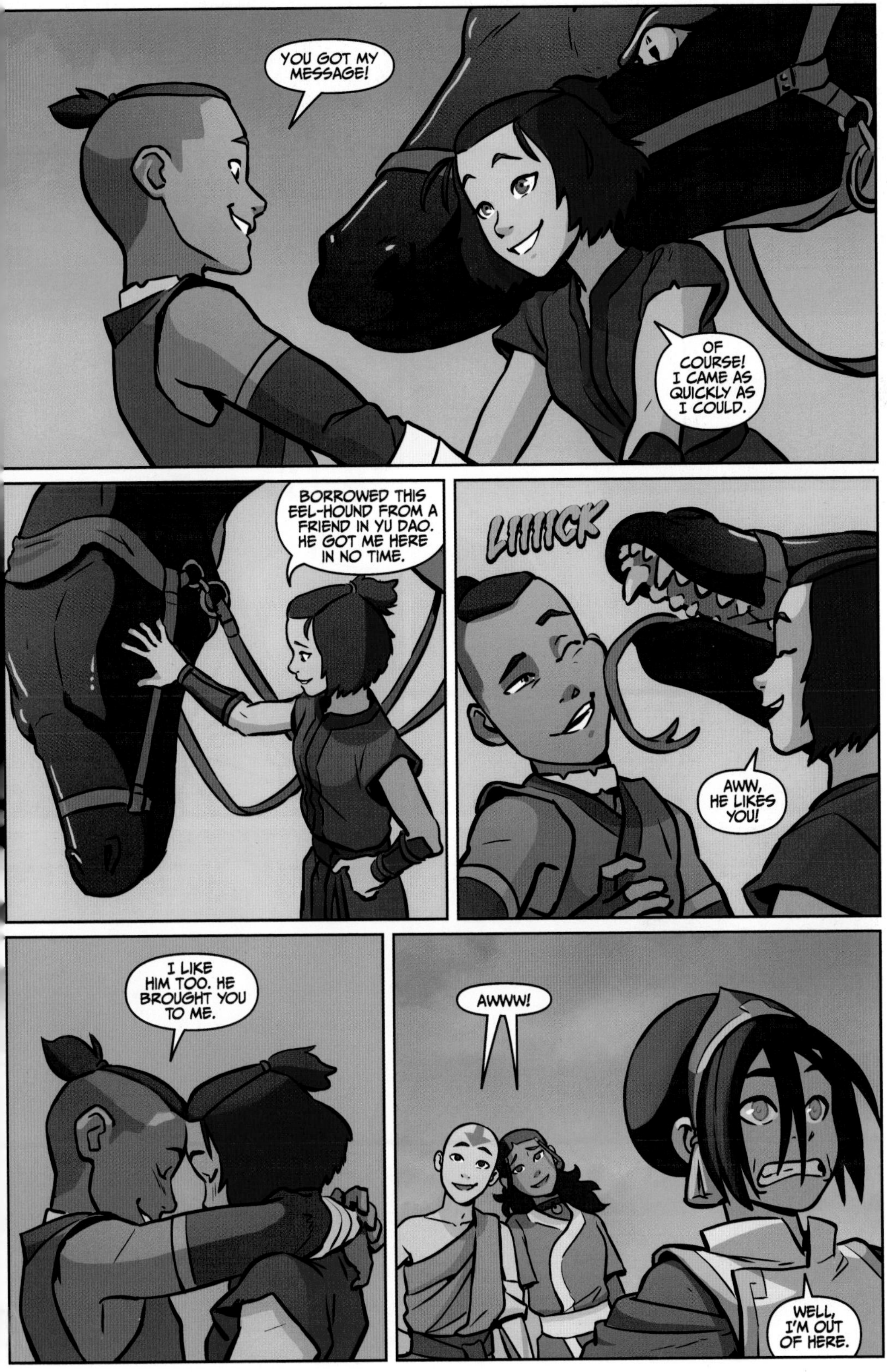
YOU GOT MY MESSAGE!
OF COURSE! I CAME AS QUICKLY AS I COULD.
BORROWED THIS EEL-HOUND FROM A FRIEND IN YU DAO. HE GOT ME HERE IN NO TIME.
LIIIICK
AWW, HE LIKES YOU!
I LIKE HIM TOO. HE BROUGHT YOU TO ME.
AWWW!
WELL, I'M OUT OF HERE.

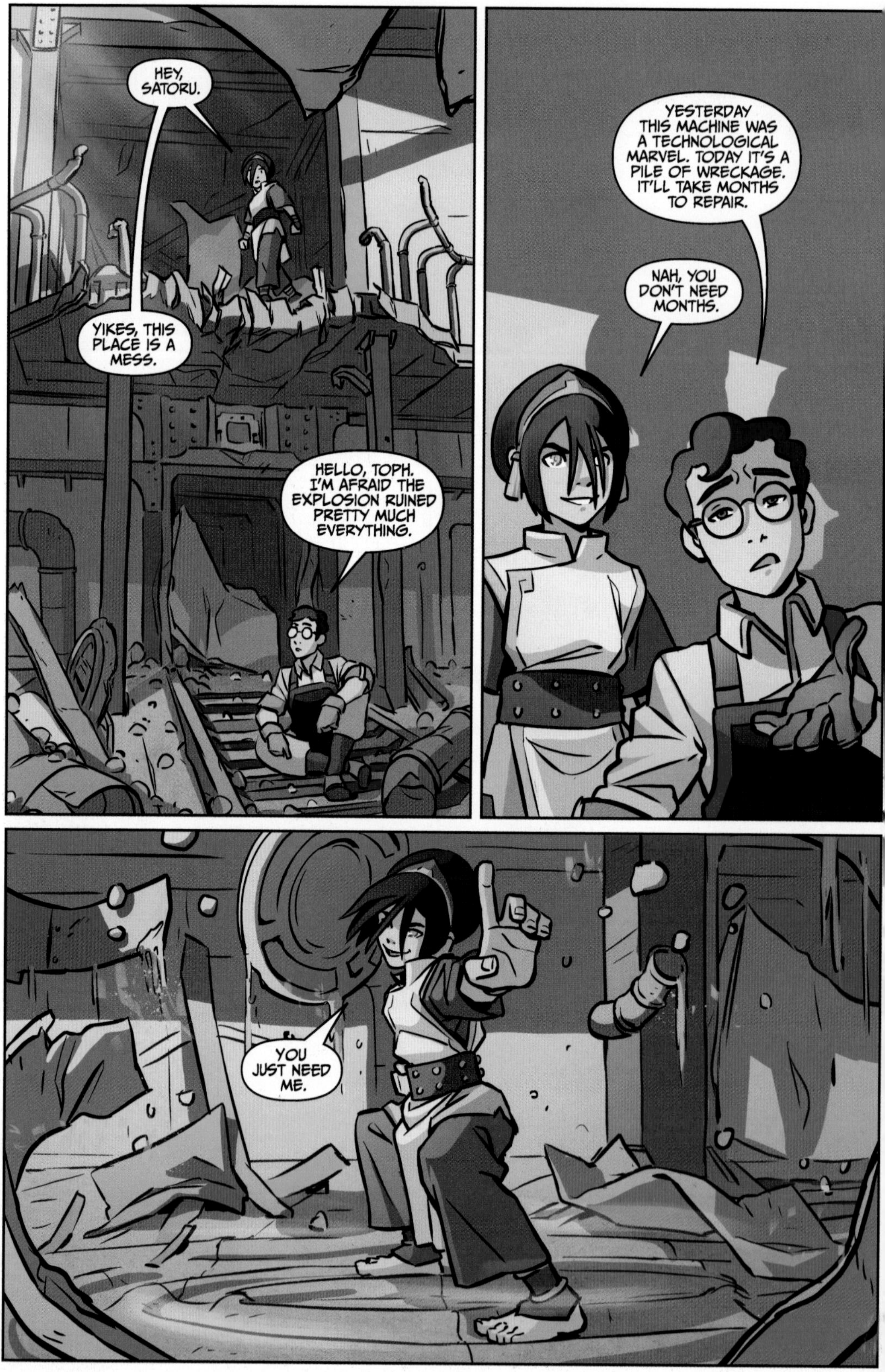
HEY, SATORU.
YIKES, THIS PLACE IS A MESS.
HELLO, TOPH. I'M AFRAID THE EXPLOSION RUINED PRETTY MUCH EVERYTHING.
YESTERDAY THIS MACHINE WAS A TECHNOLOGICAL MARVEL. TODAY IT'S A PILE OF WRECKAGE. IT'LL TAKE MONTHS TO REPAIR.
NAH, YOU DON'T NEED MONTHS.
YOU JUST NEED ME.

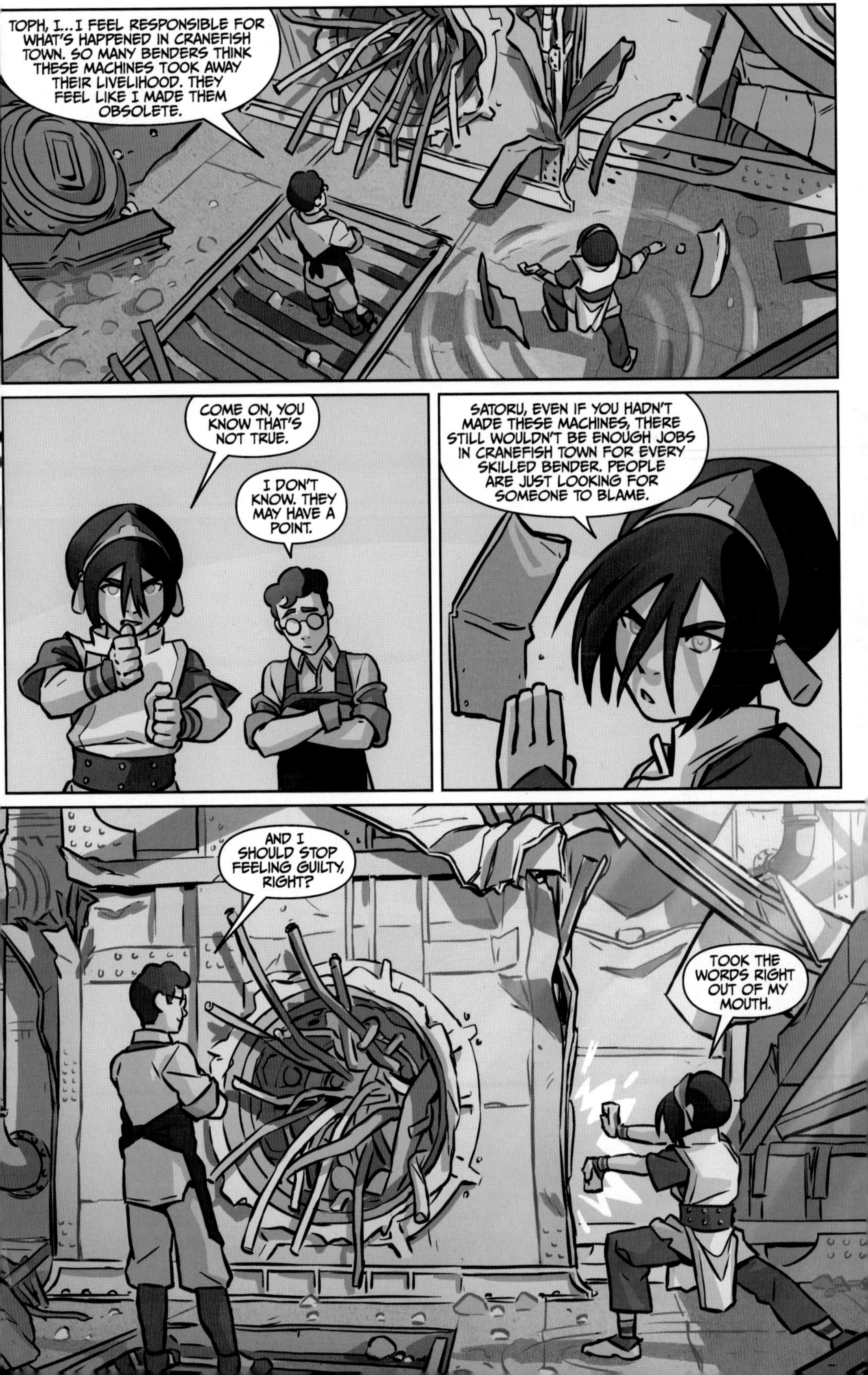
TOPH, I...I FEEL RESPONSIBLE FOR WHAT'S HAPPENED IN CRANEFISH TOWN. SO MANY BENDERS THINK THESE MACHINES TOOK AWAY THEIR LIVELIHOOD. THEY FEEL LIKE I MADE THEM OBSOLETE.
COME ON, YOU KNOW THAT'S NOT TRUE.
I DON'T KNOW. THEY MAY HAVE A POINT.
SATORU, EVEN IF YOU HADN'T MADE THESE MACHINES, THERE STILL WOULDN'T BE ENOUGH JOBS IN CRANEFISH TOWN FOR EVERY SKILLED BENDER. PEOPLE ARE JUST LOOKING FOR SOMEONE TO BLAME.
AND I SHOULD STOP FEELING GUILTY, RIGHT?
TOOK THE WORDS RIGHT OUT OF MY MOUTH.

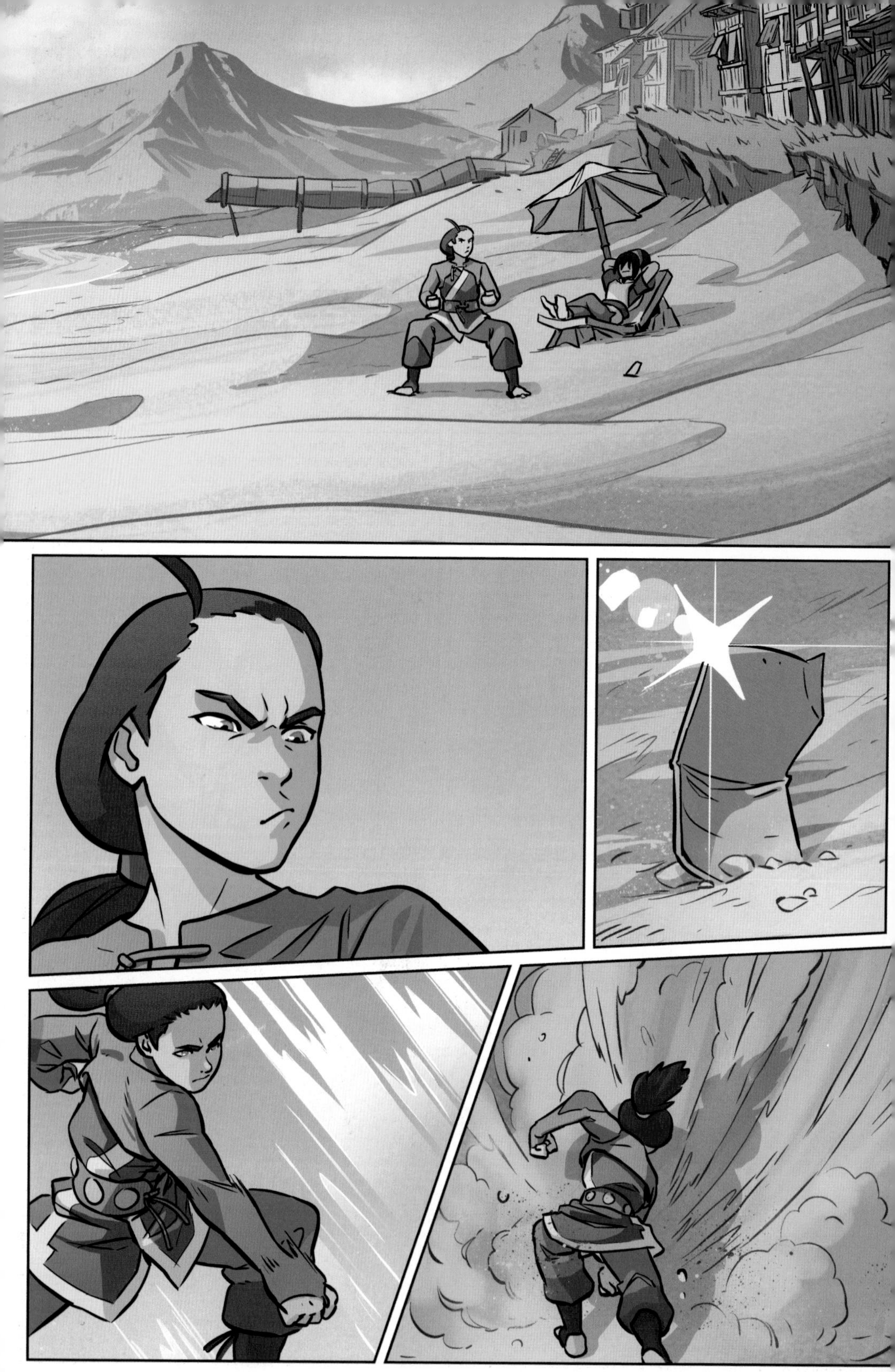

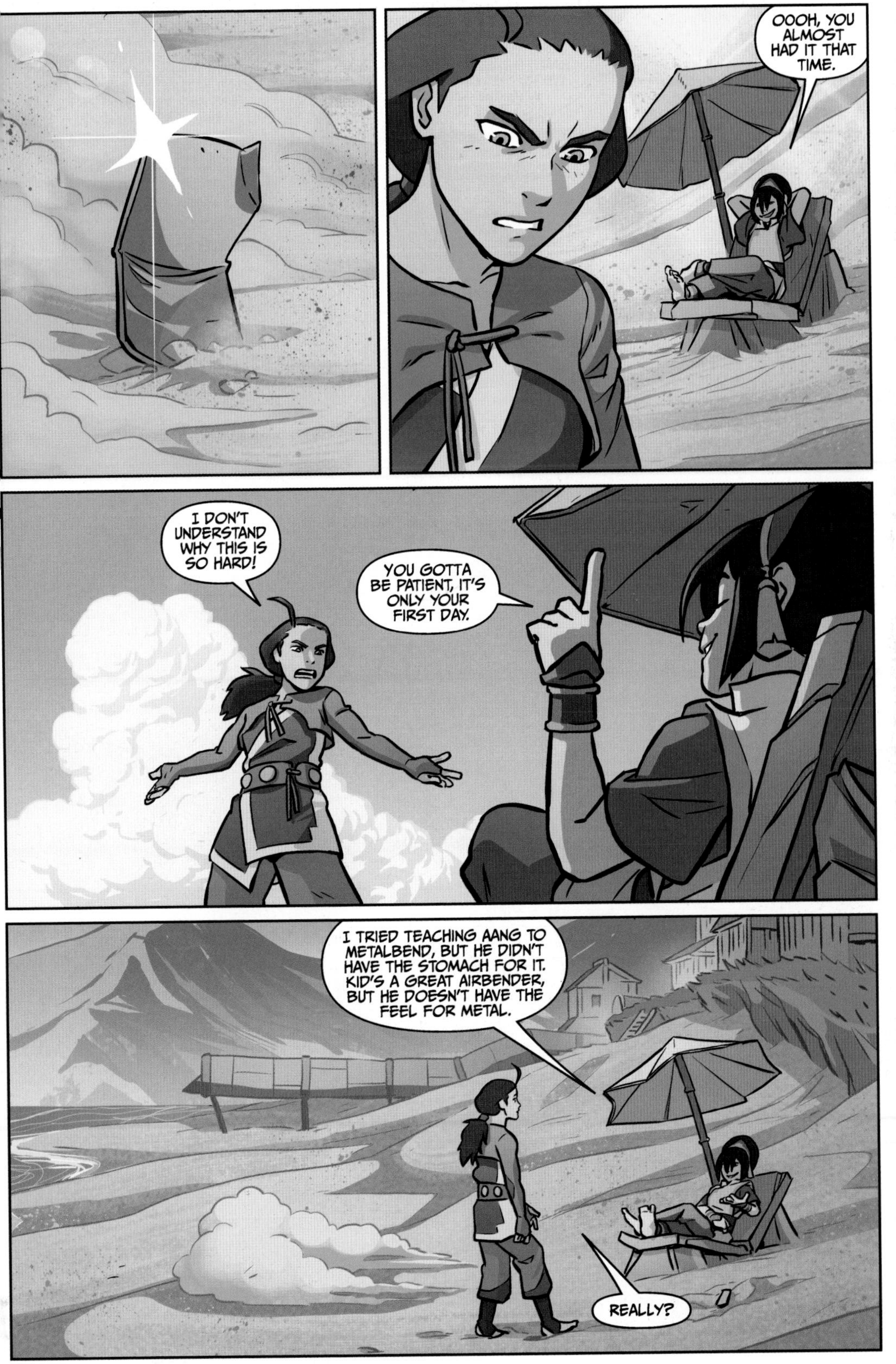
OOOH, YOU ALMOST HAD IT THAT TIME.
I DON'T UNDERSTAND WHY THIS IS SO HARD!
YOU GOTTA BE PATIENT, IT'S ONLY YOUR FIRST DAY.
I TRIED TEACHING AANG TO METALBEND, BUT HE DIDN'T HAVE THE STOMACH FOR IT. KID'S A GREAT AIRBENDER, BUT HE DOESN'T HAVE THE FEEL FOR METAL.
REALLY?

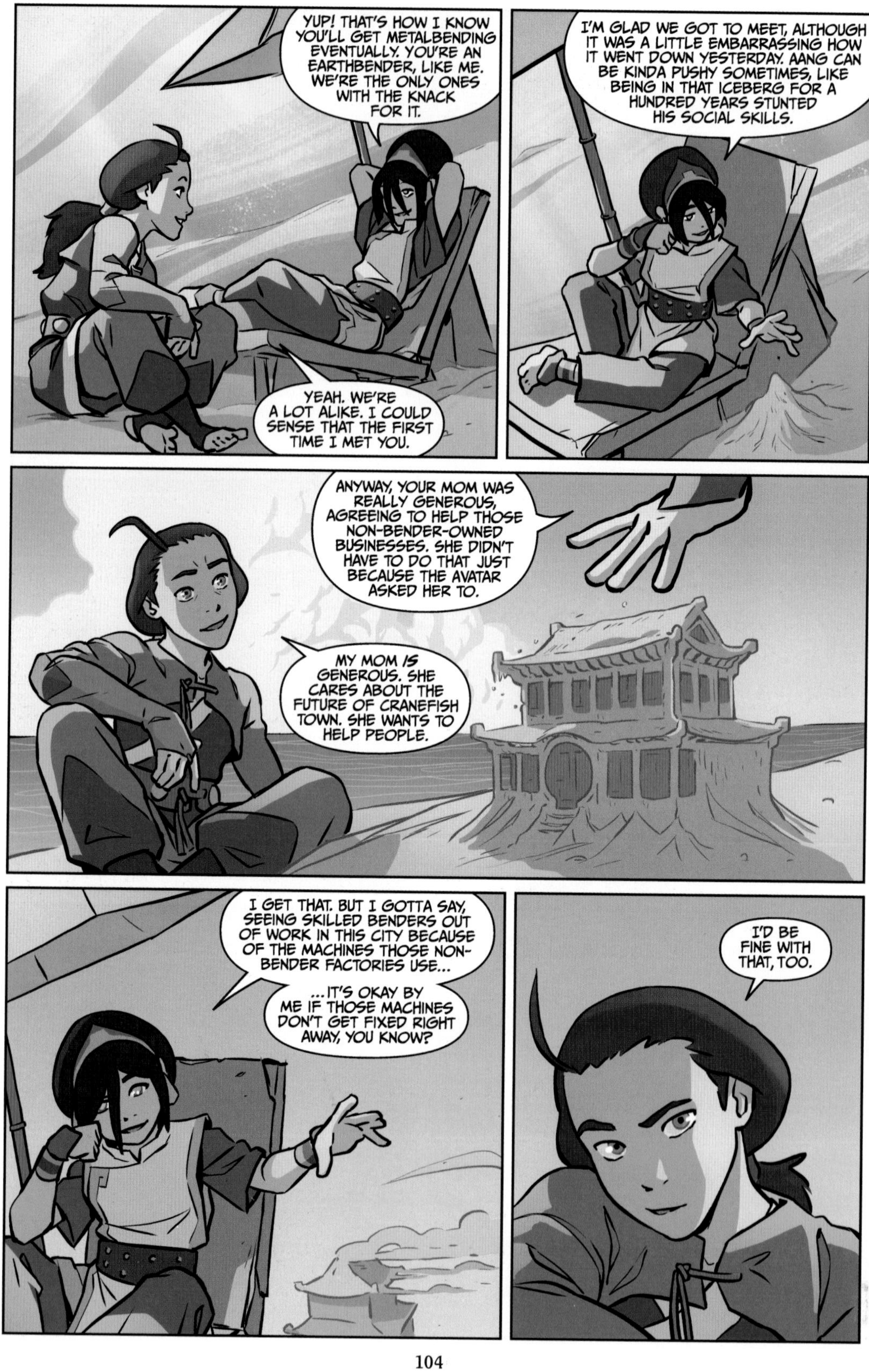
YUP! THAT'S HOW I KNOW YOU'LL GET METALBENDING EVENTUALLY. YOU'RE AN EARTHBENDER, LIKE ME. WE'RE THE ONLY ONES WITH THE KNACK FOR IT.
YEAH. WE'RE A LOT ALIKE. I COULD SENSE THAT THE FIRST TIME I MET YOU.
I'M GLAD WE GOT TO MEET, ALTHOUGH IT WAS A LITTLE EMBARRASSING HOW IT WENT DOWN YESTERDAY. AANG CAN BE KINDA PUSHY SOMETIMES, LIKE BEING IN THAT ICEBERG FOR A HUNDRED YEARS STUNTED HIS SOCIAL SKILLS.
ANYWAY, YOUR MOM WAS REALLY GENEROUS, AGREEING TO HELP THOSE NON-BENDER-OWNED BUSINESSES. SHE DIDN'T HAVE TO DO THAT JUST BECAUSE THE AVATAR ASKED HER TO.
MY MOM *IS* GENEROUS. SHE CARES ABOUT THE FUTURE OF CRANEFISH TOWN. SHE WANTS TO HELP PEOPLE.
I GET THAT. BUT I GOTTA SAY, SEEING SKILLED BENDERS OUT OF WORK IN THIS CITY BECAUSE OF THE MACHINES THOSE NON-BENDER FACTORIES USE...
...IT'S OKAY BY ME IF THOSE MACHINES DON'T GET FIXED RIGHT AWAY, YOU KNOW?
I'D BE FINE WITH THAT, TOO.

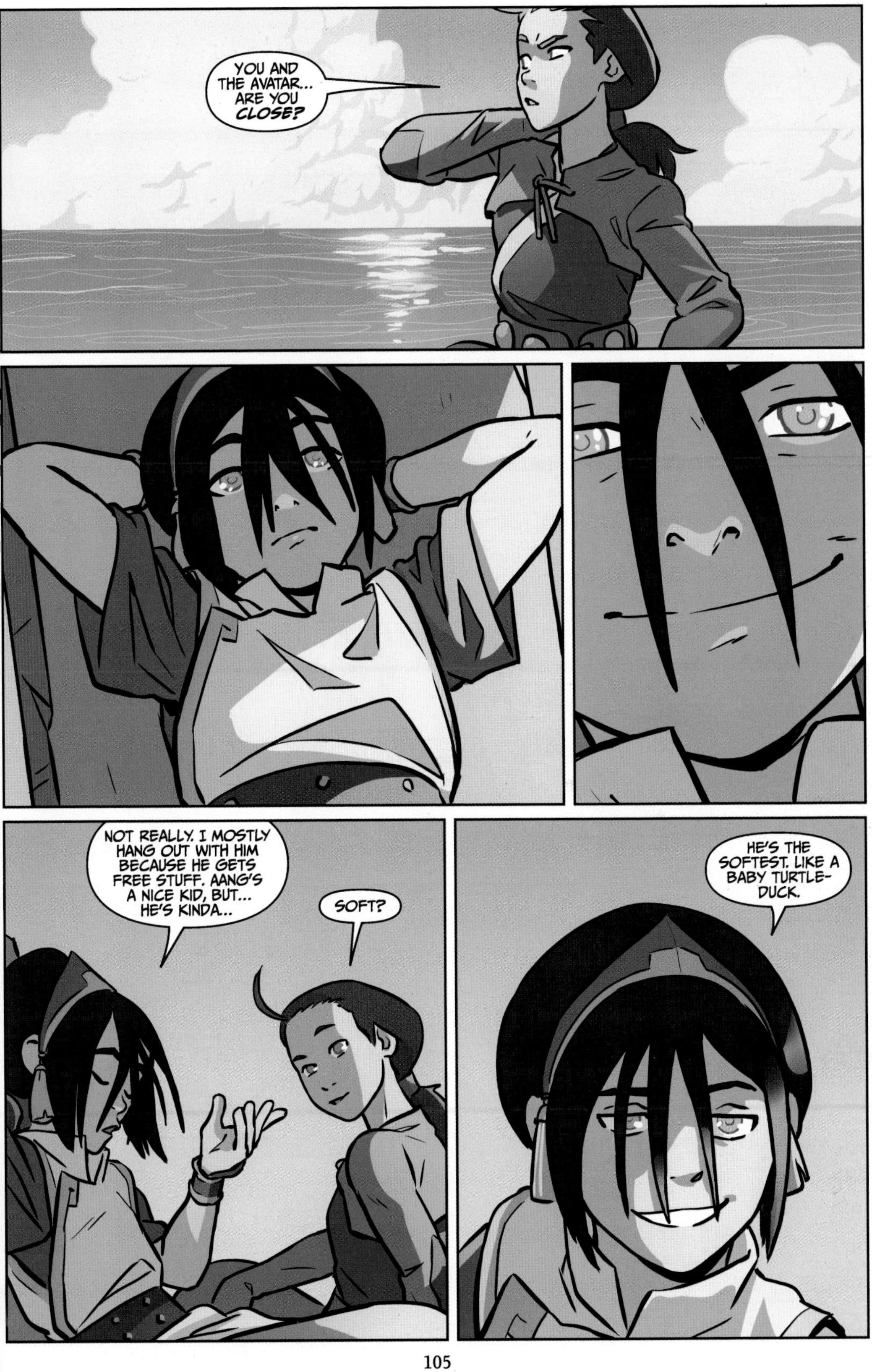
YOU AND THE AVATAR... ARE YOU CLOSE?
NOT REALLY. I MOSTLY HANG OUT WITH HIM BECAUSE HE GETS FREE STUFF. AANG'S A NICE KID, BUT... HE'S KINDA...
SOFT?
HE'S THE SOFTEST. LIKE A BABY TURTLE-DUCK.

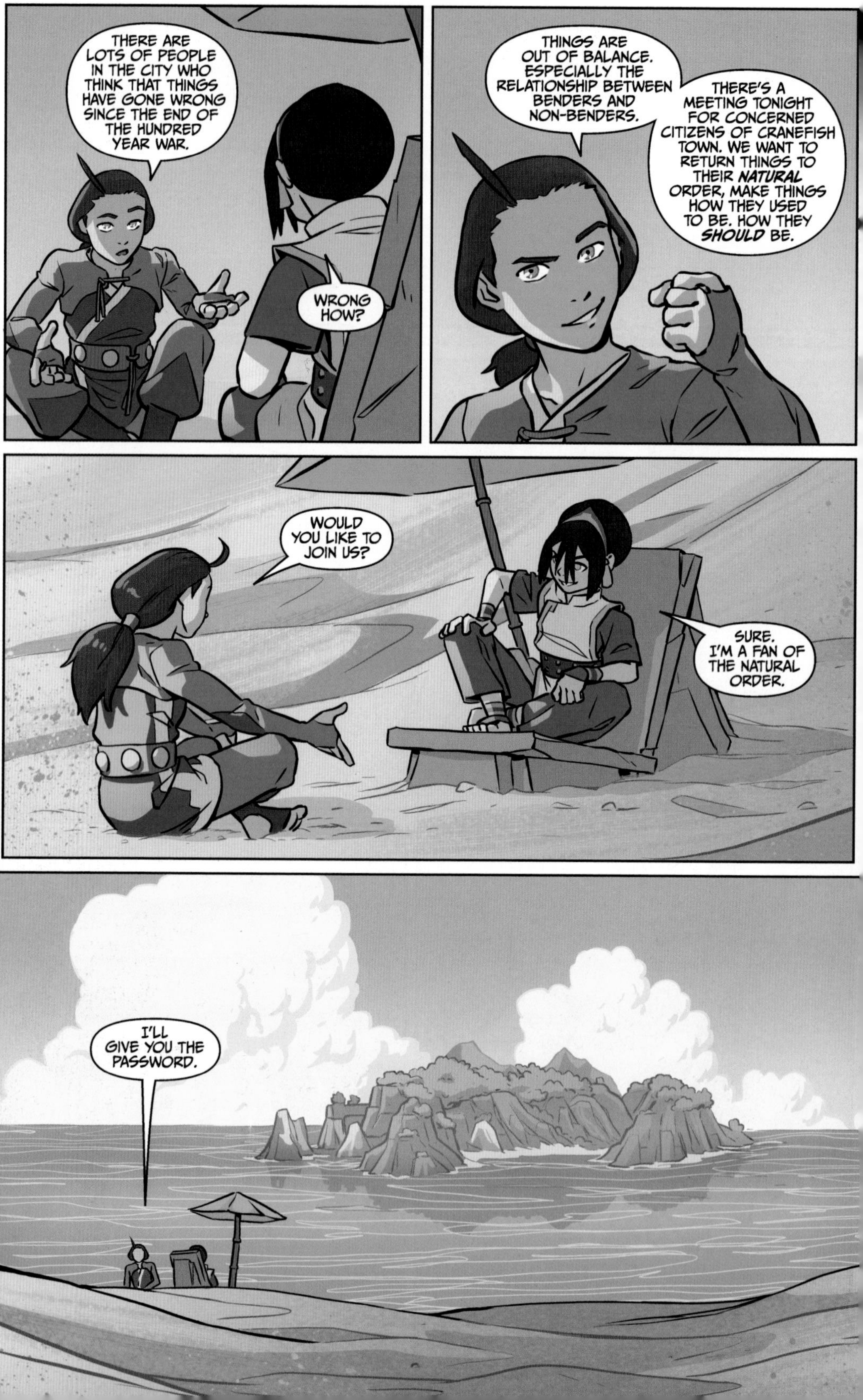
THERE ARE LOTS OF PEOPLE IN THE CITY WHO THINK THAT THINGS HAVE GONE WRONG SINCE THE END OF THE HUNDRED YEAR WAR.
WRONG HOW?
THINGS ARE OUT OF BALANCE. ESPECIALLY THE RELATIONSHIP BETWEEN BENDERS AND NON-BENDERS.
THERE'S A MEETING TONIGHT FOR CONCERNED CITIZENS OF CRANEFISH TOWN. WE WANT TO RETURN THINGS TO THEIR *NATURAL* ORDER, MAKE THINGS HOW THEY USED TO BE. HOW THEY ***SHOULD*** BE.
WOULD YOU LIKE TO JOIN US?
SURE. I'M A FAN OF THE NATURAL ORDER.
I'LL GIVE YOU THE PASSWORD.

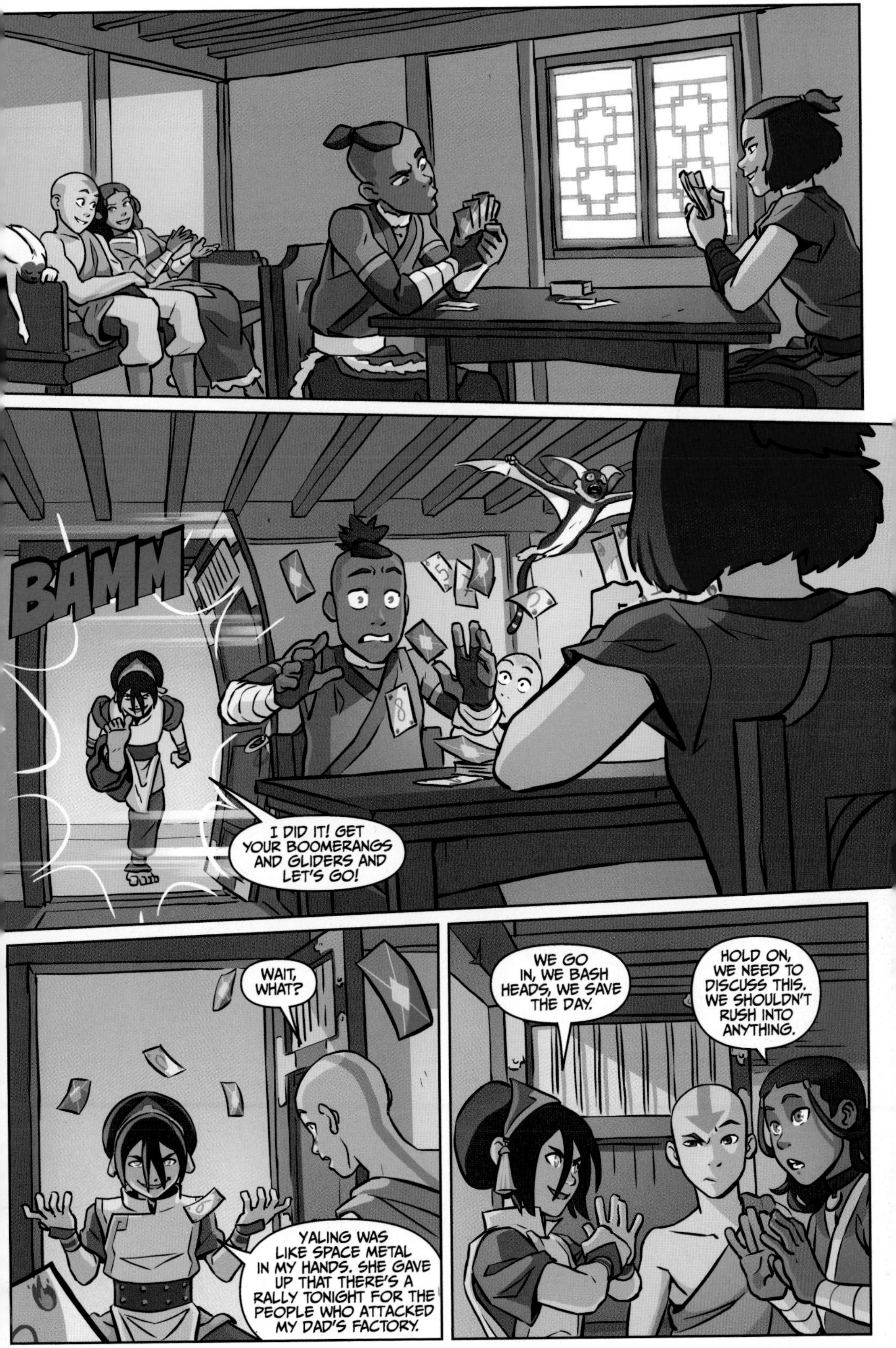
BAMM
I DID IT! GET YOUR BOOMERANGS AND GLIDERS AND LET'S GO!
WAIT, WHAT?
YALING WAS LIKE SPACE METAL IN MY HANDS. SHE GAVE UP THAT THERE'S A RALLY TONIGHT FOR THE PEOPLE WHO ATTACKED MY DAD'S FACTORY.
WE GO IN, WE BASH HEADS, WE SAVE THE DAY.
HOLD ON, WE NEED TO DISCUSS THIS. WE SHOULDN'T RUSH INTO ANYTHING.

WHAT'S TO DISCUSS?

WE DON'T KNOW WHY THE FACTORIES WERE ATTACKED, OR WHAT LILING'S INVOLVEMENT IS. SHE'S ON CRANEFISH TOWN'S BUSINESS COUNCIL. WE CAN'T ARREST HER WITHOUT PROOF SHE DID SOMETHING WRONG.

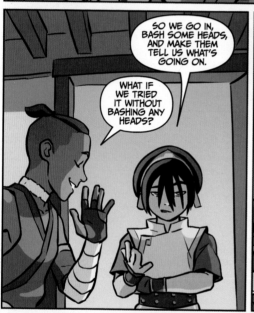

SO WE GO IN, BASH SOME HEADS, AND MAKE THEM TELL US WHAT'S GOING ON.

WHAT IF WE TRIED IT WITHOUT BASHING ANY HEADS?

WE *COULD* DO THAT, BUT... *WHY?*

WHAT ABOUT THIS. TOPH GOES TO THE MEETING WITH YALING, AND THE REST OF US DISGUISE OURSELVES AND SNEAK IN AFTER HER. THEN WE CAN GATHER INFORMATION.

SEEMS LIKE LESS FUN, BUT IF THAT'S THE WAY YOU WANT TO PLAY IT.

I THINK IT'S A GOOD PLAN.

IT'S A *GREAT* PLAN. ALSO, IT MEANS—

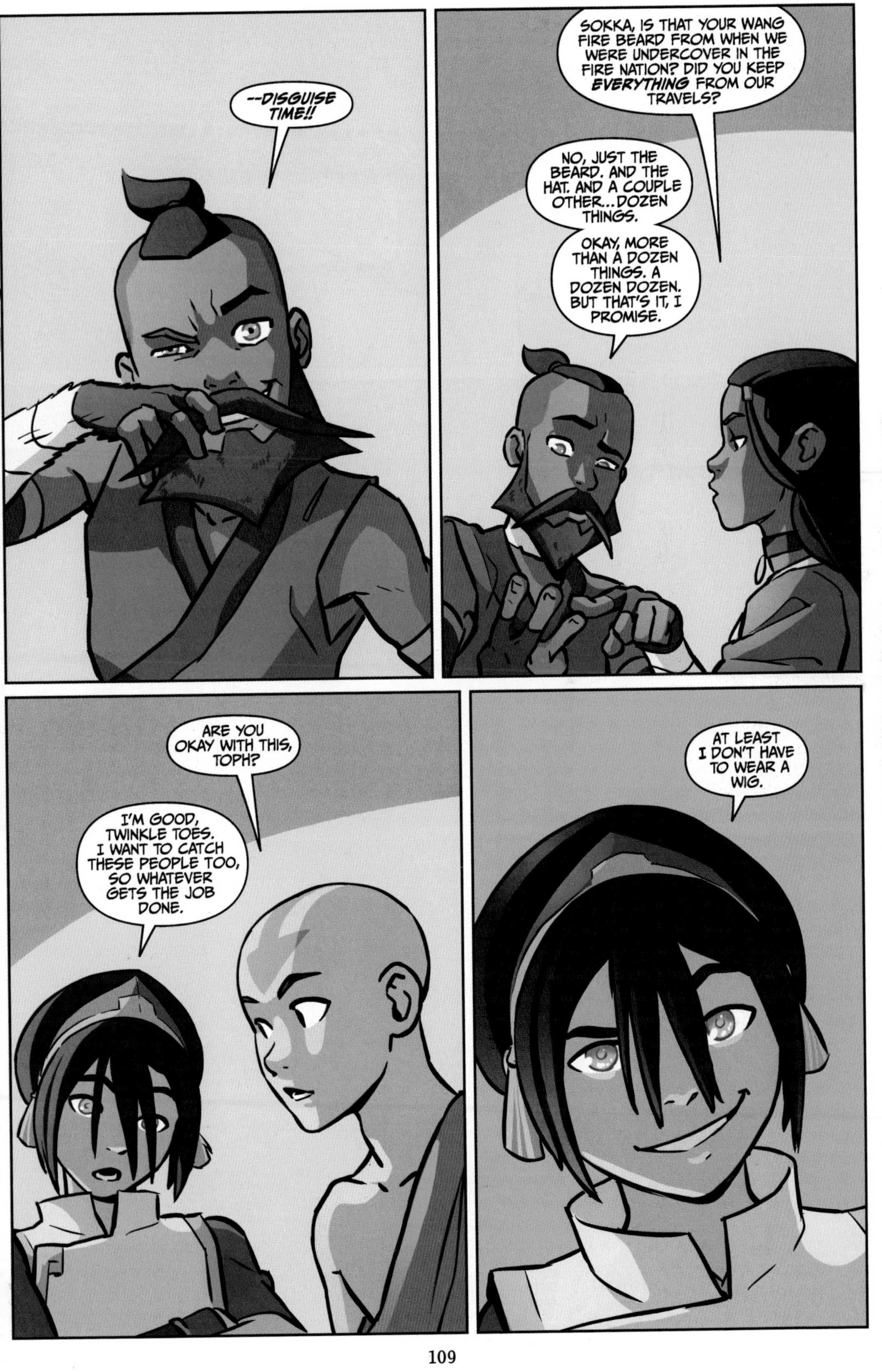
--DISGUISE TIME!!
SOKKA, IS THAT YOUR WANG FIRE BEARD FROM WHEN WE WERE UNDERCOVER IN THE FIRE NATION? DID YOU KEEP EVERYTHING FROM OUR TRAVELS?
NO, JUST THE BEARD. AND THE HAT. AND A COUPLE OTHER... DOZEN THINGS.
OKAY, MORE THAN A DOZEN THINGS. A DOZEN DOZEN. BUT THAT'S IT, I PROMISE.
ARE YOU OKAY WITH THIS, TOPH?
I'M GOOD, TWINKLE TOES. I WANT TO CATCH THESE PEOPLE TOO, SO WHATEVER GETS THE JOB DONE.
AT LEAST I DON'T HAVE TO WEAR A WIG.

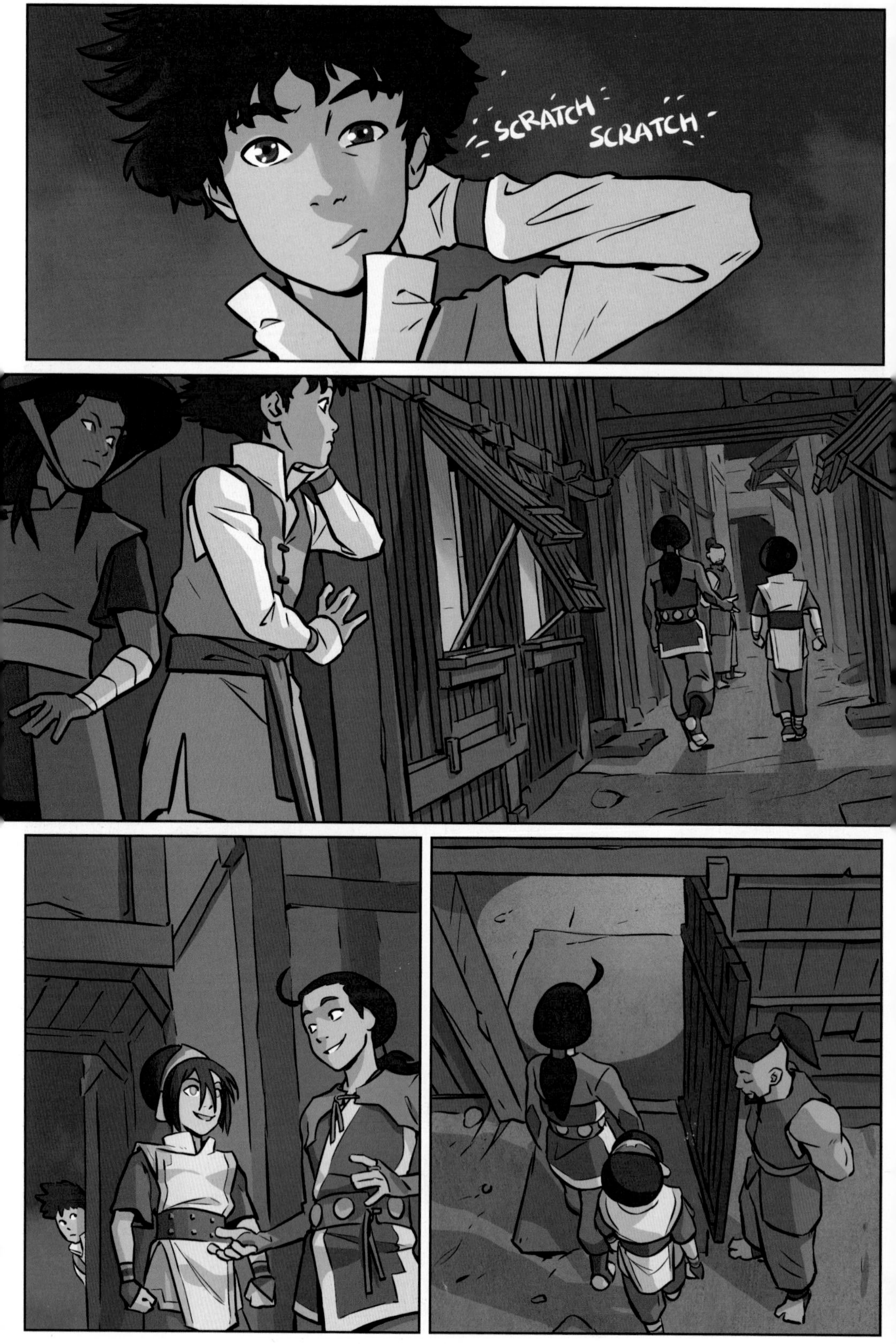
SCRATCH
SCRATCH

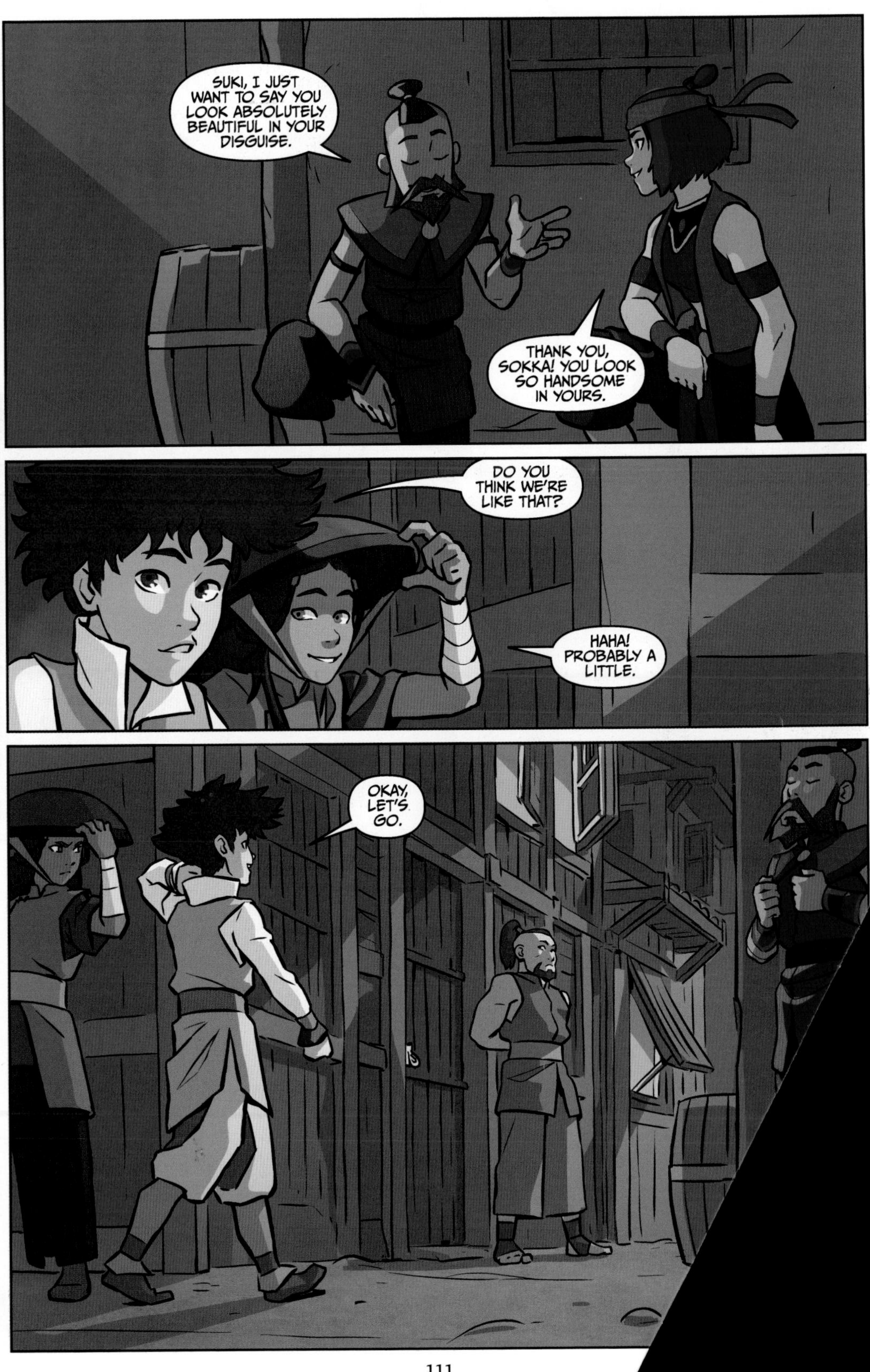
SUKI, I JUST WANT TO SAY YOU LOOK ABSOLUTELY BEAUTIFUL IN YOUR DISGUISE.
THANK YOU, SOKKA! YOU LOOK SO HANDSOME IN YOURS.
DO YOU THINK WE'RE LIKE THAT?
HAHA! PROBABLY A LITTLE.
OKAY, LET'S GO.

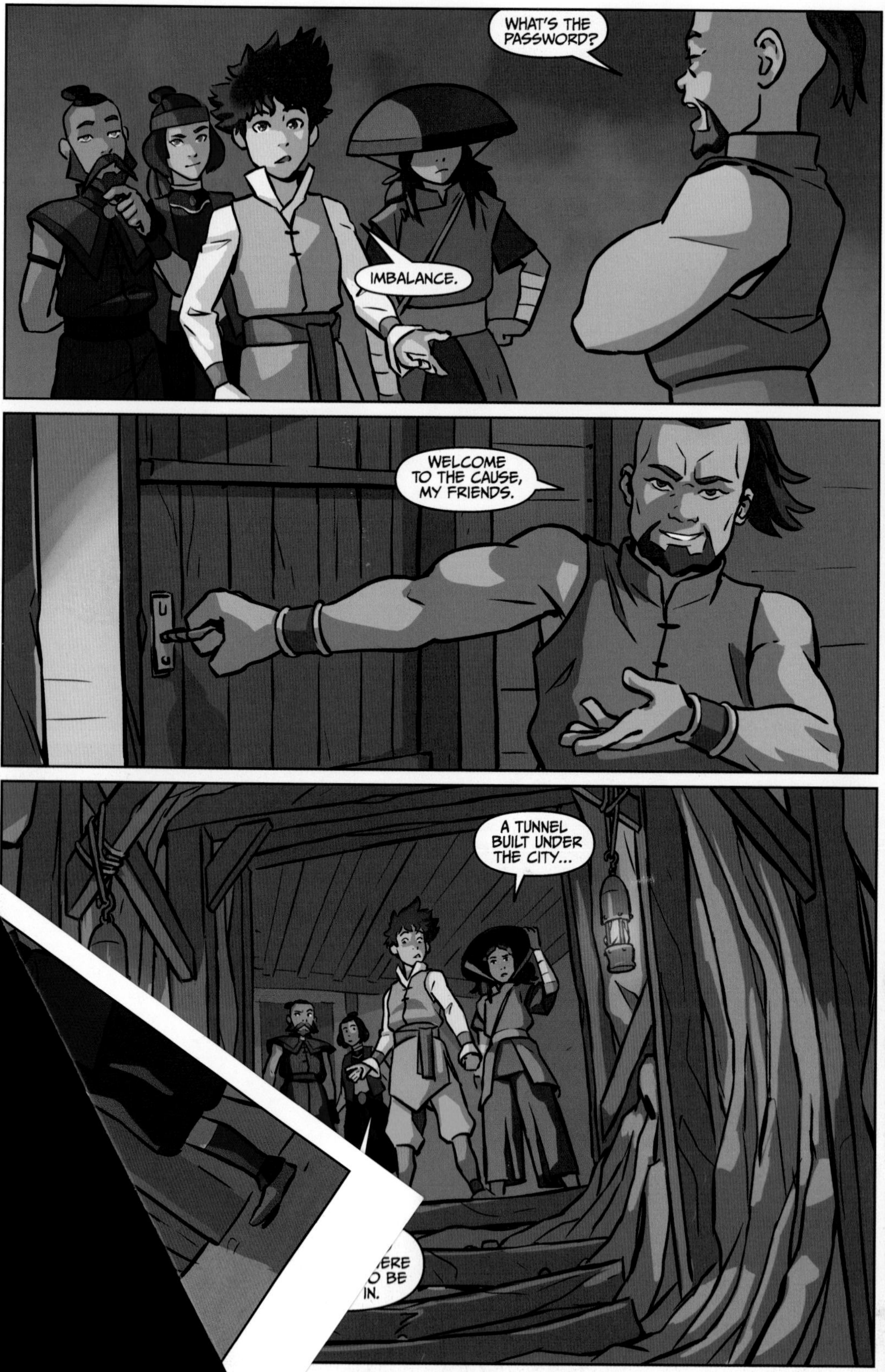
WHAT'S THE PASSWORD?
IMBALANCE.
WELCOME TO THE CAUSE, MY FRIENDS.
A TUNNEL BUILT UNDER THE CITY...

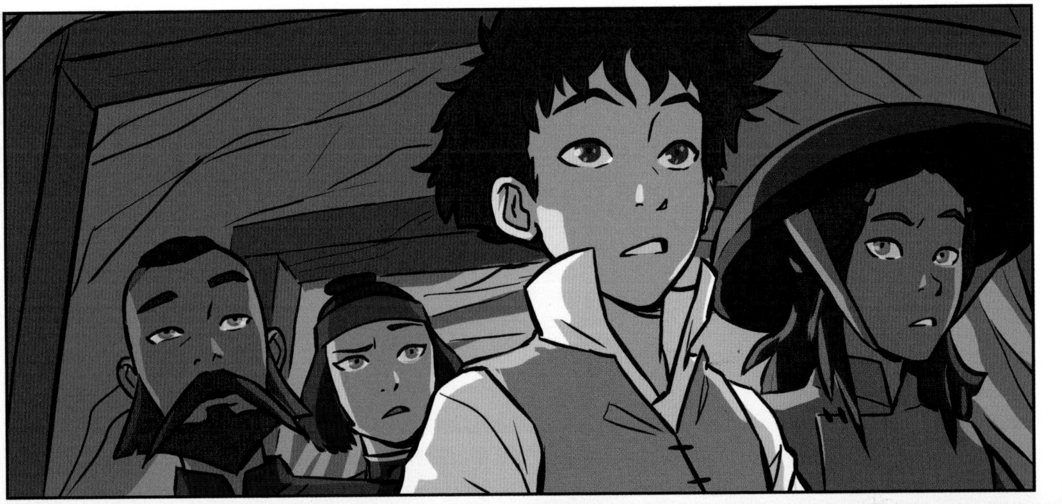

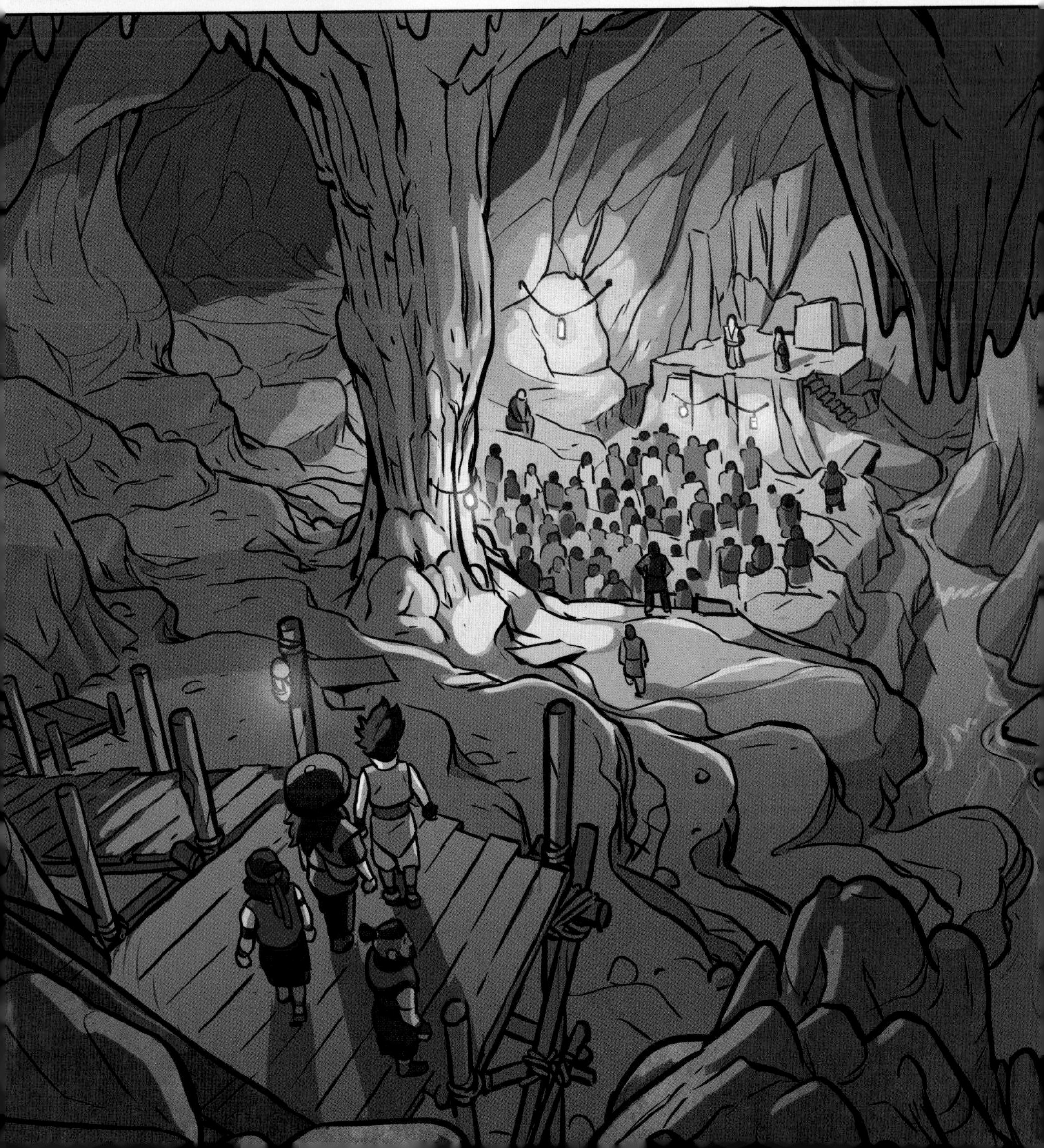

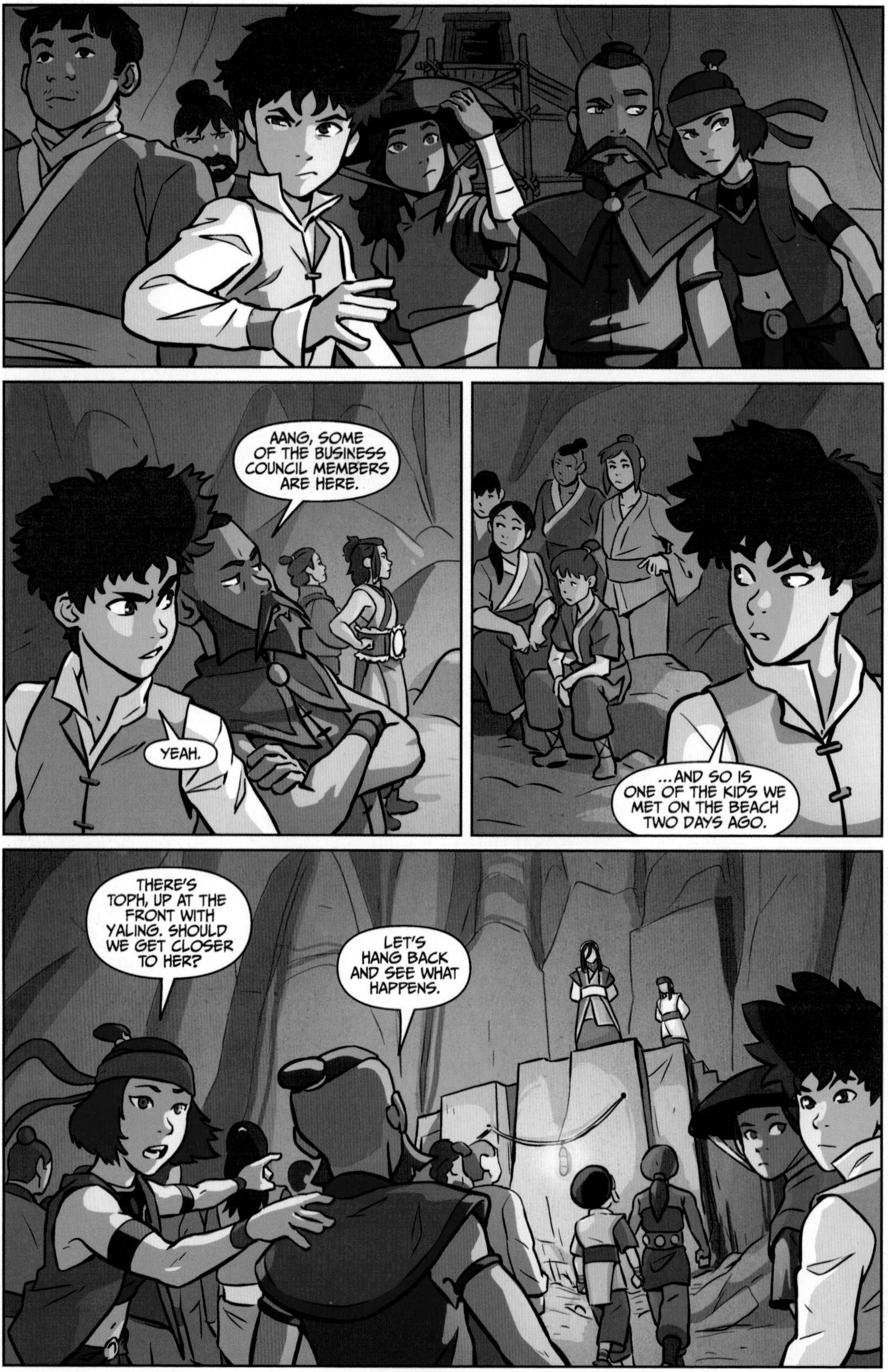
AANG, SOME OF THE BUSINESS COUNCIL MEMBERS ARE HERE.
YEAH.
...AND SO IS ONE OF THE KIDS WE MET ON THE BEACH TWO DAYS AGO.
THERE'S TOPH, UP AT THE FRONT WITH YALING. SHOULD WE GET CLOSER TO HER?
LET'S HANG BACK AND SEE WHAT HAPPENS.

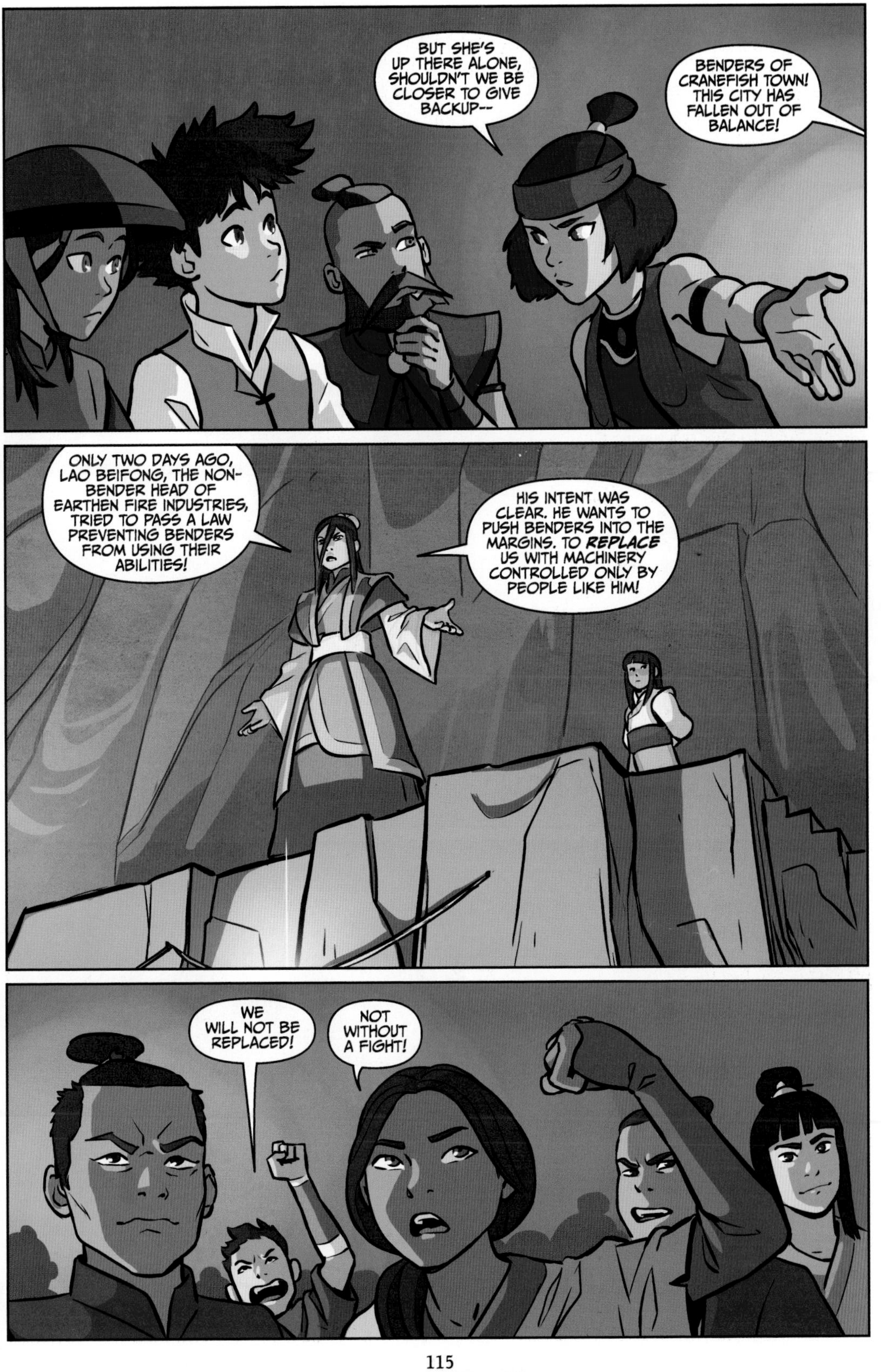
BUT SHE'S UP THERE ALONE, SHOULDN'T WE BE CLOSER TO GIVE BACKUP--
BENDERS OF CRANEFISH TOWN! THIS CITY HAS FALLEN OUT OF BALANCE!
ONLY TWO DAYS AGO, LAO BEIFONG, THE NON-BENDER HEAD OF EARTHEN FIRE INDUSTRIES, TRIED TO PASS A LAW PREVENTING BENDERS FROM USING THEIR ABILITIES!
HIS INTENT WAS CLEAR. HE WANTS TO PUSH BENDERS INTO THE MARGINS. TO REPLACE US WITH MACHINERY CONTROLLED ONLY BY PEOPLE LIKE HIM!
WE WILL NOT BE REPLACED!
NOT WITHOUT A FIGHT!

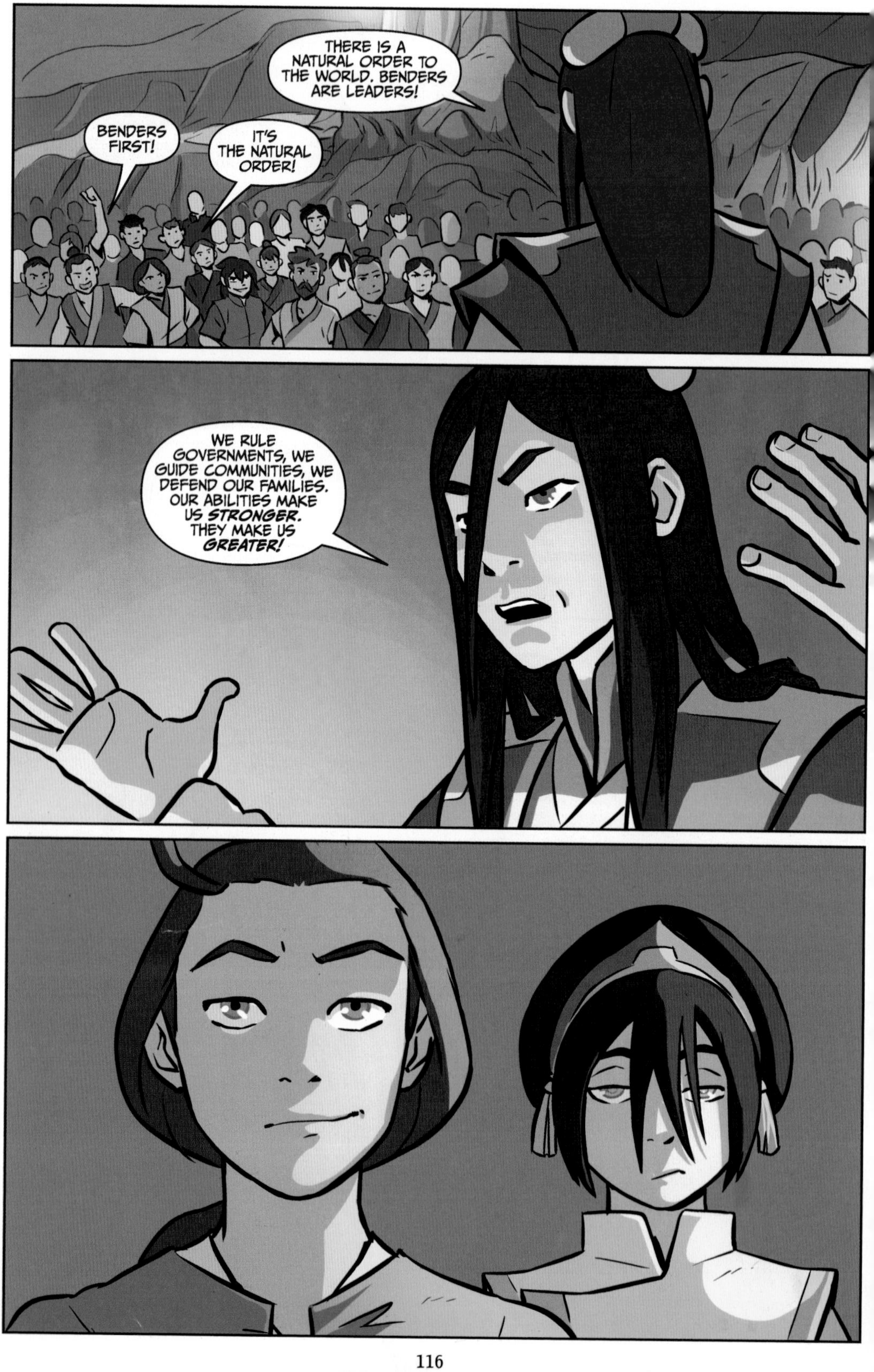
THERE IS A NATURAL ORDER TO THE WORLD. BENDERS ARE LEADERS!
BENDERS FIRST!
IT'S THE NATURAL ORDER!
WE RULE GOVERNMENTS, WE GUIDE COMMUNITIES, WE DEFEND OUR FAMILIES. OUR ABILITIES MAKE US STRONGER. THEY MAKE US GREATER!

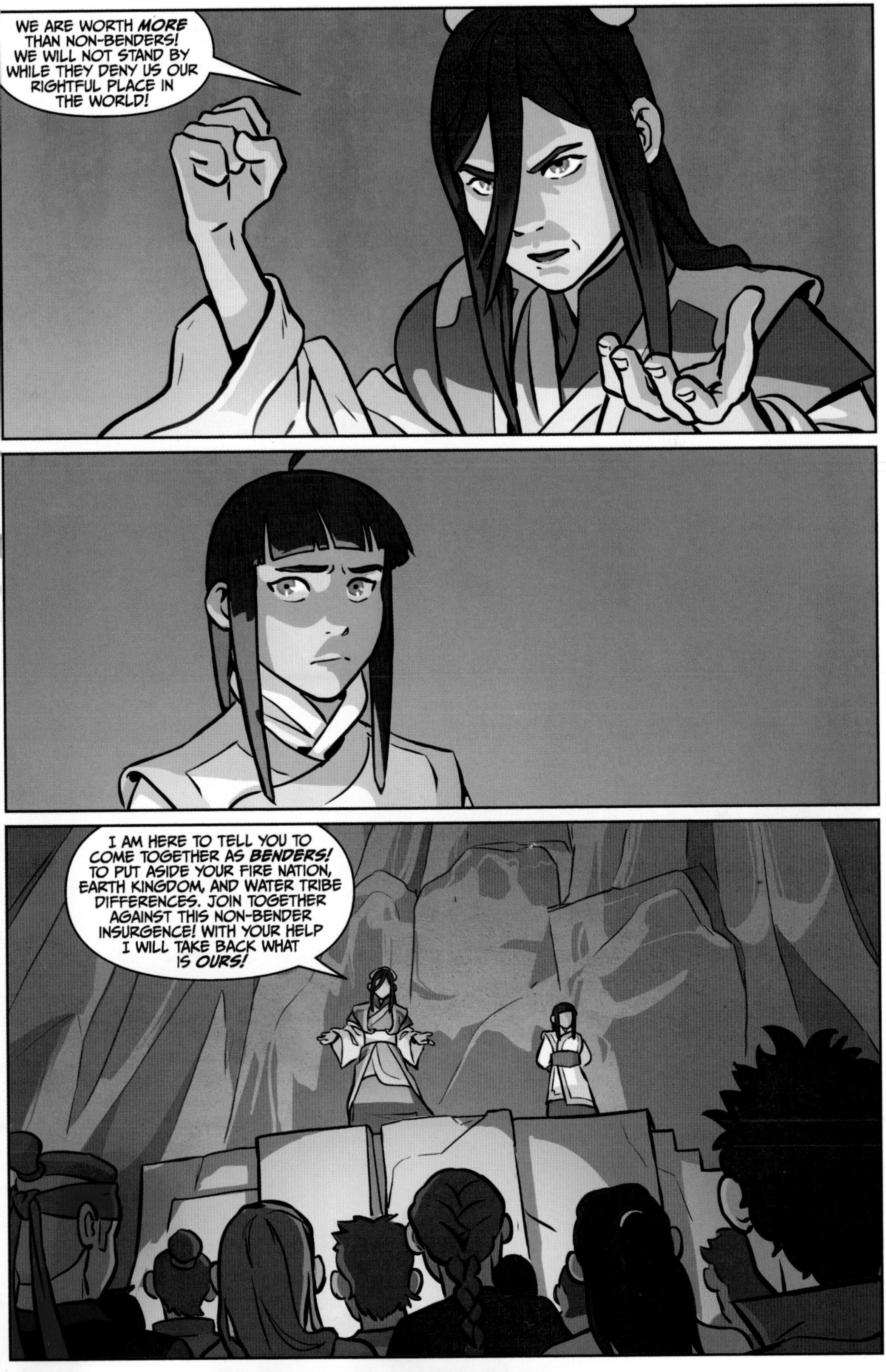
WE ARE WORTH MORE THAN NON-BENDERS! WE WILL NOT STAND BY WHILE THEY DENY US OUR RIGHTFUL PLACE IN THE WORLD!
I AM HERE TO TELL YOU TO COME TOGETHER AS BENDERS! TO PUT ASIDE YOUR FIRE NATION, EARTH KINGDOM, AND WATER TRIBE DIFFERENCES. JOIN TOGETHER AGAINST THIS NON-BENDER INSURGENCE! WITH YOUR HELP I WILL TAKE BACK WHAT IS OURS!

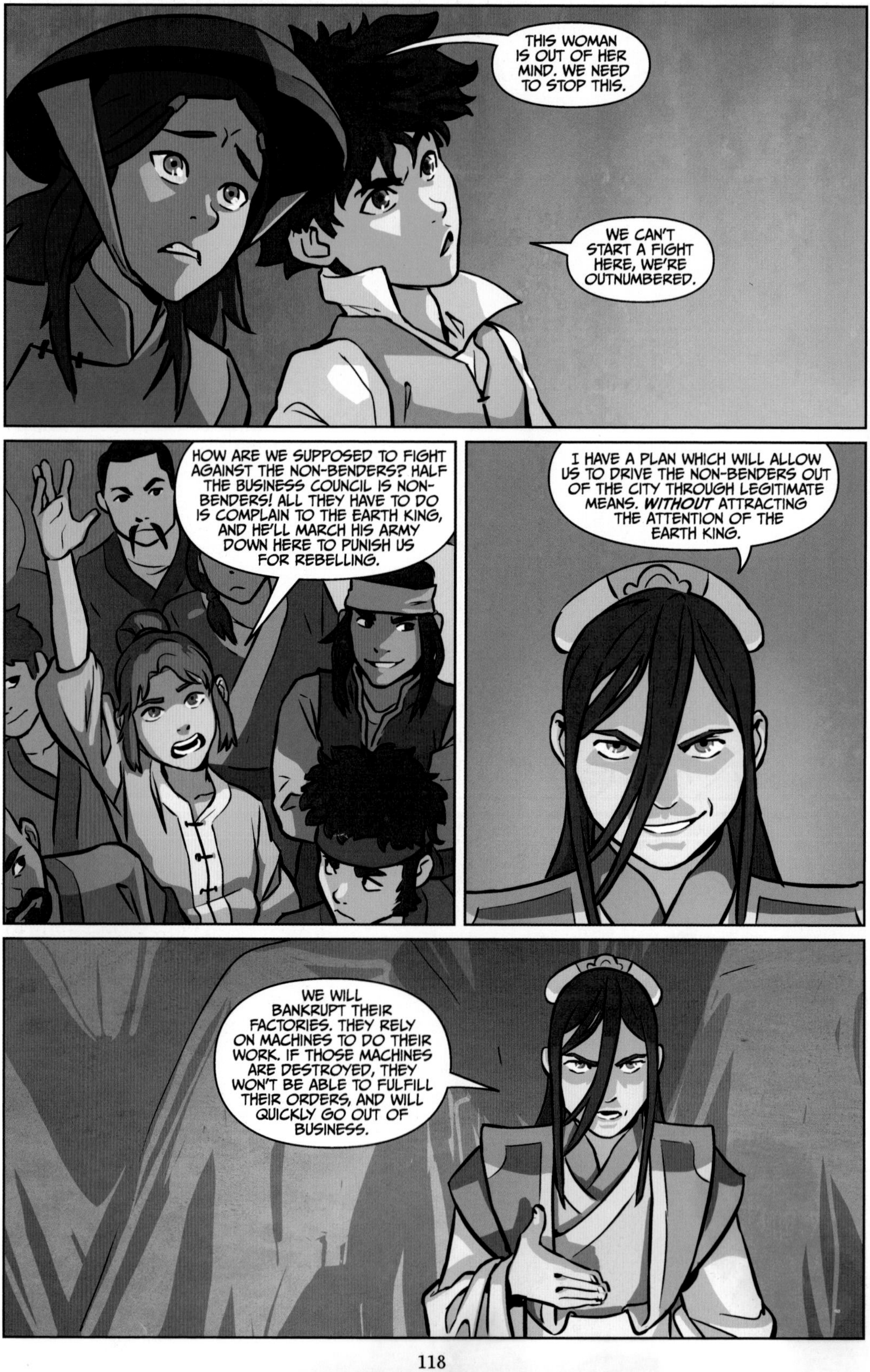
THIS WOMAN IS OUT OF HER MIND. WE NEED TO STOP THIS.
WE CAN'T START A FIGHT HERE, WE'RE OUTNUMBERED.
HOW ARE WE SUPPOSED TO FIGHT AGAINST THE NON-BENDERS? HALF THE BUSINESS COUNCIL IS NON-BENDERS! ALL THEY HAVE TO DO IS COMPLAIN TO THE EARTH KING, AND HE'LL MARCH HIS ARMY DOWN HERE TO PUNISH US FOR REBELLING.
I HAVE A PLAN WHICH WILL ALLOW US TO DRIVE THE NON-BENDERS OUT OF THE CITY THROUGH LEGITIMATE MEANS. *WITHOUT* ATTRACTING THE ATTENTION OF THE EARTH KING.
WE WILL BANKRUPT THEIR FACTORIES. THEY RELY ON MACHINES TO DO THEIR WORK. IF THOSE MACHINES ARE DESTROYED, THEY WON'T BE ABLE TO FULFILL THEIR ORDERS, AND WILL QUICKLY GO OUT OF BUSINESS.

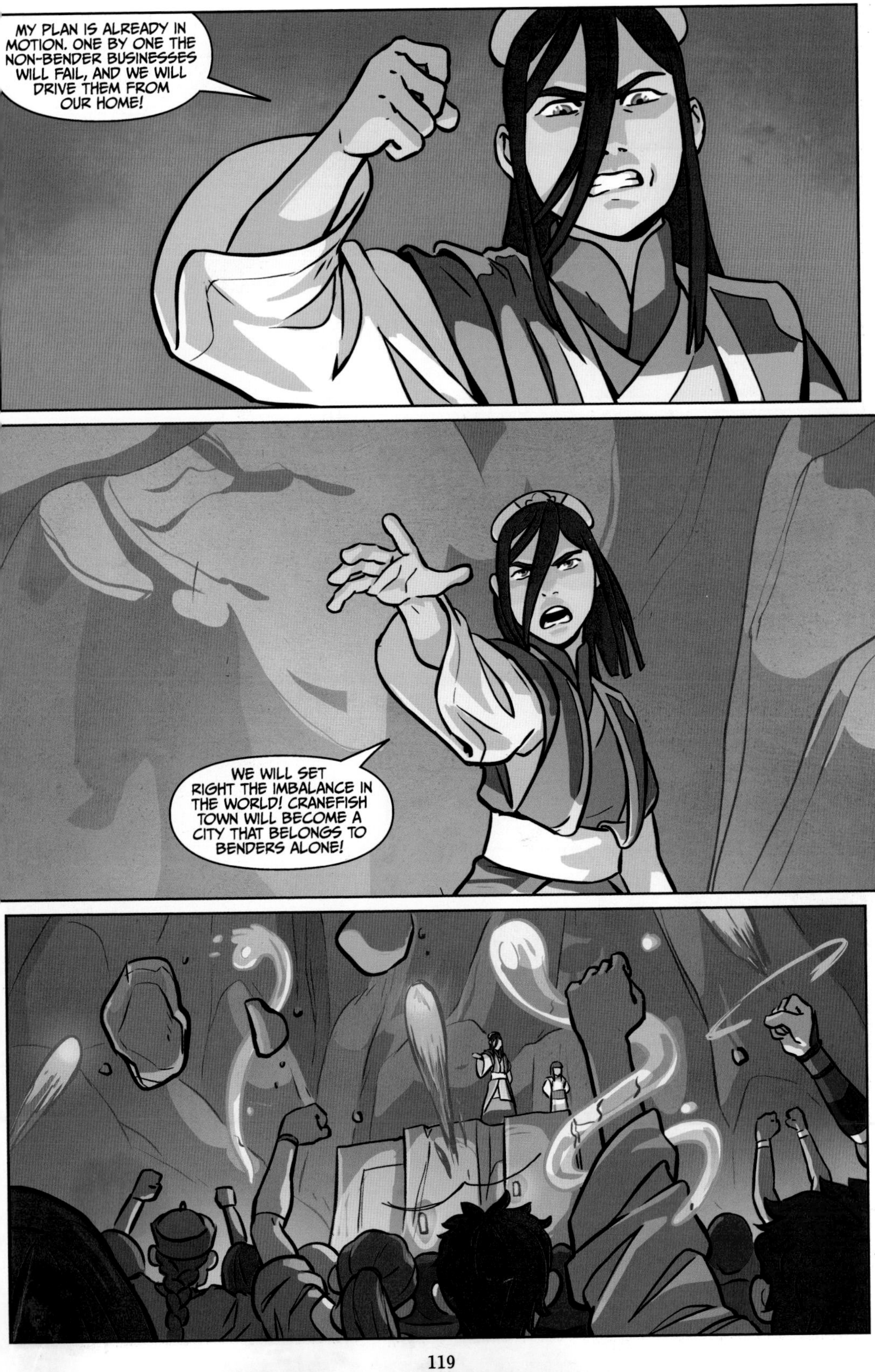
MY PLAN IS ALREADY IN MOTION. ONE BY ONE THE NON-BENDER BUSINESSES WILL FAIL, AND WE WILL DRIVE THEM FROM OUR HOME!
WE WILL SET RIGHT THE IMBALANCE IN THE WORLD! CRANEFISH TOWN WILL BECOME A CITY THAT BELONGS TO BENDERS ALONE!

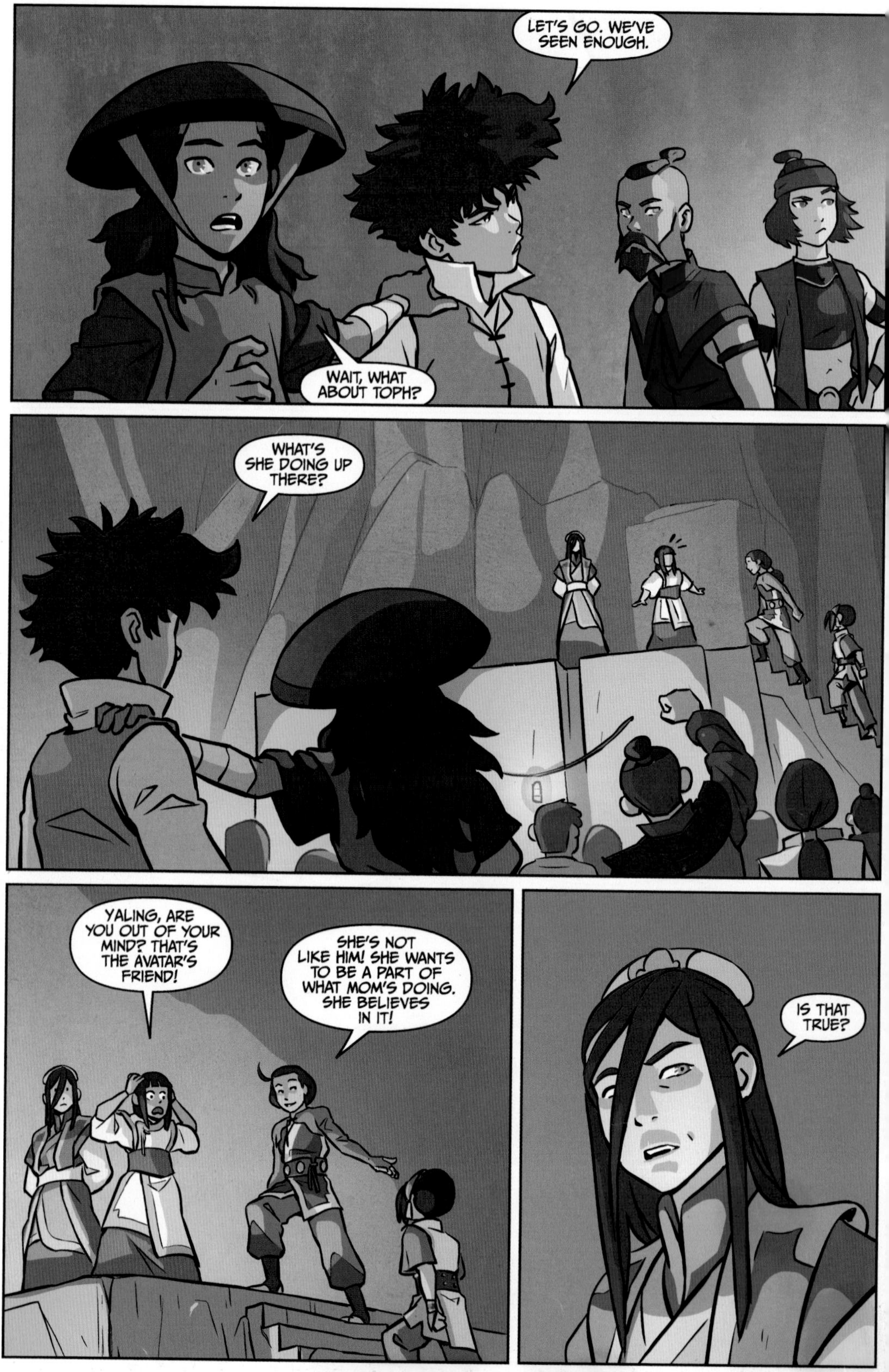
LET'S GO. WE'VE SEEN ENOUGH.
WAIT, WHAT ABOUT TOPH?
WHAT'S SHE DOING UP THERE?
YALING, ARE YOU OUT OF YOUR MIND? THAT'S THE AVATAR'S FRIEND!
SHE'S NOT LIKE HIM! SHE WANTS TO BE A PART OF WHAT MOM'S DOING. SHE BELIEVES IN IT!
IS THAT TRUE?

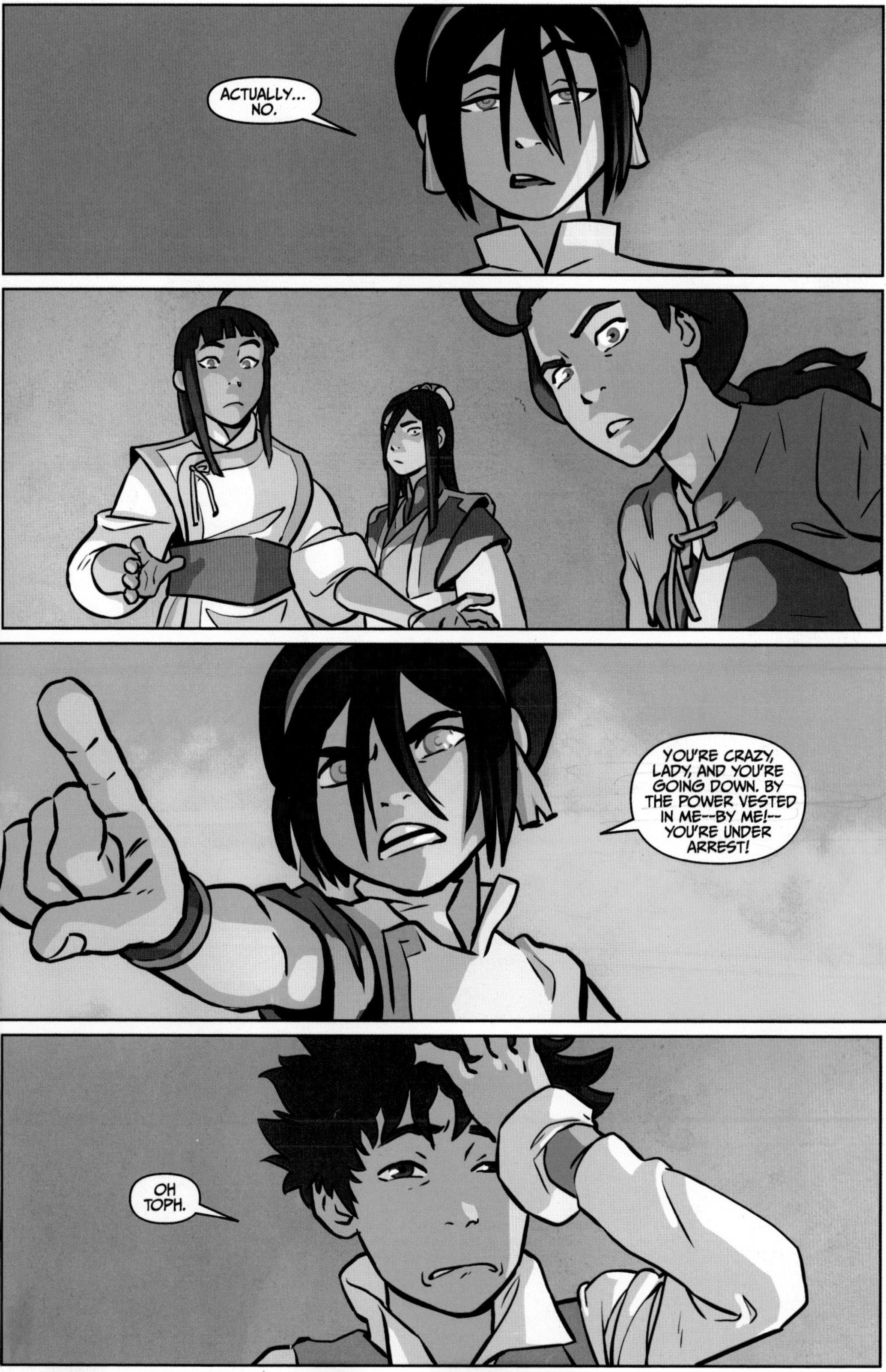
ACTUALLY... NO.
YOU'RE CRAZY, LADY, AND YOU'RE GOING DOWN. BY THE POWER VESTED IN ME--BY ME!--YOU'RE UNDER ARREST!
OH TOPH.

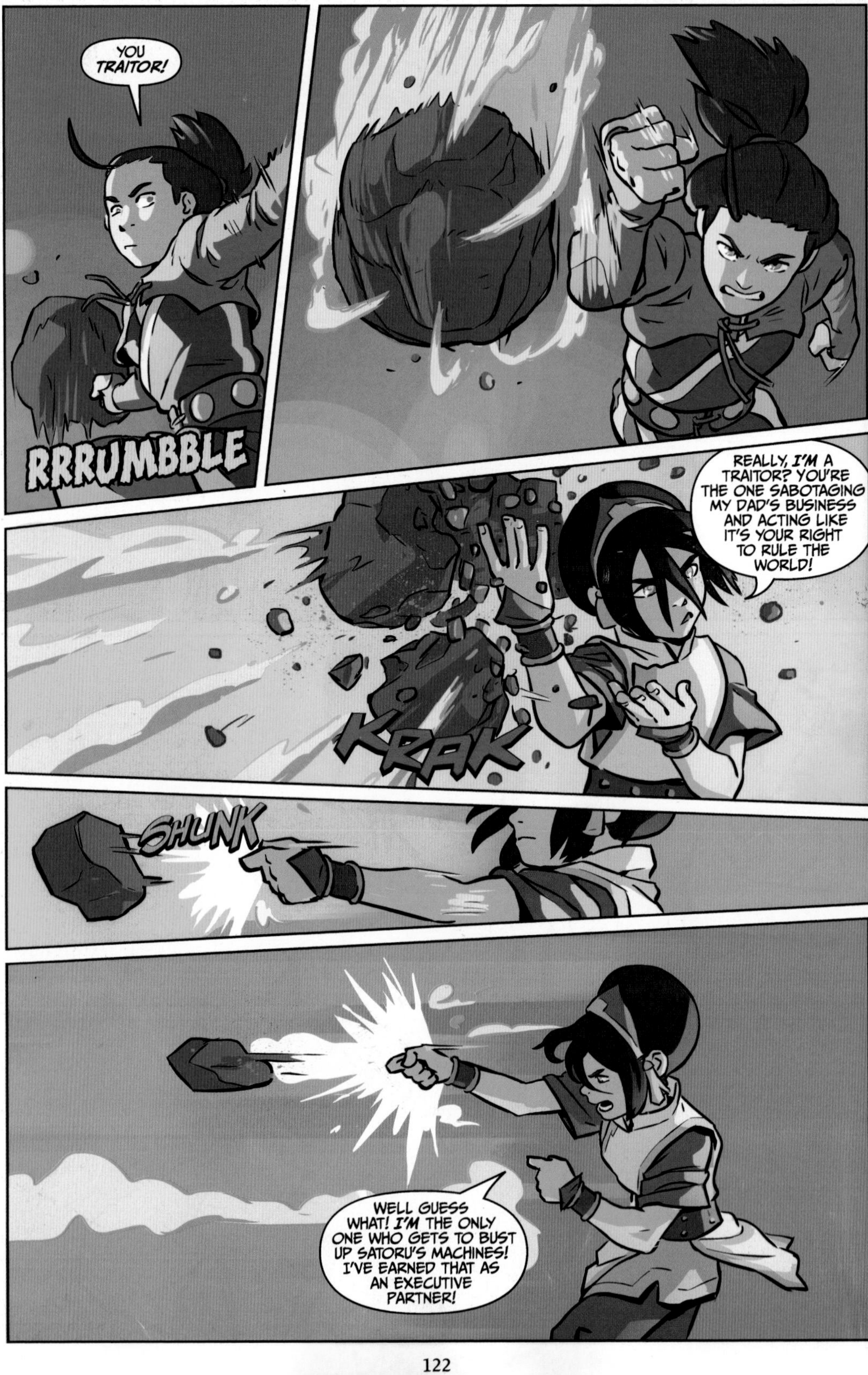
YOU TRAITOR!
RRRUMBBLE
REALLY, I'M A TRAITOR? YOU'RE THE ONE SABOTAGING MY DAD'S BUSINESS AND ACTING LIKE IT'S YOUR RIGHT TO RULE THE WORLD!
KRAK
SHUNK
WELL GUESS WHAT! I'M THE ONLY ONE WHO GETS TO BUST UP SATORU'S MACHINES! I'VE EARNED THAT AS AN EXECUTIVE PARTNER!

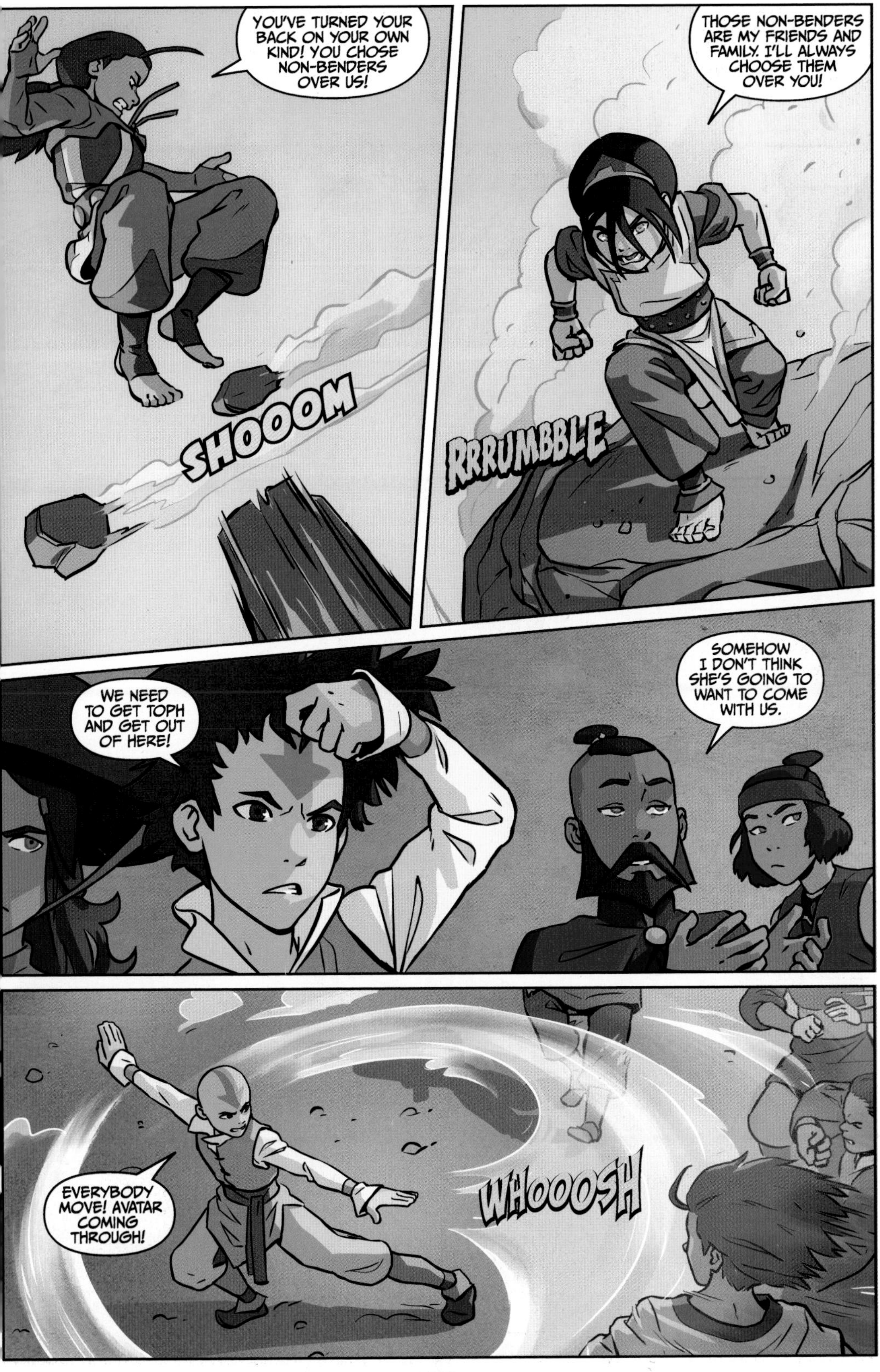
YOU'VE TURNED YOUR BACK ON YOUR OWN KIND! YOU CHOSE NON-BENDERS OVER US!
SHOOOM
THOSE NON-BENDERS ARE MY FRIENDS AND FAMILY. I'LL ALWAYS CHOOSE THEM OVER YOU!
RRRUMBBLE
WE NEED TO GET TOPH AND GET OUT OF HERE!
SOMEHOW I DON'T THINK SHE'S GOING TO WANT TO COME WITH US.
EVERYBODY MOVE! AVATAR COMING THROUGH!
WHOOOSH

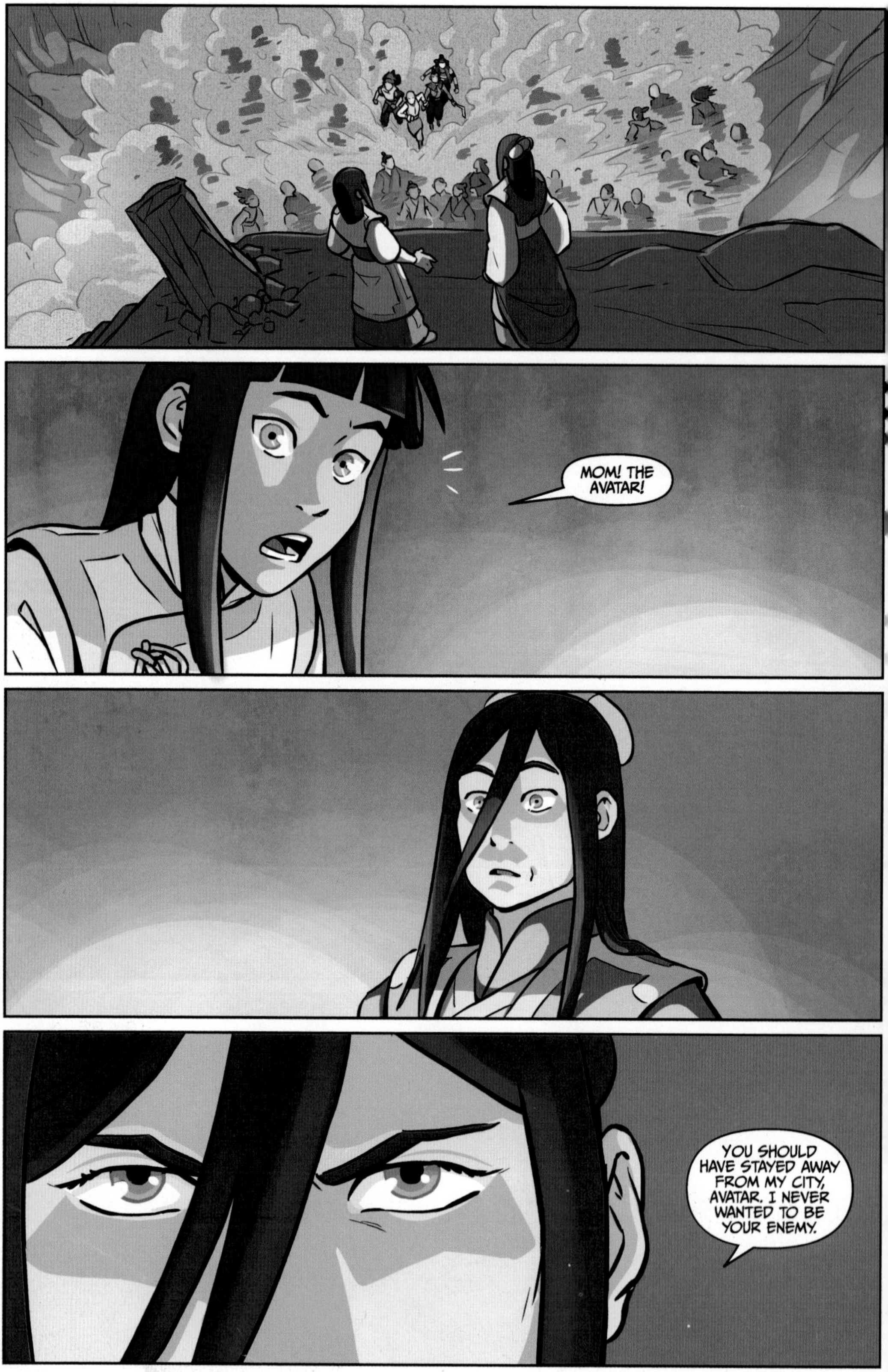
MOM! THE AVATAR!
YOU SHOULD HAVE STAYED AWAY FROM MY CITY, AVATAR. I NEVER WANTED TO BE YOUR ENEMY.

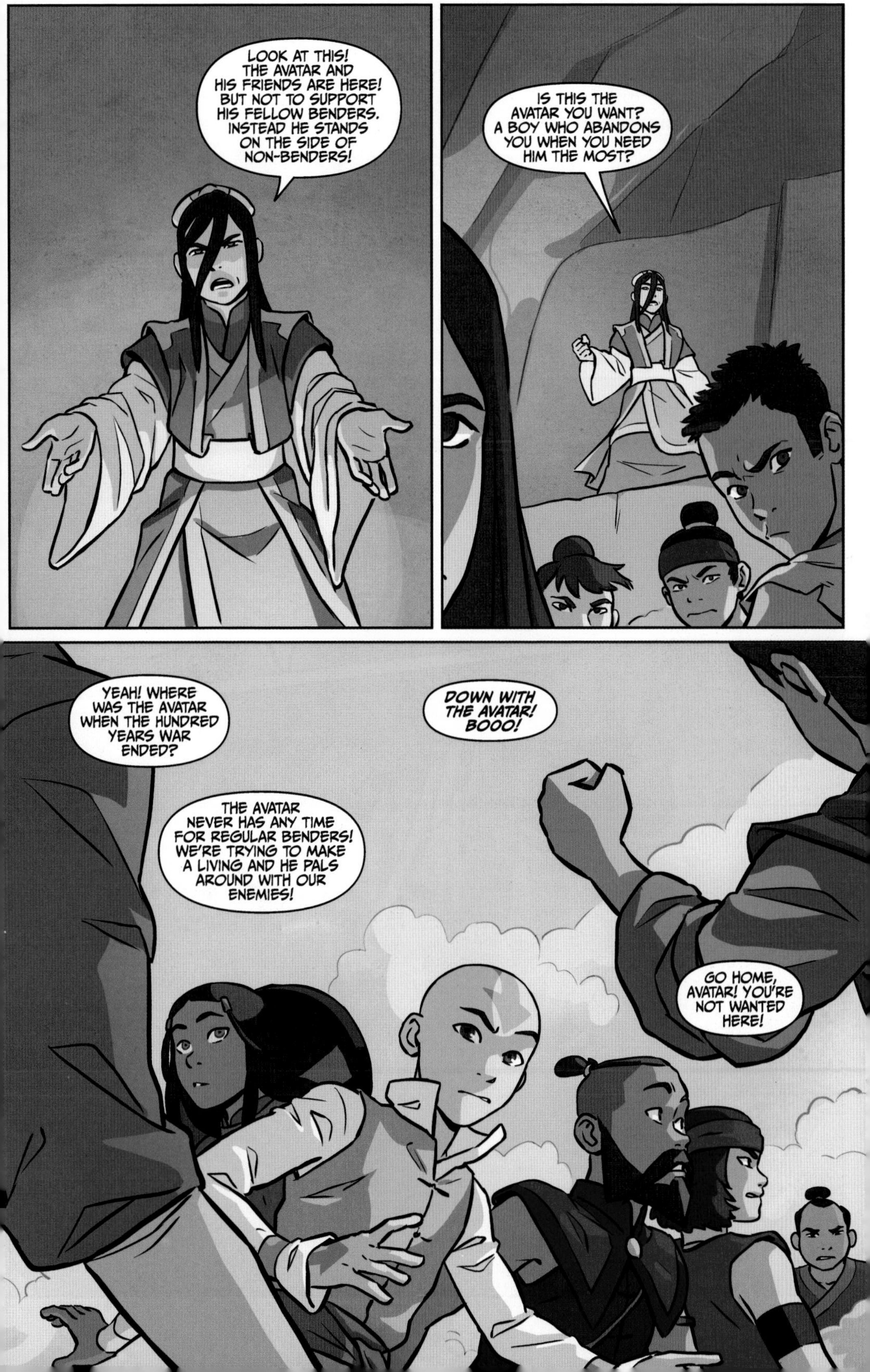
LOOK AT THIS! THE AVATAR AND HIS FRIENDS ARE HERE! BUT NOT TO SUPPORT HIS FELLOW BENDERS. INSTEAD HE STANDS ON THE SIDE OF NON-BENDERS!
IS THIS THE AVATAR YOU WANT? A BOY WHO ABANDONS YOU WHEN YOU NEED HIM THE MOST?
YEAH! WHERE WAS THE AVATAR WHEN THE HUNDRED YEARS WAR ENDED?
DOWN WITH THE AVATAR! BOOO!
THE AVATAR NEVER HAS ANY TIME FOR REGULAR BENDERS! WE'RE TRYING TO MAKE A LIVING AND HE PALS AROUND WITH OUR ENEMIES!
GO HOME, AVATAR! YOU'RE NOT WANTED HERE!

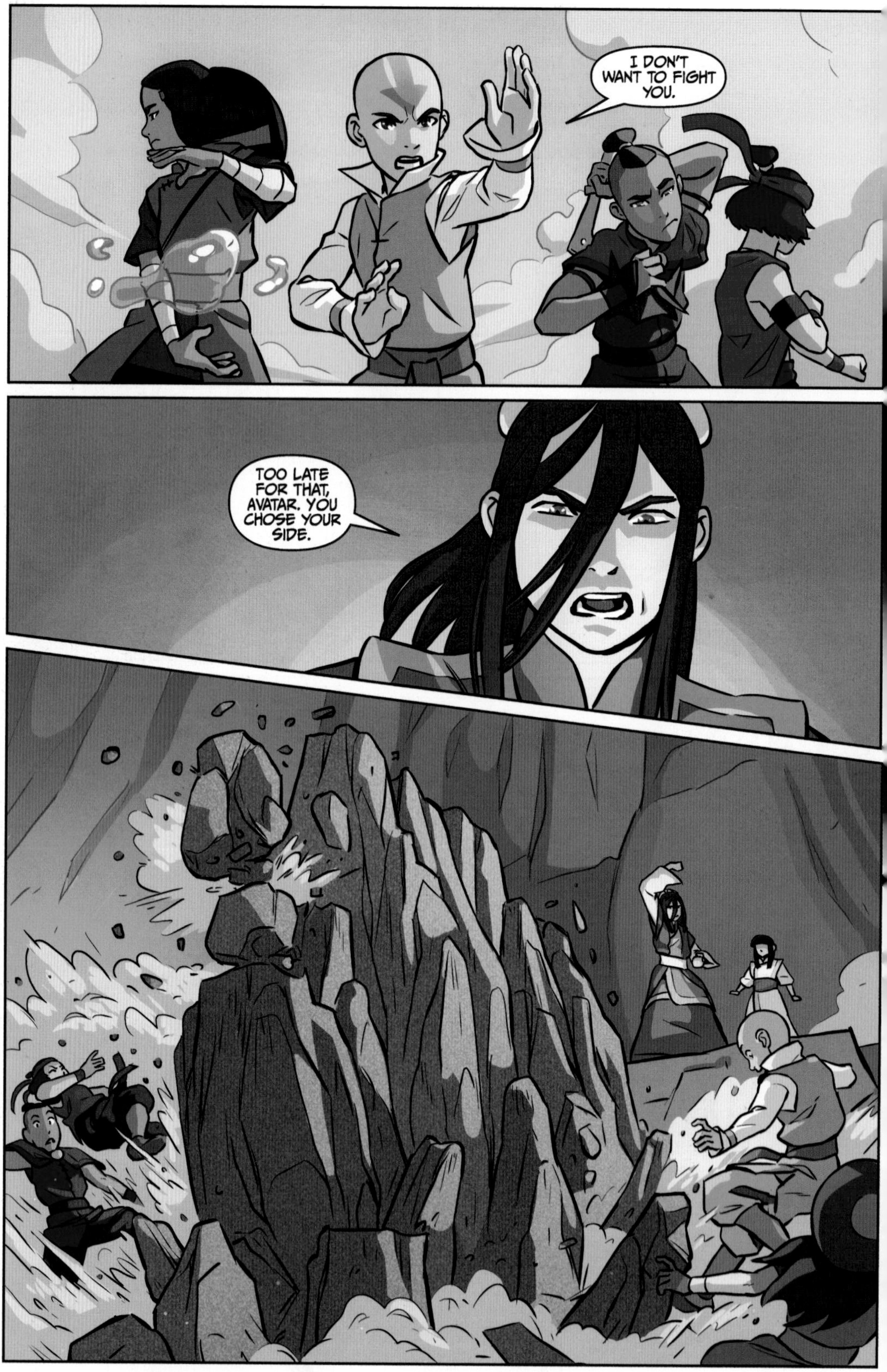
I DON'T WANT TO FIGHT YOU.
TOO LATE FOR THAT, AVATAR. YOU CHOSE YOUR SIDE.

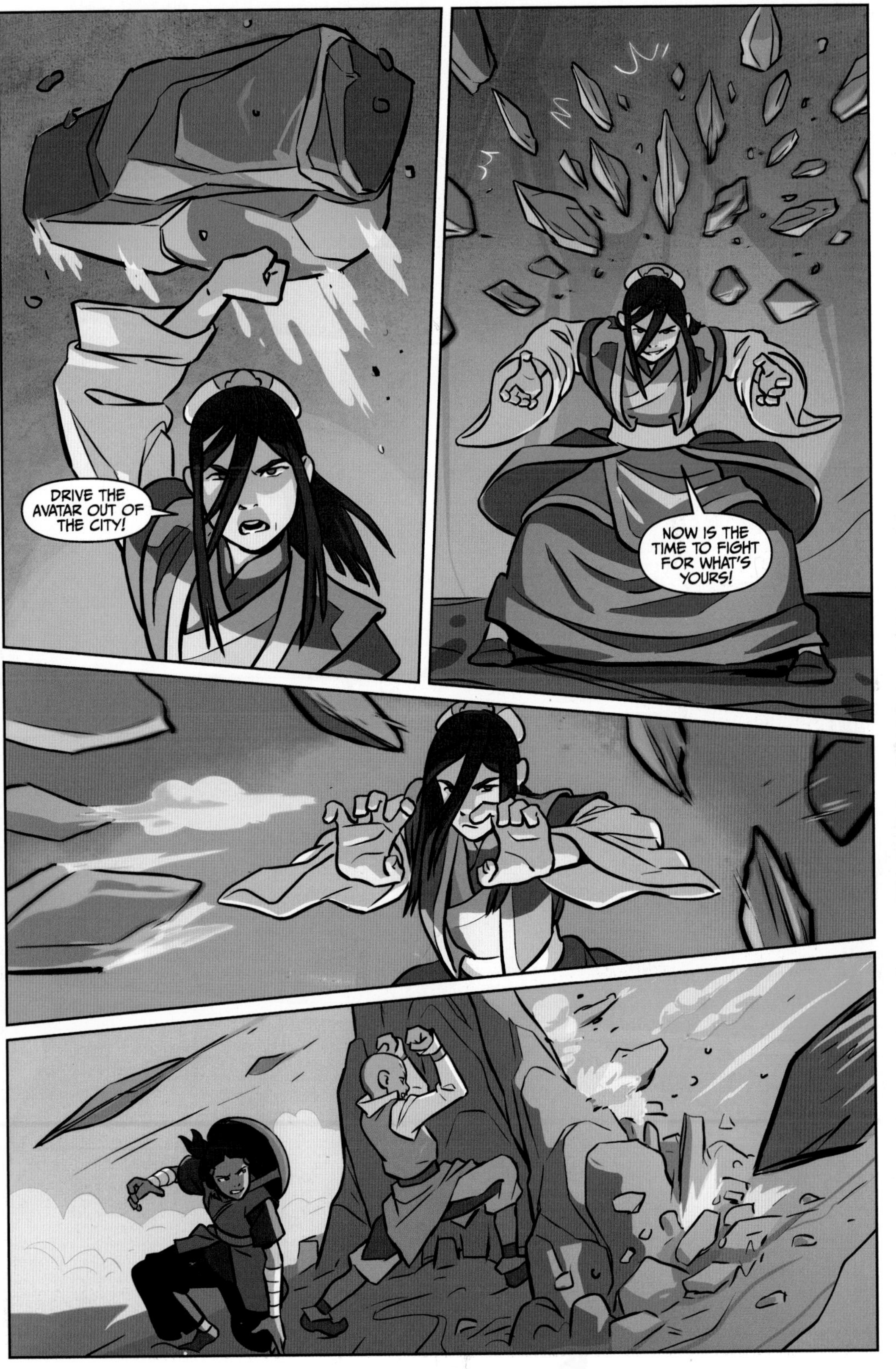
DRIVE THE AVATAR OUT OF THE CITY!
NOW IS THE TIME TO FIGHT FOR WHAT'S YOURS!

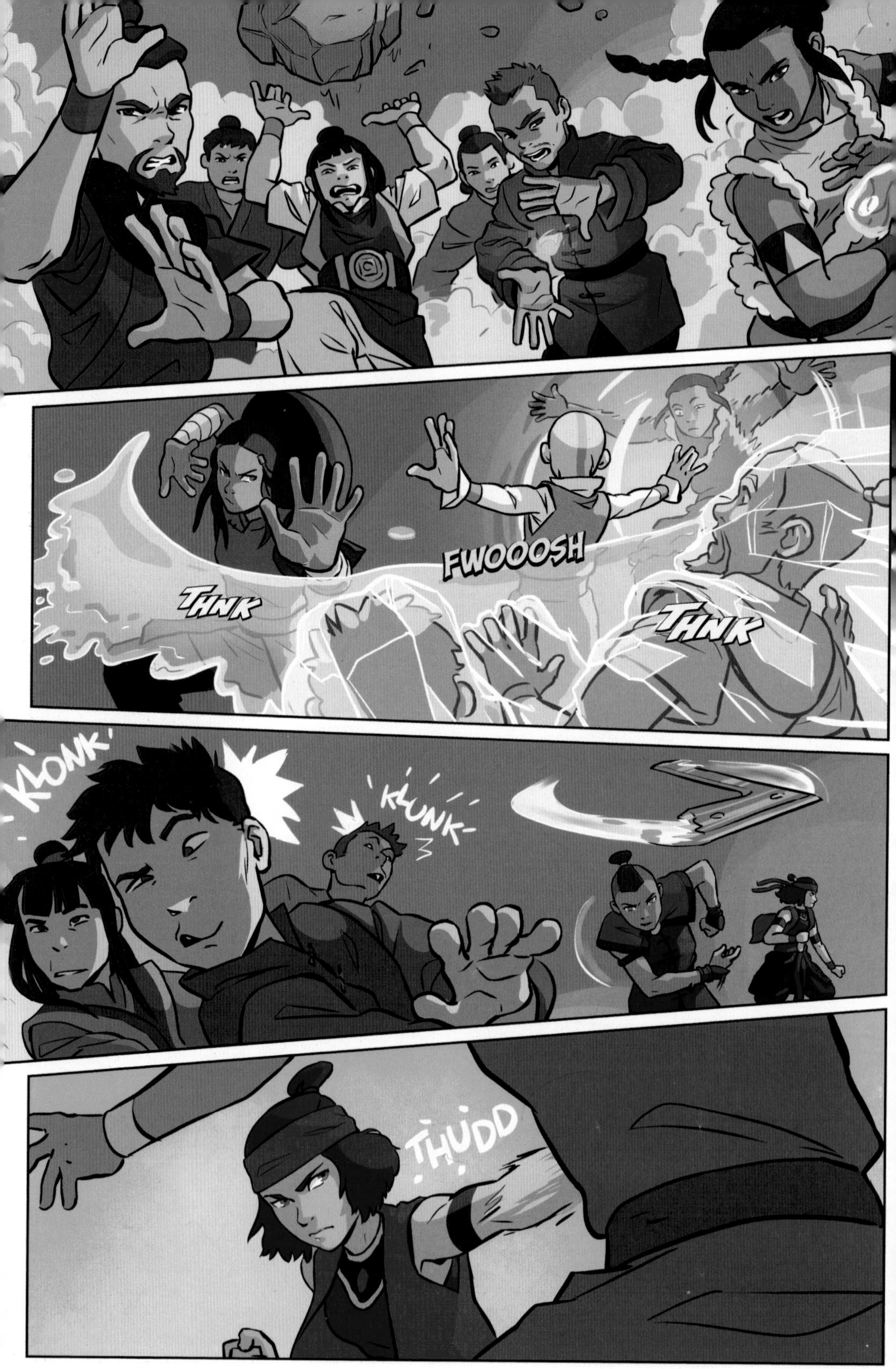

FWOOOSH
THNK
THNK
KLONK
KLUNK
THUDD

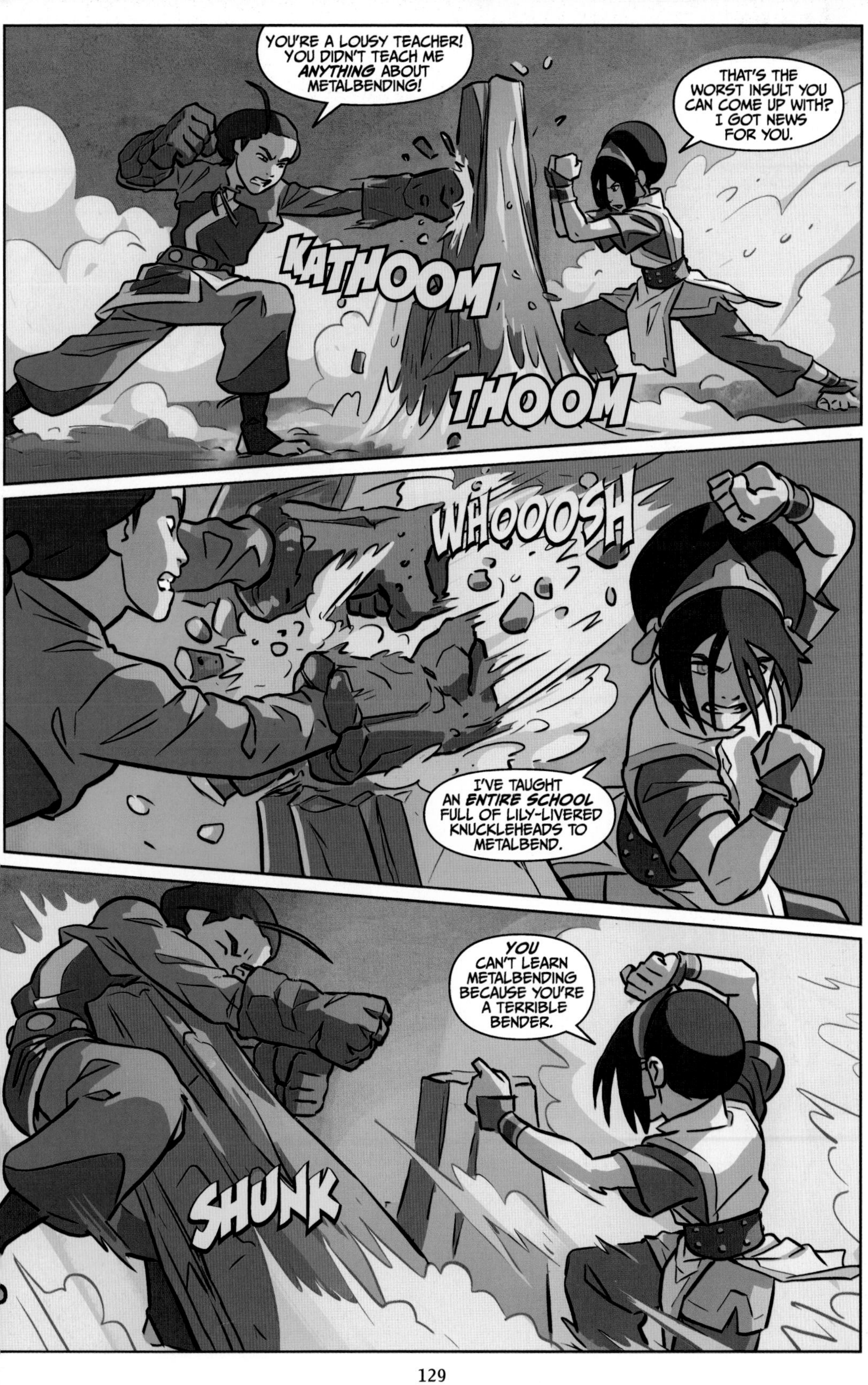
YOU'RE A LOUSY TEACHER! YOU DIDN'T TEACH ME *ANYTHING* ABOUT METALBENDING!
THAT'S THE WORST INSULT YOU CAN COME UP WITH? I GOT NEWS FOR YOU.
KATHOOM
THOOM
WHOOOSH
I'VE TAUGHT AN **ENTIRE SCHOOL** FULL OF LILY-LIVERED KNUCKLEHEADS TO METALBEND.
YOU CAN'T LEARN METALBENDING BECAUSE YOU'RE A TERRIBLE BENDER.
SHUNK

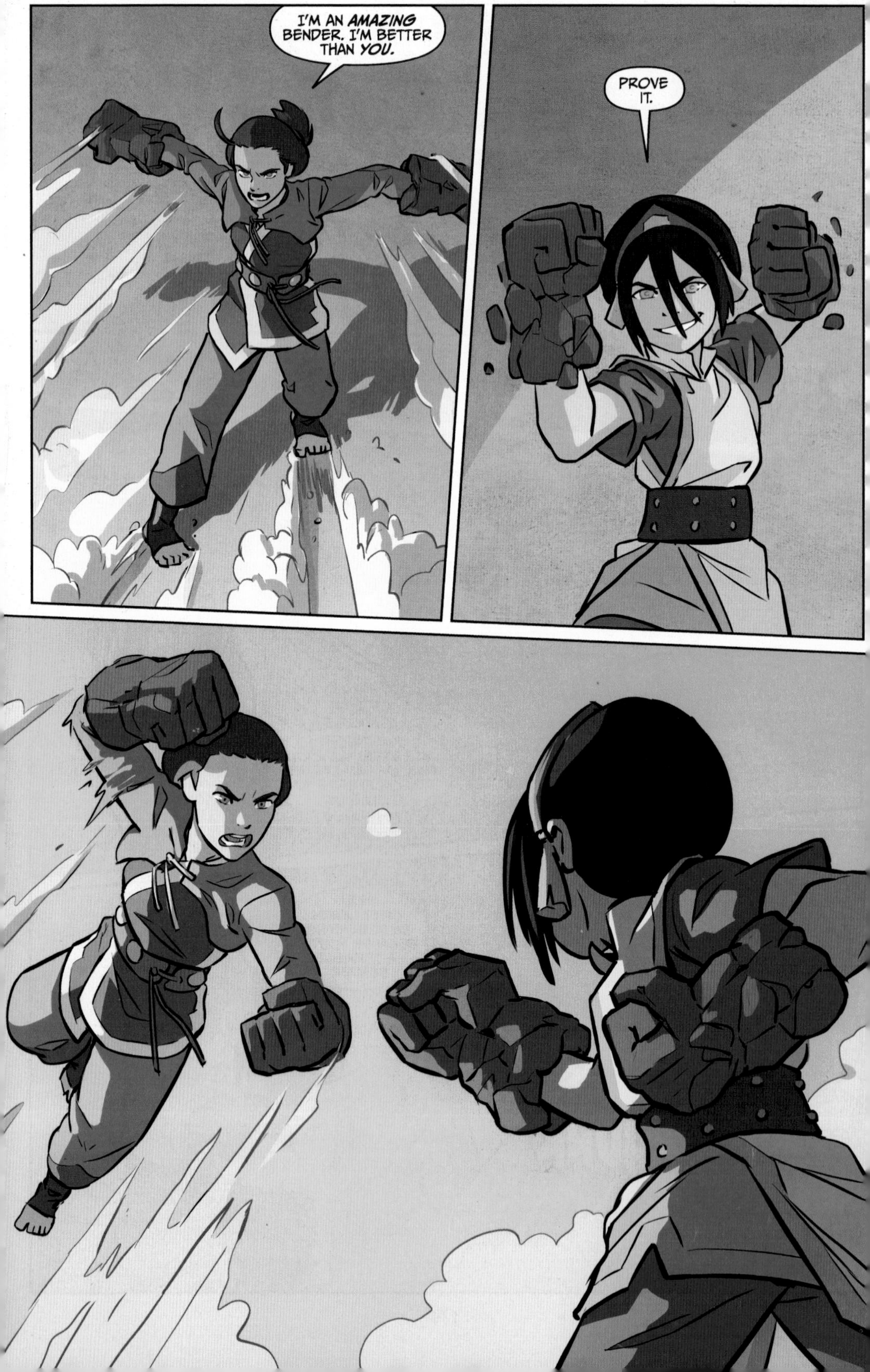
I'M AN *AMAZING* BENDER. I'M BETTER THAN *YOU.*
PROVE IT.

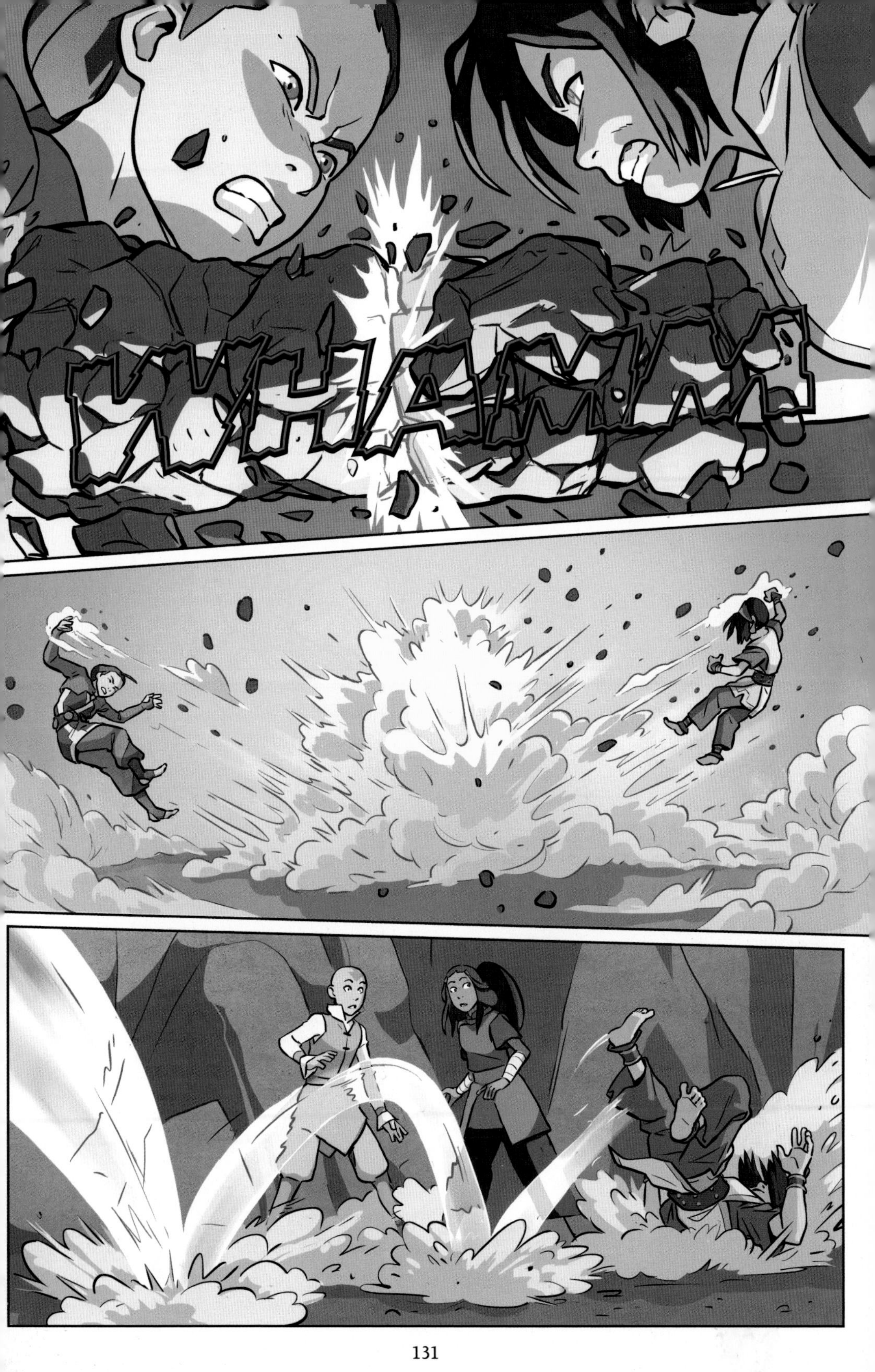
KWHAMM

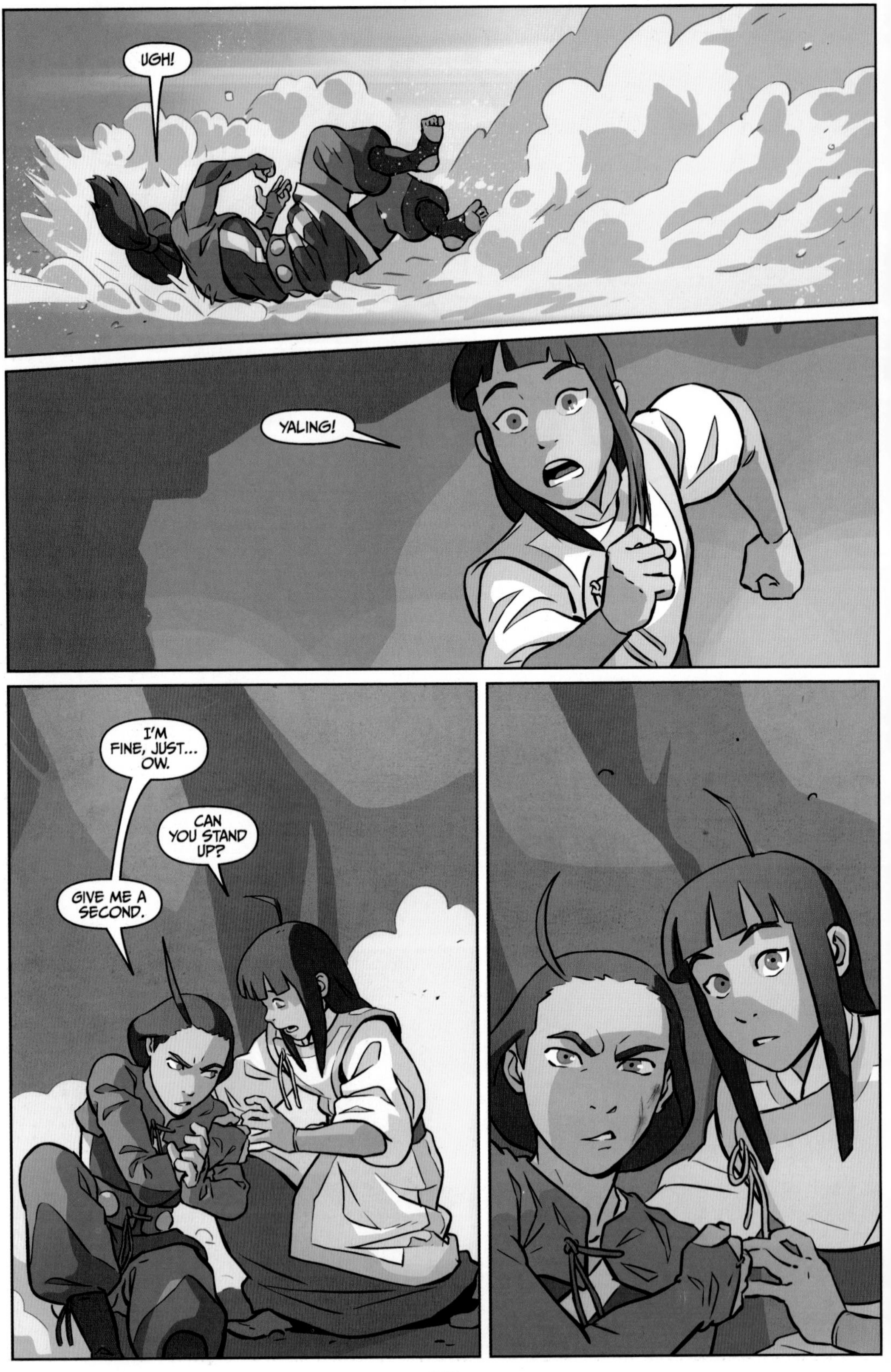
UGH!
YALING!
I'M FINE, JUST... OW.
CAN YOU STAND UP?
GIVE ME A SECOND.

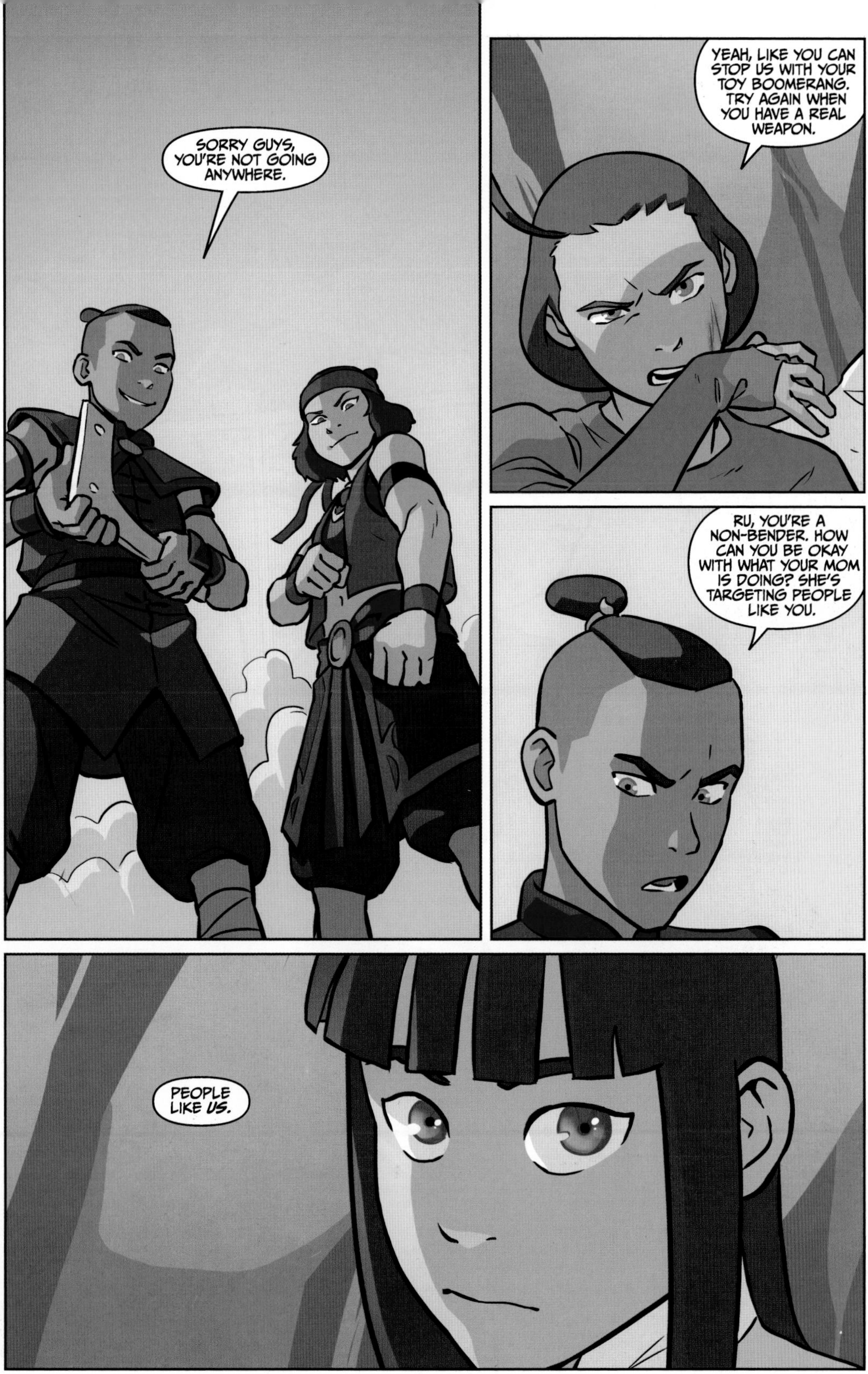
SORRY GUYS, YOU'RE NOT GOING ANYWHERE.
YEAH, LIKE YOU CAN STOP US WITH YOUR TOY BOOMERANG. TRY AGAIN WHEN YOU HAVE A REAL WEAPON.
RU, YOU'RE A NON-BENDER. HOW CAN YOU BE OKAY WITH WHAT YOUR MOM IS DOING? SHE'S TARGETING PEOPLE LIKE YOU.
PEOPLE LIKE *US*.

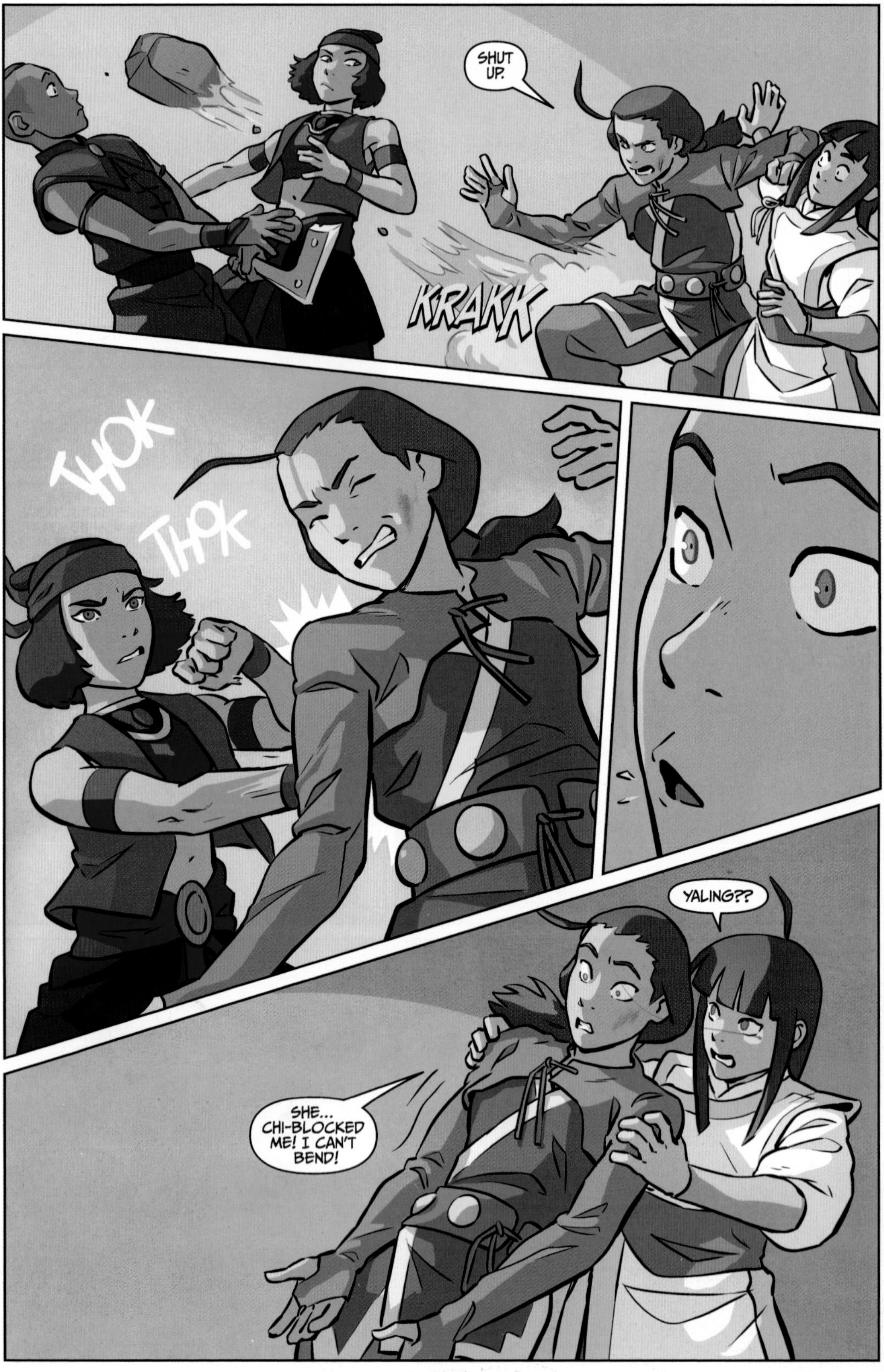
SHUT UP.
KRAKK
THOK
THOK
YALING??
SHE... CHI-BLOCKED ME! I CAN'T BEND!

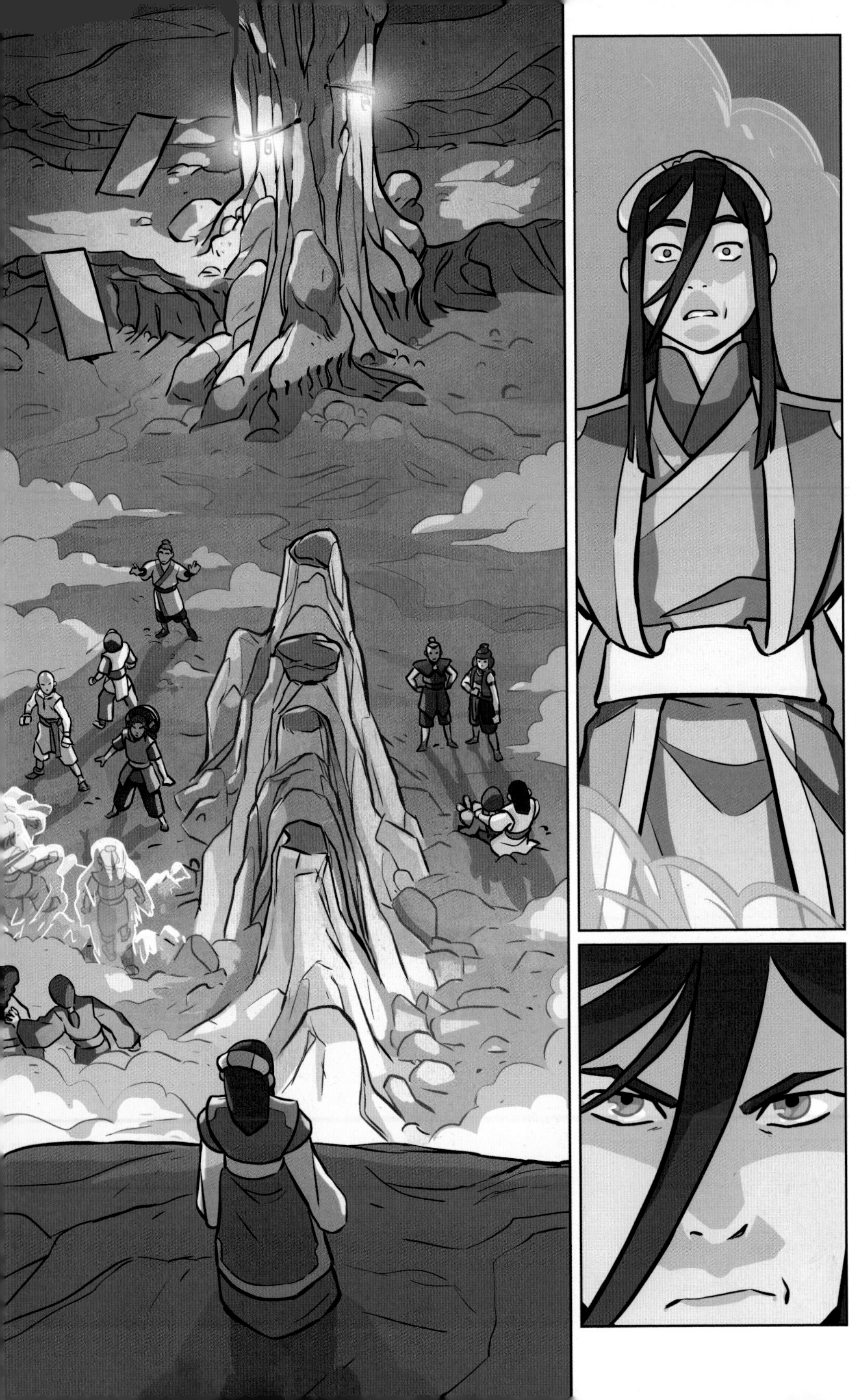

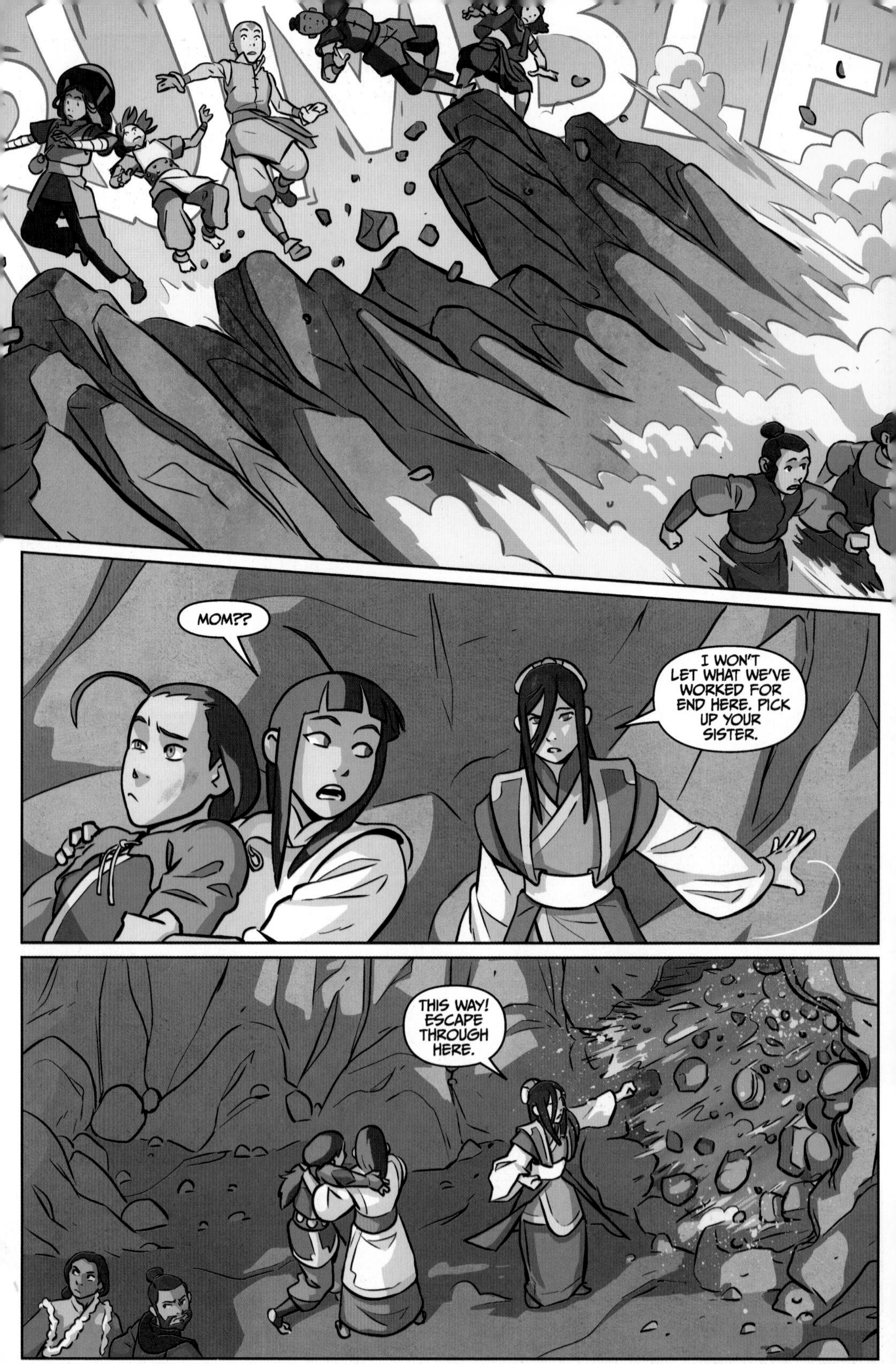
MOM??
I WON'T LET WHAT WE'VE WORKED FOR END HERE. PICK UP YOUR SISTER.
THIS WAY! ESCAPE THROUGH HERE.

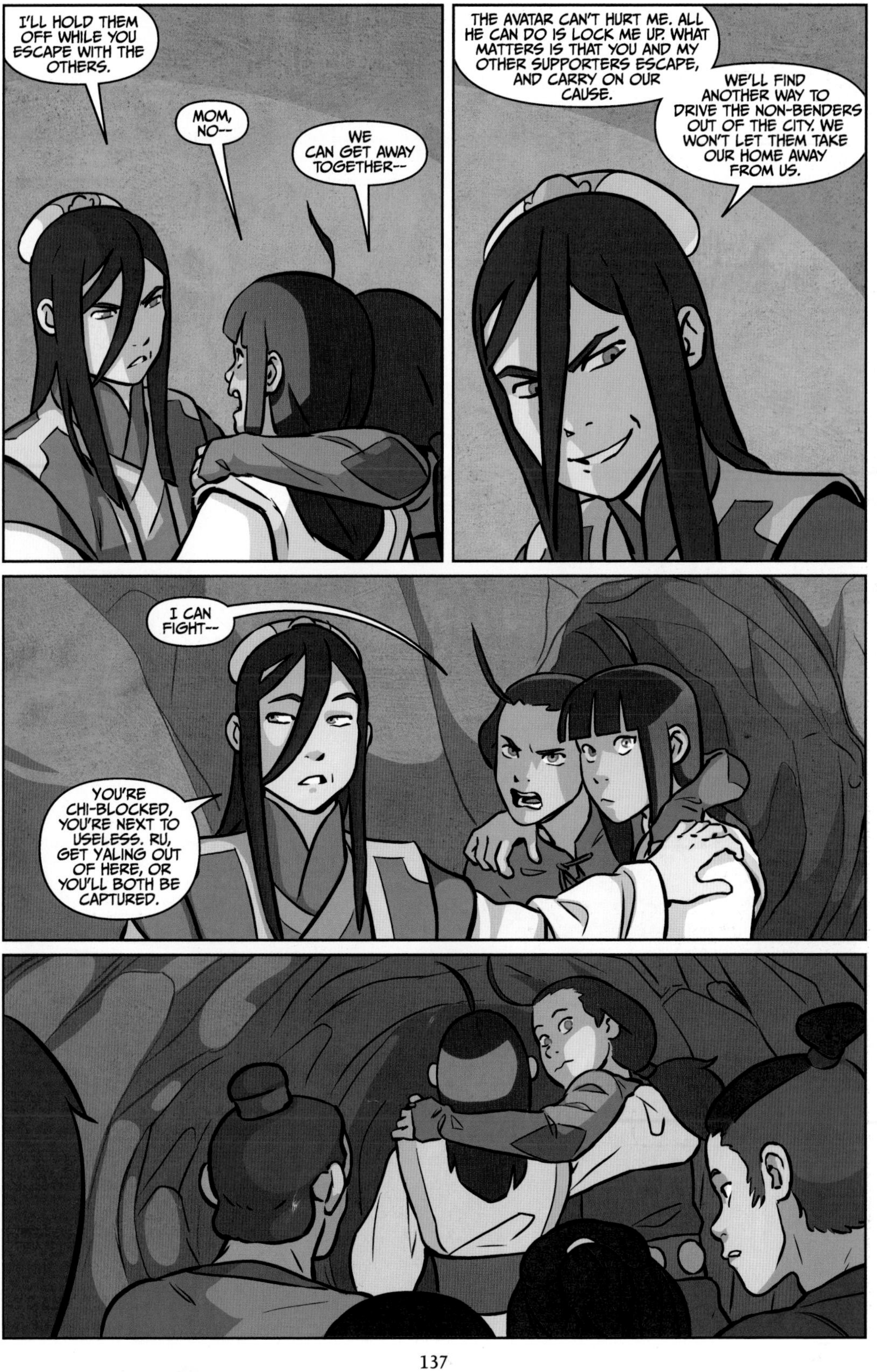

I'LL HOLD THEM OFF WHILE YOU ESCAPE WITH THE OTHERS.
MOM, NO--
WE CAN GET AWAY TOGETHER--
THE AVATAR CAN'T HURT ME. ALL HE CAN DO IS LOCK ME UP. WHAT MATTERS IS THAT YOU AND MY OTHER SUPPORTERS ESCAPE, AND CARRY ON OUR CAUSE.
WE'LL FIND ANOTHER WAY TO DRIVE THE NON-BENDERS OUT OF THE CITY. WE WON'T LET THEM TAKE OUR HOME AWAY FROM US.
I CAN FIGHT--
YOU'RE CHI-BLOCKED, YOU'RE NEXT TO USELESS. RU, GET YALING OUT OF HERE, OR YOU'LL BOTH BE CAPTURED.

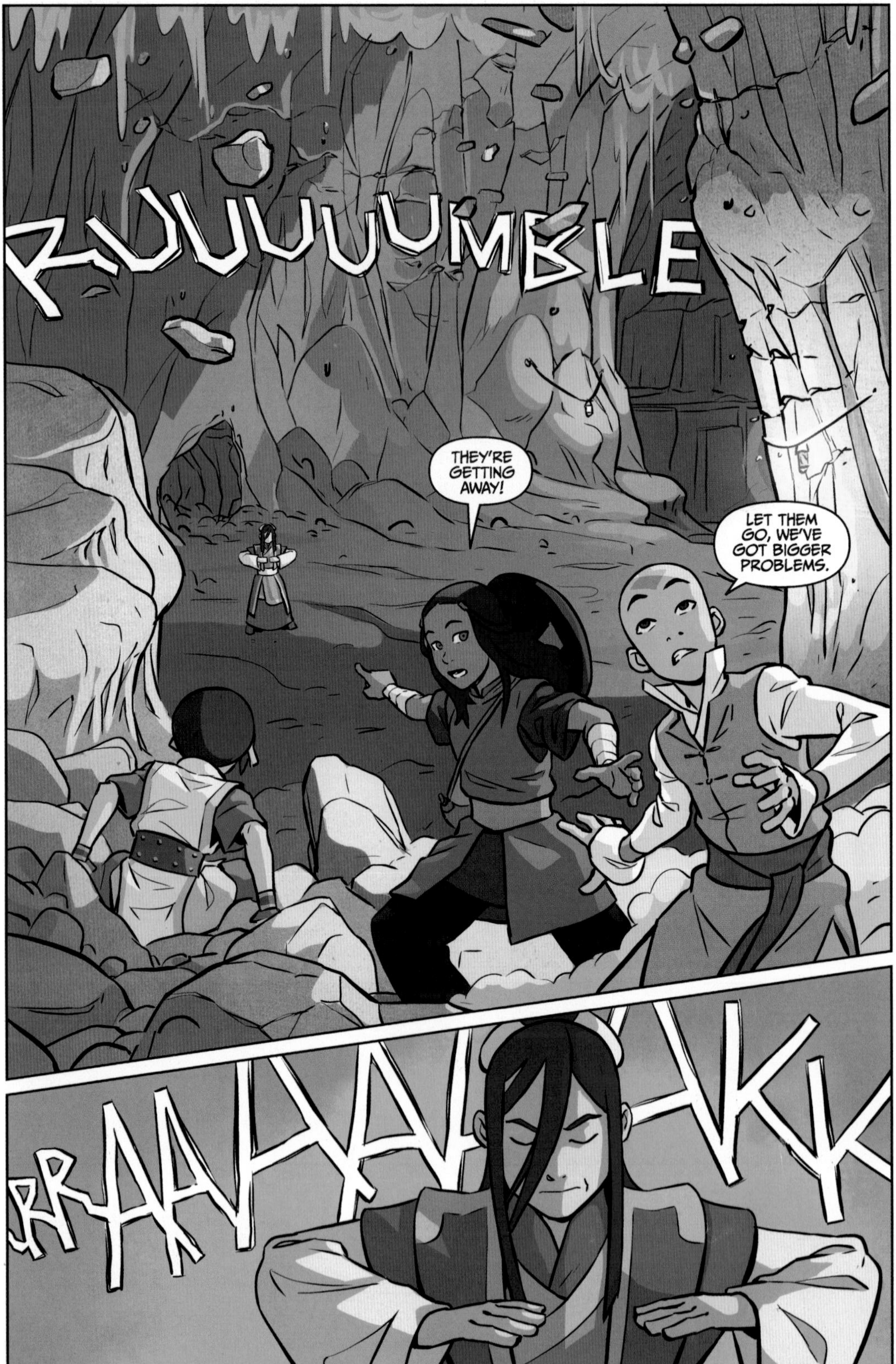
RUUUUUMBLE
THEY'RE GETTING AWAY!
LET THEM GO, WE'VE GOT BIGGER PROBLEMS.

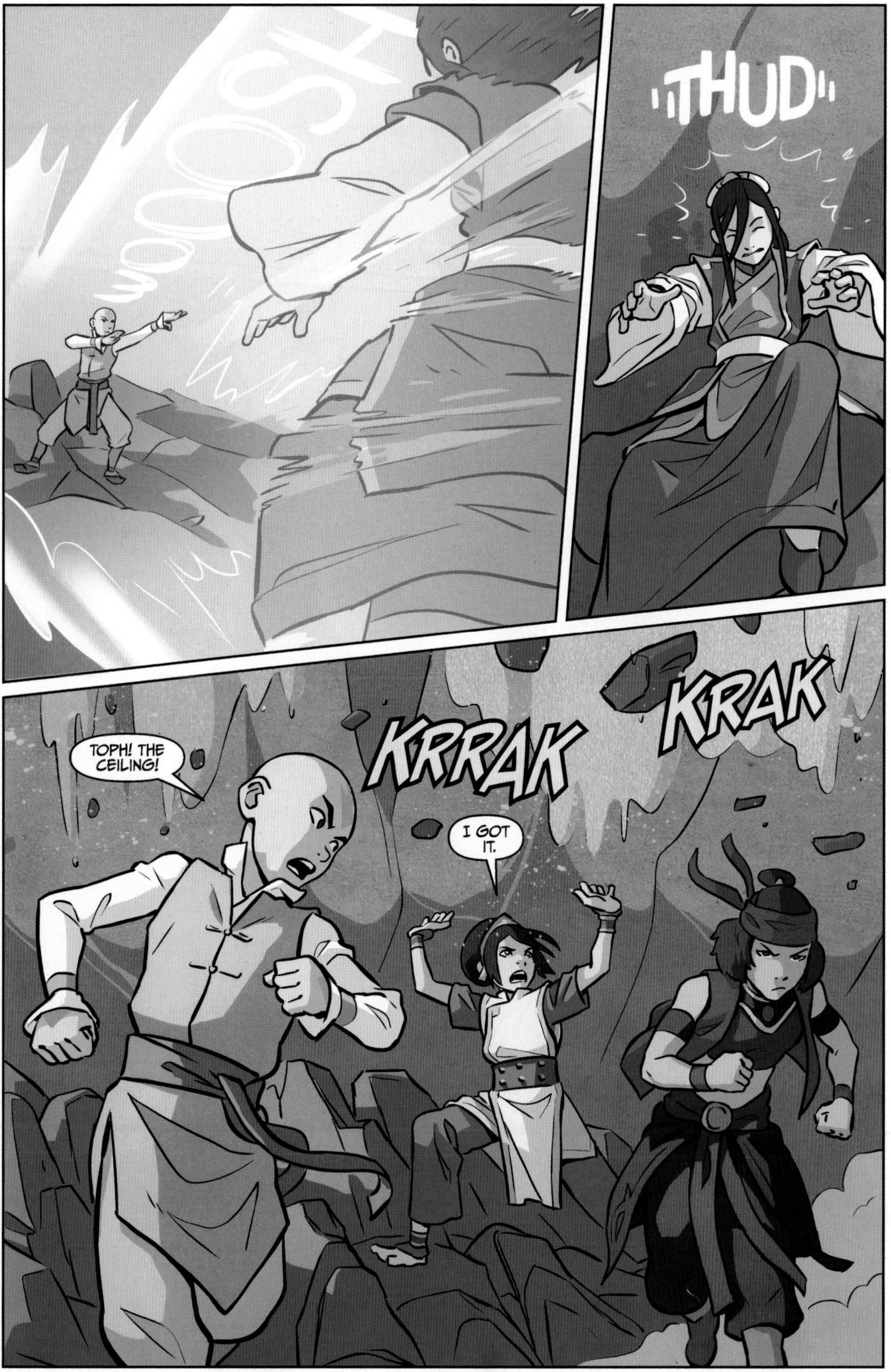
THUD
TOPH! THE CEILING!
KRRAK
I GOT IT.
KRAK

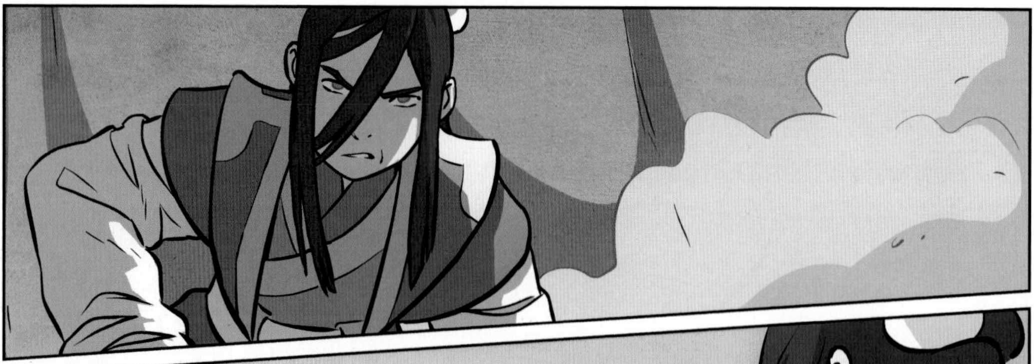

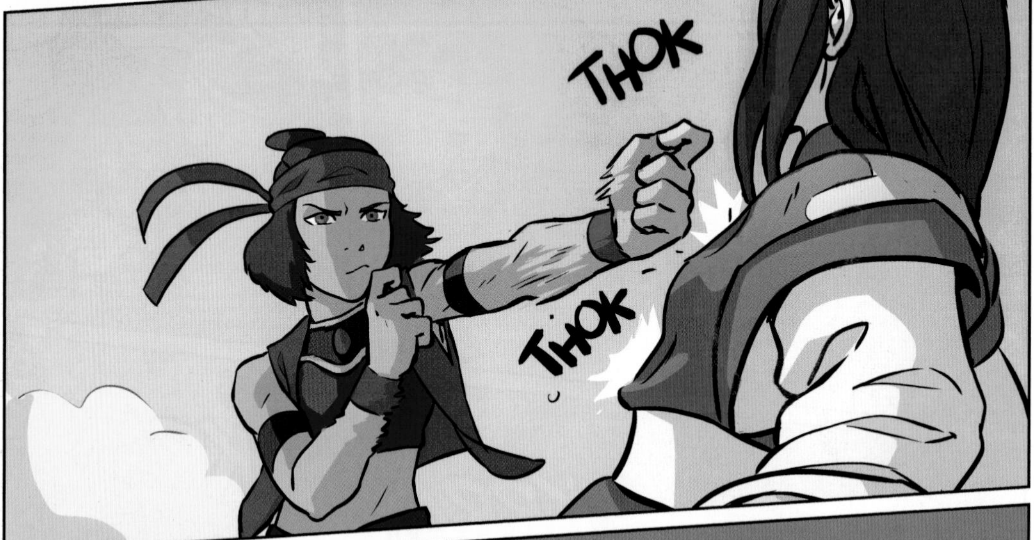
THOK
THOK

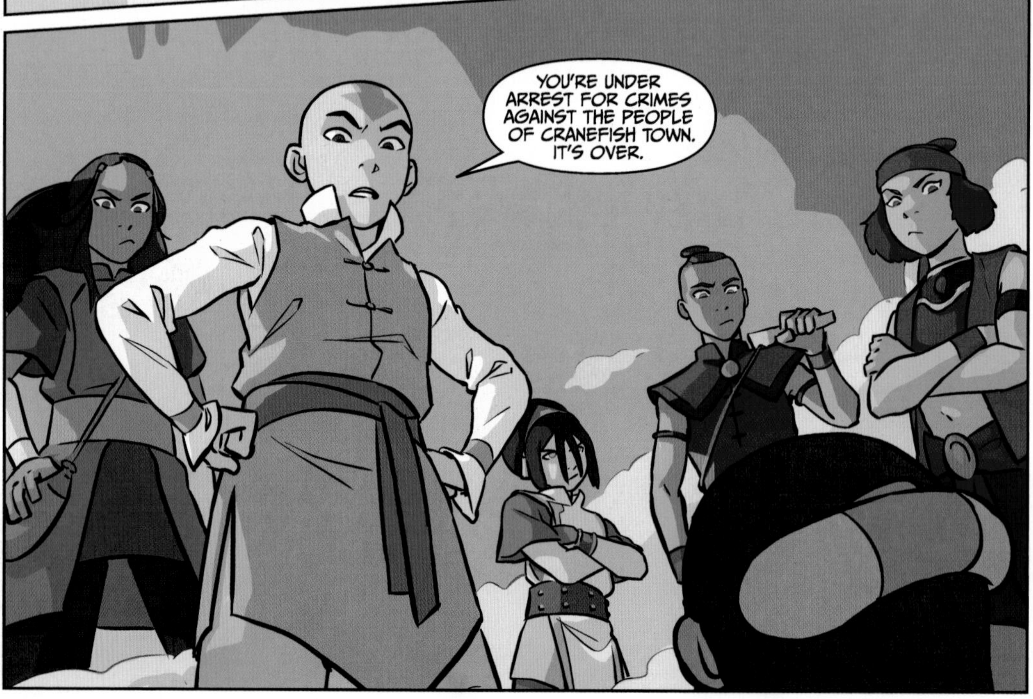
YOU'RE UNDER ARREST FOR CRIMES AGAINST THE PEOPLE OF CRANEFISH TOWN. IT'S OVER.

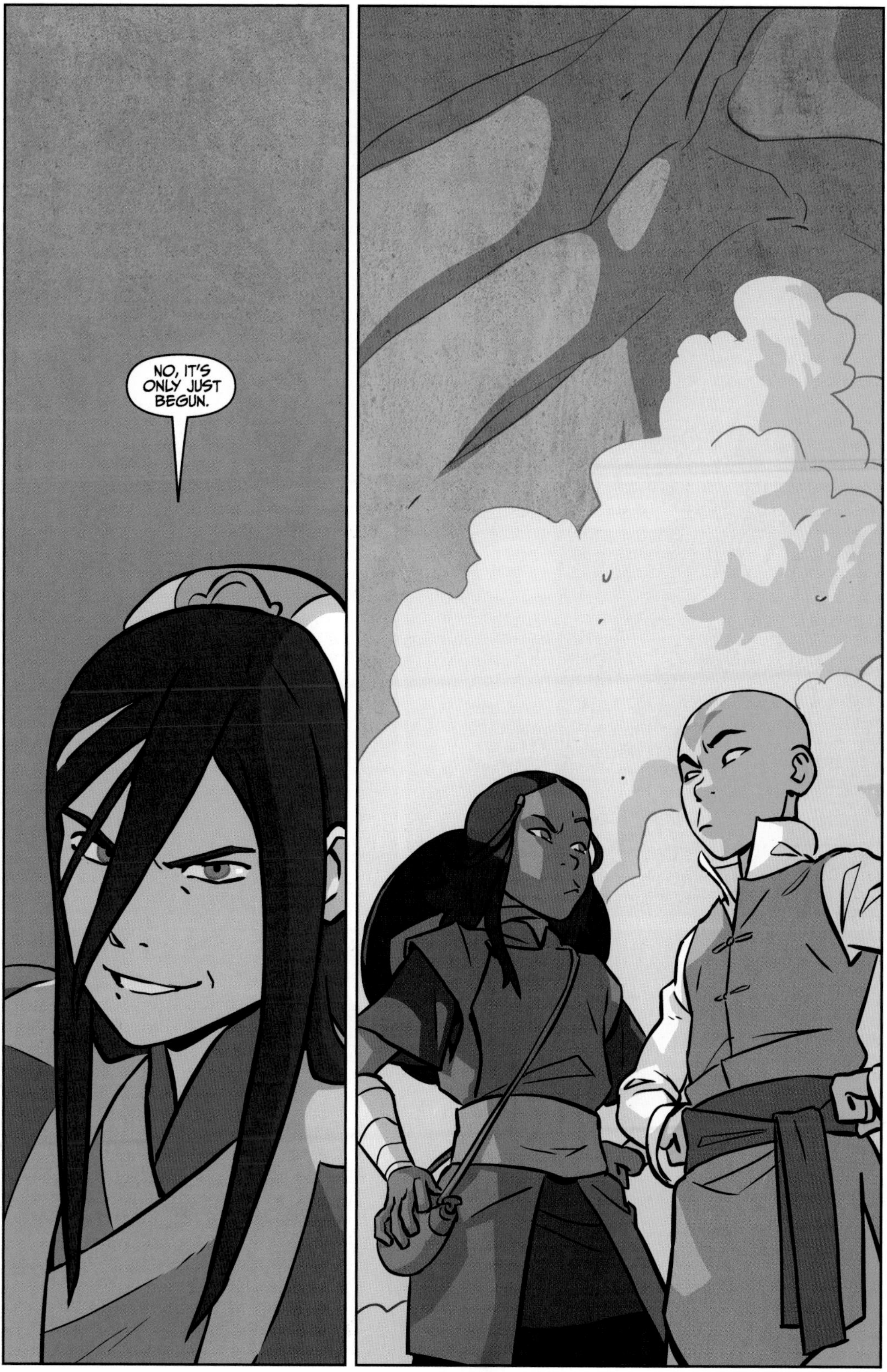
NO, IT'S ONLY JUST BEGUN.

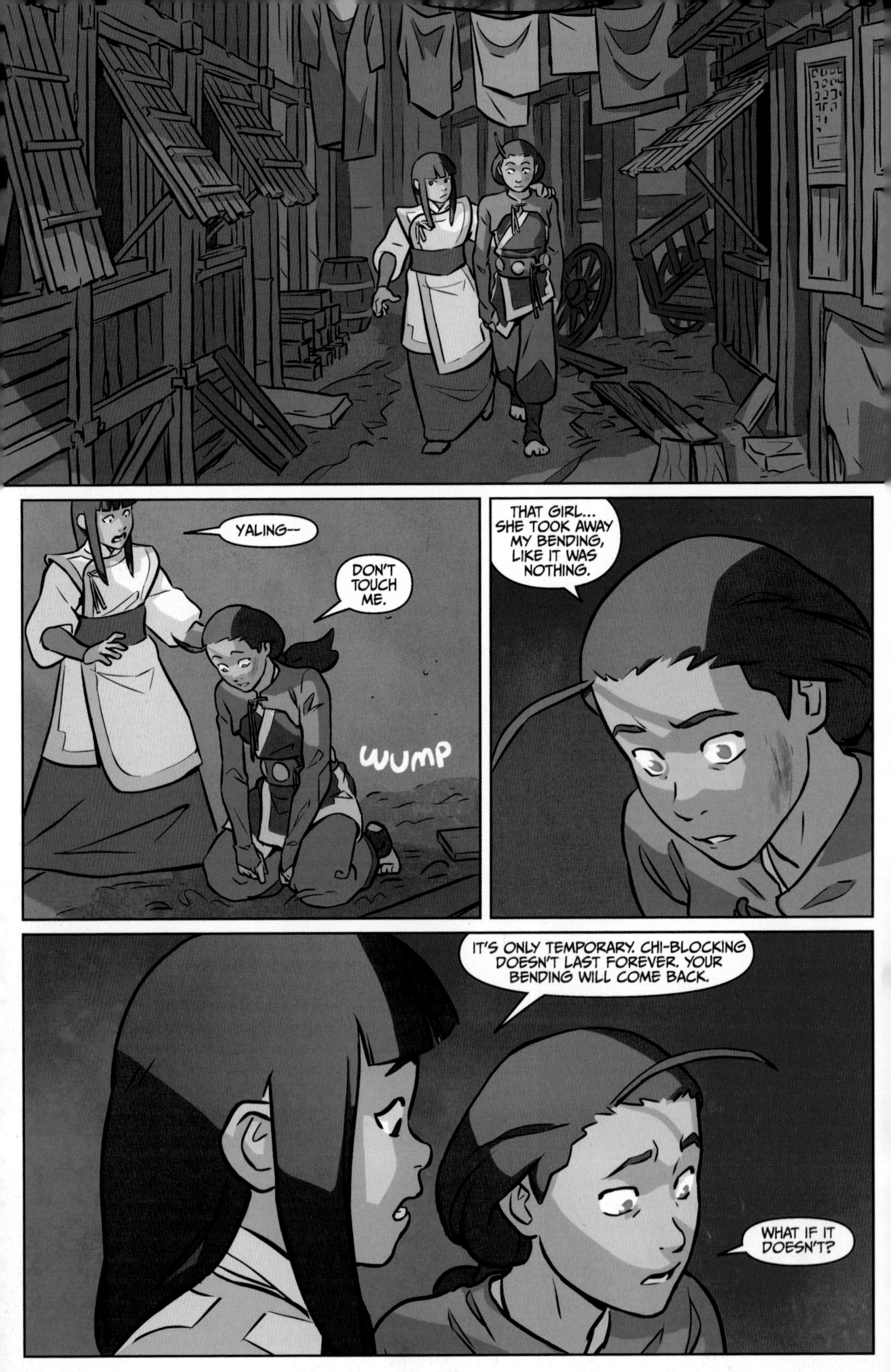
YALING--
DON'T TOUCH ME.
WUMP
THAT GIRL... SHE TOOK AWAY MY BENDING, LIKE IT WAS NOTHING.
IT'S ONLY TEMPORARY. CHI-BLOCKING DOESN'T LAST FOREVER. YOUR BENDING WILL COME BACK.
WHAT IF IT DOESN'T?

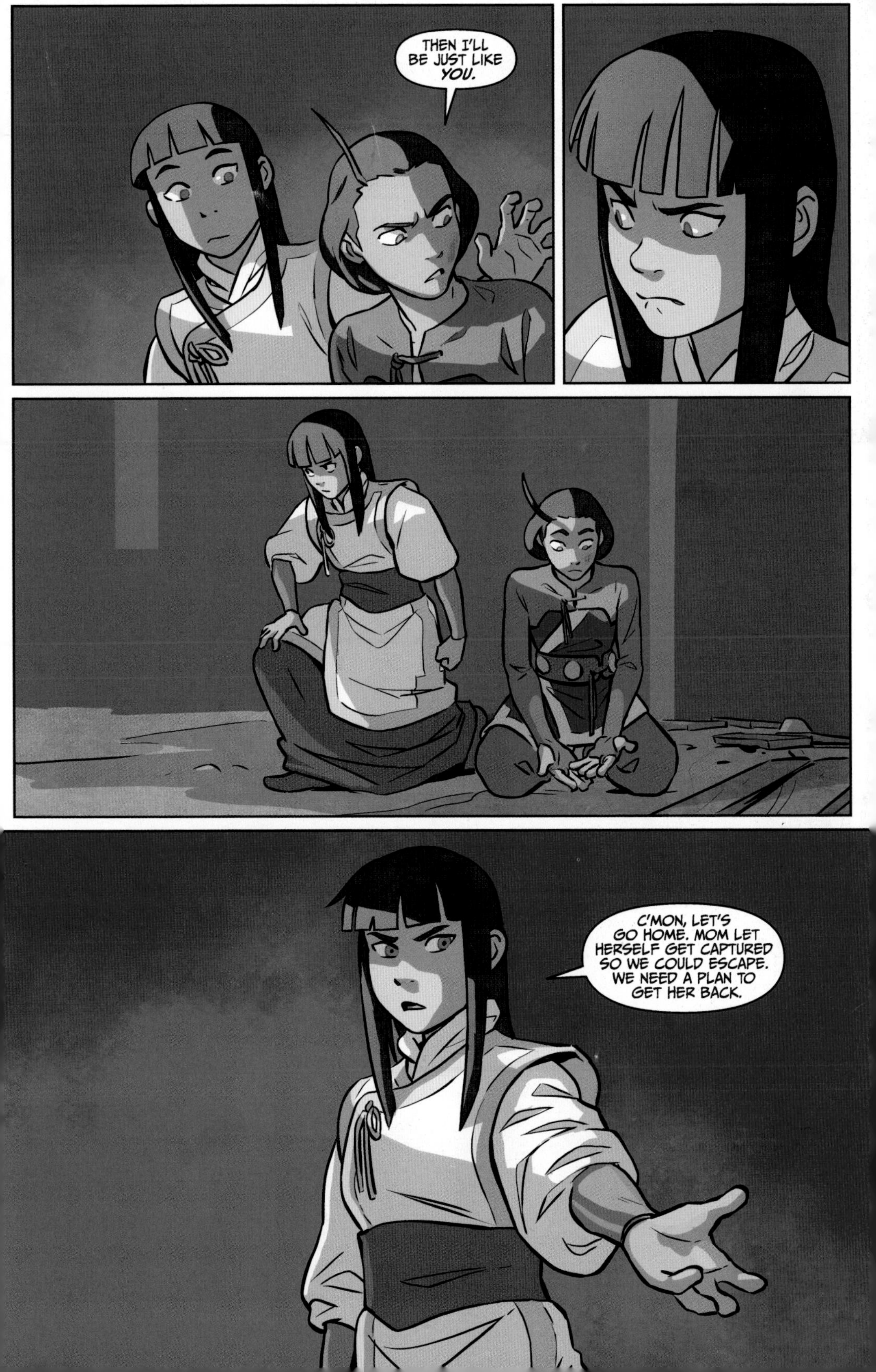
THEN I'LL BE JUST LIKE *YOU.*
C'MON, LET'S GO HOME. MOM LET HERSELF GET CAPTURED SO WE COULD ESCAPE. WE NEED A PLAN TO GET HER BACK.

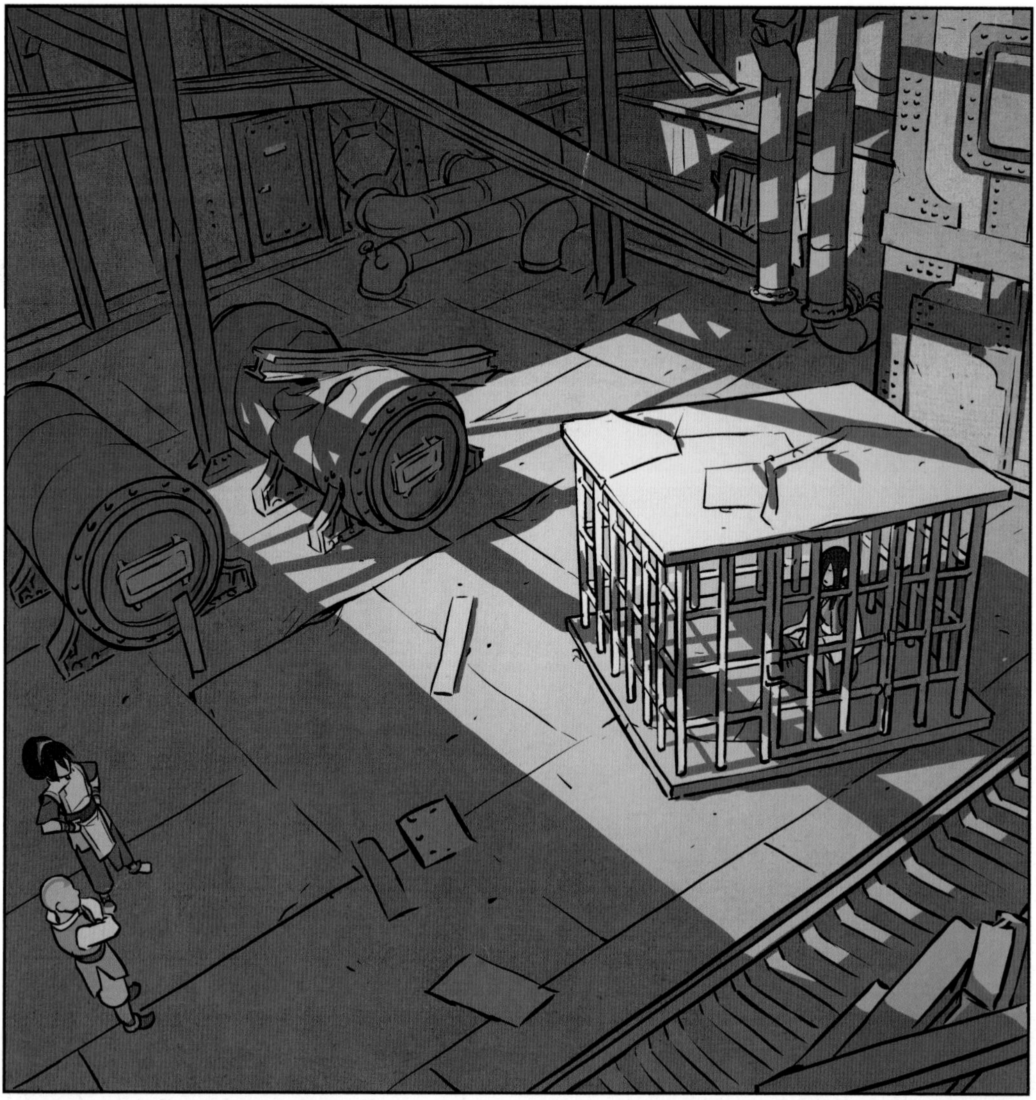

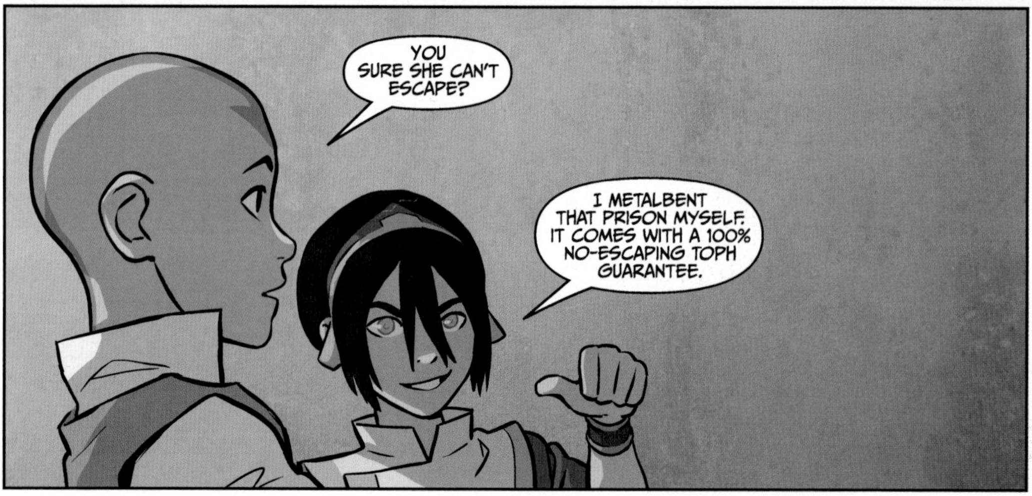
YOU SURE SHE CAN'T ESCAPE?
I METALBENT THAT PRISON MYSELF. IT COMES WITH A 100% NO-ESCAPING TOPH GUARANTEE.

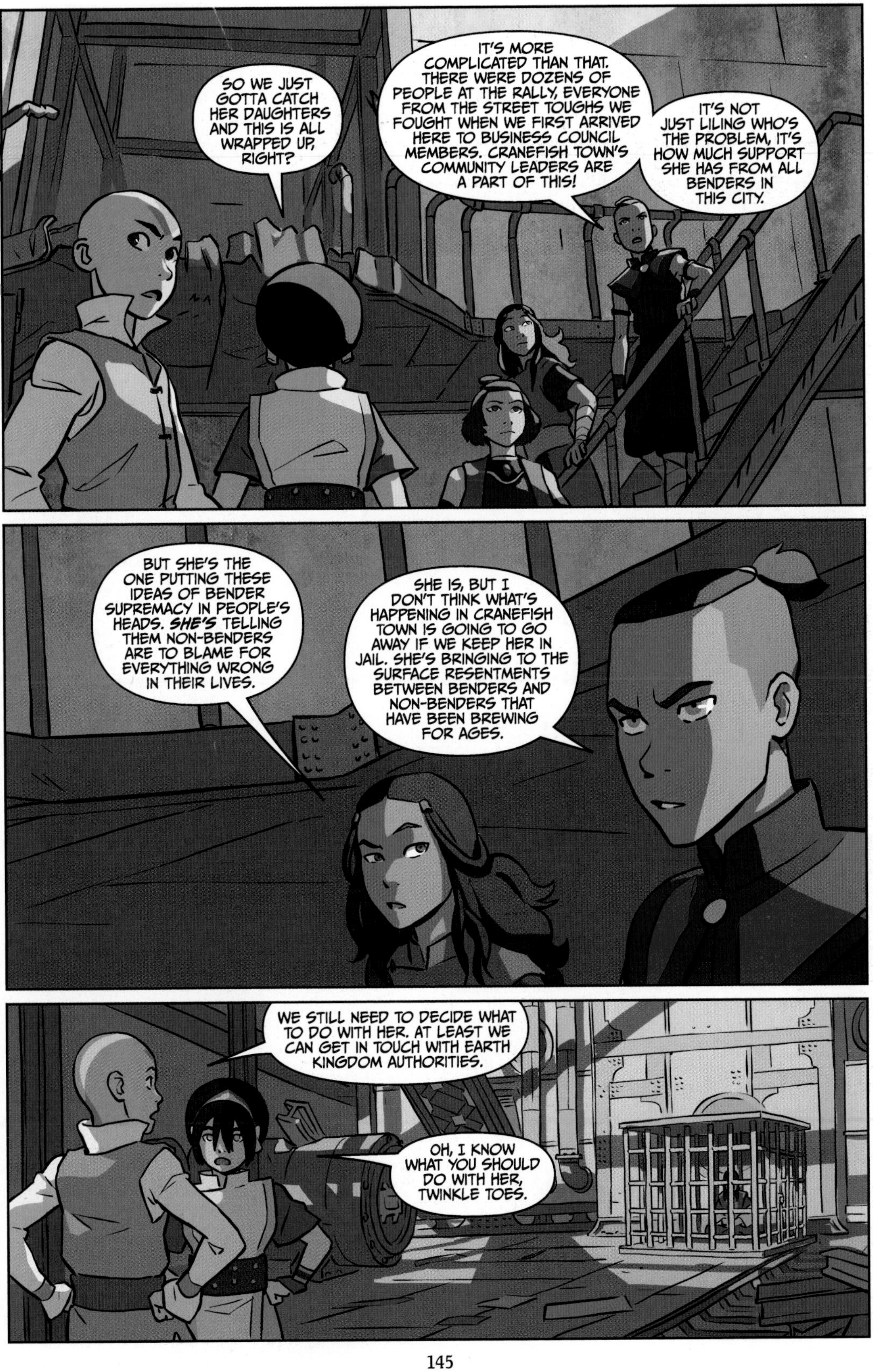
SO WE JUST GOTTA CATCH HER DAUGHTERS AND THIS IS ALL WRAPPED UP, RIGHT?
IT'S MORE COMPLICATED THAN THAT. THERE WERE DOZENS OF PEOPLE AT THE RALLY, EVERYONE FROM THE STREET TOUGHS WE FOUGHT WHEN WE FIRST ARRIVED HERE TO BUSINESS COUNCIL MEMBERS. CRANEFISH TOWN'S COMMUNITY LEADERS ARE A PART OF THIS!
IT'S NOT JUST LILING WHO'S THE PROBLEM, IT'S HOW MUCH SUPPORT SHE HAS FROM ALL BENDERS IN THIS CITY.
BUT SHE'S THE ONE PUTTING THESE IDEAS OF BENDER SUPREMACY IN PEOPLE'S HEADS. SHE'S TELLING THEM NON-BENDERS ARE TO BLAME FOR EVERYTHING WRONG IN THEIR LIVES.
SHE IS, BUT I DON'T THINK WHAT'S HAPPENING IN CRANEFISH TOWN IS GOING TO GO AWAY IF WE KEEP HER IN JAIL. SHE'S BRINGING TO THE SURFACE RESENTMENTS BETWEEN BENDERS AND NON-BENDERS THAT HAVE BEEN BREWING FOR AGES.
WE STILL NEED TO DECIDE WHAT TO DO WITH HER. AT LEAST WE CAN GET IN TOUCH WITH EARTH KINGDOM AUTHORITIES.
OH, I KNOW WHAT YOU SHOULD DO WITH HER, TWINKLE TOES.

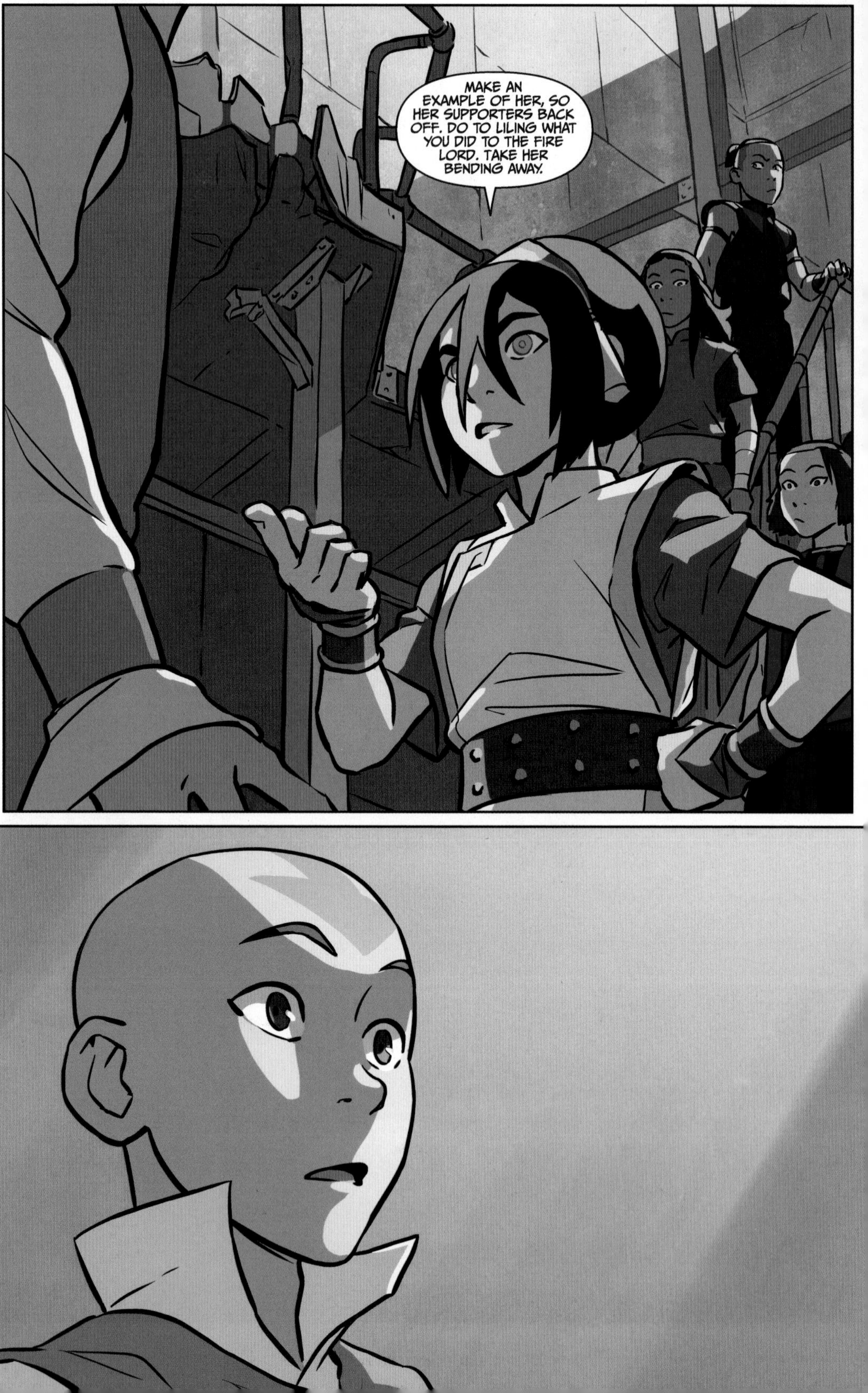
MAKE AN EXAMPLE OF HER, SO HER SUPPORTERS BACK OFF. DO TO LILING WHAT YOU DID TO THE FIRE LORD. TAKE HER BENDING AWAY.

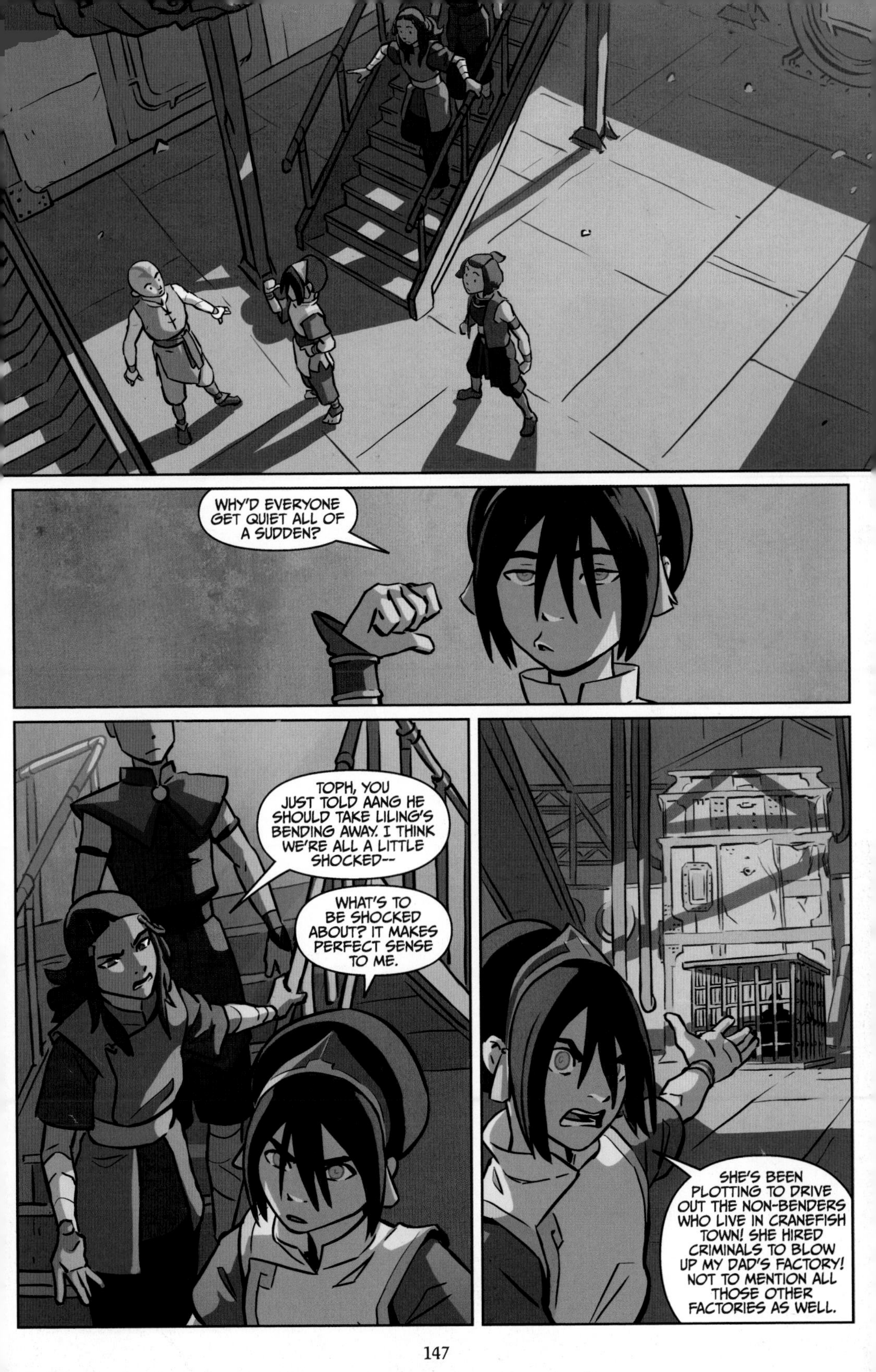
WHY'D EVERYONE GET QUIET ALL OF A SUDDEN?
TOPH, YOU JUST TOLD AANG HE SHOULD TAKE LILING'S BENDING AWAY. I THINK WE'RE ALL A LITTLE SHOCKED--
WHAT'S TO BE SHOCKED ABOUT? IT MAKES PERFECT SENSE TO ME.
SHE'S BEEN PLOTTING TO DRIVE OUT THE NON-BENDERS WHO LIVE IN CRANEFISH TOWN! SHE HIRED CRIMINALS TO BLOW UP MY DAD'S FACTORY! NOT TO MENTION ALL THOSE OTHER FACTORIES AS WELL.

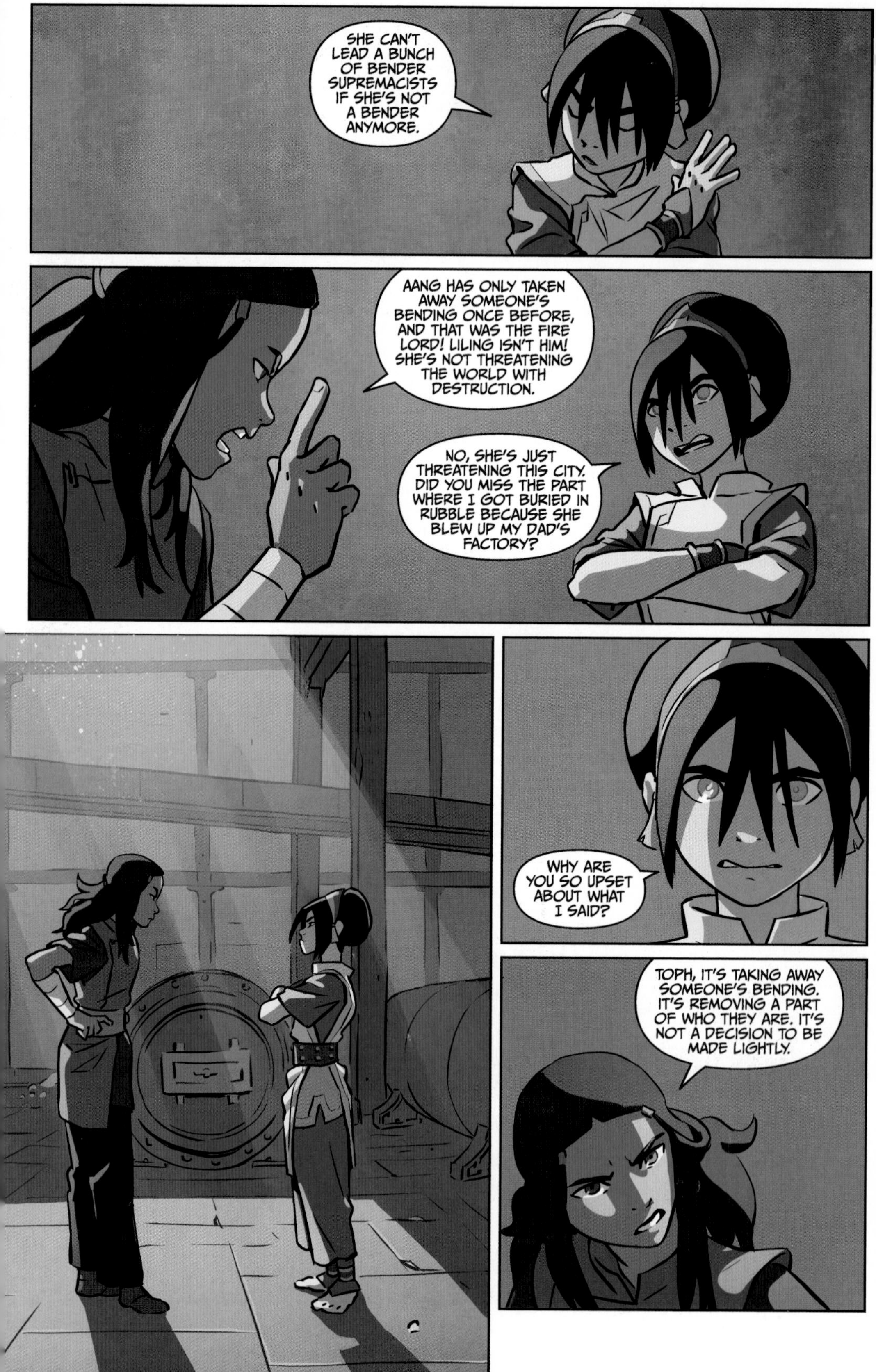
SHE CAN'T LEAD A BUNCH OF BENDER SUPREMACISTS IF SHE'S NOT A BENDER ANYMORE.
AANG HAS ONLY TAKEN AWAY SOMEONE'S BENDING ONCE BEFORE, AND THAT WAS THE FIRE LORD! LILING ISN'T HIM! SHE'S NOT THREATENING THE WORLD WITH DESTRUCTION.
NO, SHE'S JUST THREATENING THIS CITY. DID YOU MISS THE PART WHERE I GOT BURIED IN RUBBLE BECAUSE SHE BLEW UP MY DAD'S FACTORY?
WHY ARE YOU SO UPSET ABOUT WHAT I SAID?
TOPH, IT'S TAKING AWAY SOMEONE'S BENDING. IT'S REMOVING A PART OF WHO THEY ARE. IT'S NOT A DECISION TO BE MADE LIGHTLY.

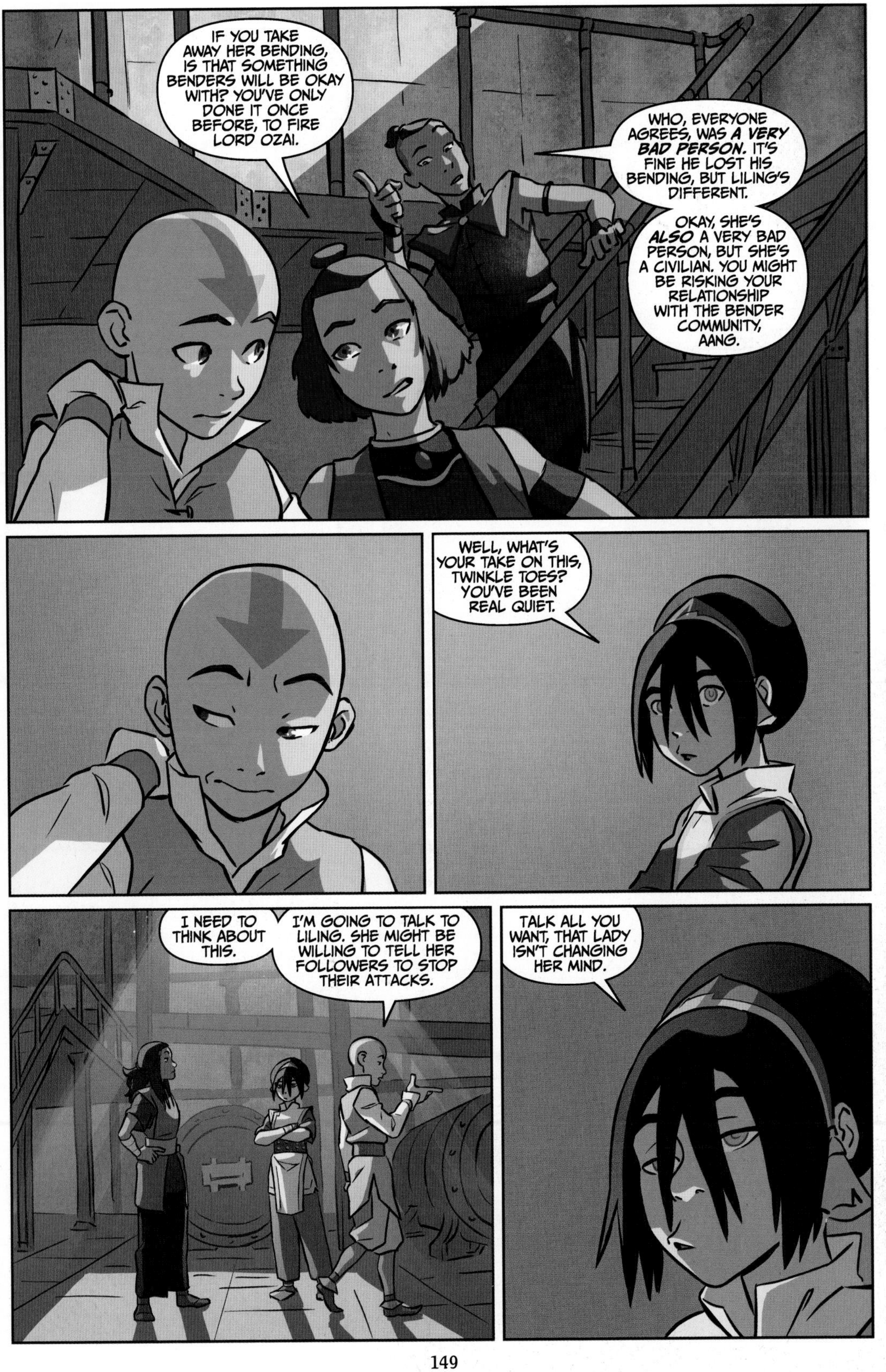
IF YOU TAKE AWAY HER BENDING, IS THAT SOMETHING BENDERS WILL BE OKAY WITH? YOU'VE ONLY DONE IT ONCE BEFORE, TO FIRE LORD OZAI.
WHO, EVERYONE AGREES, WAS ***A VERY BAD PERSON.*** IT'S FINE HE LOST HIS BENDING, BUT LILING'S DIFFERENT.
OKAY, SHE'S ***ALSO*** A VERY BAD PERSON, BUT SHE'S A CIVILIAN. YOU MIGHT BE RISKING YOUR RELATIONSHIP WITH THE BENDER COMMUNITY, AANG.
WELL, WHAT'S YOUR TAKE ON THIS, TWINKLE TOES? YOU'VE BEEN REAL QUIET.
I NEED TO THINK ABOUT THIS.
I'M GOING TO TALK TO LILING. SHE MIGHT BE WILLING TO TELL HER FOLLOWERS TO STOP THEIR ATTACKS.
TALK ALL YOU WANT, THAT LADY ISN'T CHANGING HER MIND.

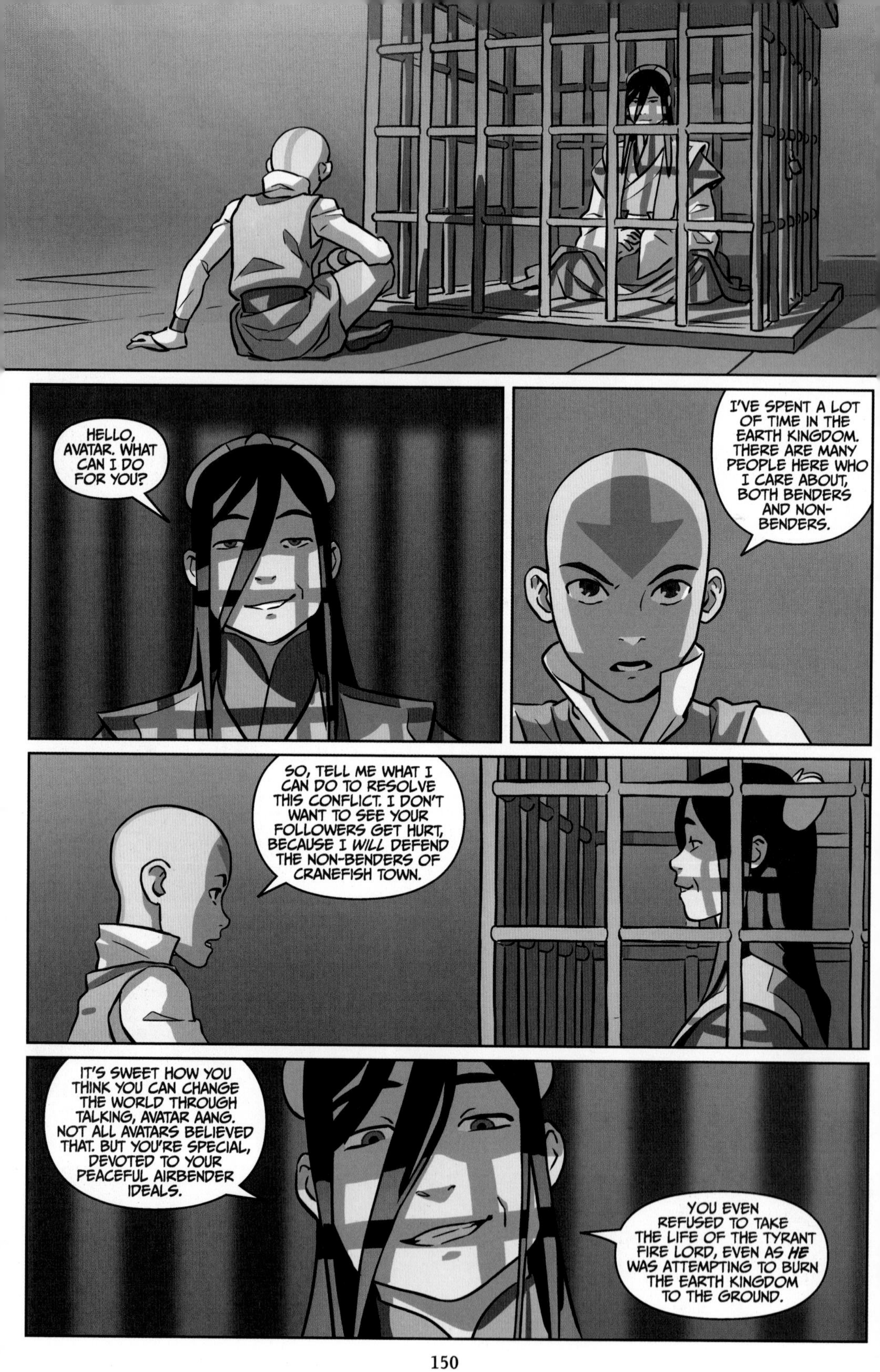
HELLO, AVATAR. WHAT CAN I DO FOR YOU?
I'VE SPENT A LOT OF TIME IN THE EARTH KINGDOM. THERE ARE MANY PEOPLE HERE WHO I CARE ABOUT, BOTH BENDERS AND NON-BENDERS.
SO, TELL ME WHAT I CAN DO TO RESOLVE THIS CONFLICT. I DON'T WANT TO SEE YOUR FOLLOWERS GET HURT, BECAUSE I *WILL* DEFEND THE NON-BENDERS OF CRANEFISH TOWN.
IT'S SWEET HOW YOU THINK YOU CAN CHANGE THE WORLD THROUGH TALKING, AVATAR AANG. NOT ALL AVATARS BELIEVED THAT. BUT YOU'RE SPECIAL, DEVOTED TO YOUR PEACEFUL AIRBENDER IDEALS.
YOU EVEN REFUSED TO TAKE THE LIFE OF THE TYRANT FIRE LORD, EVEN AS *HE* WAS ATTEMPTING TO BURN THE EARTH KINGDOM TO THE GROUND.

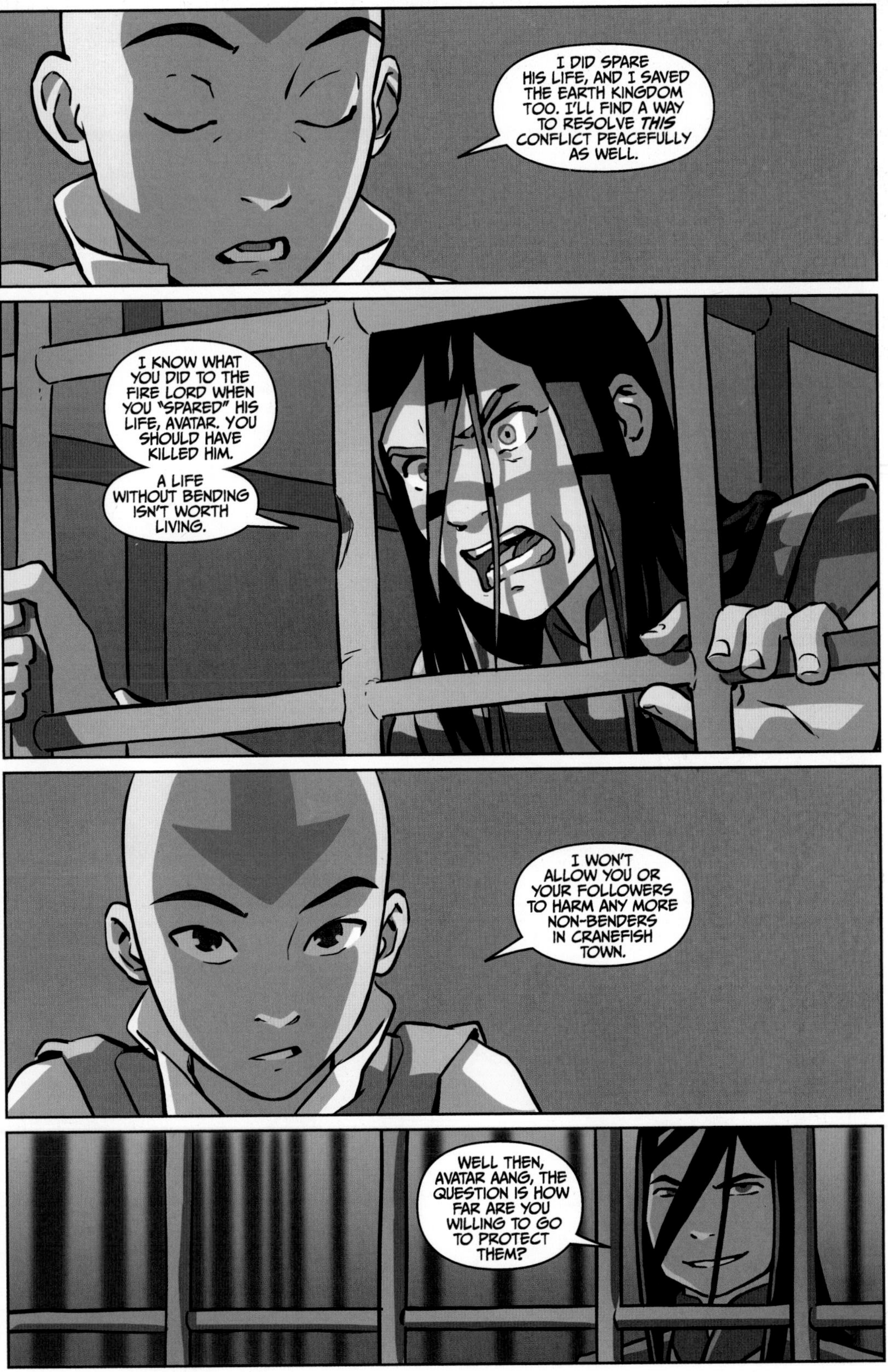
I DID SPARE HIS LIFE, AND I SAVED THE EARTH KINGDOM TOO. I'LL FIND A WAY TO RESOLVE *THIS* CONFLICT PEACEFULLY AS WELL.
I KNOW WHAT YOU DID TO THE FIRE LORD WHEN YOU "SPARED" HIS LIFE, AVATAR. YOU SHOULD HAVE KILLED HIM.
A LIFE WITHOUT BENDING ISN'T WORTH LIVING.
I WON'T ALLOW YOU OR YOUR FOLLOWERS TO HARM ANY MORE NON-BENDERS IN CRANEFISH TOWN.
WELL THEN, AVATAR AANG, THE QUESTION IS HOW FAR ARE YOU WILLING TO GO TO PROTECT THEM?

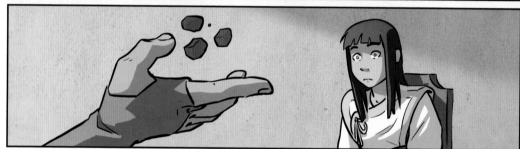

THE CHI-BLOCKING'S WORN OFF. I HAVE MY BENDING BACK.

TIME TO GO GET MOM.

THEY'RE KEEPING HER AT EARTHEN FIRE INDUSTRIES. IT'S GUARDED BY THE AVATAR, HIS FRIENDS, AND LAO'S SECURITY GUARDS. WE COULD GO IN THE MIDDLE OF THE NIGHT, SNEAK IN--

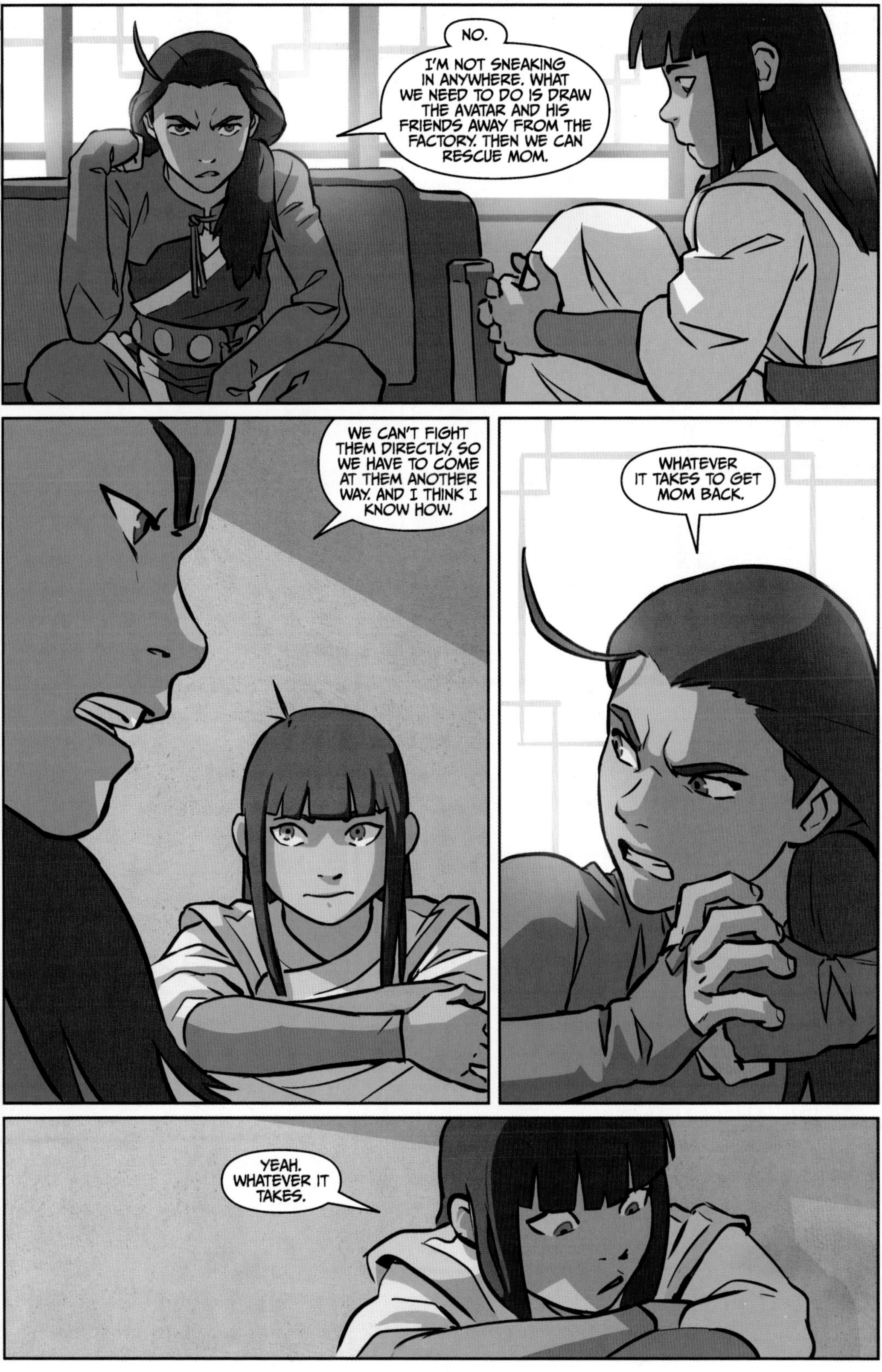
NO.
I'M NOT SNEAKING IN ANYWHERE. WHAT WE NEED TO DO IS DRAW THE AVATAR AND HIS FRIENDS AWAY FROM THE FACTORY. THEN WE CAN RESCUE MOM.
WE CAN'T FIGHT THEM DIRECTLY, SO WE HAVE TO COME AT THEM ANOTHER WAY. AND I THINK I KNOW HOW.
WHATEVER IT TAKES TO GET MOM BACK.
YEAH. WHATEVER IT TAKES.

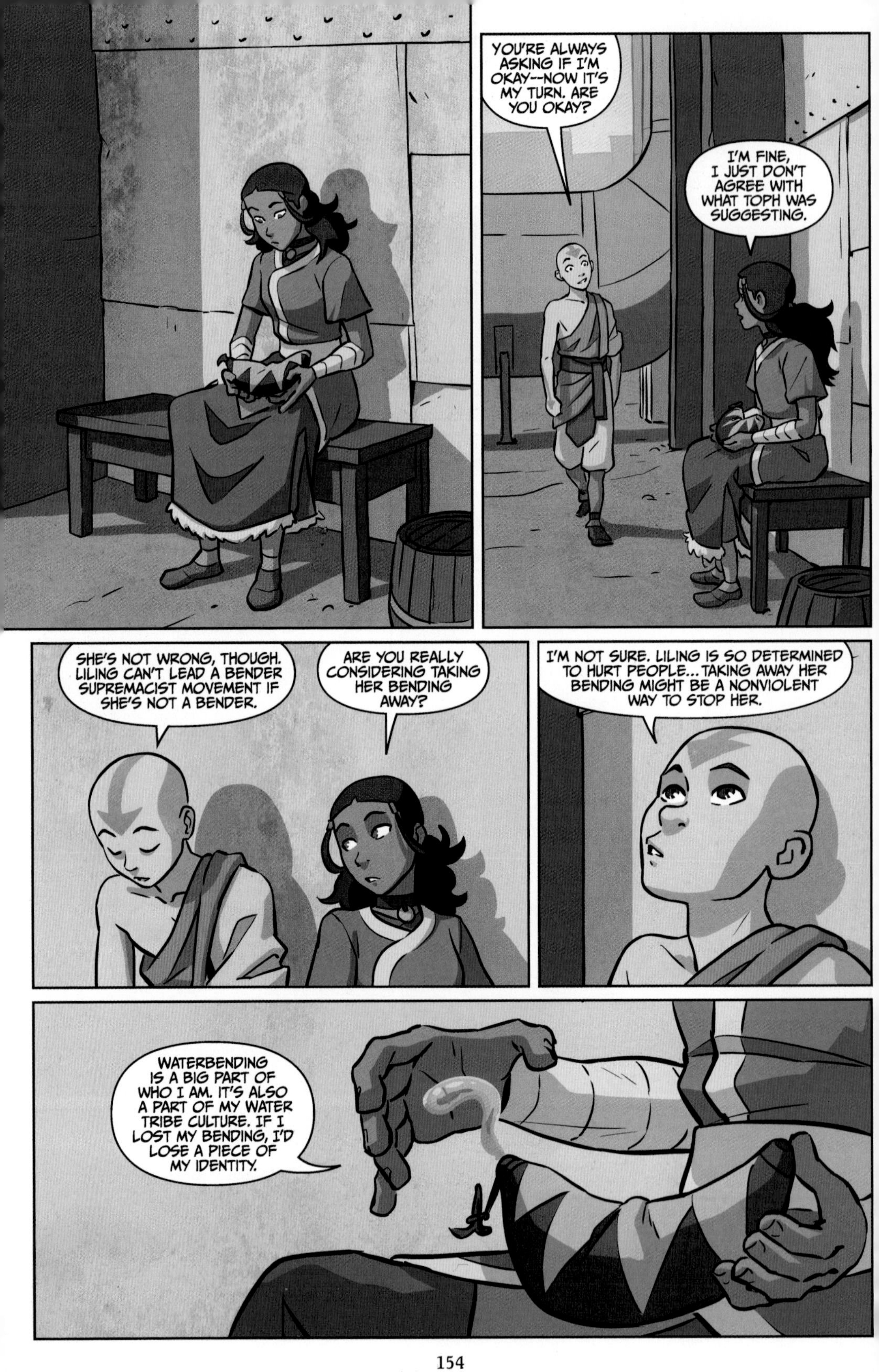
YOU'RE ALWAYS ASKING IF I'M OKAY--NOW IT'S MY TURN. ARE YOU OKAY?
I'M FINE, I JUST DON'T AGREE WITH WHAT TOPH WAS SUGGESTING.
SHE'S NOT WRONG, THOUGH. LILING CAN'T LEAD A BENDER SUPREMACIST MOVEMENT IF SHE'S NOT A BENDER.
ARE YOU REALLY CONSIDERING TAKING HER BENDING AWAY?
I'M NOT SURE. LILING IS SO DETERMINED TO HURT PEOPLE...TAKING AWAY HER BENDING MIGHT BE A NONVIOLENT WAY TO STOP HER.
WATERBENDING IS A BIG PART OF WHO I AM. IT'S ALSO A PART OF MY WATER TRIBE CULTURE. IF I LOST MY BENDING, I'D LOSE A PIECE OF MY IDENTITY.

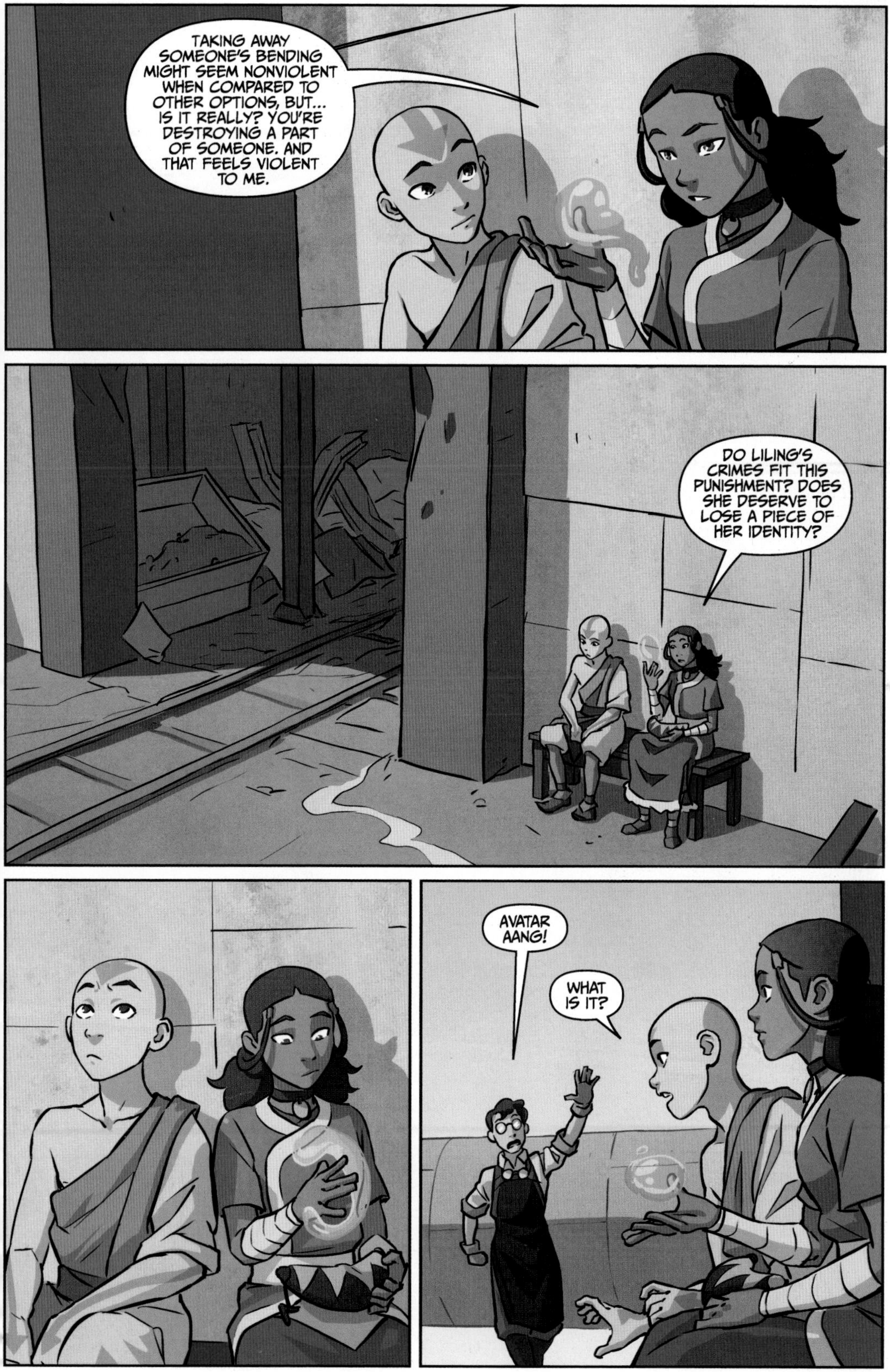
TAKING AWAY SOMEONE'S BENDING MIGHT SEEM NONVIOLENT WHEN COMPARED TO OTHER OPTIONS, BUT... IS IT REALLY? YOU'RE DESTROYING A PART OF SOMEONE. AND THAT FEELS VIOLENT TO ME.
DO LILING'S CRIMES FIT THIS PUNISHMENT? DOES SHE DESERVE TO LOSE A PIECE OF HER IDENTITY?
AVATAR AANG!
WHAT IS IT?

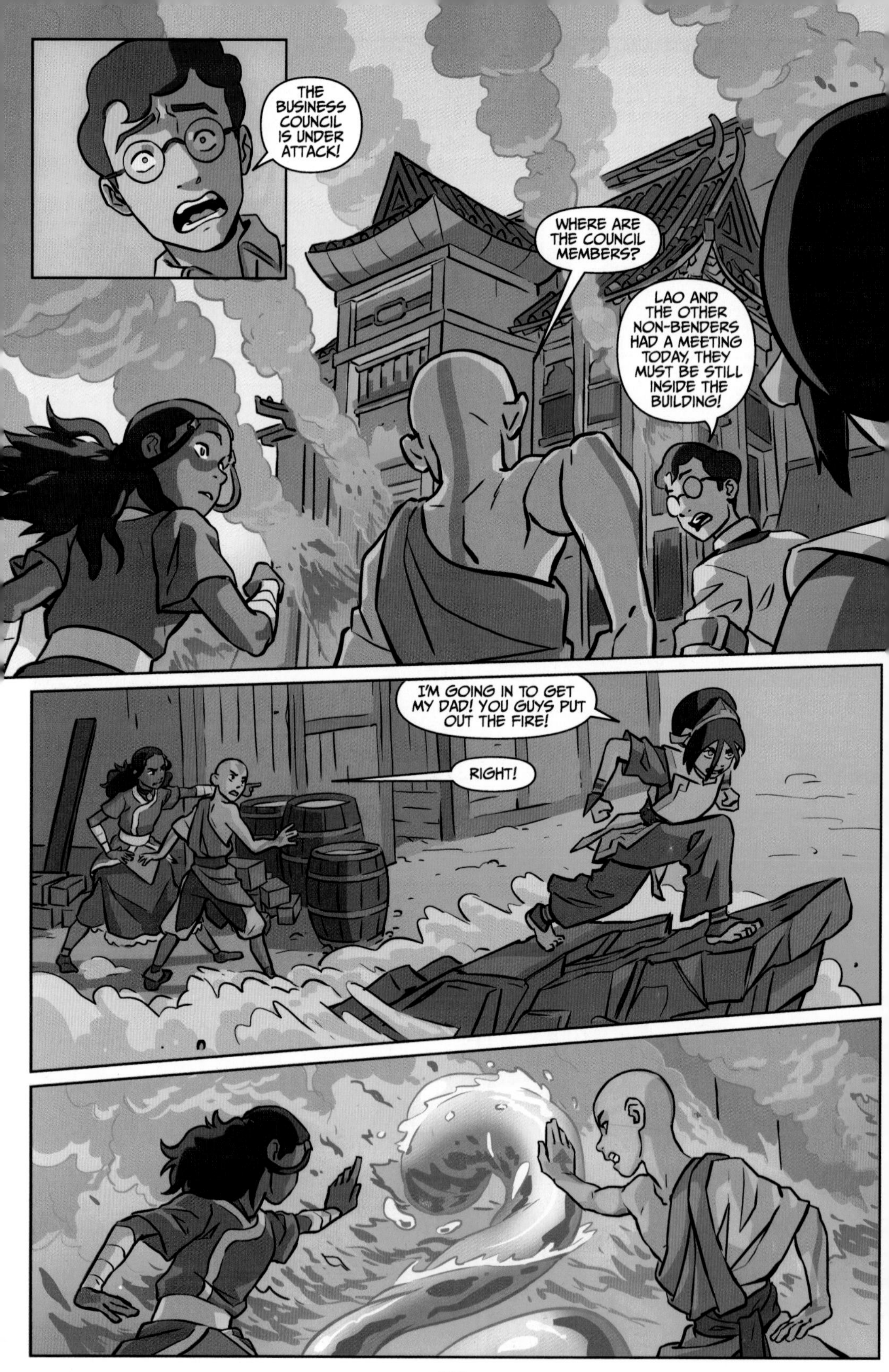
THE BUSINESS COUNCIL IS UNDER ATTACK!
WHERE ARE THE COUNCIL MEMBERS?
LAO AND THE OTHER NON-BENDERS HAD A MEETING TODAY, THEY MUST BE STILL INSIDE THE BUILDING!
I'M GOING IN TO GET MY DAD! YOU GUYS PUT OUT THE FIRE!
RIGHT!

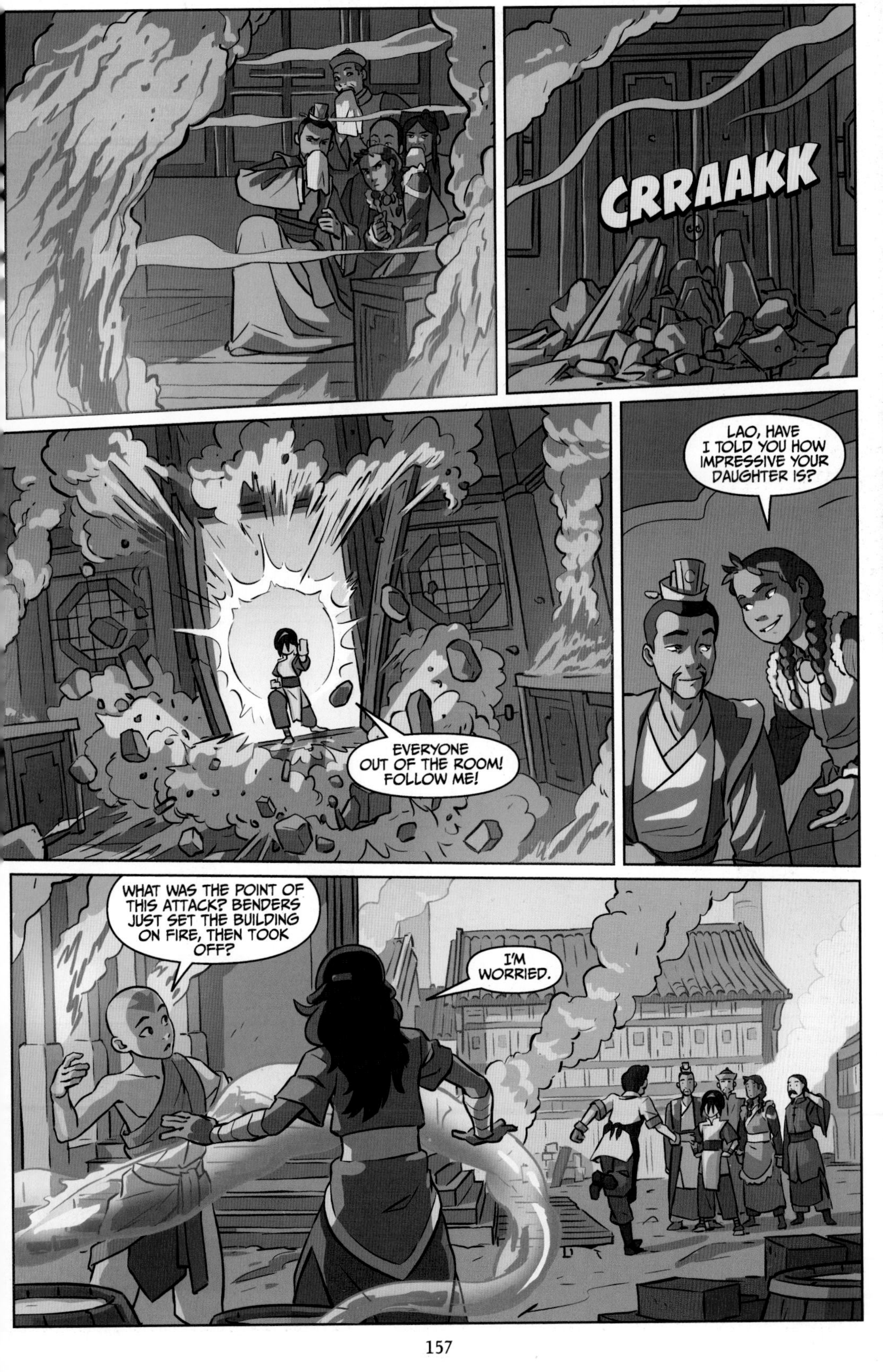
CRRAAKK
EVERYONE OUT OF THE ROOM! FOLLOW ME!
LAO, HAVE I TOLD YOU HOW IMPRESSIVE YOUR DAUGHTER IS?
WHAT WAS THE POINT OF THIS ATTACK? BENDERS JUST SET THE BUILDING ON FIRE, THEN TOOK OFF?
I'M WORRIED.

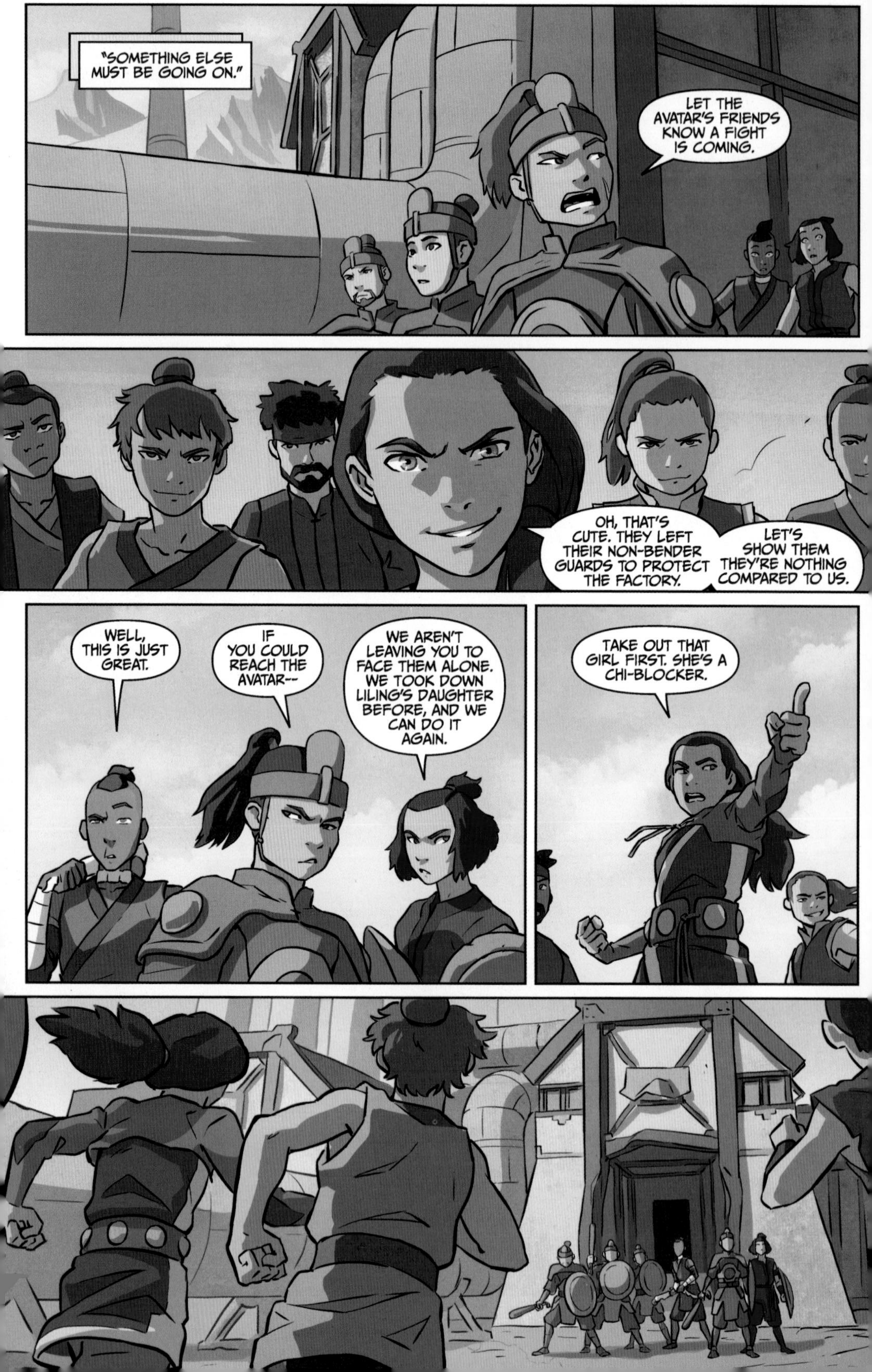
"SOMETHING ELSE MUST BE GOING ON."
LET THE AVATAR'S FRIENDS KNOW A FIGHT IS COMING.
OH, THAT'S CUTE. THEY LEFT THEIR NON-BENDER GUARDS TO PROTECT THE FACTORY.
LET'S SHOW THEM THEY'RE NOTHING COMPARED TO US.
WELL, THIS IS JUST GREAT.
IF YOU COULD REACH THE AVATAR--
WE AREN'T LEAVING YOU TO FACE THEM ALONE. WE TOOK DOWN LILING'S DAUGHTER BEFORE, AND WE CAN DO IT AGAIN.
TAKE OUT THAT GIRL FIRST. SHE'S A CHI-BLOCKER.

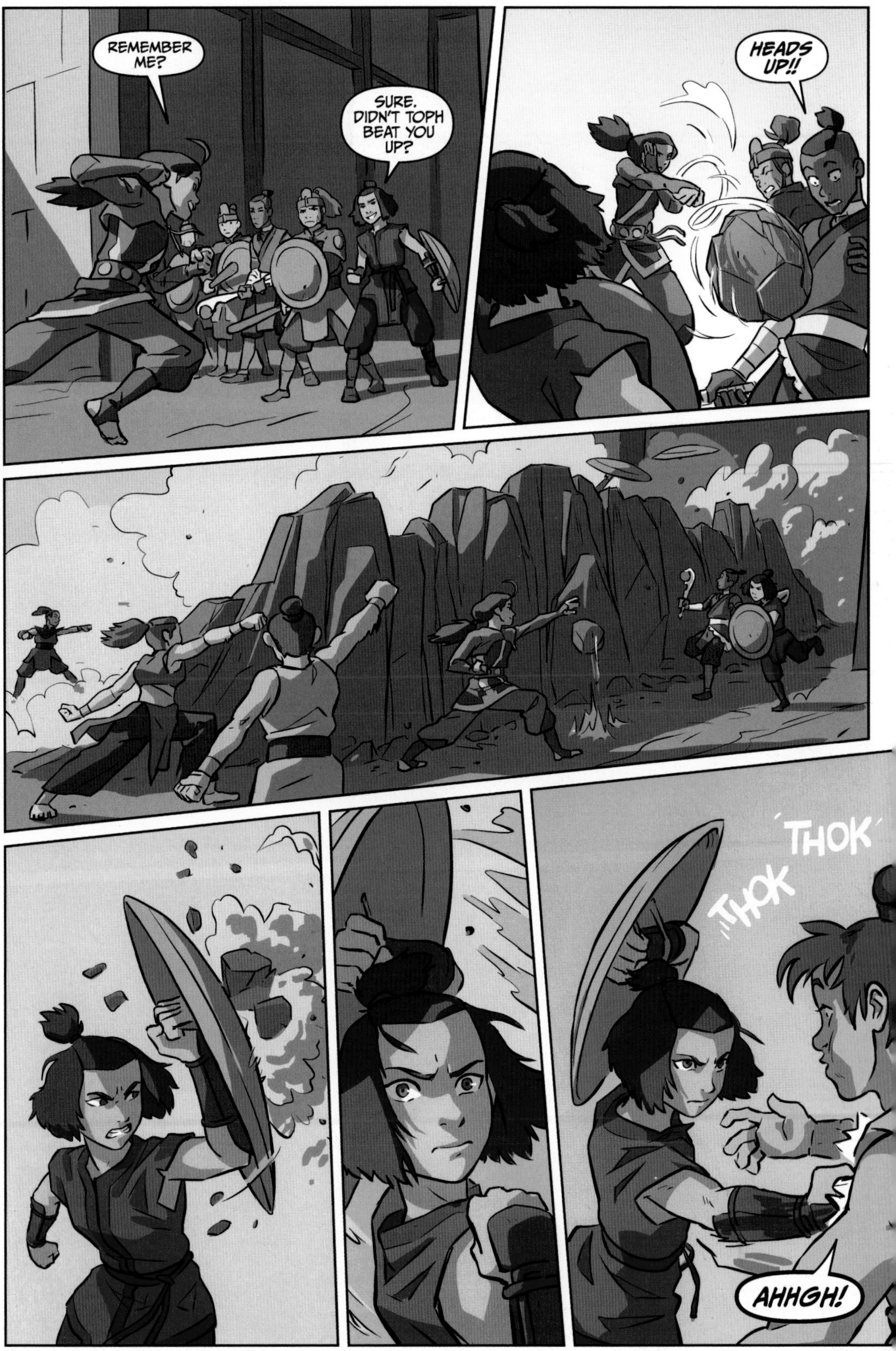
REMEMBER ME?
SURE. DIDN'T TOPH BEAT YOU UP?
HEADS UP!!
THOK
THOK
AHHGH!

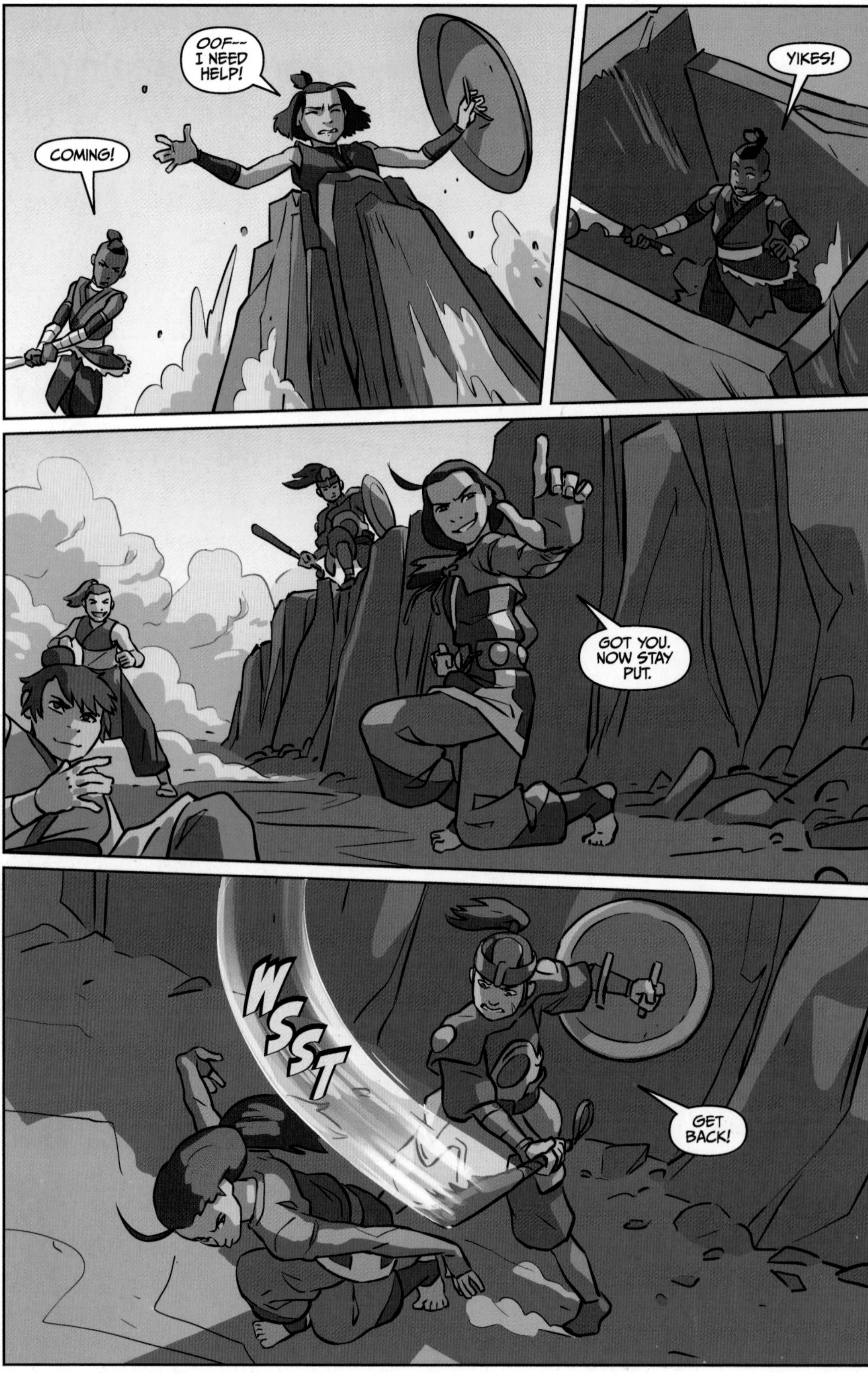
OOF-- I NEED HELP!
COMING!
YIKES!
GOT YOU. NOW STAY PUT.
WSST
GET BACK!

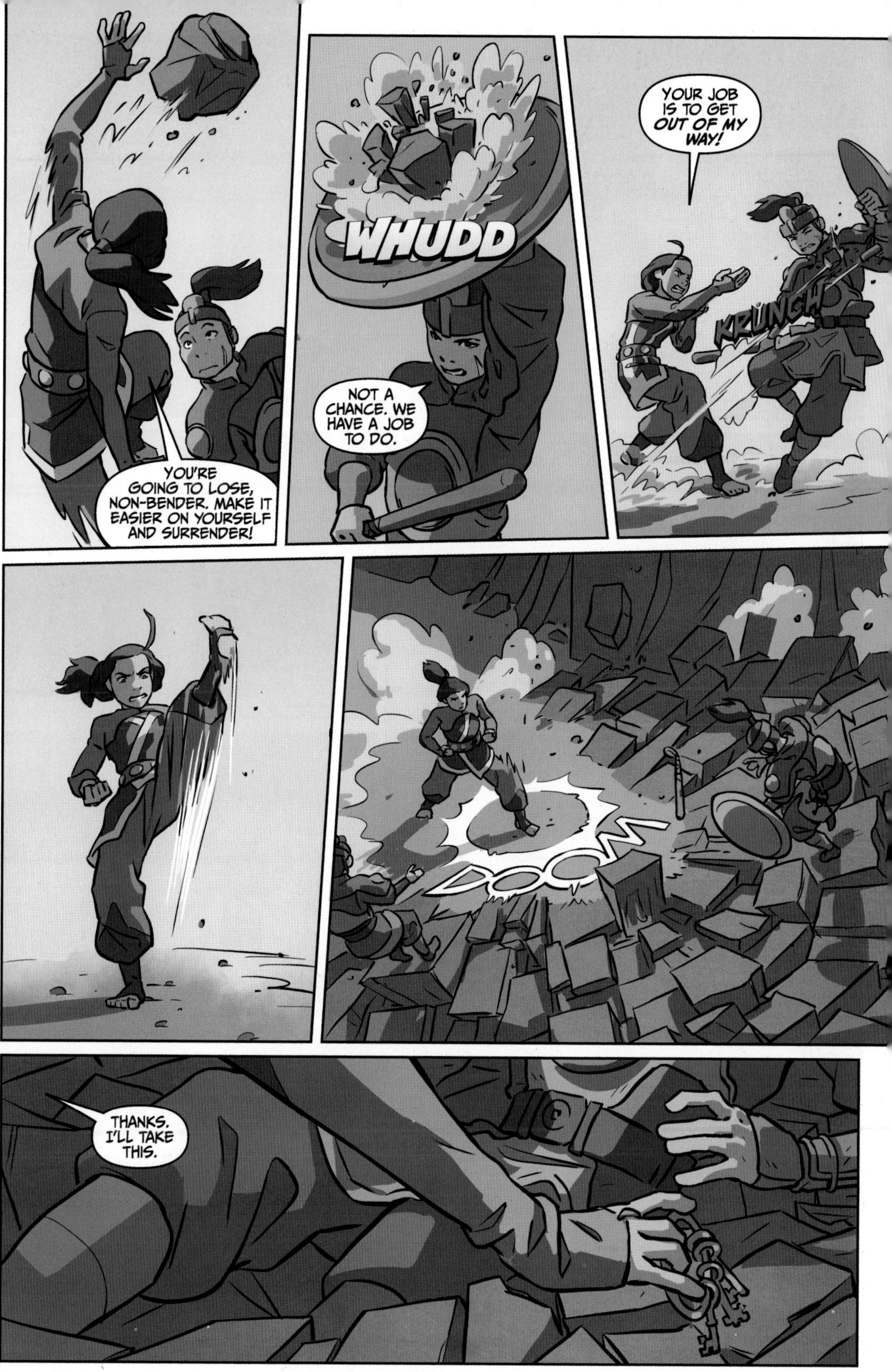
YOU'RE GOING TO LOSE, NON-BENDER. MAKE IT EASIER ON YOURSELF AND SURRENDER!
WHUDD
NOT A CHANCE. WE HAVE A JOB TO DO.
YOUR JOB IS TO GET OUT OF MY WAY!
KRUNCH
DOOM
THANKS. I'LL TAKE THIS.

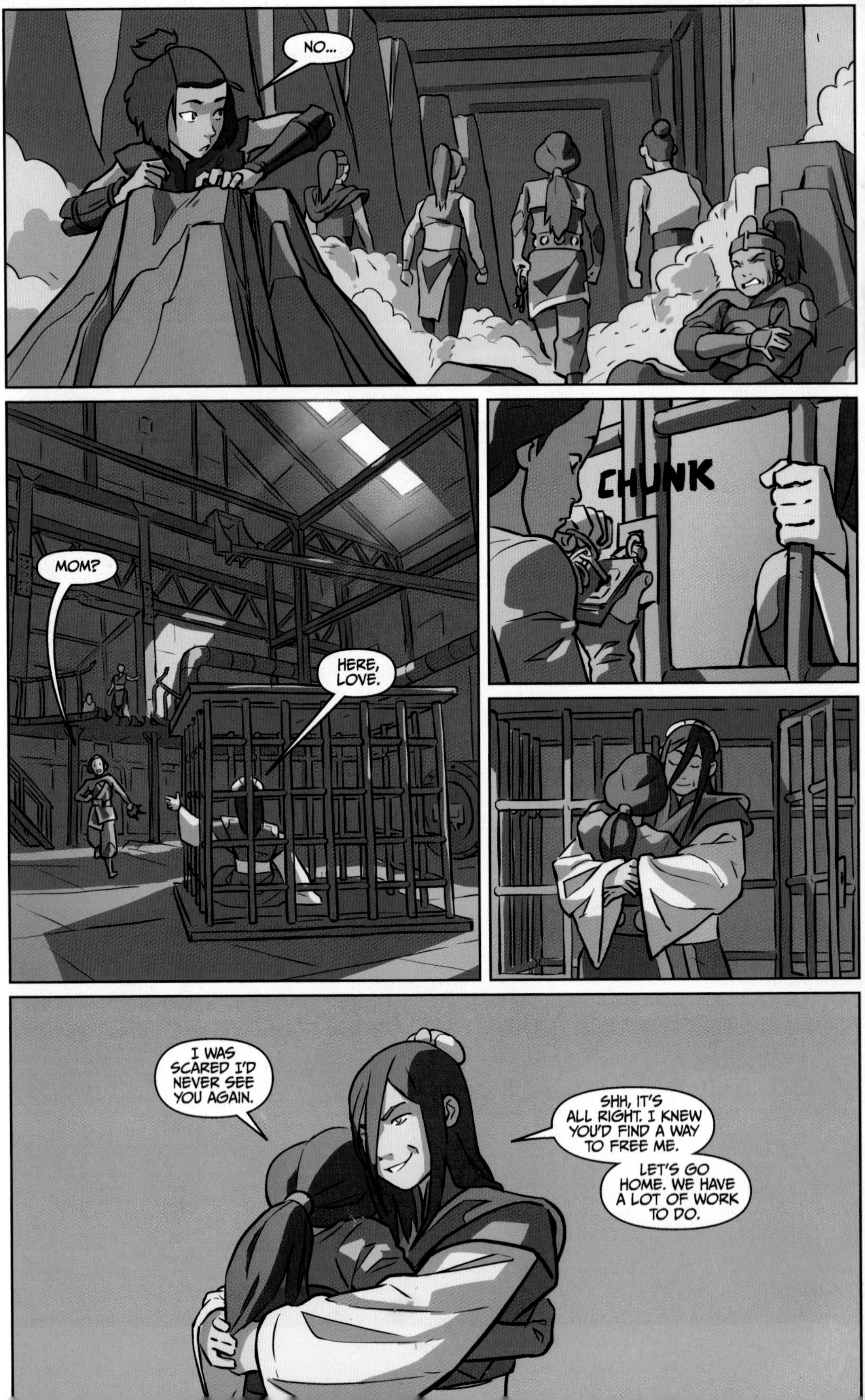
NO...
MOM?
HERE, LOVE.
CHUNK
I WAS SCARED I'D NEVER SEE YOU AGAIN.
SHH, IT'S ALL RIGHT. I KNEW YOU'D FIND A WAY TO FREE ME.
LET'S GO HOME. WE HAVE A LOT OF WORK TO DO.

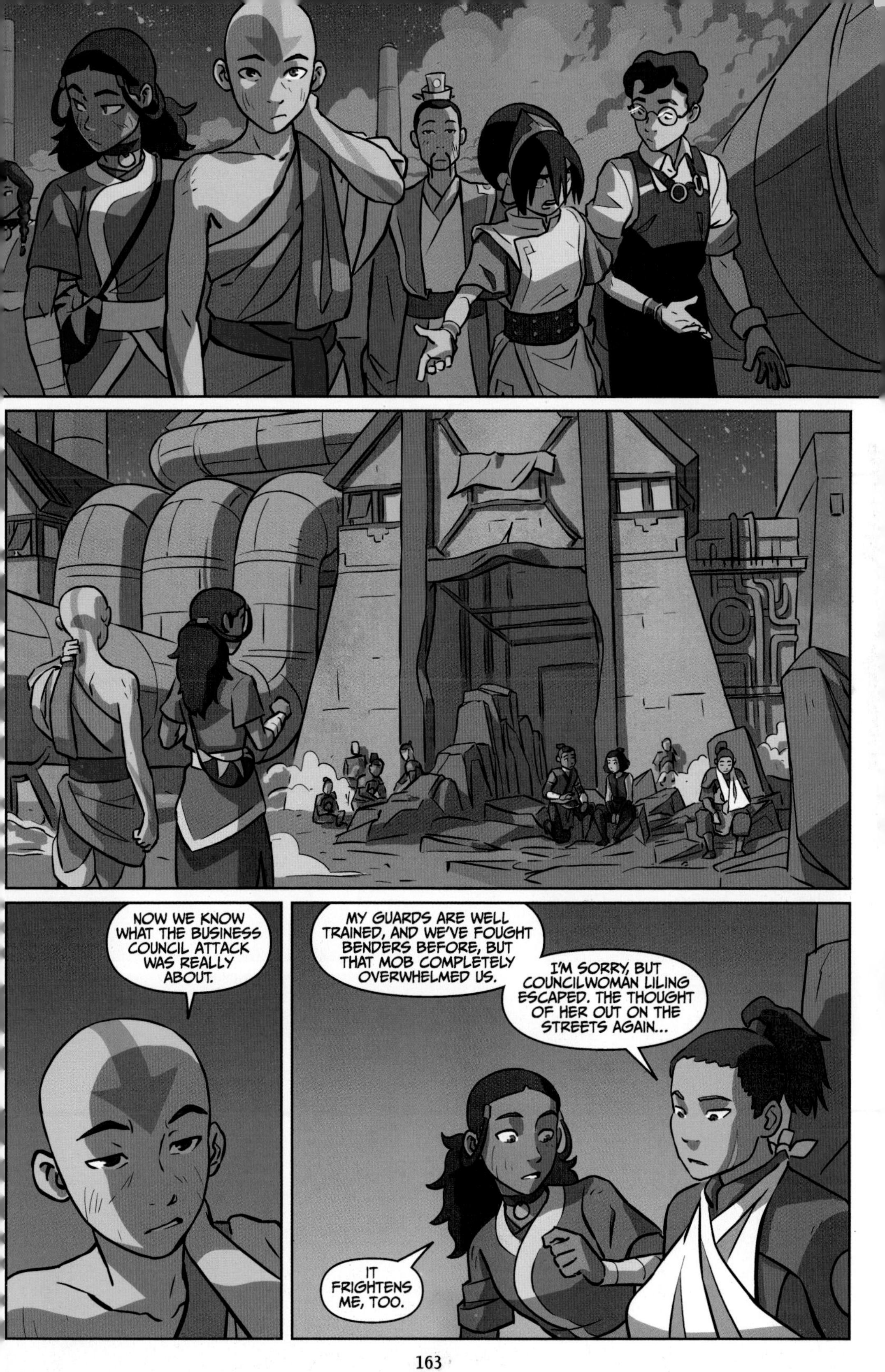
NOW WE KNOW WHAT THE BUSINESS COUNCIL ATTACK WAS REALLY ABOUT.
MY GUARDS ARE WELL TRAINED, AND WE'VE FOUGHT BENDERS BEFORE, BUT THAT MOB COMPLETELY OVERWHELMED US.
I'M SORRY, BUT COUNCILWOMAN LILING ESCAPED. THE THOUGHT OF HER OUT ON THE STREETS AGAIN...
IT FRIGHTENS ME, TOO.

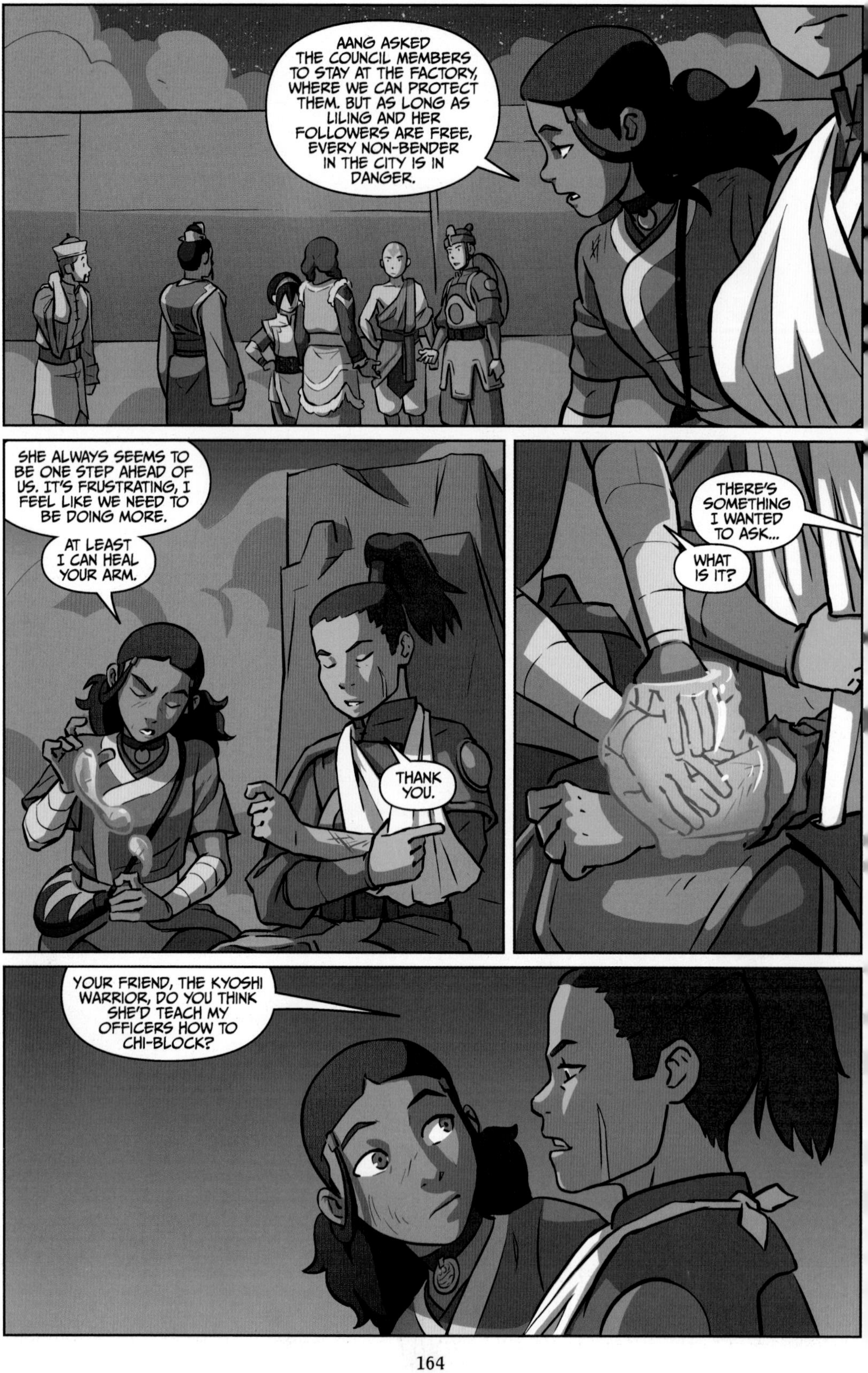
AANG ASKED THE COUNCIL MEMBERS TO STAY AT THE FACTORY, WHERE WE CAN PROTECT THEM. BUT AS LONG AS LILING AND HER FOLLOWERS ARE FREE, EVERY NON-BENDER IN THE CITY IS IN DANGER.
SHE ALWAYS SEEMS TO BE ONE STEP AHEAD OF US. IT'S FRUSTRATING, I FEEL LIKE WE NEED TO BE DOING MORE.
AT LEAST I CAN HEAL YOUR ARM.
THANK YOU.
THERE'S SOMETHING I WANTED TO ASK...
WHAT IS IT?
YOUR FRIEND, THE KYOSHI WARRIOR, DO YOU THINK SHE'D TEACH MY OFFICERS HOW TO CHI-BLOCK?

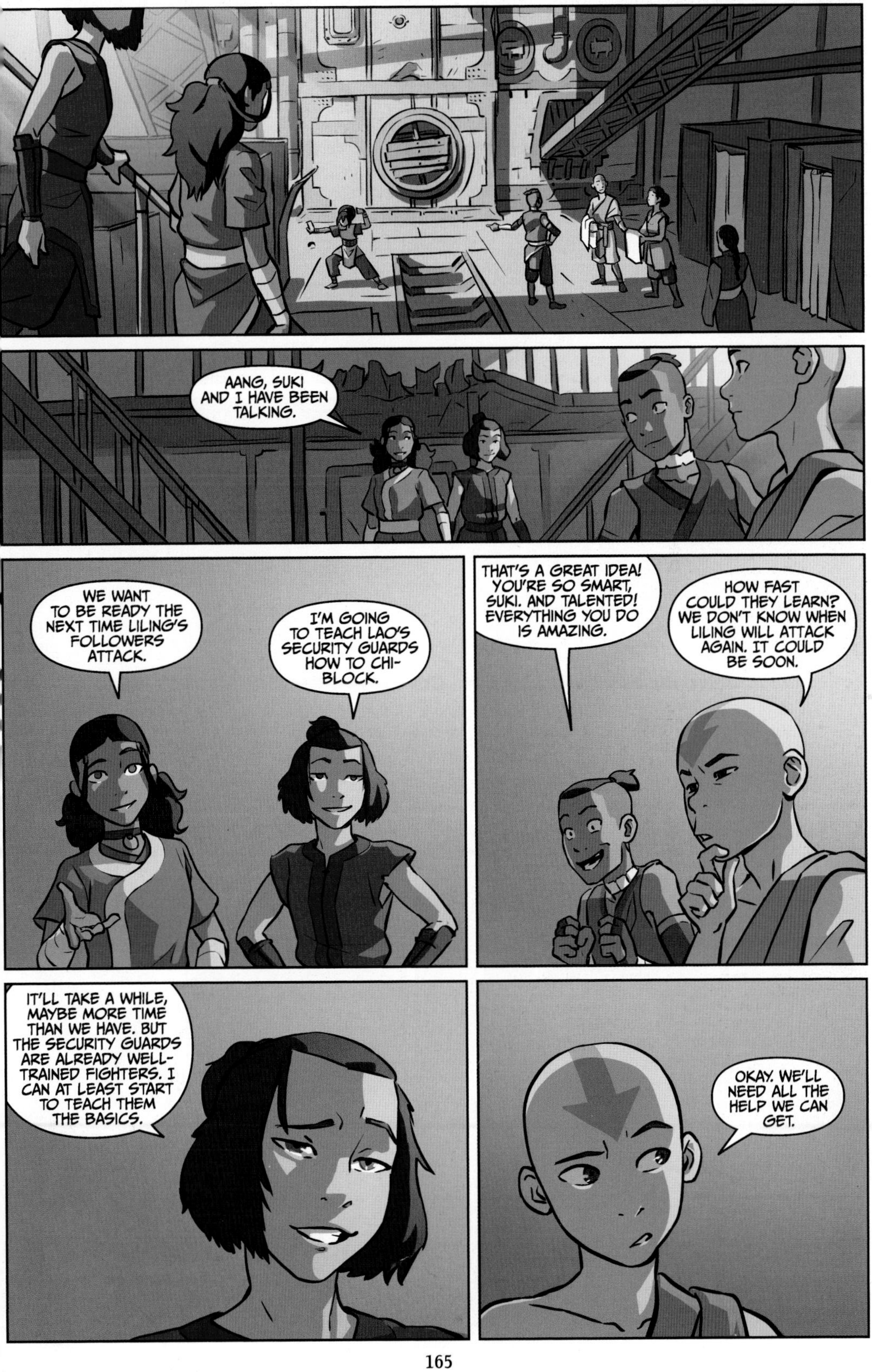
AANG, SUKI AND I HAVE BEEN TALKING.
WE WANT TO BE READY THE NEXT TIME LILING'S FOLLOWERS ATTACK.
I'M GOING TO TEACH LAO'S SECURITY GUARDS HOW TO CHI-BLOCK.
THAT'S A GREAT IDEA! YOU'RE SO SMART, SUKI. AND TALENTED! EVERYTHING YOU DO IS AMAZING.
HOW FAST COULD THEY LEARN? WE DON'T KNOW WHEN LILING WILL ATTACK AGAIN. IT COULD BE SOON.
IT'LL TAKE A WHILE, MAYBE MORE TIME THAN WE HAVE. BUT THE SECURITY GUARDS ARE ALREADY WELL-TRAINED FIGHTERS. I CAN AT LEAST START TO TEACH THEM THE BASICS.
OKAY. WE'LL NEED ALL THE HELP WE CAN GET.

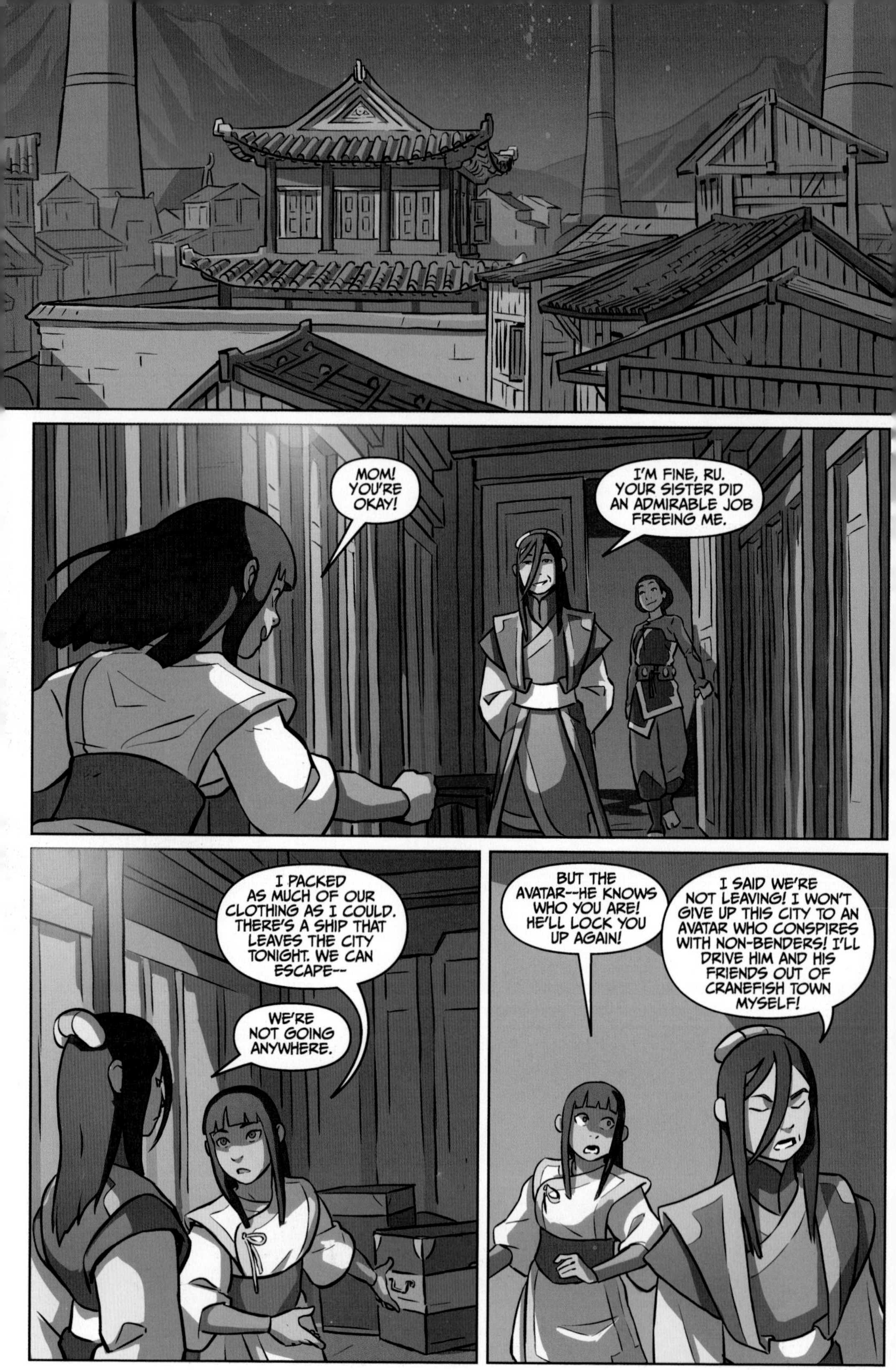
MOM! YOU'RE OKAY!
I'M FINE, RU. YOUR SISTER DID AN ADMIRABLE JOB FREEING ME.
I PACKED AS MUCH OF OUR CLOTHING AS I COULD. THERE'S A SHIP THAT LEAVES THE CITY TONIGHT. WE CAN ESCAPE--
WE'RE NOT GOING ANYWHERE.
BUT THE AVATAR--HE KNOWS WHO YOU ARE! HE'LL LOCK YOU UP AGAIN!
I SAID WE'RE NOT LEAVING! I WON'T GIVE UP THIS CITY TO AN AVATAR WHO CONSPIRES WITH NON-BENDERS! I'LL DRIVE HIM AND HIS FRIENDS OUT OF CRANEFISH TOWN MYSELF!

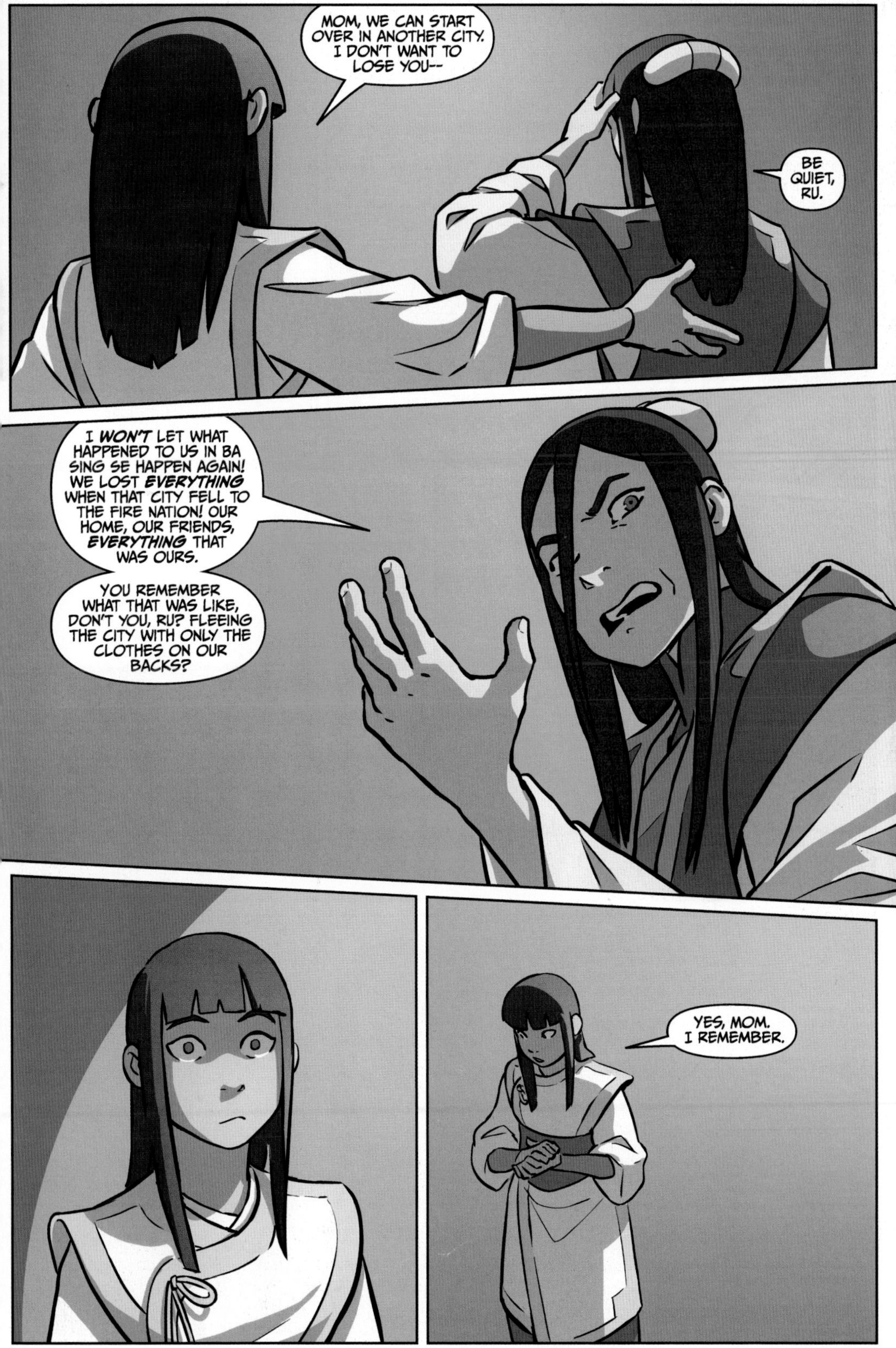
MOM, WE CAN START OVER IN ANOTHER CITY. I DON'T WANT TO LOSE YOU--
BE QUIET, RU.
I ***WON'T*** LET WHAT HAPPENED TO US IN BA SING SE HAPPEN AGAIN! WE LOST ***EVERYTHING*** WHEN THAT CITY FELL TO THE FIRE NATION! OUR HOME, OUR FRIENDS, ***EVERYTHING*** THAT WAS OURS.
YOU REMEMBER WHAT THAT WAS LIKE, DON'T YOU, RU? FLEEING THE CITY WITH ONLY THE CLOTHES ON OUR BACKS?
YES, MOM. I REMEMBER.

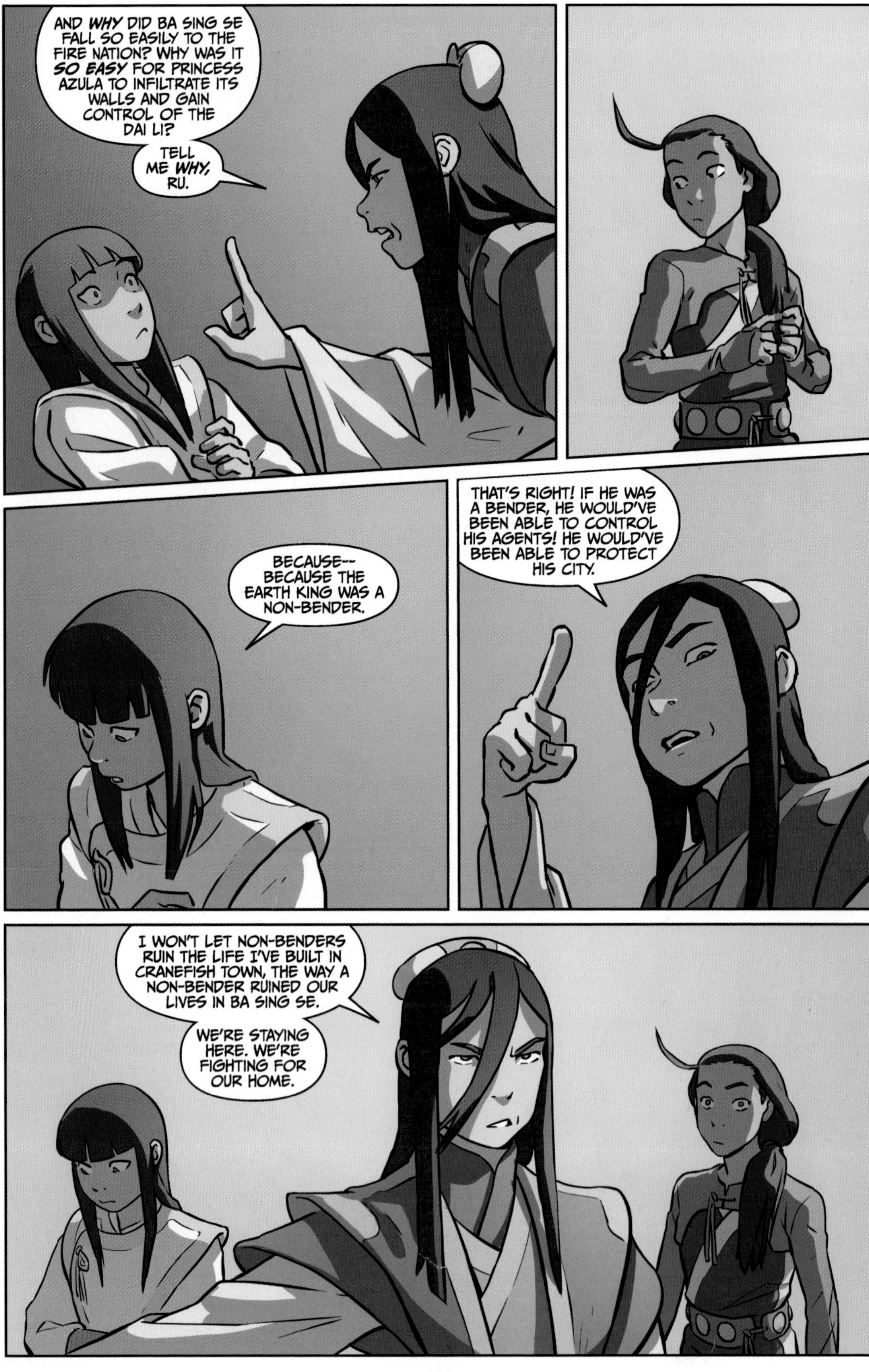
AND WHY DID BA SING SE FALL SO EASILY TO THE FIRE NATION? WHY WAS IT SO EASY FOR PRINCESS AZULA TO INFILTRATE ITS WALLS AND GAIN CONTROL OF THE DAI LI?
TELL ME WHY, RU.
BECAUSE-- BECAUSE THE EARTH KING WAS A NON-BENDER.
THAT'S RIGHT! IF HE WAS A BENDER, HE WOULD'VE BEEN ABLE TO CONTROL HIS AGENTS! HE WOULD'VE BEEN ABLE TO PROTECT HIS CITY.
I WON'T LET NON-BENDERS RUIN THE LIFE I'VE BUILT IN CRANEFISH TOWN, THE WAY A NON-BENDER RUINED OUR LIVES IN BA SING SE.
WE'RE STAYING HERE. WE'RE FIGHTING FOR OUR HOME.

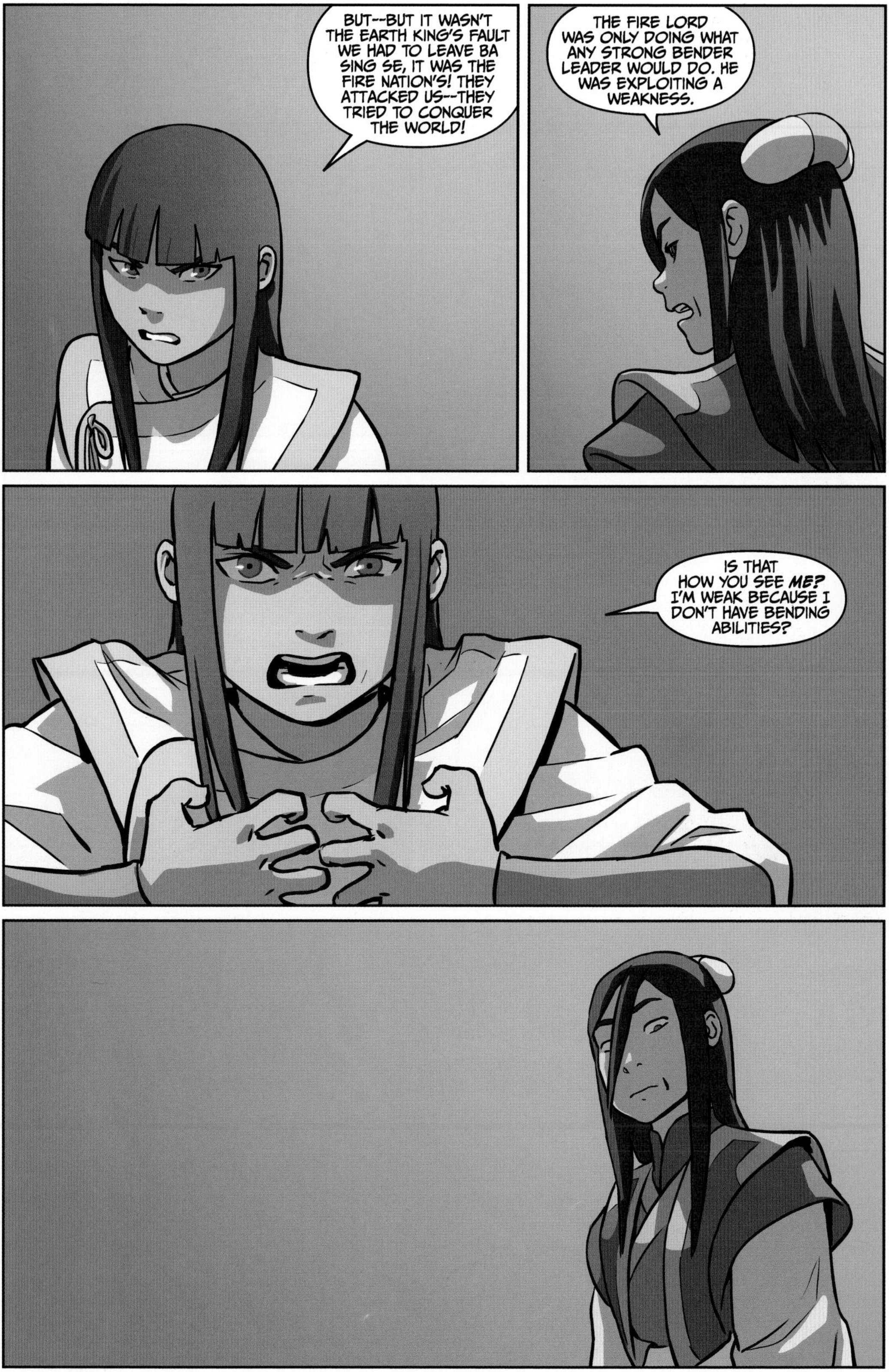
BUT--BUT IT WASN'T THE EARTH KING'S FAULT WE HAD TO LEAVE BA SING SE, IT WAS THE FIRE NATION'S! THEY ATTACKED US--THEY TRIED TO CONQUER THE WORLD!
THE FIRE LORD WAS ONLY DOING WHAT ANY STRONG BENDER LEADER WOULD DO. HE WAS EXPLOITING A WEAKNESS.
IS THAT HOW YOU SEE *ME?* I'M WEAK BECAUSE I DON'T HAVE BENDING ABILITIES?

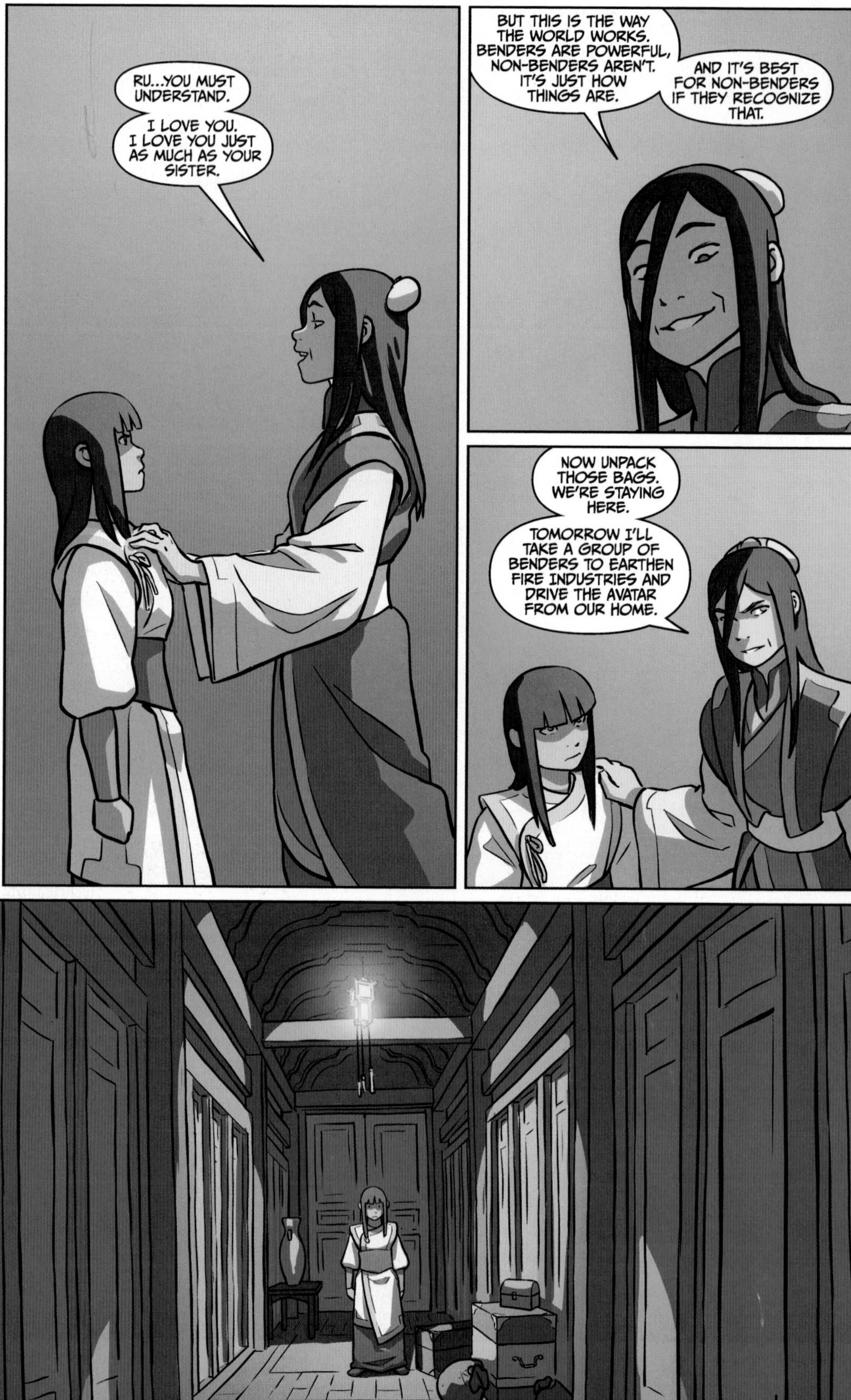
RU...YOU MUST UNDERSTAND.
I LOVE YOU. I LOVE YOU JUST AS MUCH AS YOUR SISTER.
BUT THIS IS THE WAY THE WORLD WORKS. BENDERS ARE POWERFUL, NON-BENDERS AREN'T. IT'S JUST HOW THINGS ARE.
AND IT'S BEST FOR NON-BENDERS IF THEY RECOGNIZE THAT.
NOW UNPACK THOSE BAGS. WE'RE STAYING HERE.
TOMORROW I'LL TAKE A GROUP OF BENDERS TO EARTHEN FIRE INDUSTRIES AND DRIVE THE AVATAR FROM OUR HOME.

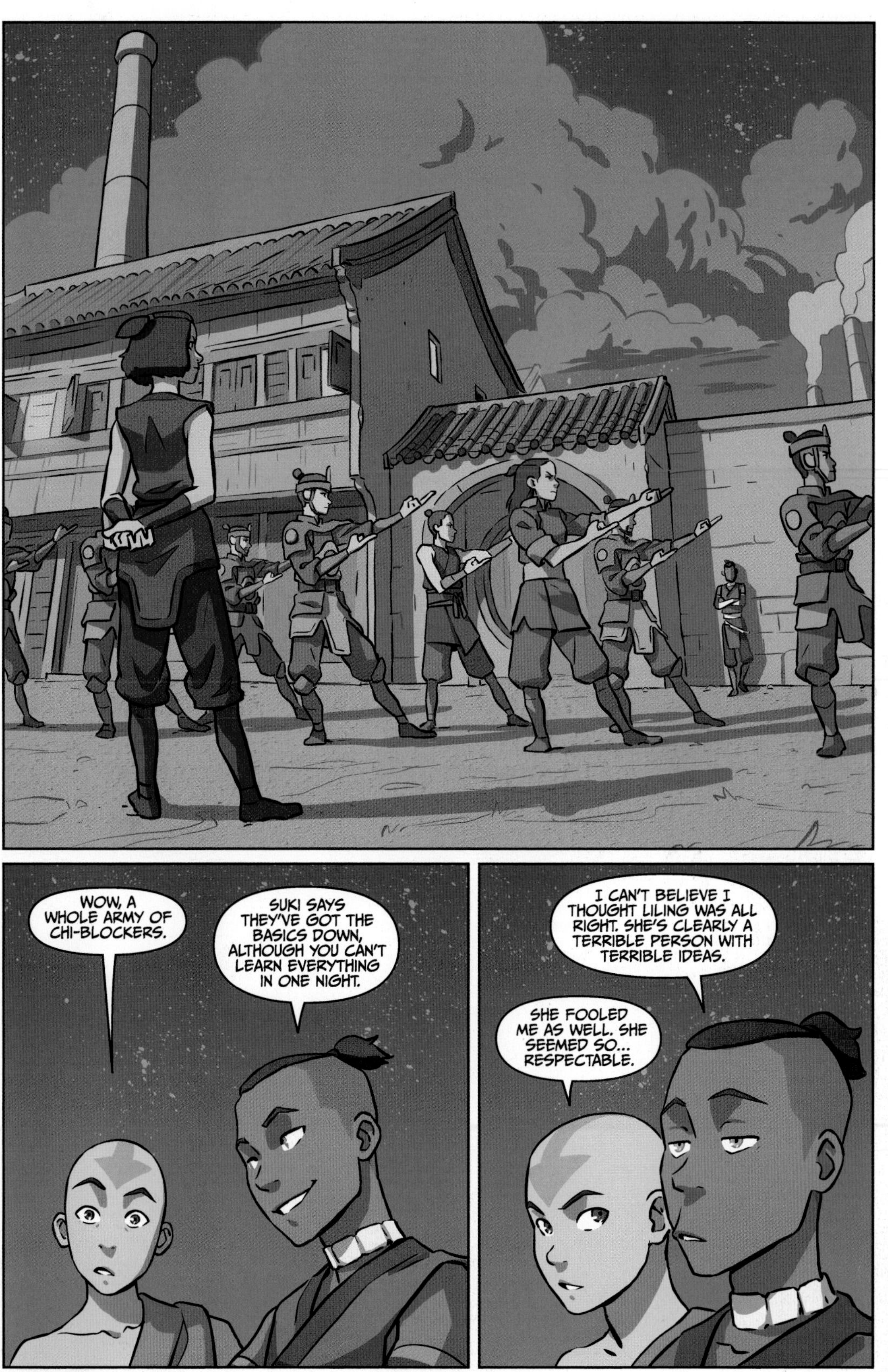
WOW, A WHOLE ARMY OF CHI-BLOCKERS.
SUKI SAYS THEY'VE GOT THE BASICS DOWN, ALTHOUGH YOU CAN'T LEARN EVERYTHING IN ONE NIGHT.
I CAN'T BELIEVE I THOUGHT LILING WAS ALL RIGHT. SHE'S CLEARLY A TERRIBLE PERSON WITH TERRIBLE IDEAS.
SHE FOOLED ME AS WELL. SHE SEEMED SO... RESPECTABLE.

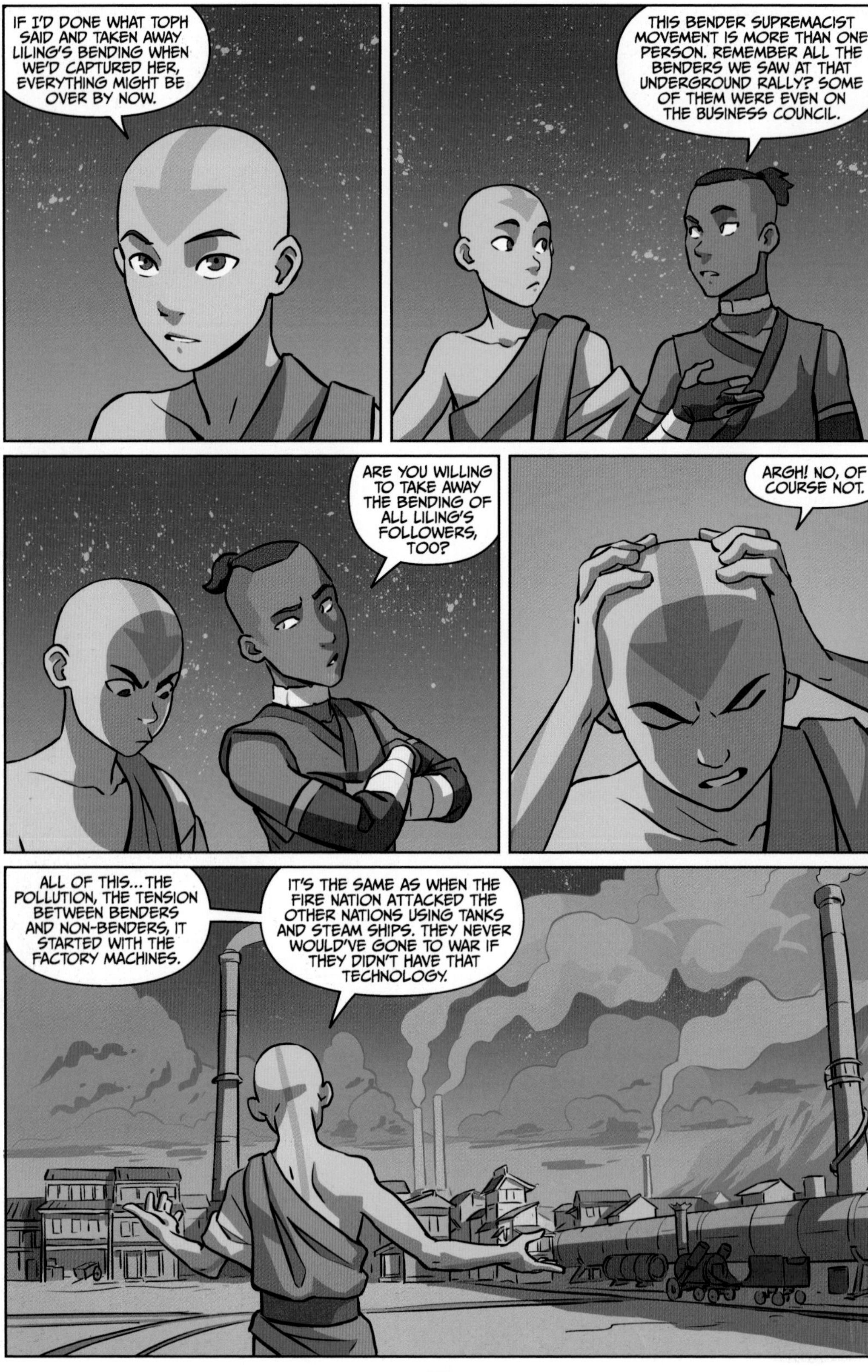
IF I'D DONE WHAT TOPH SAID AND TAKEN AWAY LILING'S BENDING WHEN WE'D CAPTURED HER, EVERYTHING MIGHT BE OVER BY NOW.
THIS BENDER SUPREMACIST MOVEMENT IS MORE THAN ONE PERSON. REMEMBER ALL THE BENDERS WE SAW AT THAT UNDERGROUND RALLY? SOME OF THEM WERE EVEN ON THE BUSINESS COUNCIL.
ARE YOU WILLING TO TAKE AWAY THE BENDING OF ALL LILING'S FOLLOWERS, TOO?
ARGH! NO, OF COURSE NOT.
ALL OF THIS... THE POLLUTION, THE TENSION BETWEEN BENDERS AND NON-BENDERS, IT STARTED WITH THE FACTORY MACHINES.
IT'S THE SAME AS WHEN THE FIRE NATION ATTACKED THE OTHER NATIONS USING TANKS AND STEAM SHIPS. THEY NEVER WOULD'VE GONE TO WAR IF THEY DIDN'T HAVE THAT TECHNOLOGY.

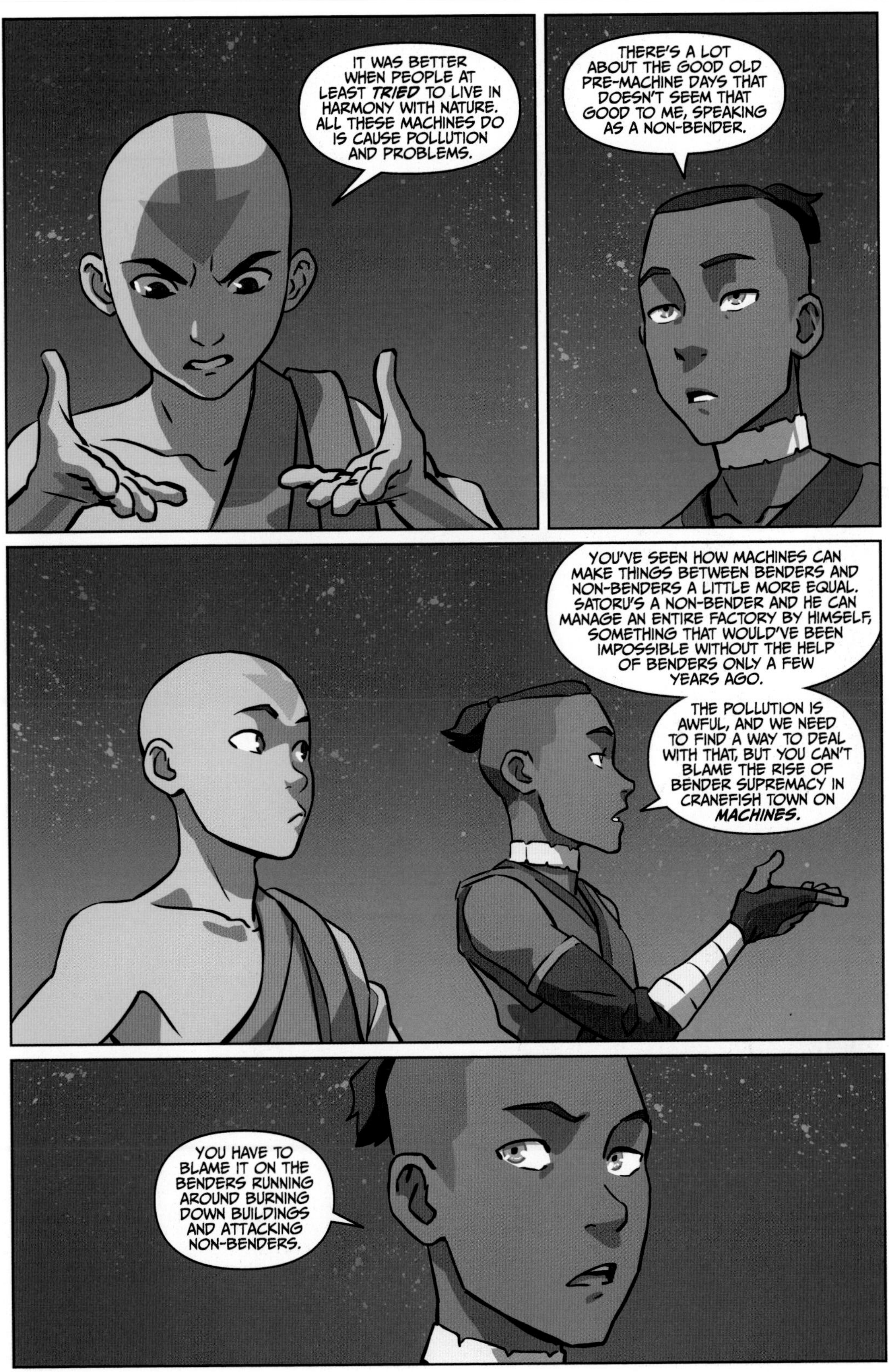
IT WAS BETTER WHEN PEOPLE AT LEAST *TRIED* TO LIVE IN HARMONY WITH NATURE. ALL THESE MACHINES DO IS CAUSE POLLUTION AND PROBLEMS.
THERE'S A LOT ABOUT THE GOOD OLD PRE-MACHINE DAYS THAT DOESN'T SEEM THAT GOOD TO ME, SPEAKING AS A NON-BENDER.
YOU'VE SEEN HOW MACHINES CAN MAKE THINGS BETWEEN BENDERS AND NON-BENDERS A LITTLE MORE EQUAL. SATORU'S A NON-BENDER AND HE CAN MANAGE AN ENTIRE FACTORY BY HIMSELF, SOMETHING THAT WOULD'VE BEEN IMPOSSIBLE WITHOUT THE HELP OF BENDERS ONLY A FEW YEARS AGO.
THE POLLUTION IS AWFUL, AND WE NEED TO FIND A WAY TO DEAL WITH THAT, BUT YOU CAN'T BLAME THE RISE OF BENDER SUPREMACY IN CRANEFISH TOWN ON *MACHINES.*
YOU HAVE TO BLAME IT ON THE BENDERS RUNNING AROUND BURNING DOWN BUILDINGS AND ATTACKING NON-BENDERS.

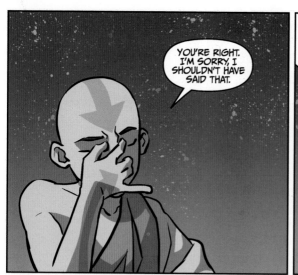

YOU'RE RIGHT. I'M SORRY, I SHOULDN'T HAVE SAID THAT.

AND THE FIRE NATION DIDN'T GO TO WAR BECAUSE THEY INVENTED STEAM SHIPS, THEY DID IT BECAUSE THE FIRE LORD WAS A GIANT JERK WHO WANTED TO RULE THE WORLD.

OKAY, OKAY, SOKKA.

SORRY, IT'S FUN TO BE RIGHT.

I'M TURNING IN, ARE YOU COMING?

NAH, I'M GOING TO WAIT FOR SUKI TO FINISH UP.

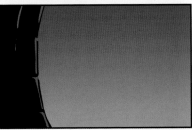

DID YOU SEE SOMEONE?

YEP. AND I THINK I KNOW WHO IT IS.

RU? IS THERE SOMETHING YOU CAME HERE TO TELL ME?

I KEEP THINKING ABOUT WHAT YOU SAID TO ME DURING THAT FIGHT IN THE CAVERN--HOW CAN I BE OKAY WITH WHAT MY MOM IS DOING?

I LOVE MY MOM AND MY SISTER, BUT THE WAY THEY TALK...THE THINGS THEY WANT TO DO... I'M *NOT* OKAY WITH IT.

BUT THEY'RE MY ONLY FAMILY! HOW COULD I TURN AGAINST THEM?

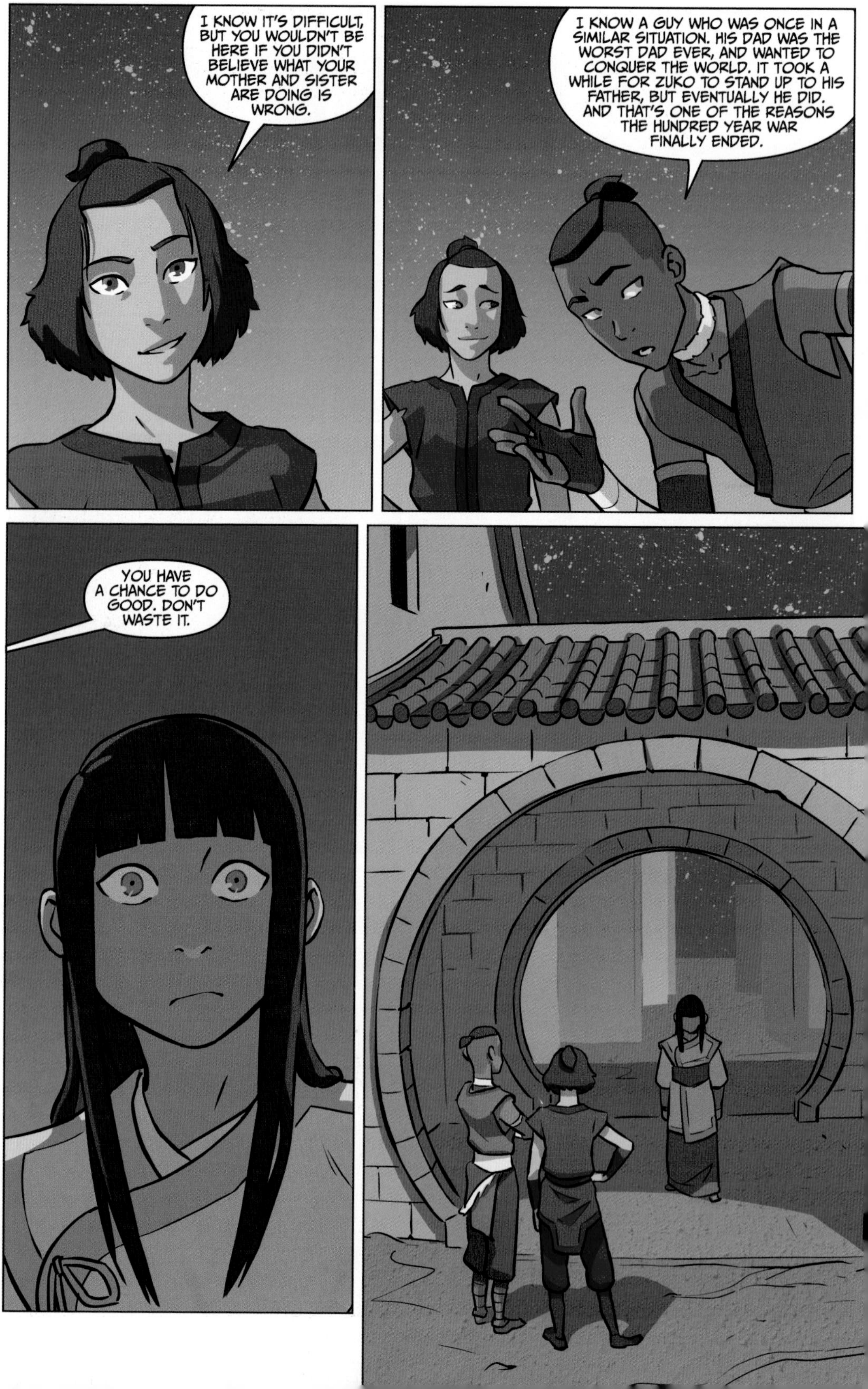
I KNOW IT'S DIFFICULT, BUT YOU WOULDN'T BE HERE IF YOU DIDN'T BELIEVE WHAT YOUR MOTHER AND SISTER ARE DOING IS WRONG.
I KNOW A GUY WHO WAS ONCE IN A SIMILAR SITUATION. HIS DAD WAS THE WORST DAD EVER, AND WANTED TO CONQUER THE WORLD. IT TOOK A WHILE FOR ZUKO TO STAND UP TO HIS FATHER, BUT EVENTUALLY HE DID. AND THAT'S ONE OF THE REASONS THE HUNDRED YEAR WAR FINALLY ENDED.
YOU HAVE A CHANCE TO DO GOOD. DON'T WASTE IT.

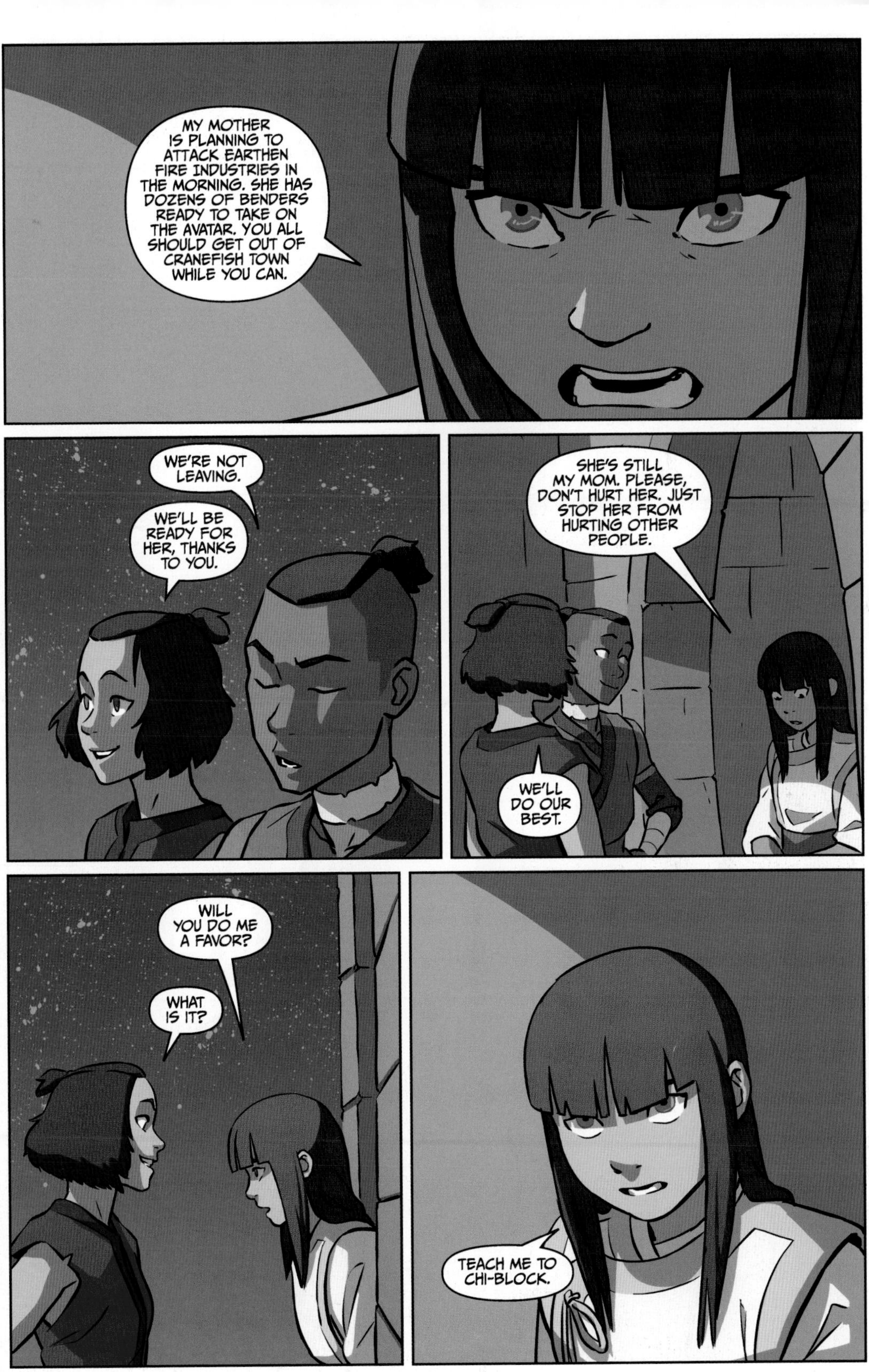
MY MOTHER IS PLANNING TO ATTACK EARTHEN FIRE INDUSTRIES IN THE MORNING. SHE HAS DOZENS OF BENDERS READY TO TAKE ON THE AVATAR. YOU ALL SHOULD GET OUT OF CRANEFISH TOWN WHILE YOU CAN.
WE'RE NOT LEAVING.
WE'LL BE READY FOR HER, THANKS TO YOU.
SHE'S STILL MY MOM. PLEASE, DON'T HURT HER. JUST STOP HER FROM HURTING OTHER PEOPLE.
WE'LL DO OUR BEST.
WILL YOU DO ME A FAVOR?
WHAT IS IT?
TEACH ME TO CHI-BLOCK.

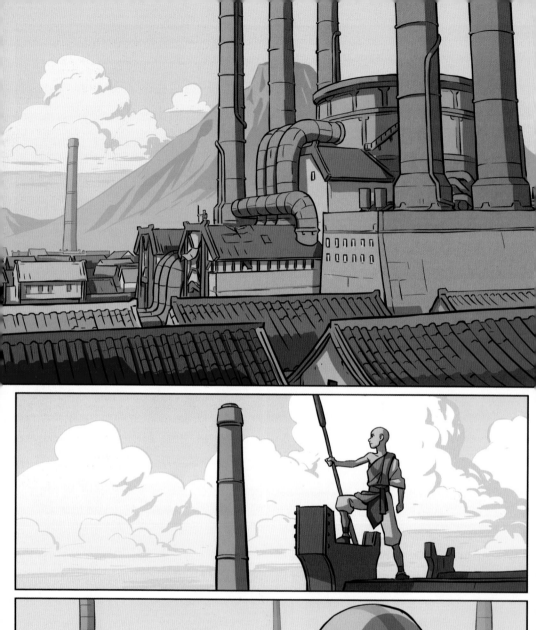

WHAT DO YOU WANT?

TO HELP, IF WE CAN. WE'VE SEEN SOME OF OUR NON-BENDER NEIGHBORS LOSE THEIR HOMES, SO WE'VE BROUGHT SUPPLIES FOR THEM.

CAN I ASK, ARE YOU BENDERS?

YES. BUT WE'RE NOT THE ONES CAUSING ALL THIS TROUBLE, AVATAR. WE CARE ABOUT THE NON-BENDERS IN CRANEFISH TOWN. WE DON'T WANT TO SEE THEM HURT.

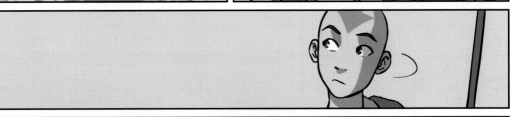

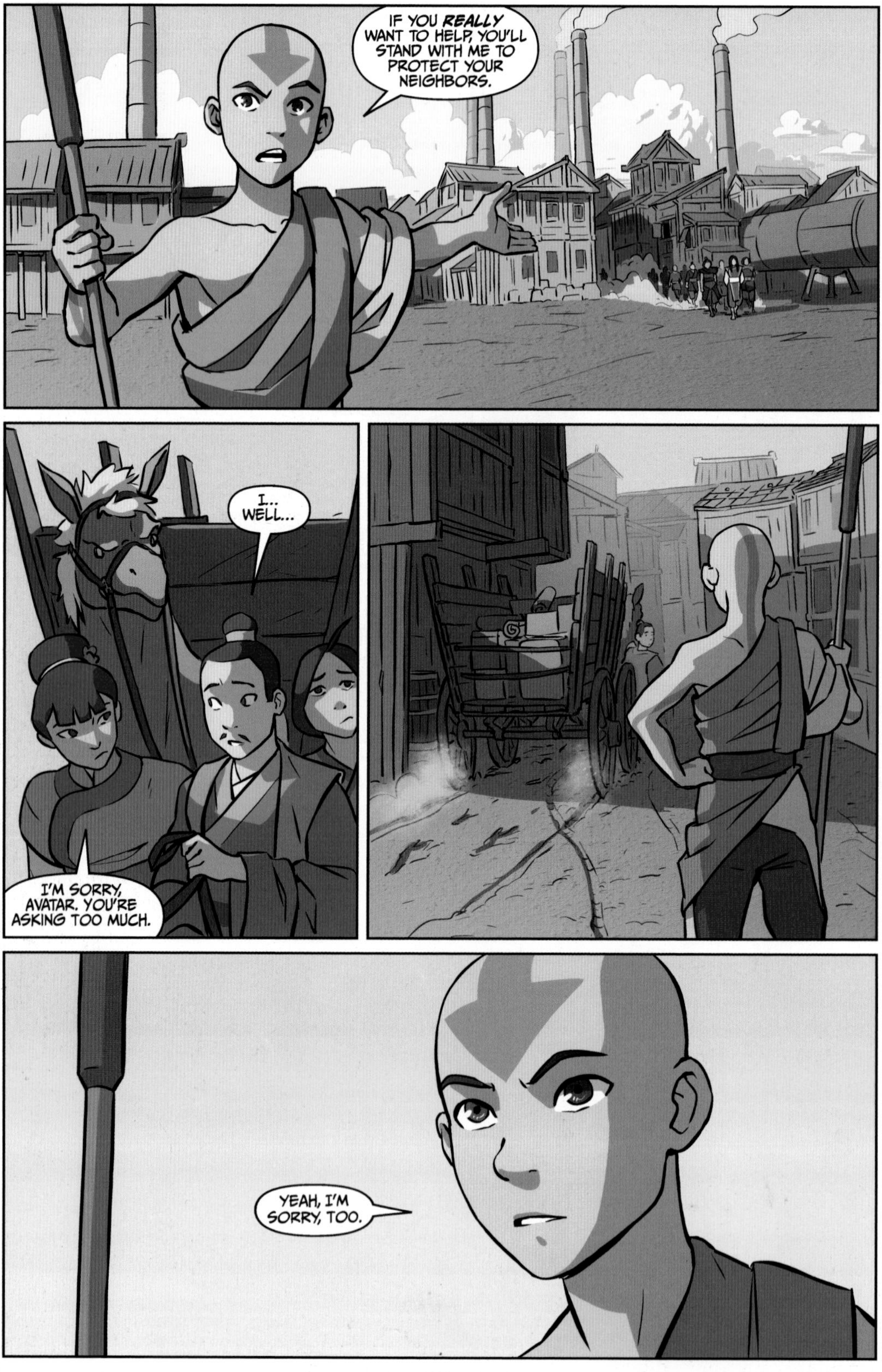
IF YOU REALLY WANT TO HELP, YOU'LL STAND WITH ME TO PROTECT YOUR NEIGHBORS.
I... WELL...
I'M SORRY, AVATAR. YOU'RE ASKING TOO MUCH.
YEAH, I'M SORRY, TOO.

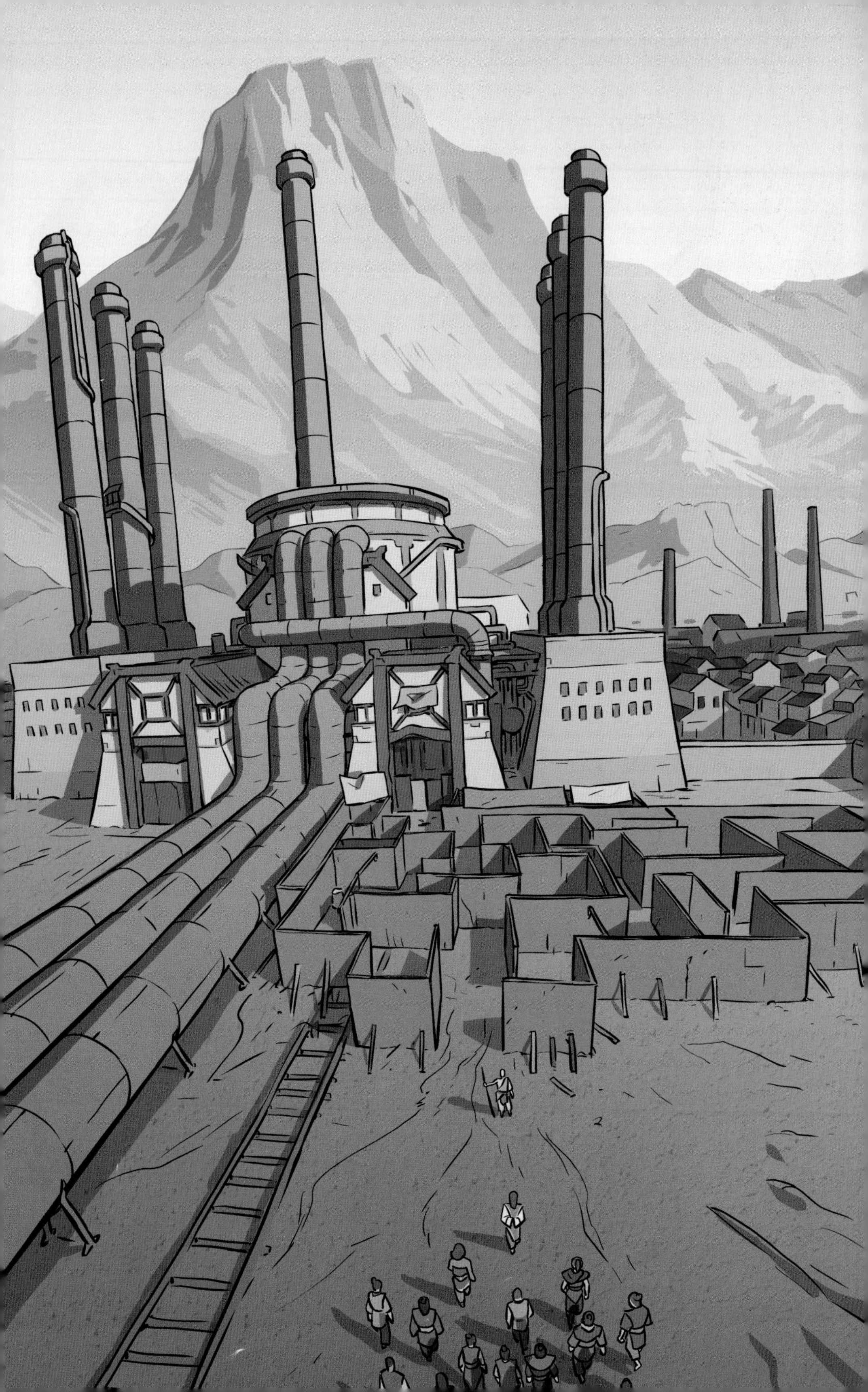

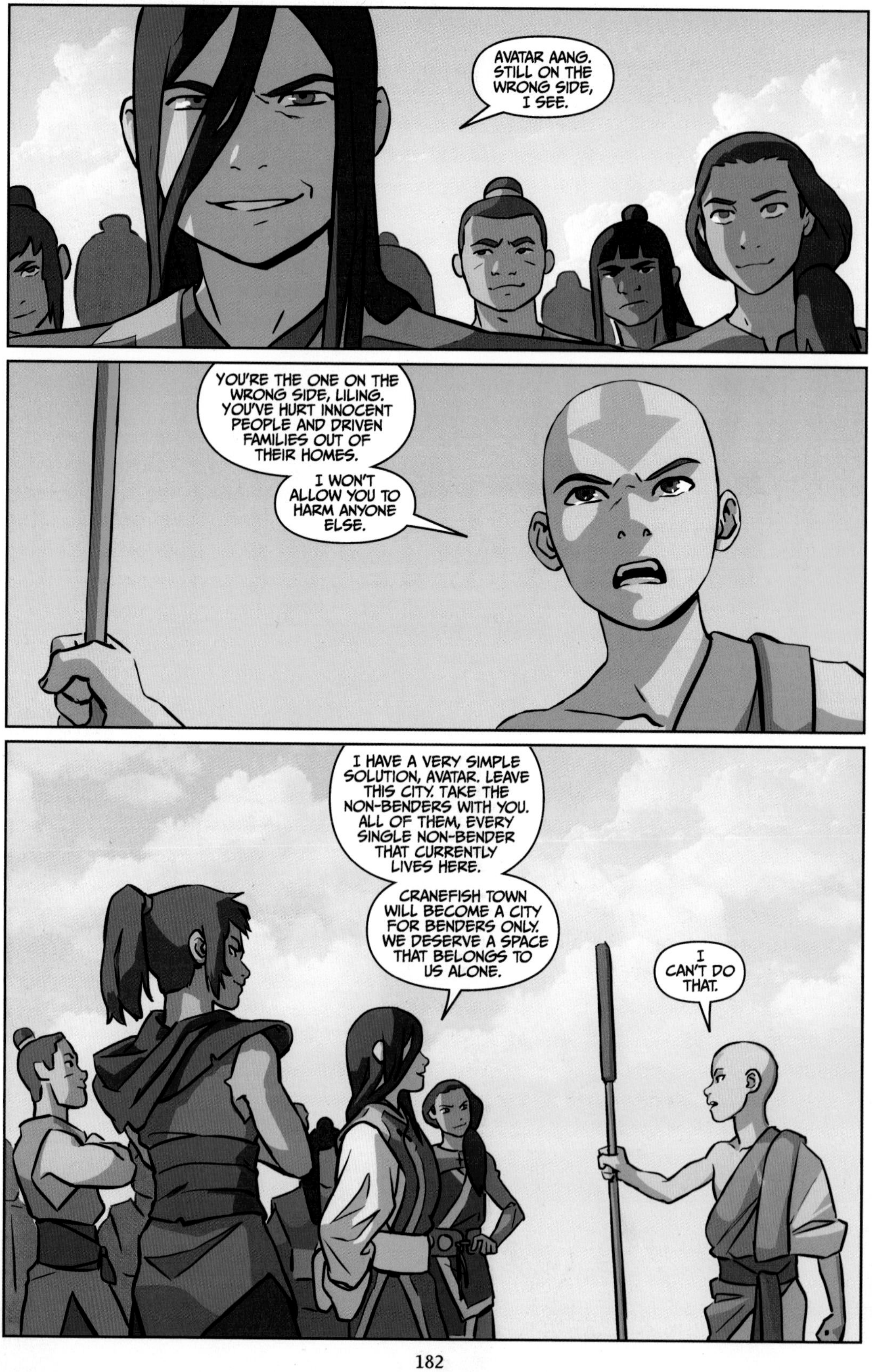
AVATAR AANG. STILL ON THE WRONG SIDE, I SEE.
YOU'RE THE ONE ON THE WRONG SIDE, LILING. YOU'VE HURT INNOCENT PEOPLE AND DRIVEN FAMILIES OUT OF THEIR HOMES.
I WON'T ALLOW YOU TO HARM ANYONE ELSE.
I HAVE A VERY SIMPLE SOLUTION, AVATAR. LEAVE THIS CITY. TAKE THE NON-BENDERS WITH YOU. ALL OF THEM, EVERY SINGLE NON-BENDER THAT CURRENTLY LIVES HERE.
CRANEFISH TOWN WILL BECOME A CITY FOR BENDERS ONLY. WE DESERVE A SPACE THAT BELONGS TO US ALONE.
I CAN'T DO THAT.

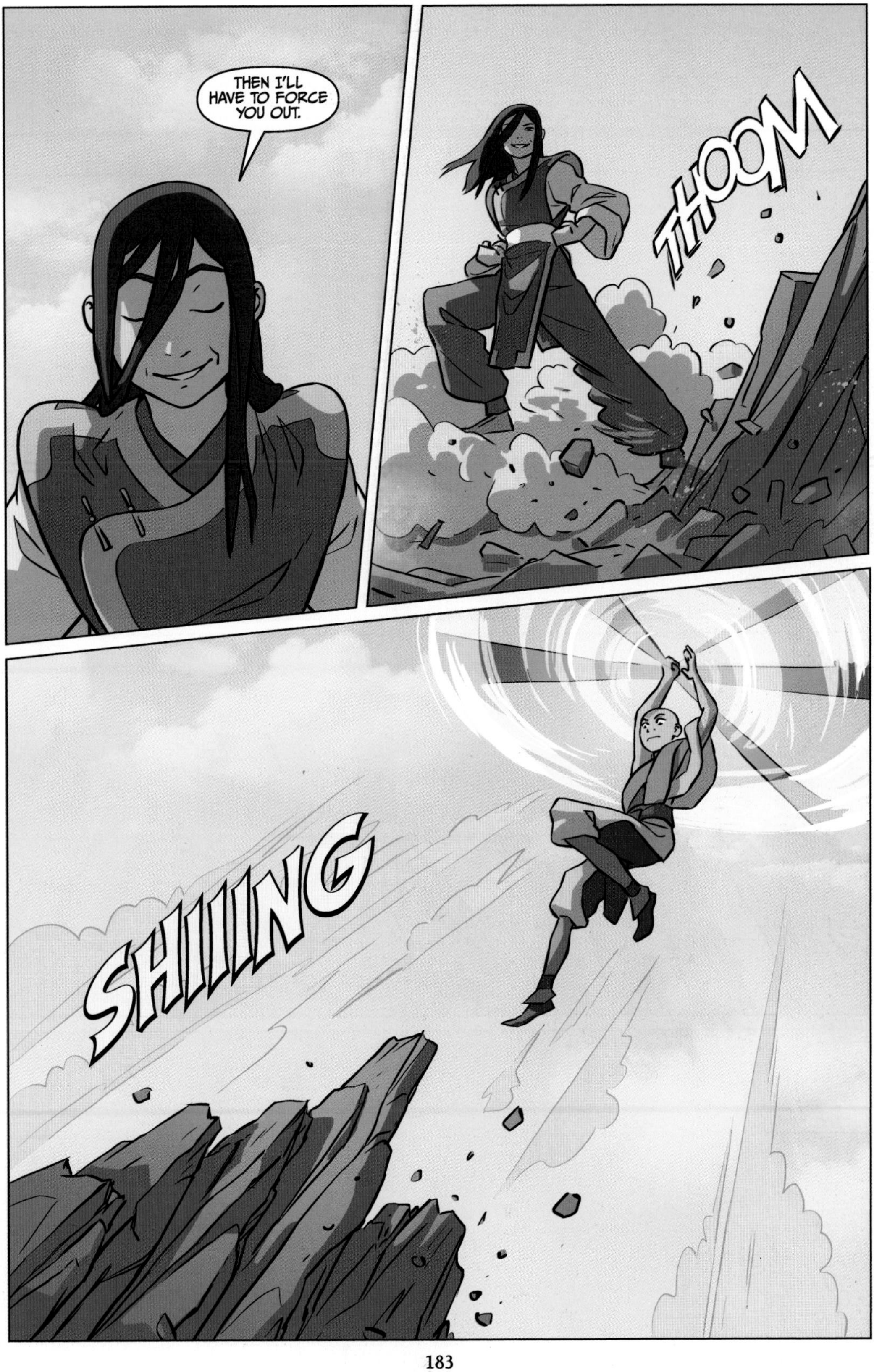
THEN I'LL HAVE TO FORCE YOU OUT.
THOOM
SHIIING

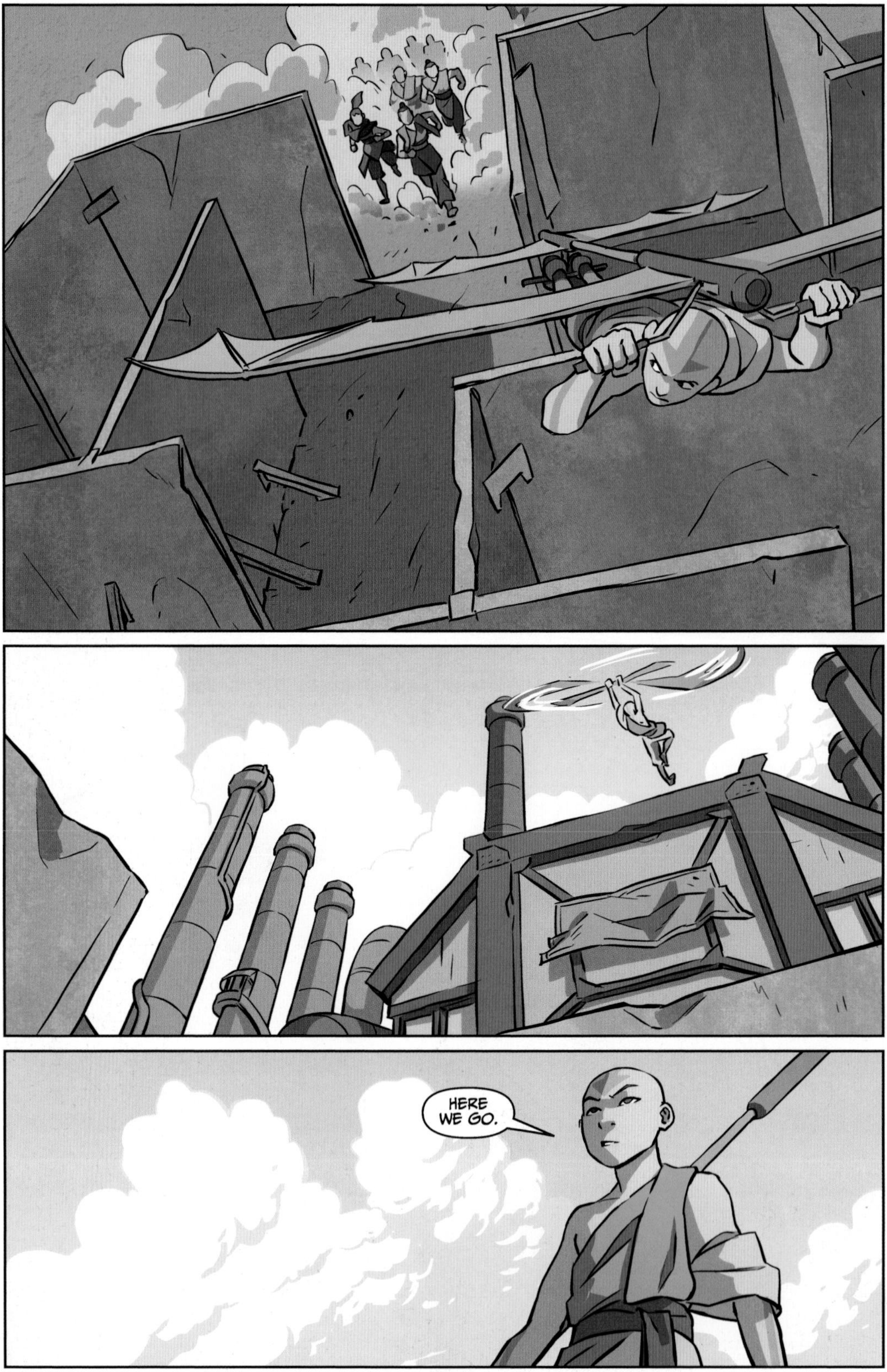
HERE WE GO.

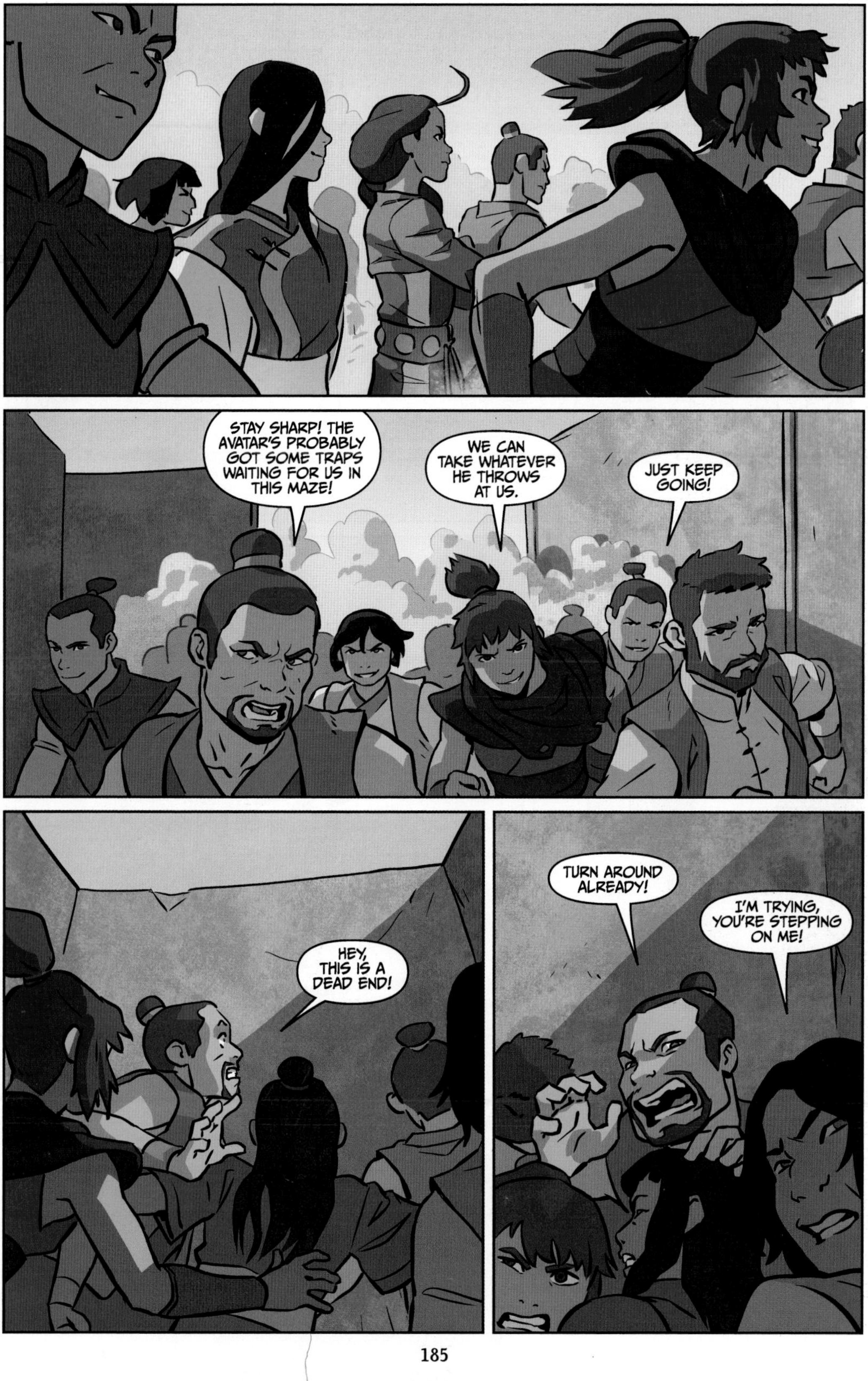
STAY SHARP! THE AVATAR'S PROBABLY GOT SOME TRAPS WAITING FOR US IN THIS MAZE!
WE CAN TAKE WHATEVER HE THROWS AT US.
JUST KEEP GOING!
HEY, THIS IS A DEAD END!
TURN AROUND ALREADY!
I'M TRYING, YOU'RE STEPPING ON ME!

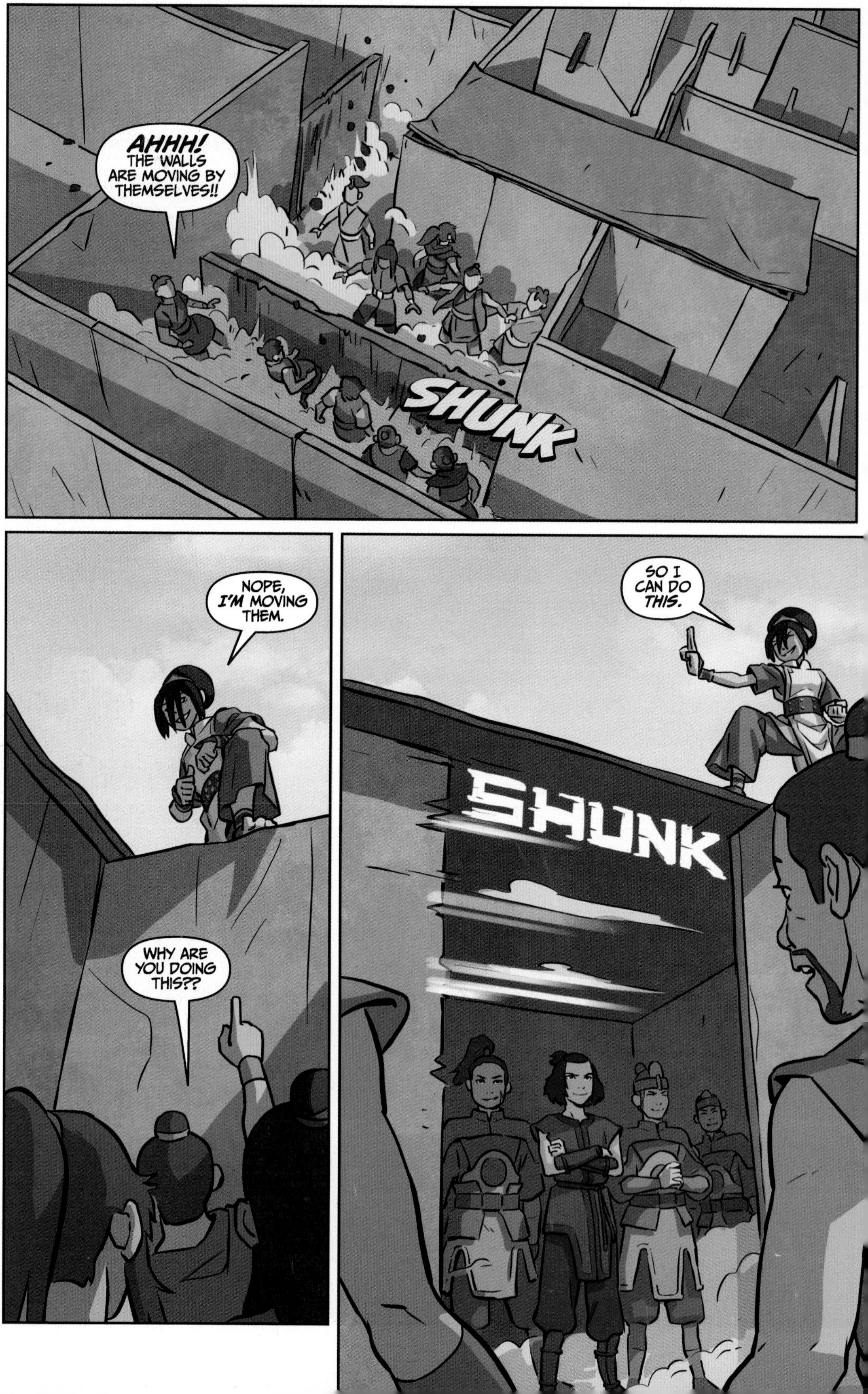
AHHH! THE WALLS ARE MOVING BY THEMSELVES!!
SHUNK
NOPE, I'M MOVING THEM.
WHY ARE YOU DOING THIS??
SO I CAN DO THIS.
SHUNK

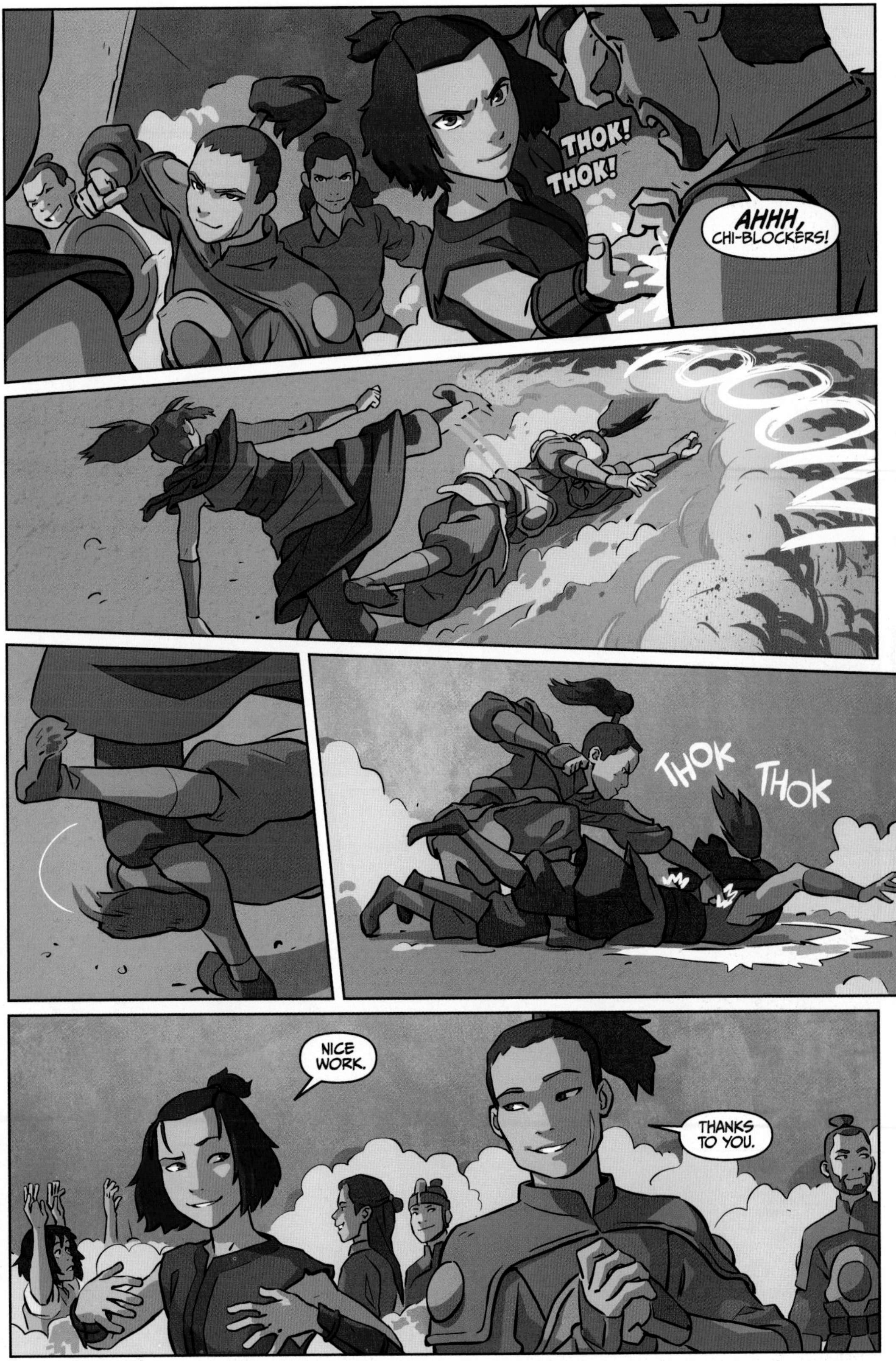
THOK!
THOK!
AHHH, CHI-BLOCKERS!
FOOOOM!
THOK
THOK
NICE WORK.
THANKS TO YOU.

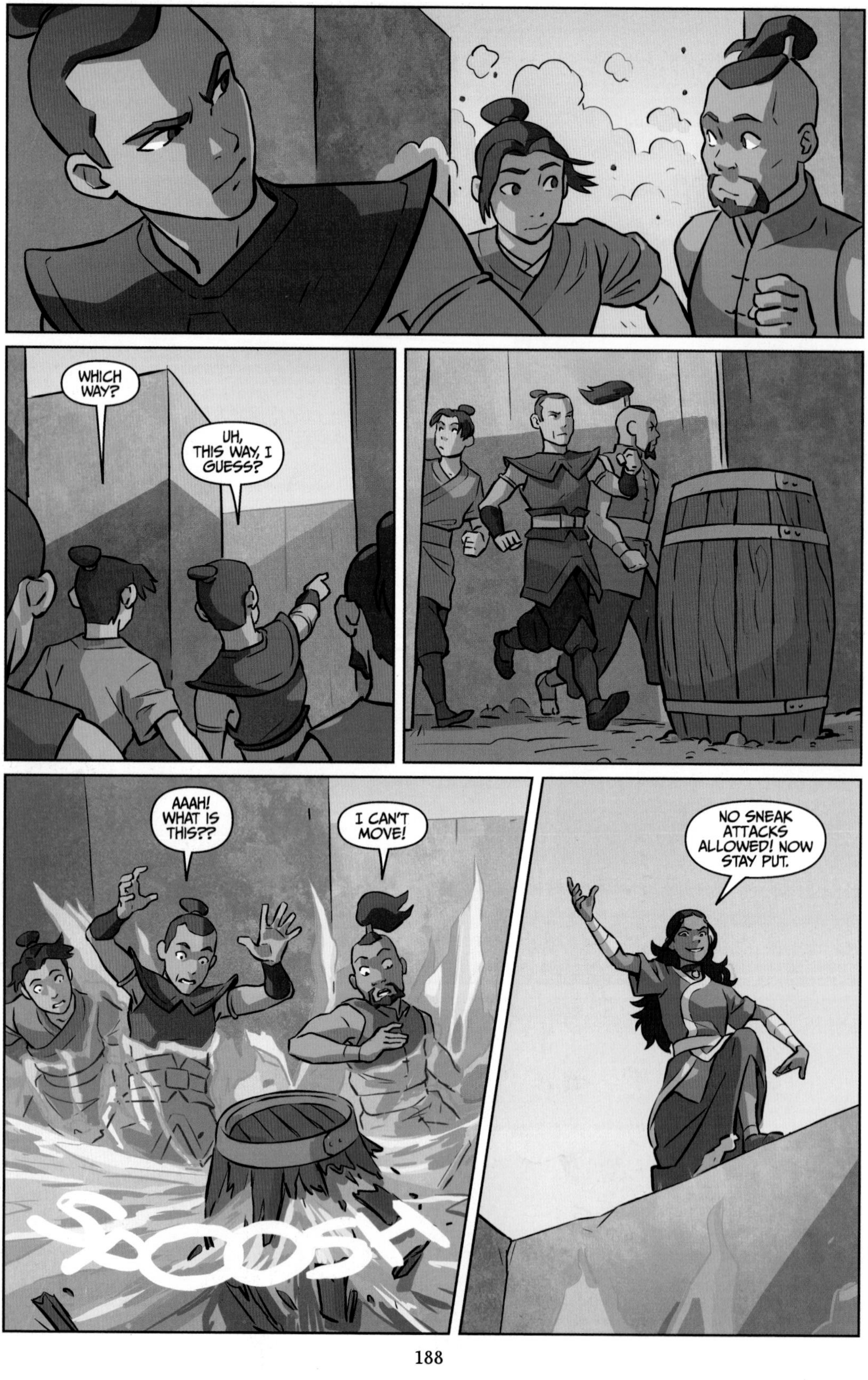
WHICH WAY?
UH, THIS WAY, I GUESS?
AAAH! WHAT IS THIS??
I CAN'T MOVE!
SOOSH
NO SNEAK ATTACKS ALLOWED! NOW STAY PUT.

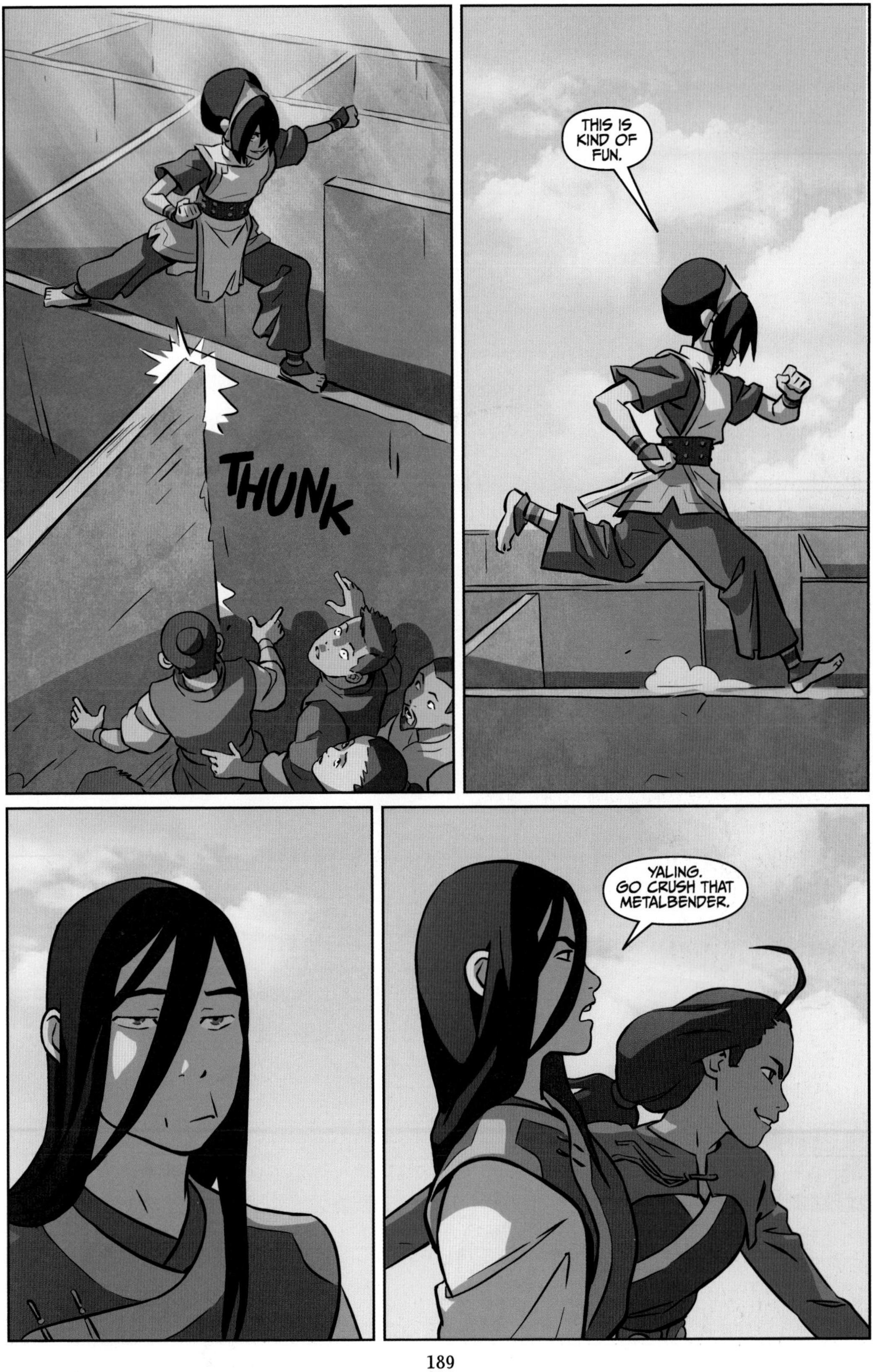
THUNK
THIS IS KIND OF FUN.
YALING. GO CRUSH THAT METALBENDER.

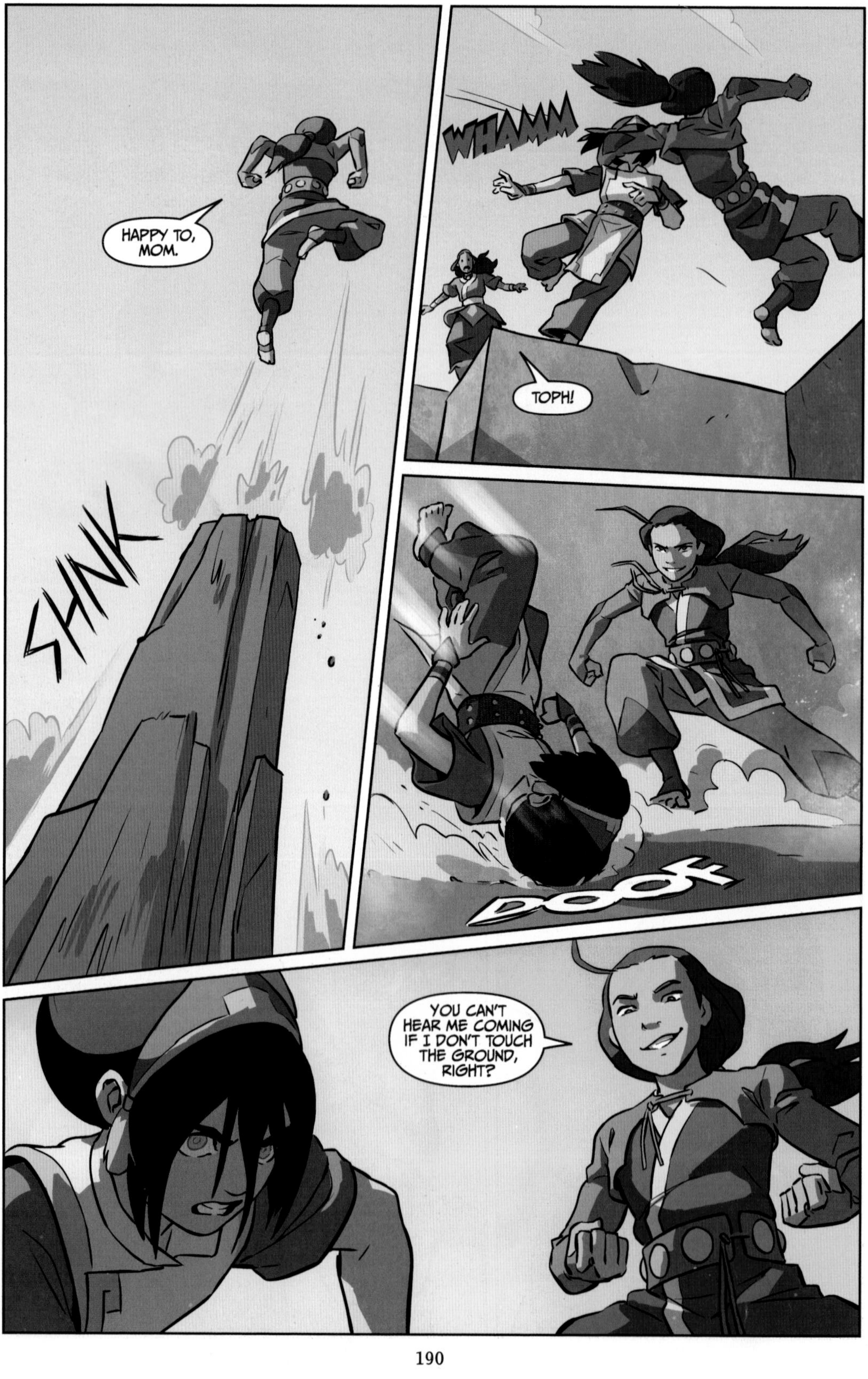
HAPPY TO, MOM.
SHNK
WHAMM
TOPH!
DOOF
YOU CAN'T HEAR ME COMING IF I DON'T TOUCH THE GROUND, RIGHT?

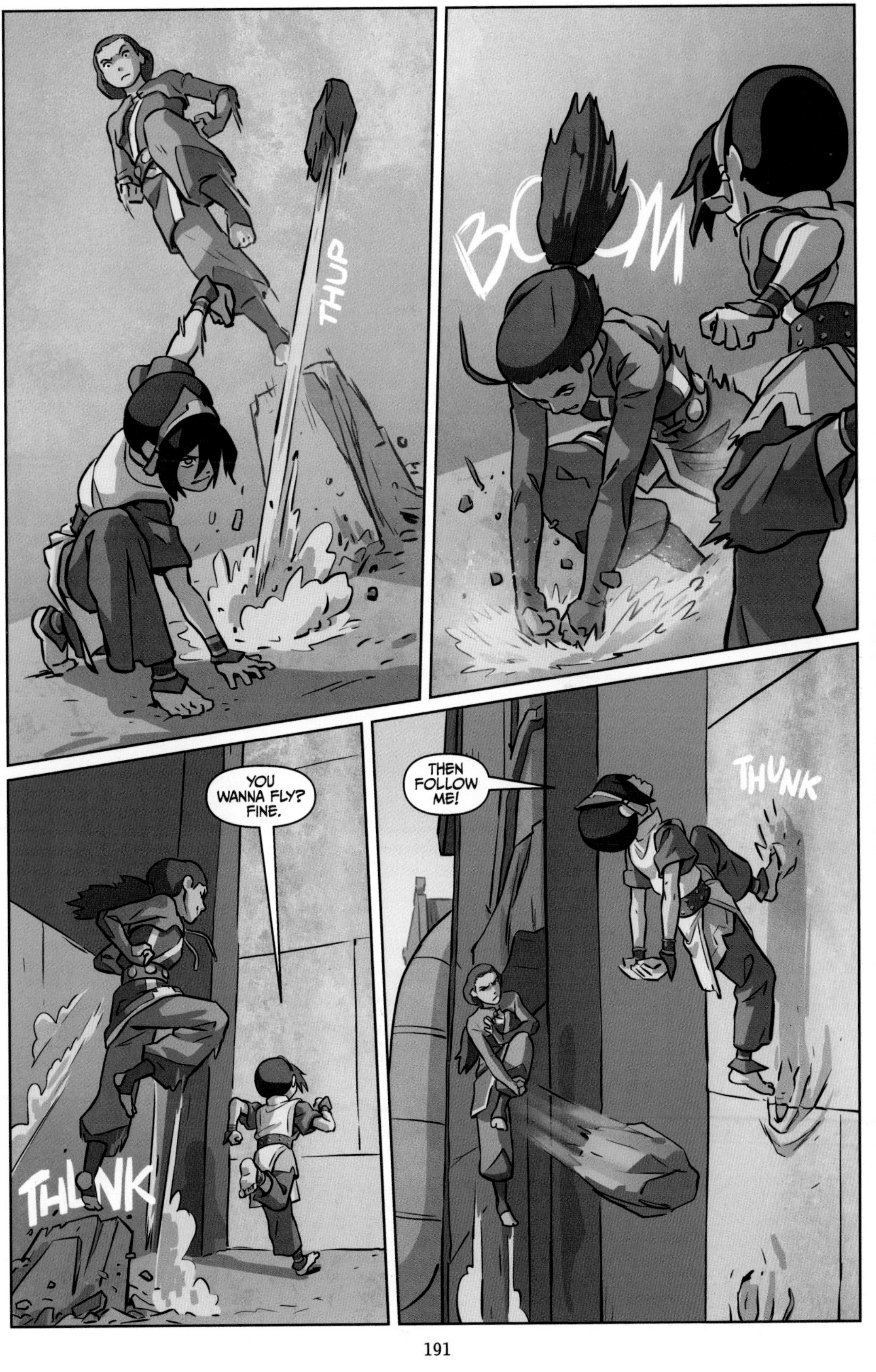
THUP
BOOM
YOU WANNA FLY? FINE.
THUNK
THEN FOLLOW ME!
THUNK

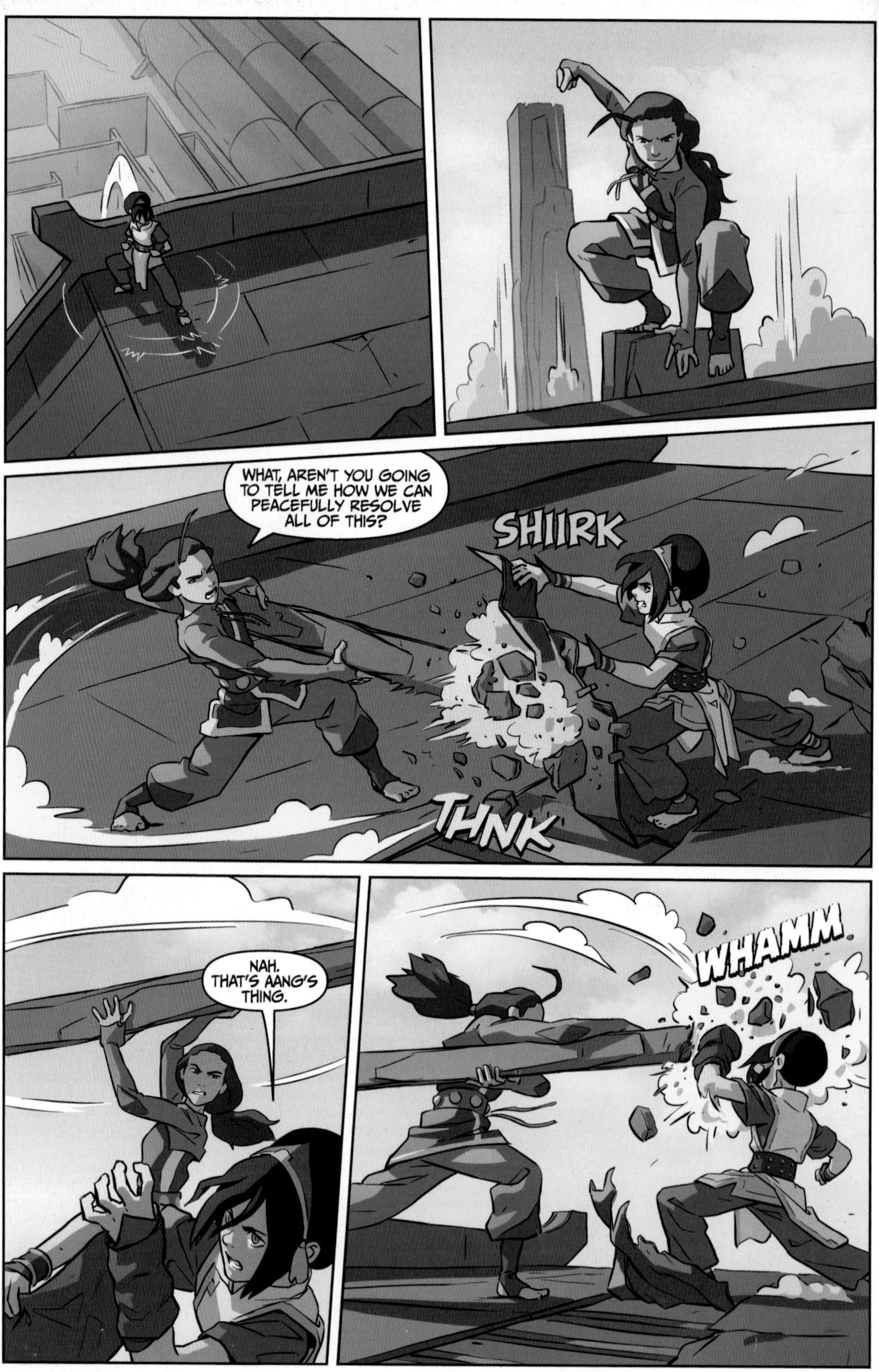
WHAT, AREN'T YOU GOING TO TELL ME HOW WE CAN PEACEFULLY RESOLVE ALL OF THIS?
SHIIRK
THNK
NAH. THAT'S AANG'S THING.
WHAMM

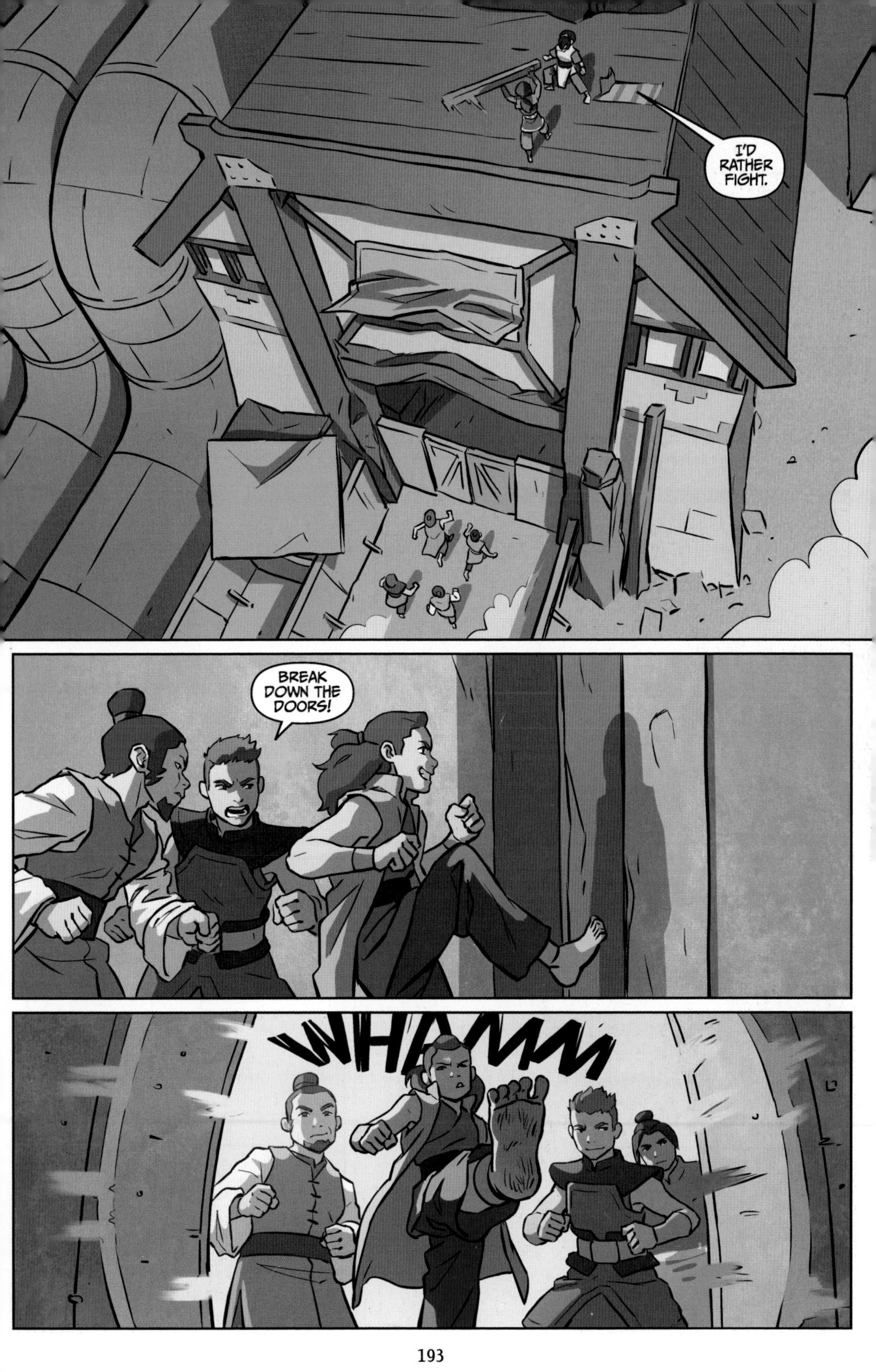
I'D RATHER FIGHT.
BREAK DOWN THE DOORS!
WHAMM

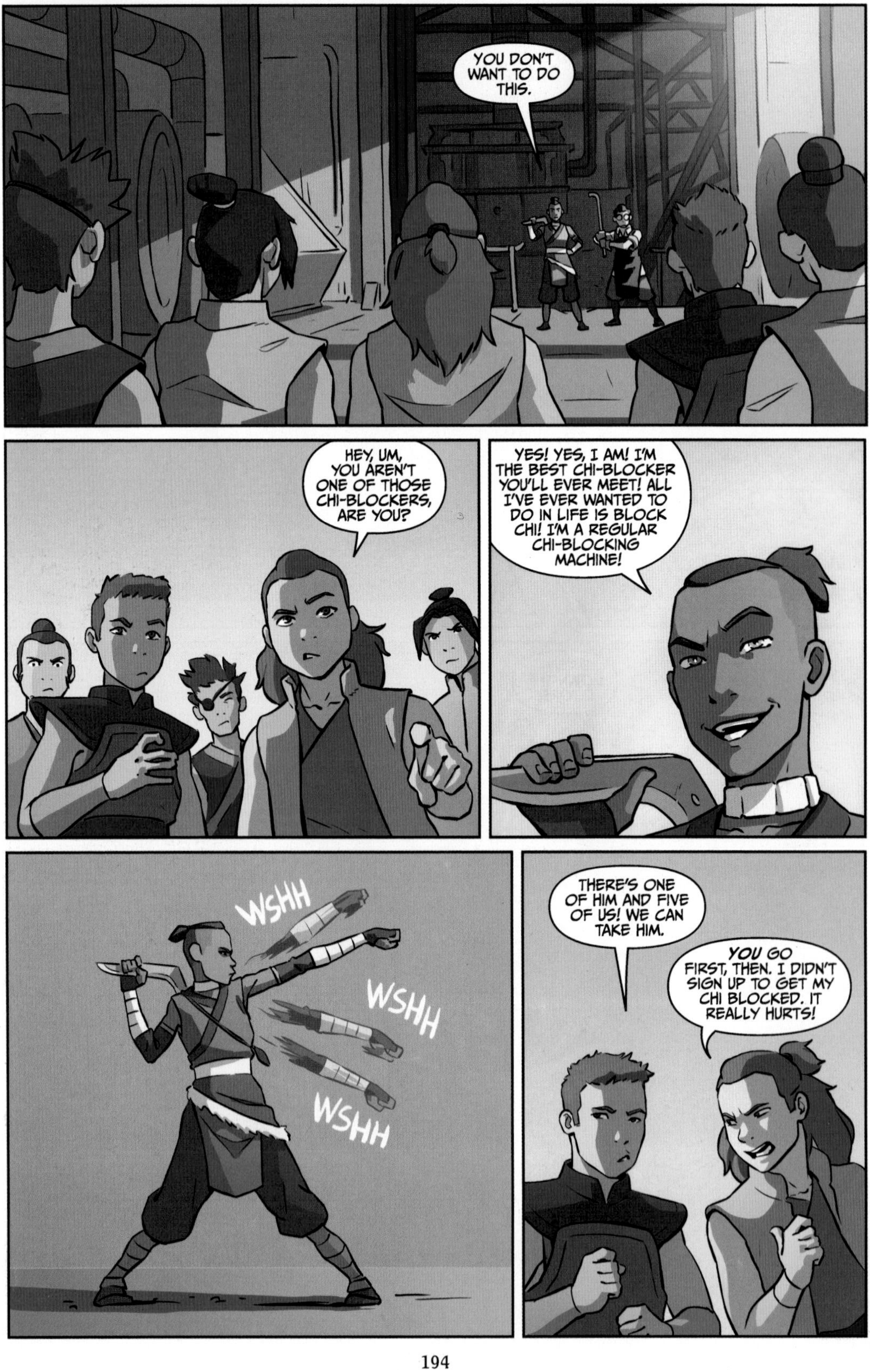
YOU DON'T WANT TO DO THIS.
HEY, UM, YOU AREN'T ONE OF THOSE CHI-BLOCKERS, ARE YOU?
YES! YES, I AM! I'M THE BEST CHI-BLOCKER YOU'LL EVER MEET! ALL I'VE EVER WANTED TO DO IN LIFE IS BLOCK CHI! I'M A REGULAR CHI-BLOCKING MACHINE!
WSHH
WSHH
WSHH
THERE'S ONE OF HIM AND FIVE OF US! WE CAN TAKE HIM.
YOU GO FIRST, THEN. I DIDN'T SIGN UP TO GET MY CHI BLOCKED. IT REALLY HURTS!

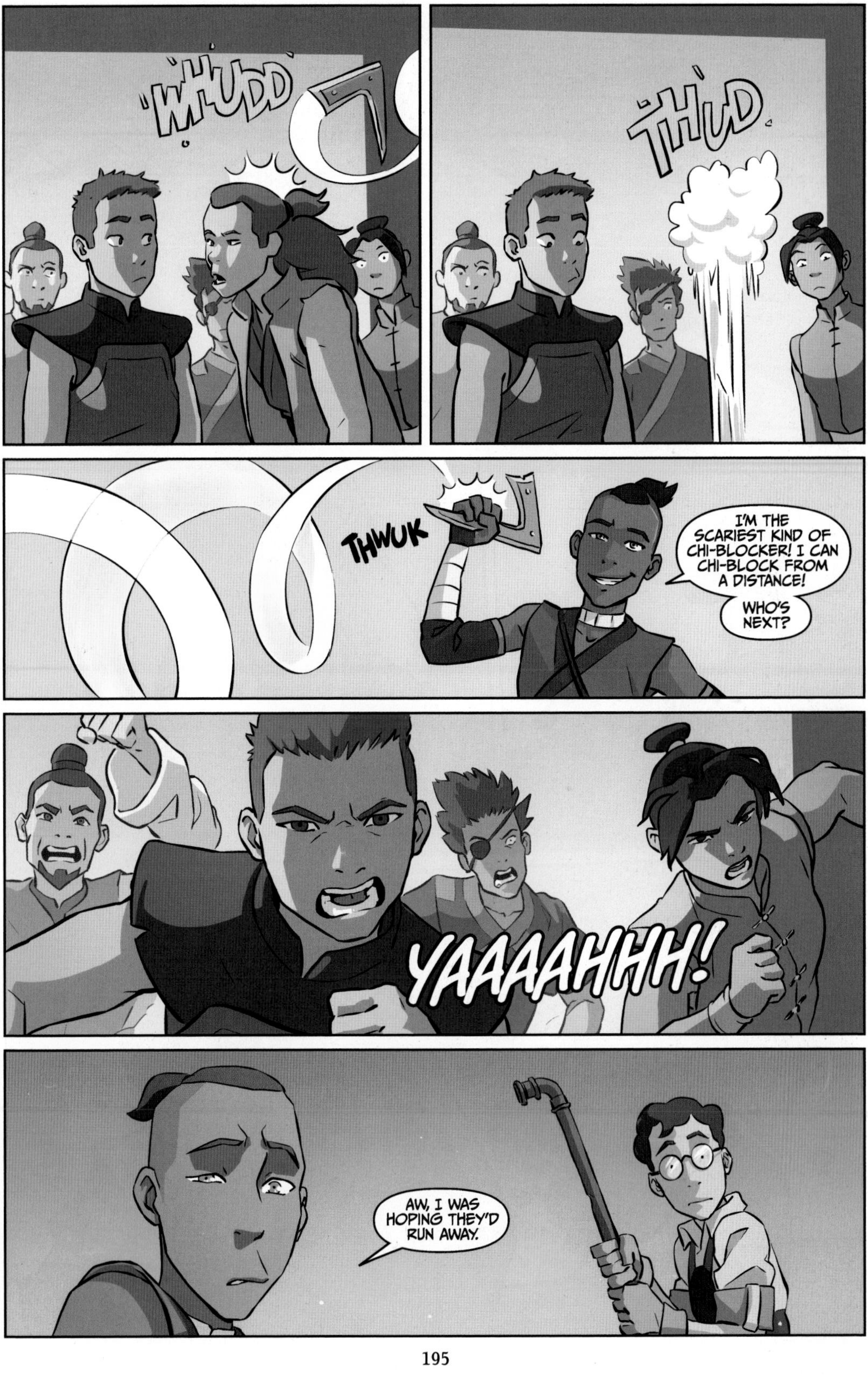
WHUDD
THUD
THWUK
I'M THE SCARIEST KIND OF CHI-BLOCKER! I CAN CHI-BLOCK FROM A DISTANCE!
WHO'S NEXT?
YAAAAHHH!
AW, I WAS HOPING THEY'D RUN AWAY.

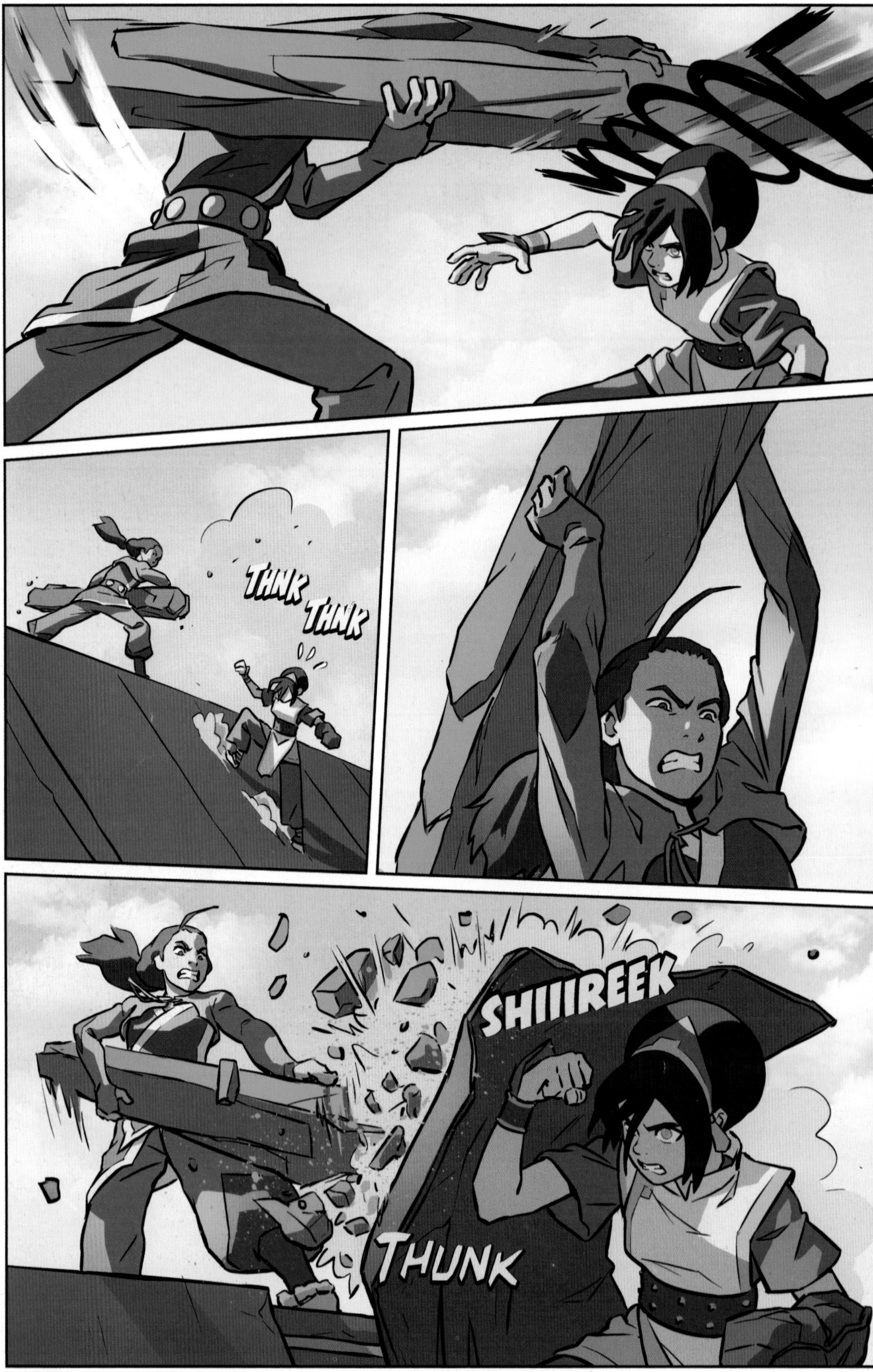
THNK
THNK
SHIIIREEK
THUNK

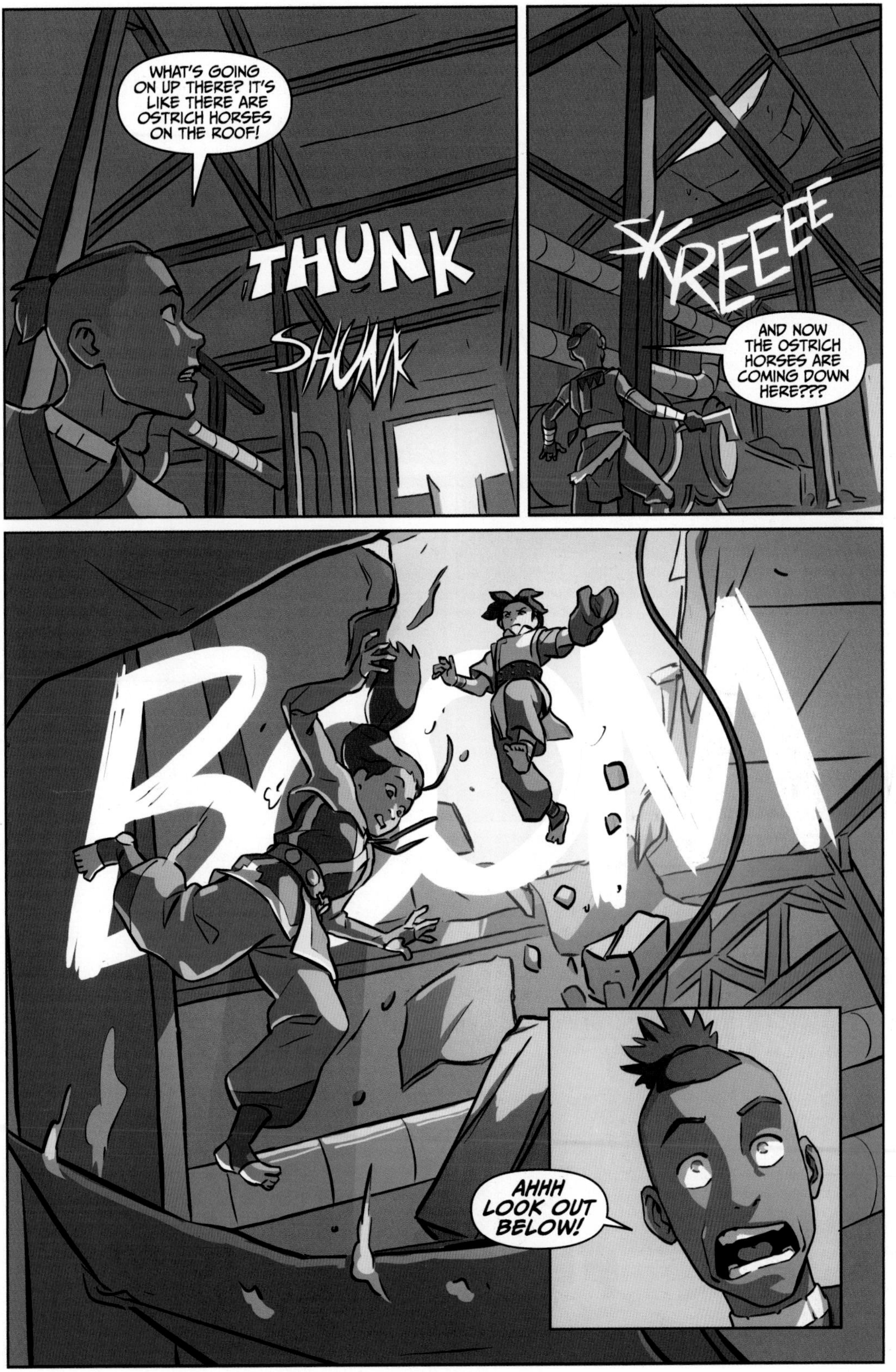
WHAT'S GOING ON UP THERE? IT'S LIKE THERE ARE OSTRICH HORSES ON THE ROOF!
THUNK
SHUNK
SKREEEE
AND NOW THE OSTRICH HORSES ARE COMING DOWN HERE???
BOOM
AHHH LOOK OUT BELOW!

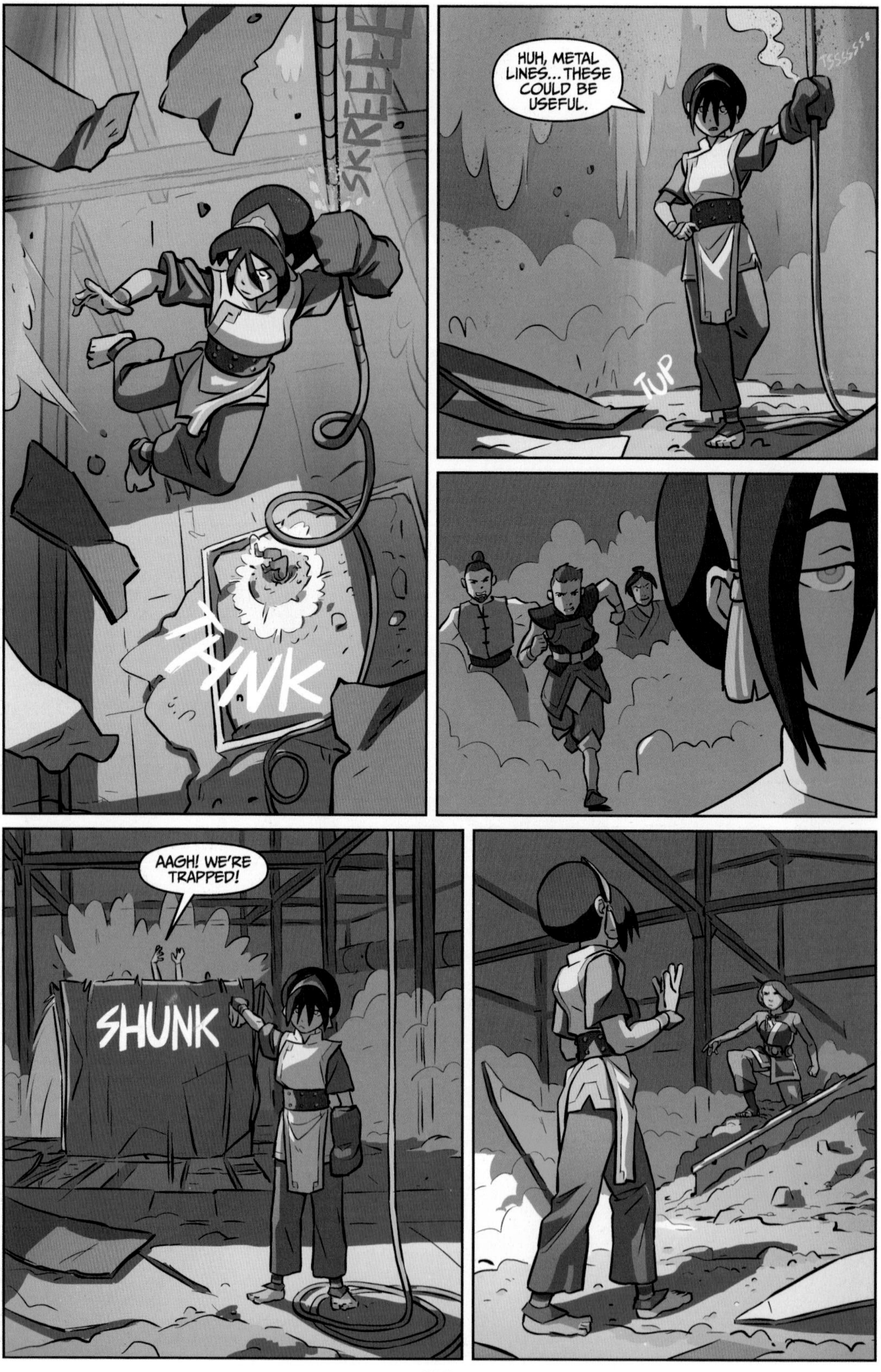
SKREEEE
HUH, METAL LINES... THESE COULD BE USEFUL.
TSSSSSSS
TUP
TANK
AAGH! WE'RE TRAPPED!
SHUNK

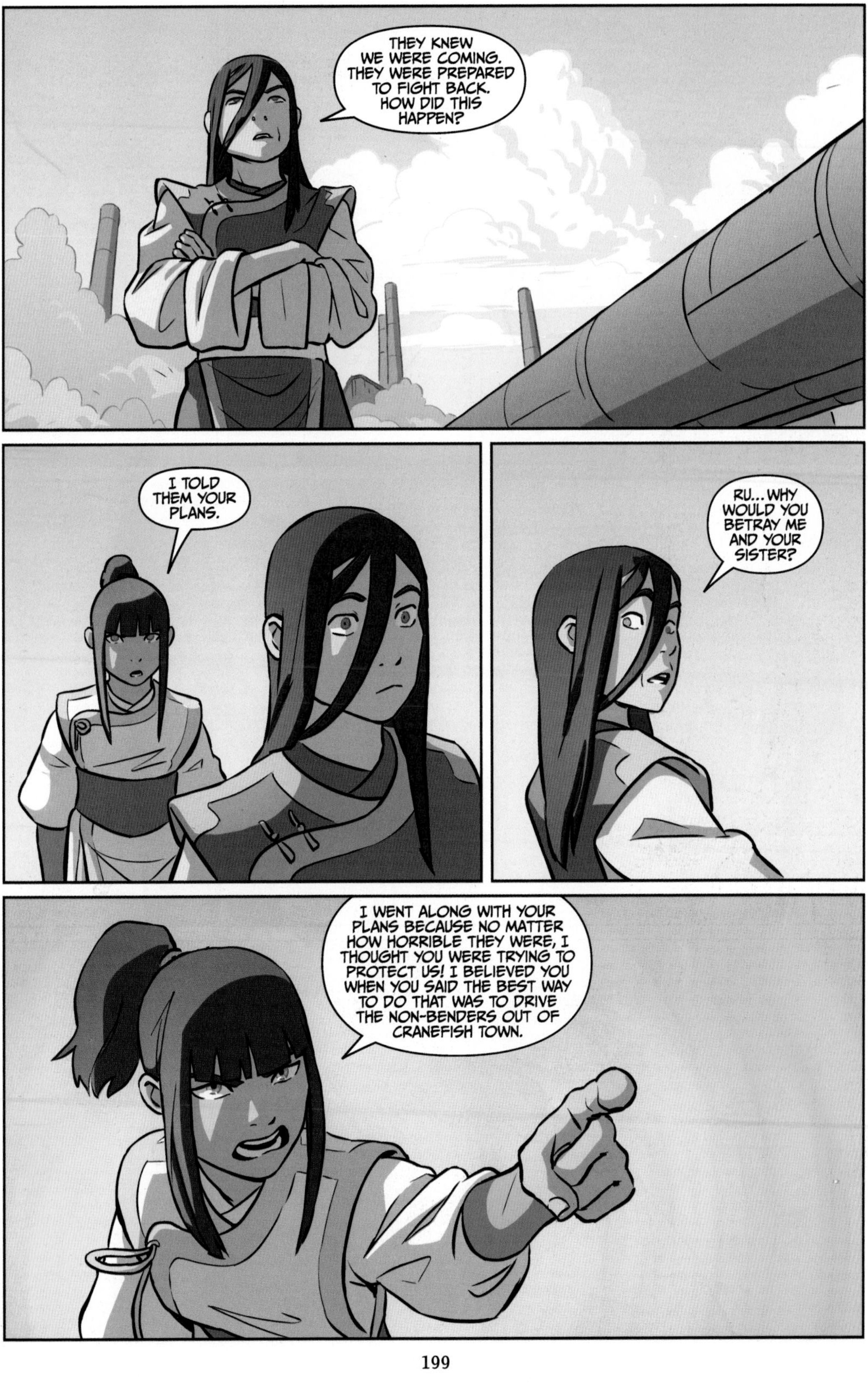
THEY KNEW WE WERE COMING. THEY WERE PREPARED TO FIGHT BACK. HOW DID THIS HAPPEN?
I TOLD THEM YOUR PLANS.
RU... WHY WOULD YOU BETRAY ME AND YOUR SISTER?
I WENT ALONG WITH YOUR PLANS BECAUSE NO MATTER HOW HORRIBLE THEY WERE, I THOUGHT YOU WERE TRYING TO PROTECT US! I BELIEVED YOU WHEN YOU SAID THE BEST WAY TO DO THAT WAS TO DRIVE THE NON-BENDERS OUT OF CRANEFISH TOWN.

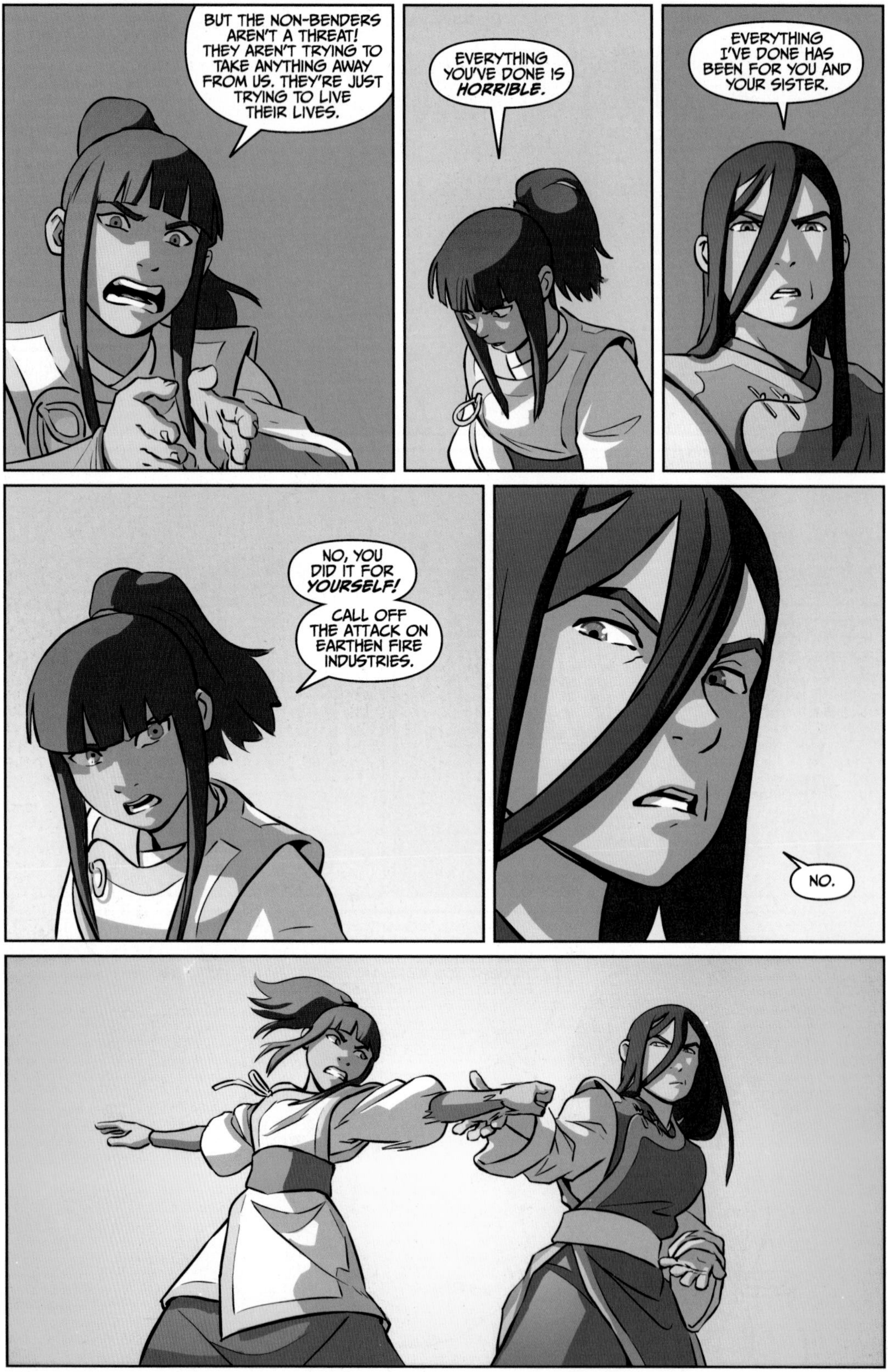
BUT THE NON-BENDERS AREN'T A THREAT! THEY AREN'T TRYING TO TAKE ANYTHING AWAY FROM US. THEY'RE JUST TRYING TO LIVE THEIR LIVES.
EVERYTHING YOU'VE DONE IS HORRIBLE.
EVERYTHING I'VE DONE HAS BEEN FOR YOU AND YOUR SISTER.
NO, YOU DID IT FOR YOURSELF!
CALL OFF THE ATTACK ON EARTHEN FIRE INDUSTRIES.
NO.

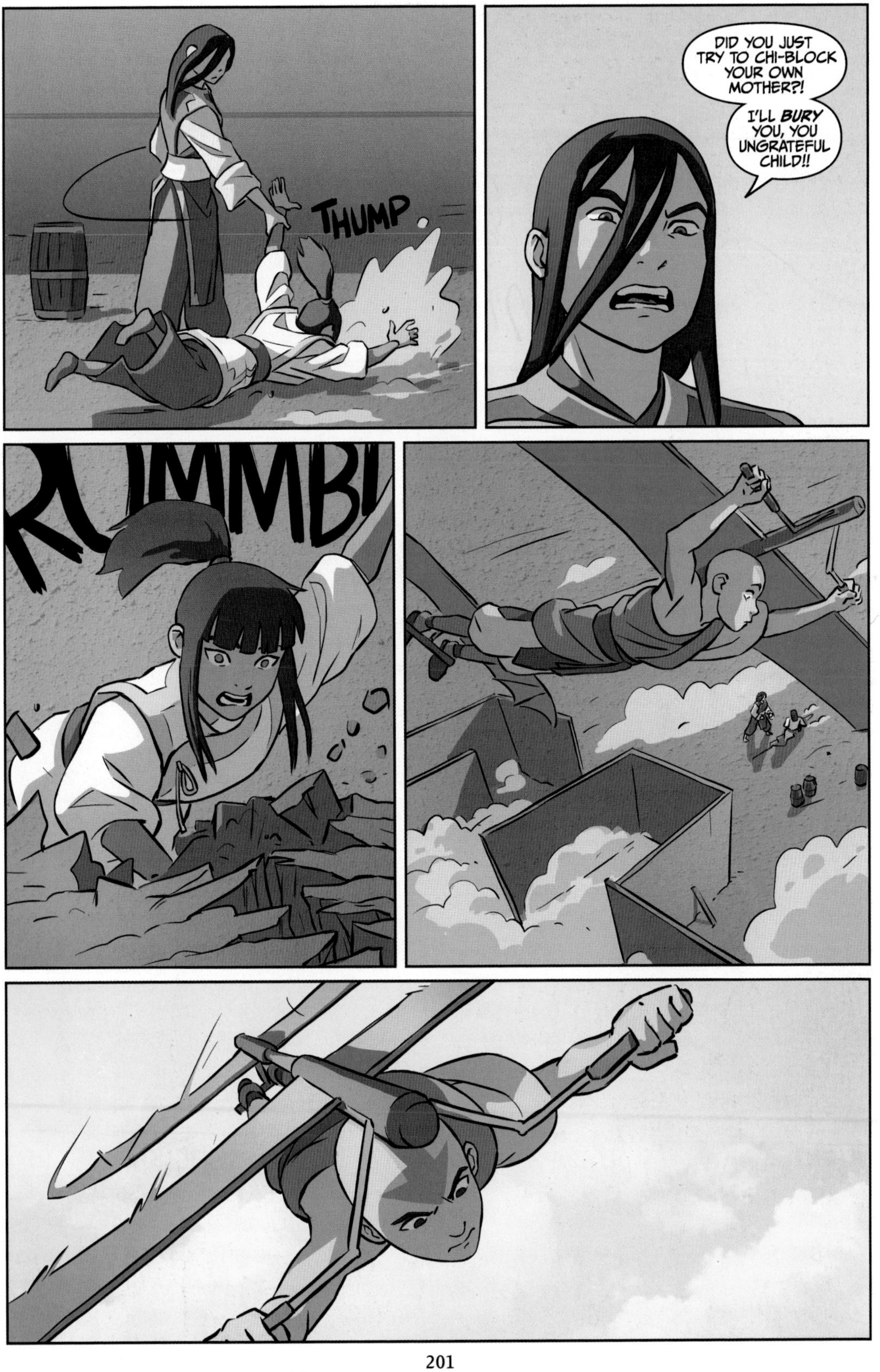
THUMP
DID YOU JUST TRY TO CHI-BLOCK YOUR OWN MOTHER?!
I'LL BURY YOU, YOU UNGRATEFUL CHILD!!
RUMMBL

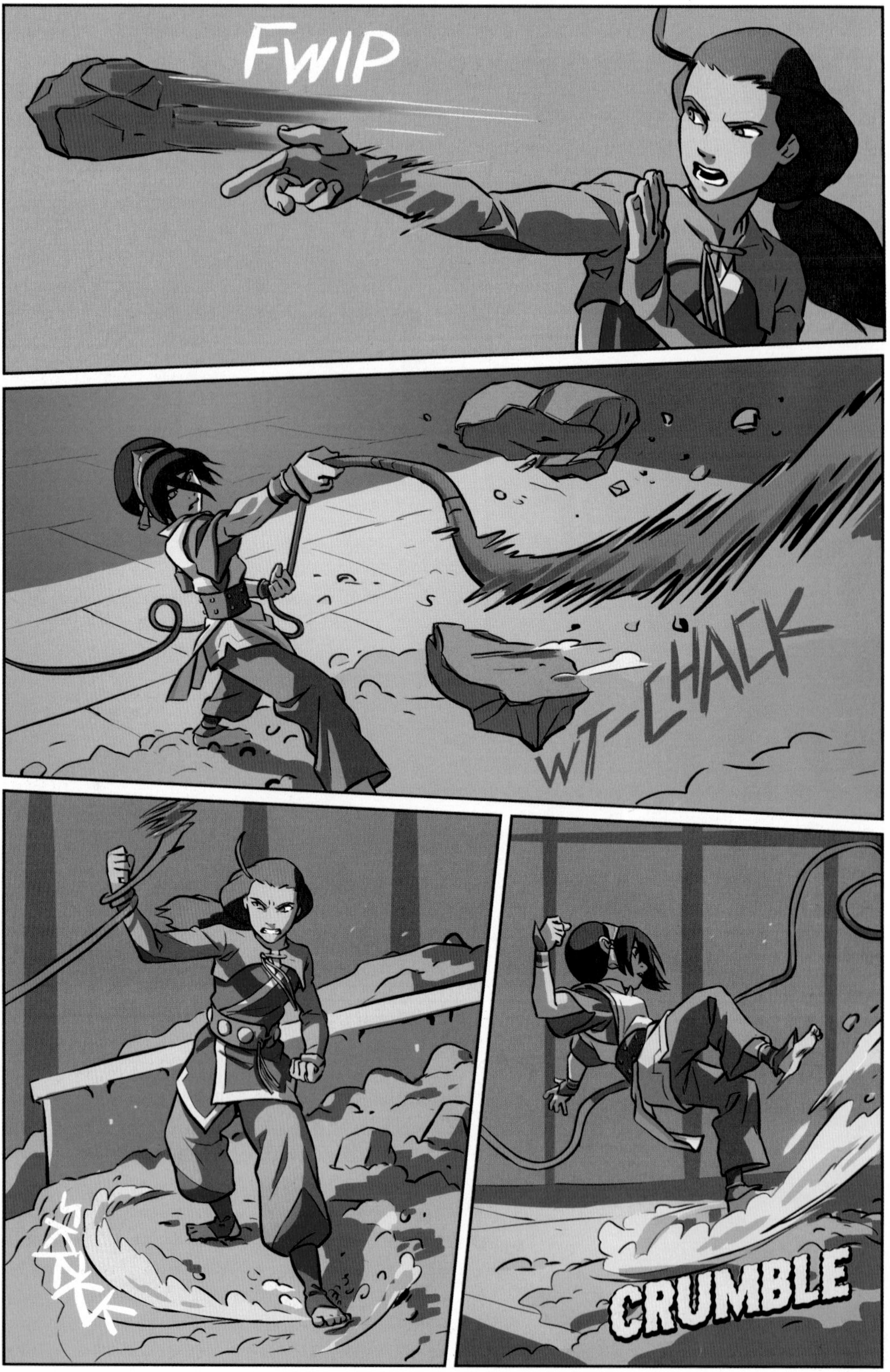
FWIP
WT-CHACK
CRUMBLE

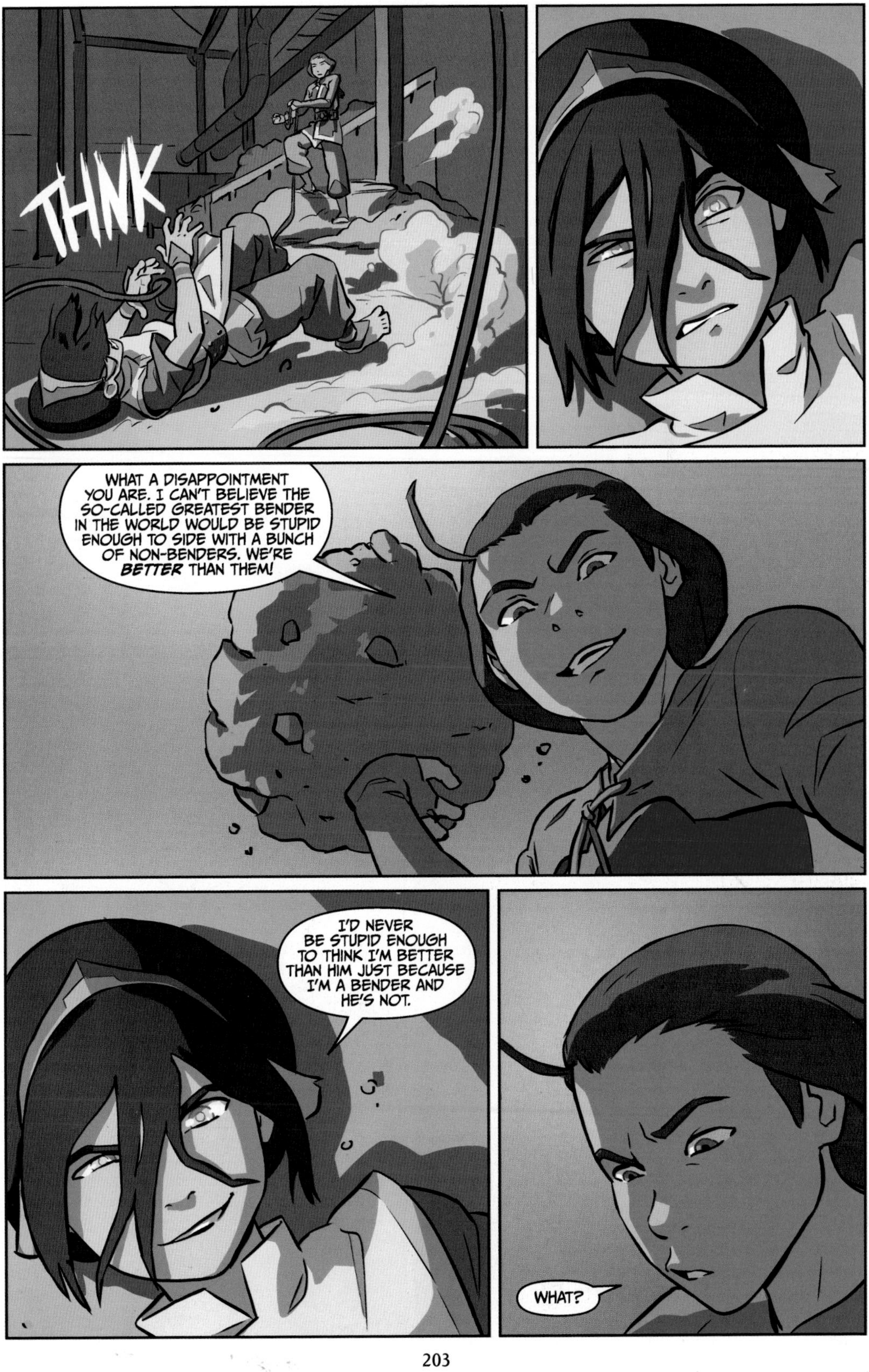
THNK
WHAT A DISAPPOINTMENT YOU ARE. I CAN'T BELIEVE THE SO-CALLED GREATEST BENDER IN THE WORLD WOULD BE STUPID ENOUGH TO SIDE WITH A BUNCH OF NON-BENDERS. WE'RE *BETTER* THAN THEM!
I'D NEVER BE STUPID ENOUGH TO THINK I'M BETTER THAN HIM JUST BECAUSE I'M A BENDER AND HE'S NOT.
WHAT?

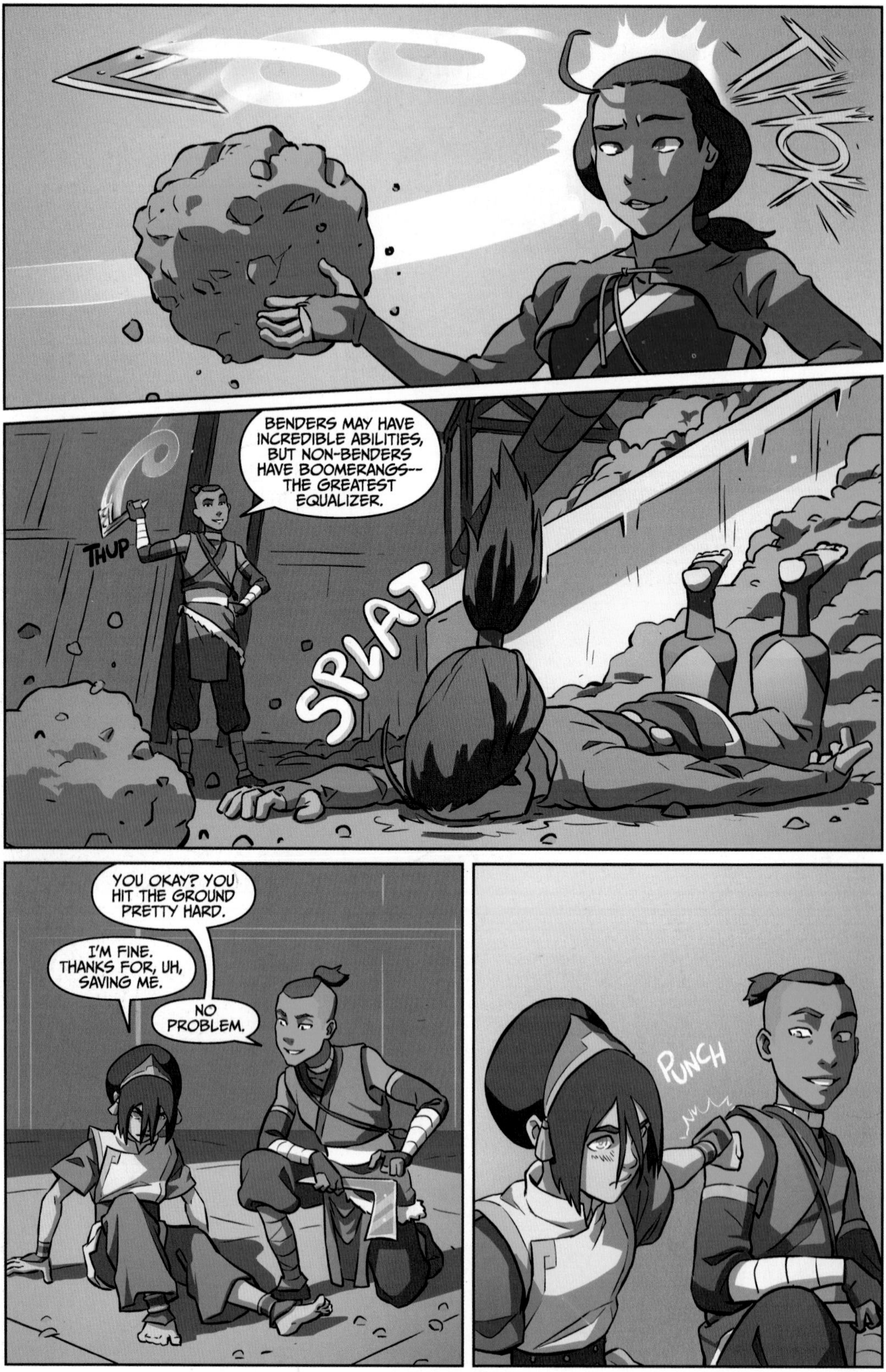
THOK
BENDERS MAY HAVE INCREDIBLE ABILITIES, BUT NON-BENDERS HAVE BOOMERANGS-- THE GREATEST EQUALIZER.
THUP
SPLAT
YOU OKAY? YOU HIT THE GROUND PRETTY HARD.
I'M FINE. THANKS FOR, UH, SAVING ME.
NO PROBLEM.
PUNCH

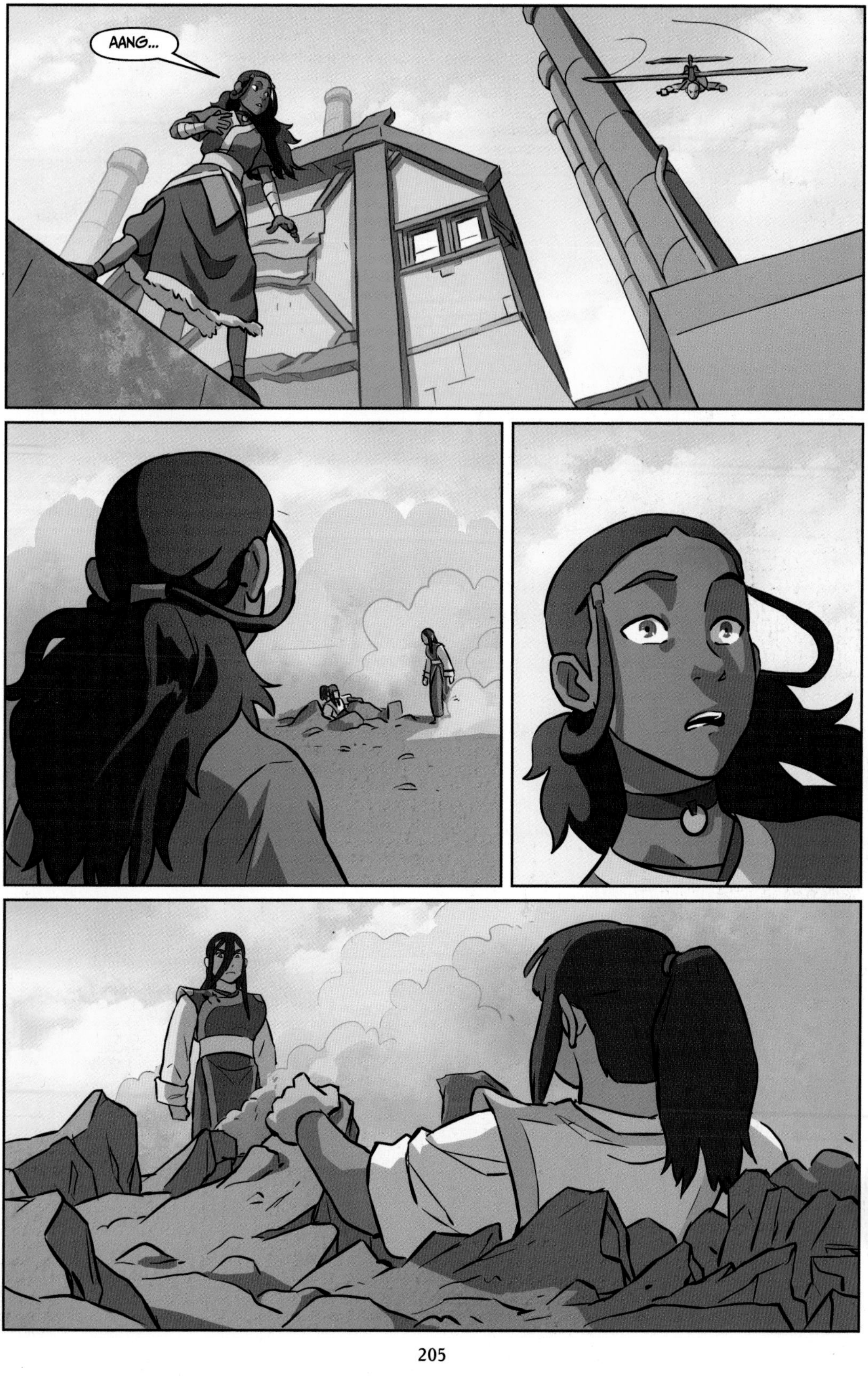
AANG...

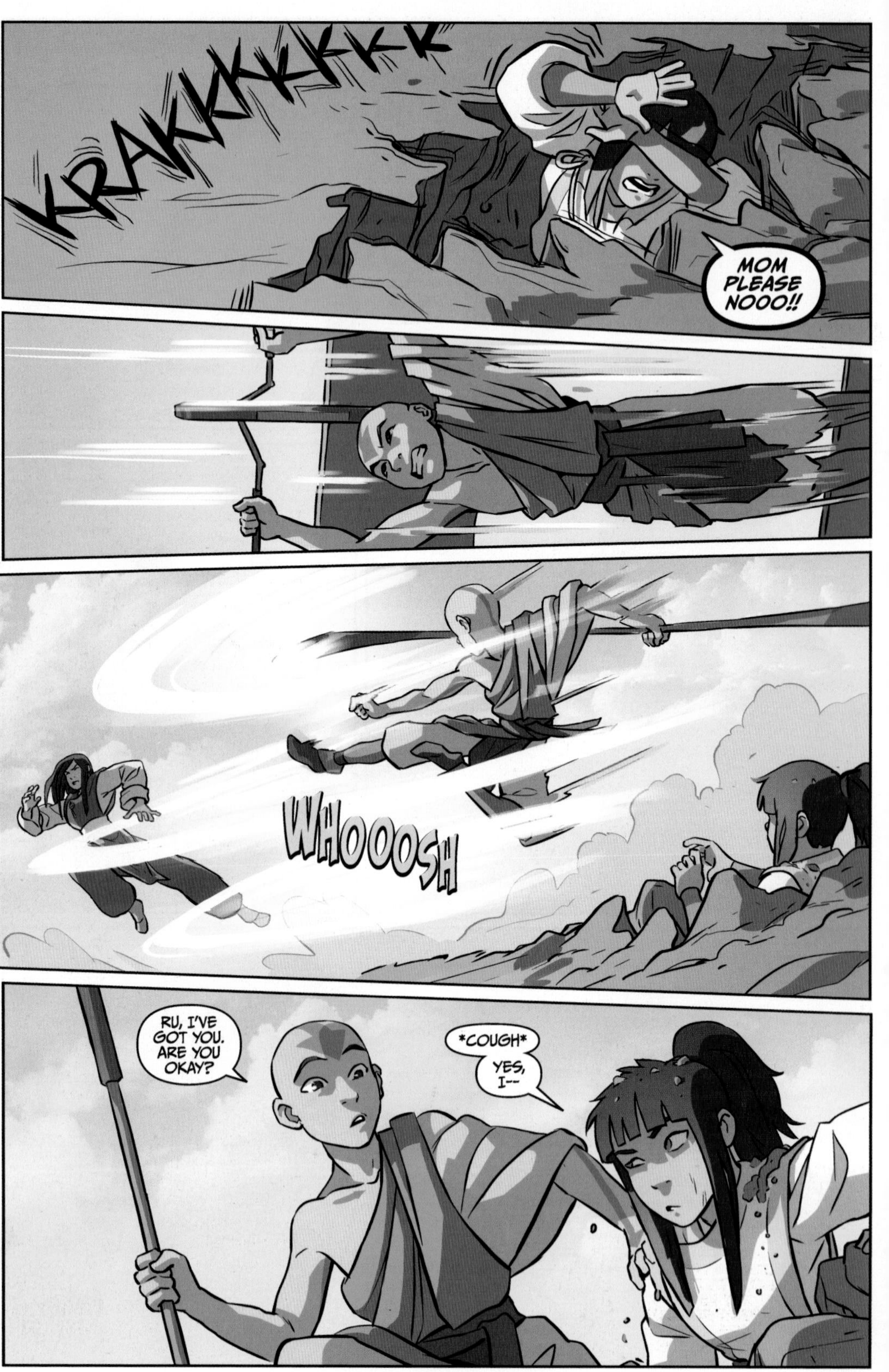
KRAKKKKKKK
MOM PLEASE NOOO!!
WHOOOSH
RU, I'VE GOT YOU. ARE YOU OKAY?
COUGH YES, I--

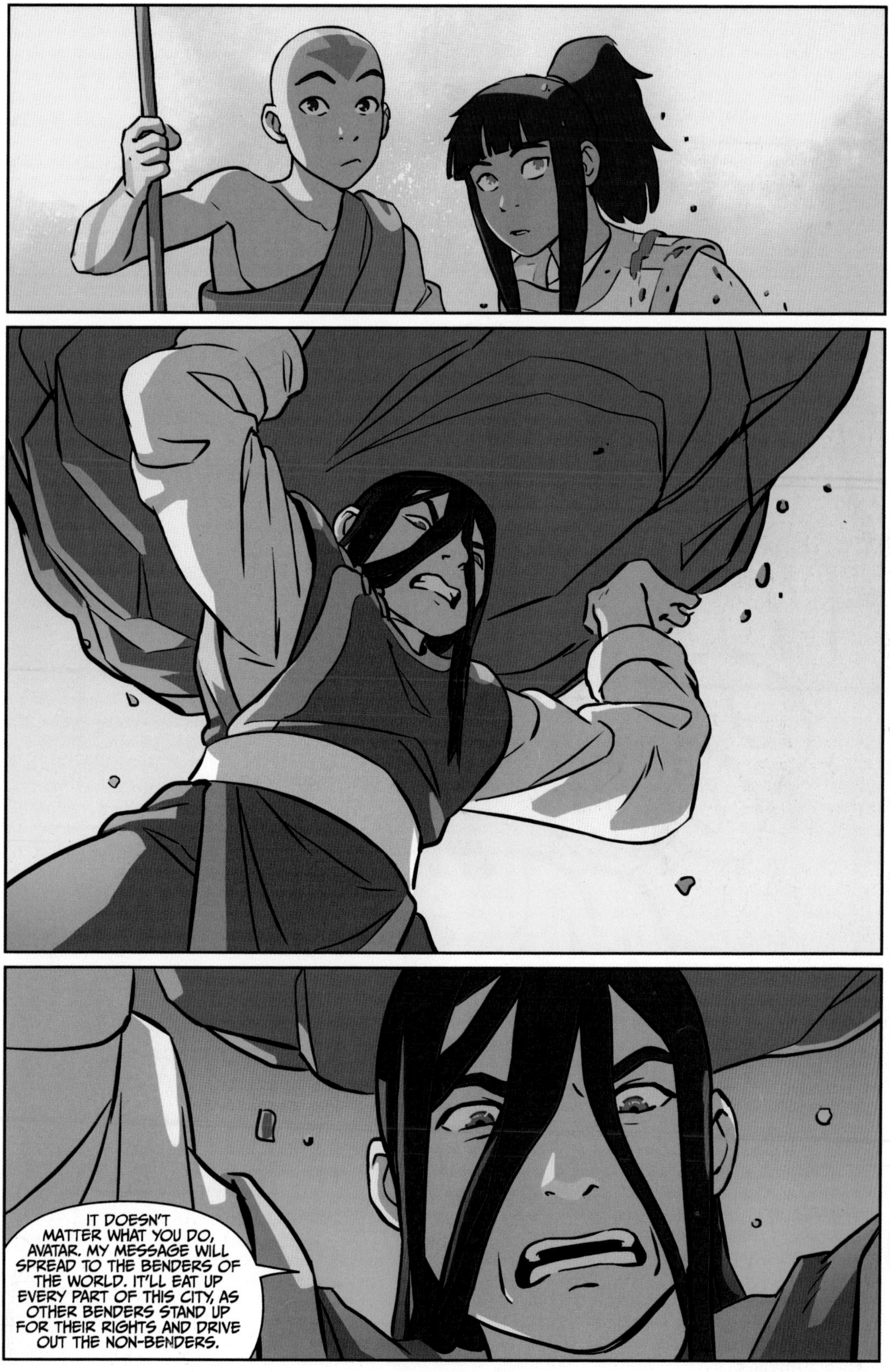
IT DOESN'T MATTER WHAT YOU DO, AVATAR. MY MESSAGE WILL SPREAD TO THE BENDERS OF THE WORLD. IT'LL EAT UP EVERY PART OF THIS CITY, AS OTHER BENDERS STAND UP FOR THEIR RIGHTS AND DRIVE OUT THE NON-BENDERS.

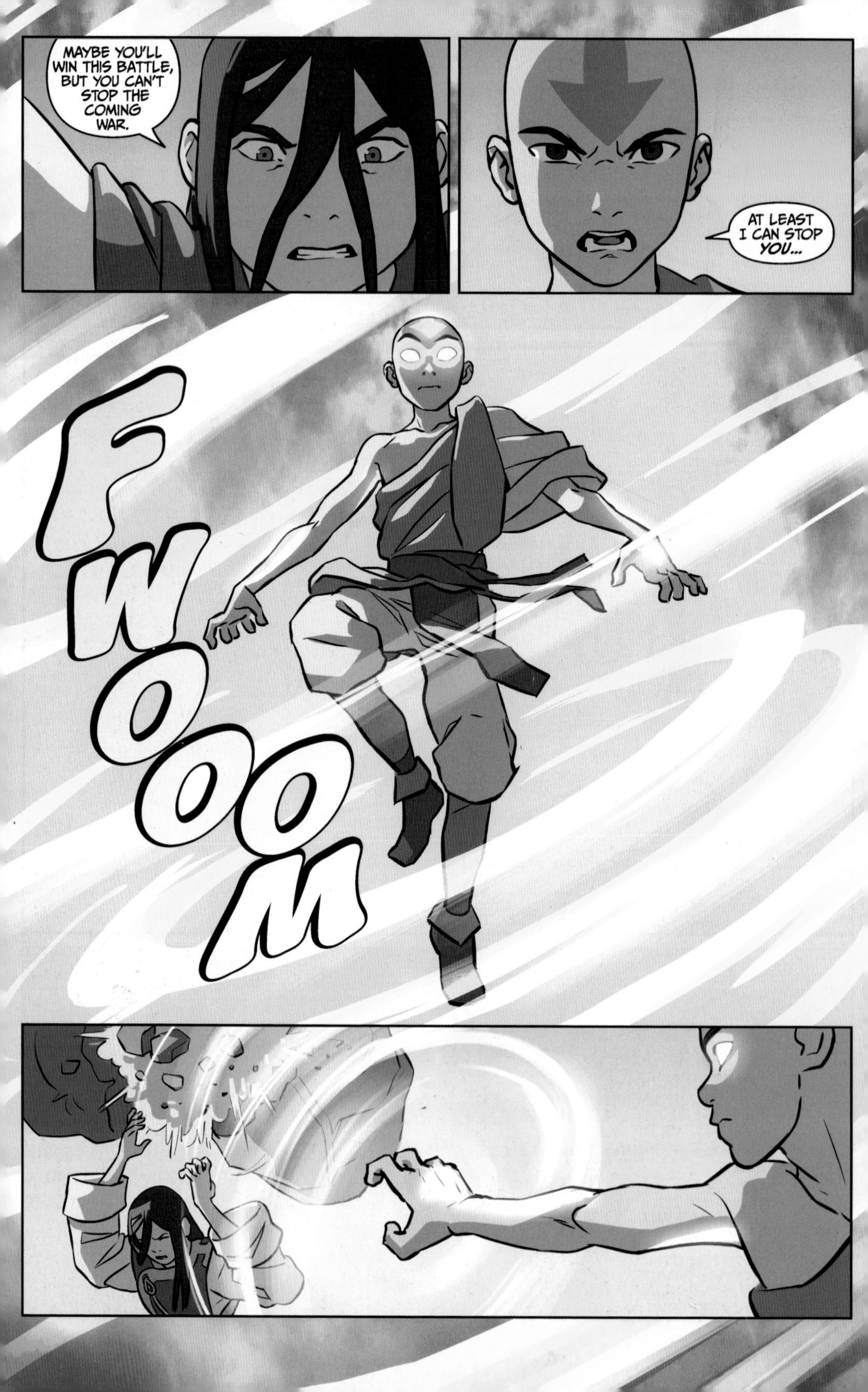
MAYBE YOU'LL WIN THIS BATTLE, BUT YOU CAN'T STOP THE COMING WAR.
AT LEAST I CAN STOP YOU...
FWOOOM

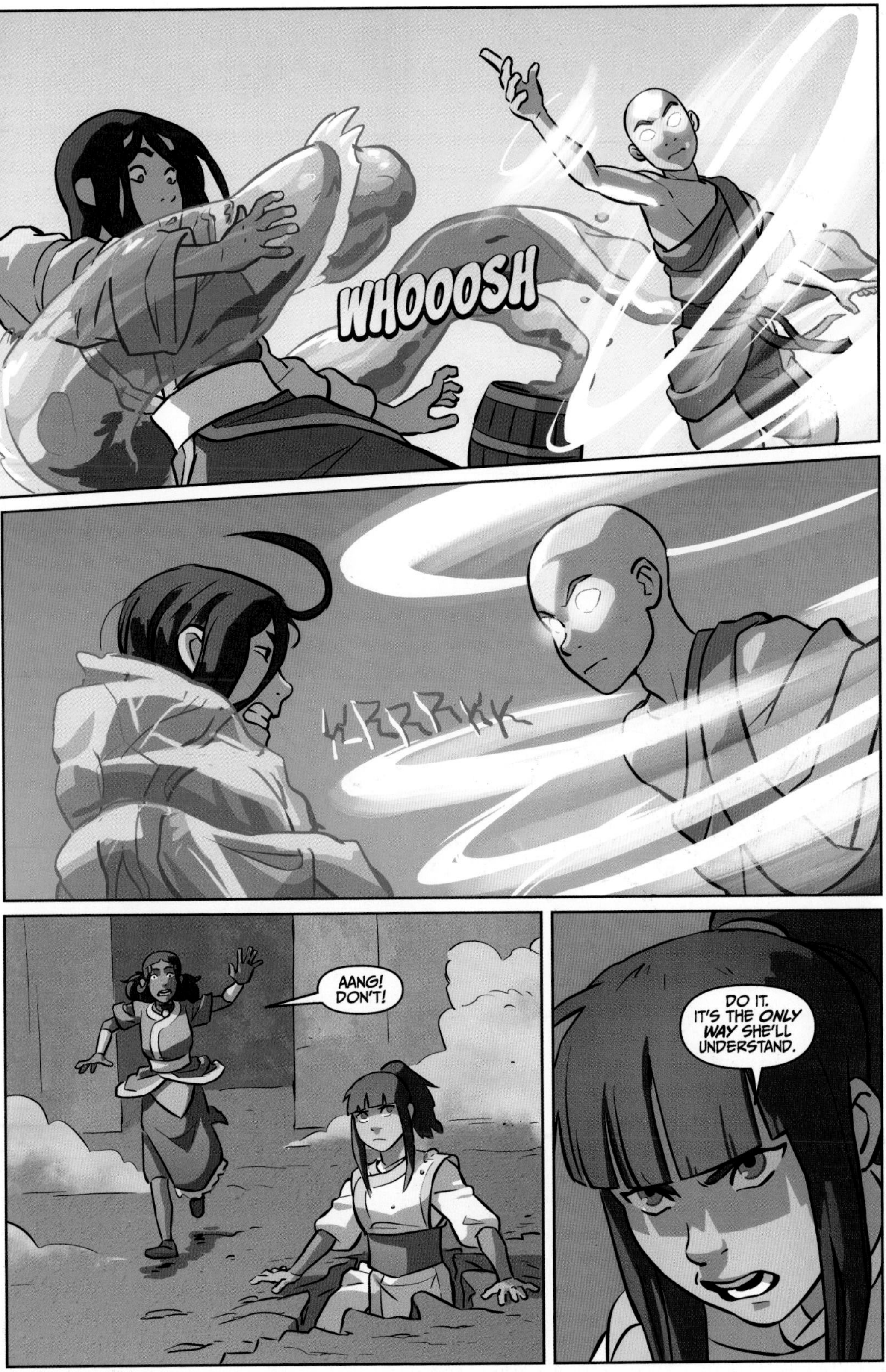
WHOOOSH
KRRRKK
AANG! DON'T!
DO IT. IT'S THE *ONLY WAY* SHE'LL UNDERSTAND.

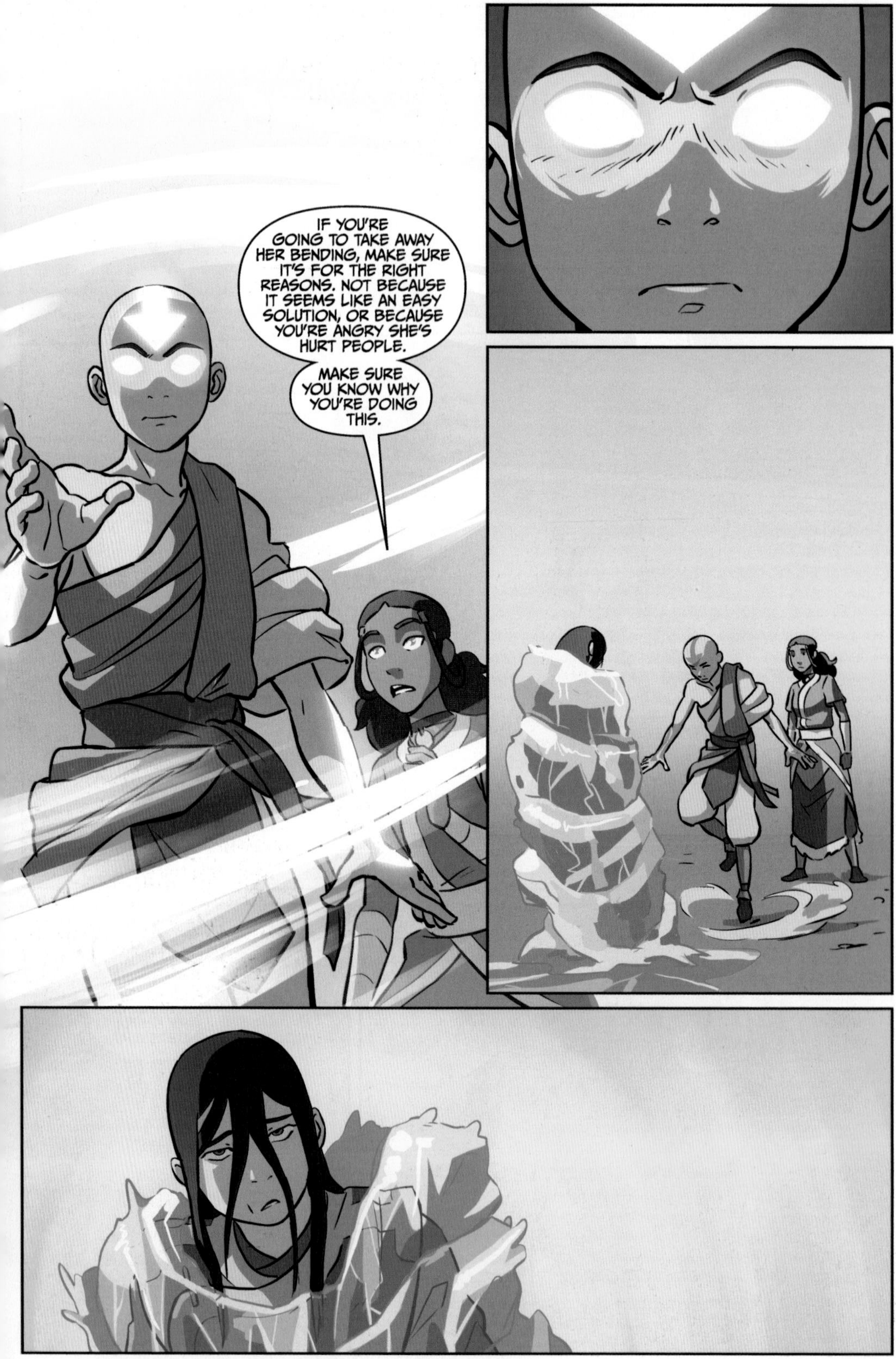
IF YOU'RE GOING TO TAKE AWAY HER BENDING, MAKE SURE IT'S FOR THE RIGHT REASONS. NOT BECAUSE IT SEEMS LIKE AN EASY SOLUTION, OR BECAUSE YOU'RE ANGRY SHE'S HURT PEOPLE.
MAKE SURE YOU KNOW WHY YOU'RE DOING THIS.

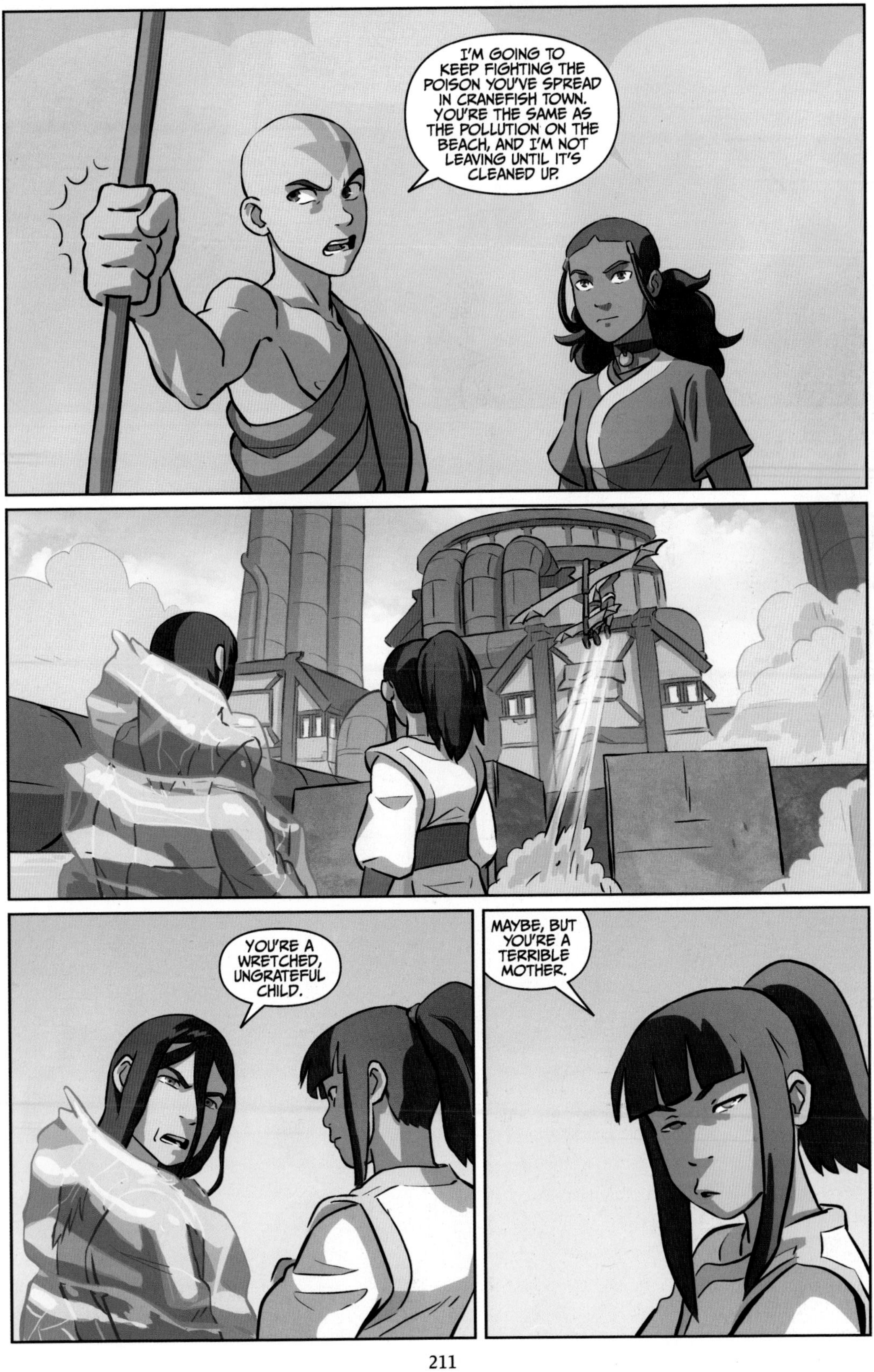
I'M GOING TO KEEP FIGHTING THE POISON YOU'VE SPREAD IN CRANEFISH TOWN. YOU'RE THE SAME AS THE POLLUTION ON THE BEACH, AND I'M NOT LEAVING UNTIL IT'S CLEANED UP.
YOU'RE A WRETCHED, UNGRATEFUL CHILD.
MAYBE, BUT YOU'RE A TERRIBLE MOTHER.

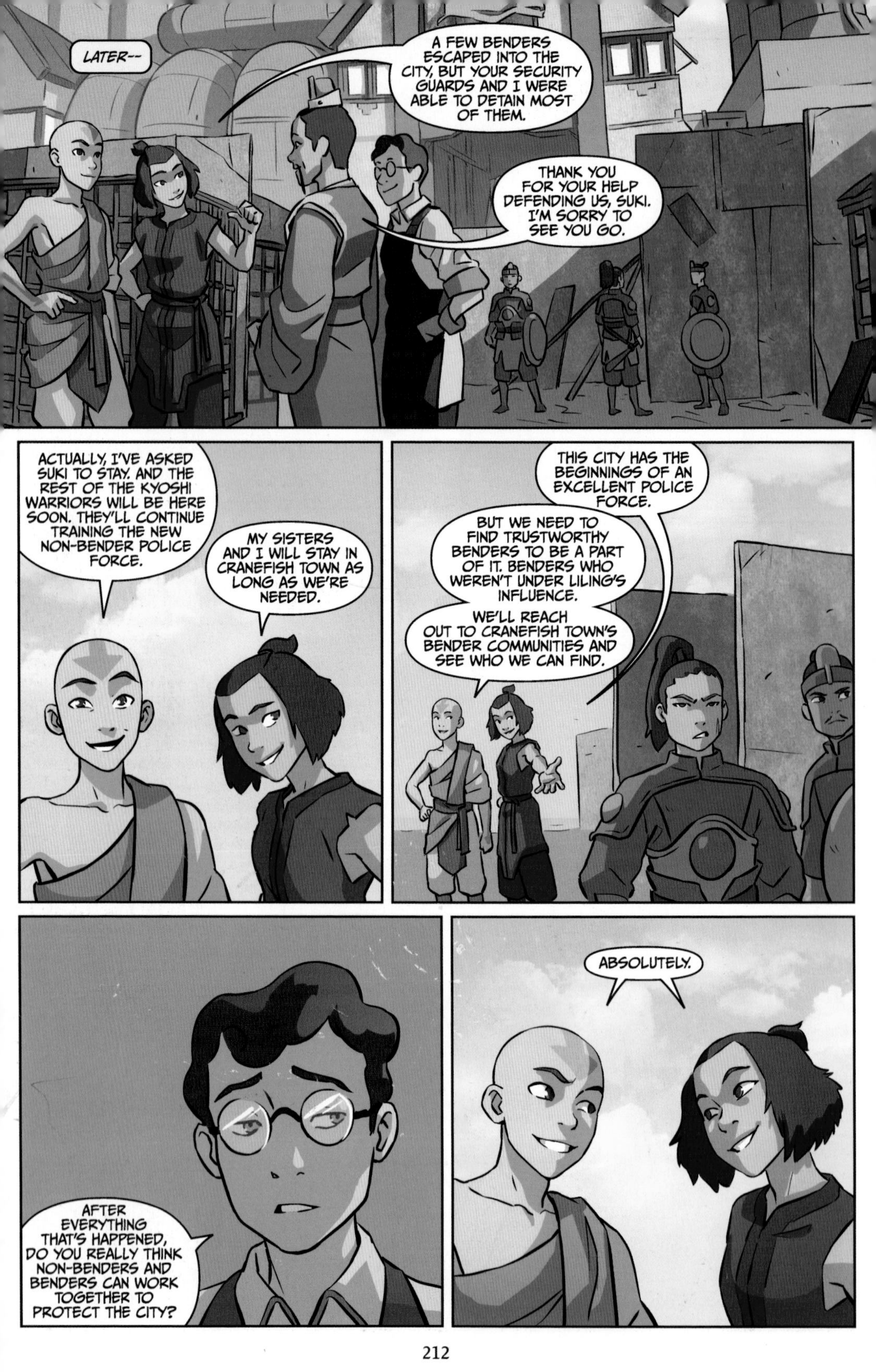
LATER--
A FEW BENDERS ESCAPED INTO THE CITY, BUT YOUR SECURITY GUARDS AND I WERE ABLE TO DETAIN MOST OF THEM.
THANK YOU FOR YOUR HELP DEFENDING US, SUKI. I'M SORRY TO SEE YOU GO.
ACTUALLY, I'VE ASKED SUKI TO STAY. AND THE REST OF THE KYOSHI WARRIORS WILL BE HERE SOON. THEY'LL CONTINUE TRAINING THE NEW NON-BENDER POLICE FORCE.
MY SISTERS AND I WILL STAY IN CRANEFISH TOWN AS LONG AS WE'RE NEEDED.
THIS CITY HAS THE BEGINNINGS OF AN EXCELLENT POLICE FORCE.
BUT WE NEED TO FIND TRUSTWORTHY BENDERS TO BE A PART OF IT. BENDERS WHO WEREN'T UNDER LILING'S INFLUENCE.
WE'LL REACH OUT TO CRANEFISH TOWN'S BENDER COMMUNITIES AND SEE WHO WE CAN FIND.
AFTER EVERYTHING THAT'S HAPPENED, DO YOU REALLY THINK NON-BENDERS AND BENDERS CAN WORK TOGETHER TO PROTECT THE CITY?
ABSOLUTELY.

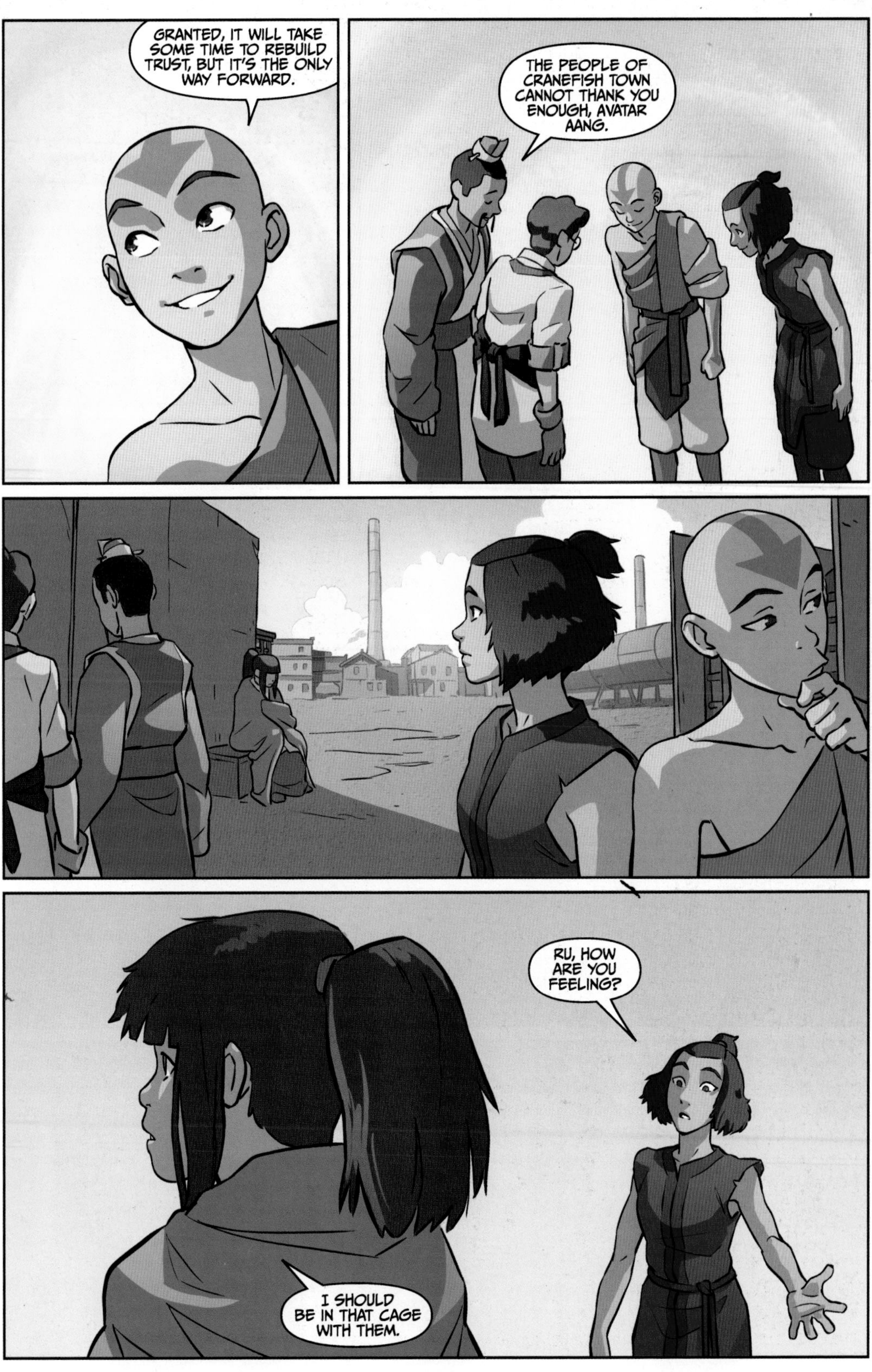
GRANTED, IT WILL TAKE SOME TIME TO REBUILD TRUST, BUT IT'S THE ONLY WAY FORWARD.
THE PEOPLE OF CRANEFISH TOWN CANNOT THANK YOU ENOUGH, AVATAR AANG.
RU, HOW ARE YOU FEELING?
I SHOULD BE IN THAT CAGE WITH THEM.

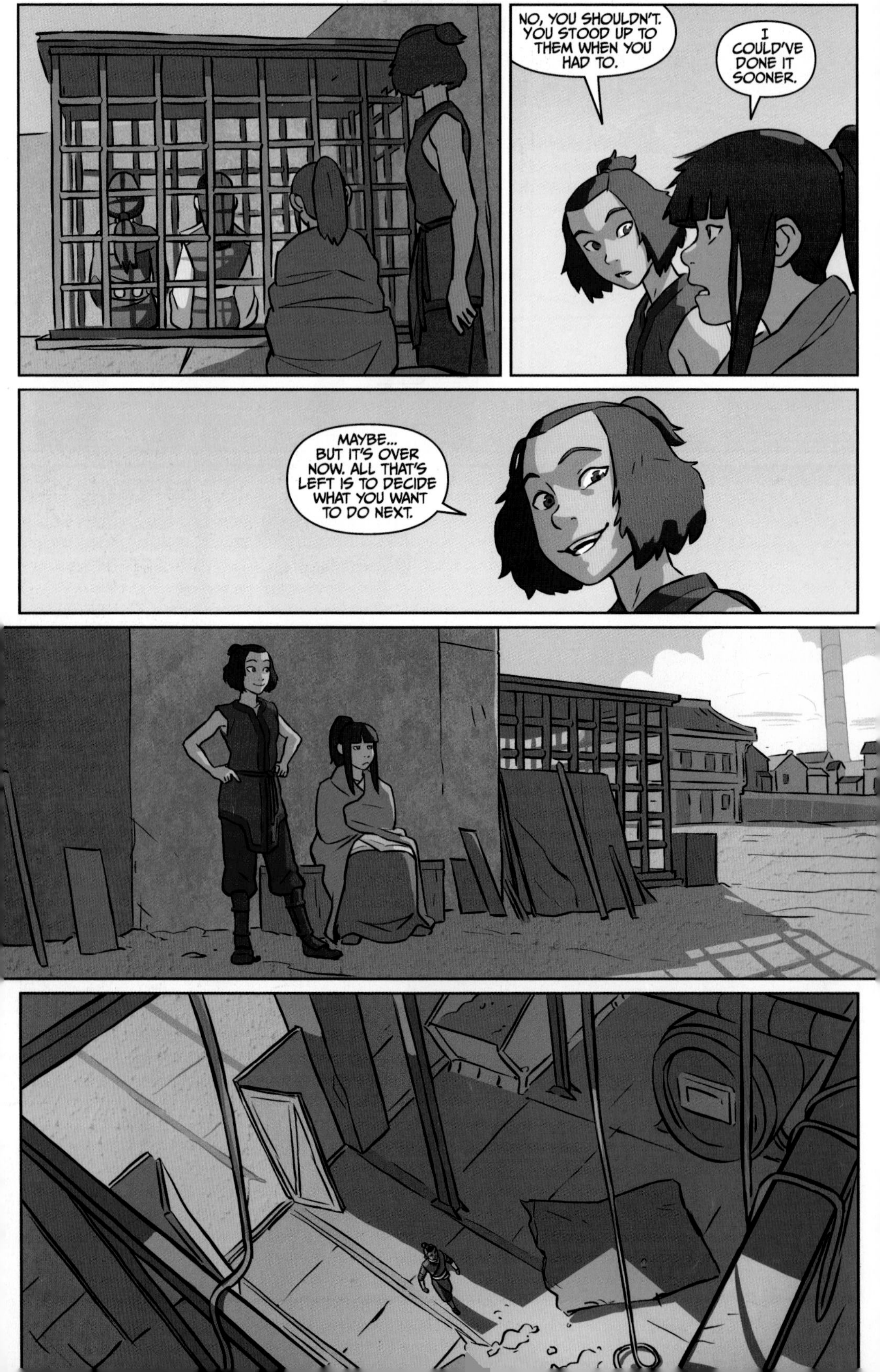
NO, YOU SHOULDN'T. YOU STOOD UP TO THEM WHEN YOU HAD TO.
I COULD'VE DONE IT SOONER.
MAYBE... BUT IT'S OVER NOW. ALL THAT'S LEFT IS TO DECIDE WHAT YOU WANT TO DO NEXT.

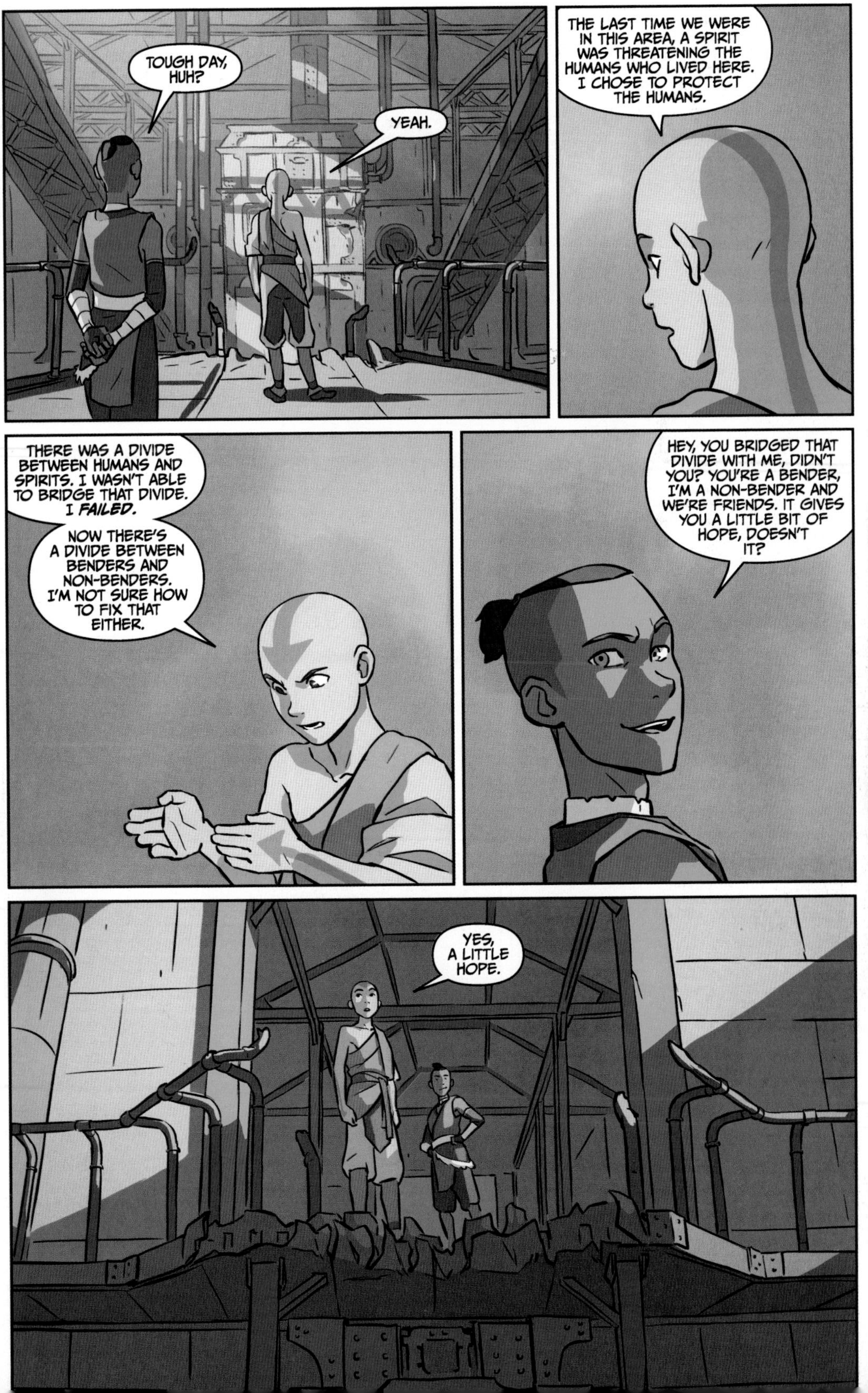
TOUGH DAY, HUH?
YEAH.
THE LAST TIME WE WERE IN THIS AREA, A SPIRIT WAS THREATENING THE HUMANS WHO LIVED HERE. I CHOSE TO PROTECT THE HUMANS.
THERE WAS A DIVIDE BETWEEN HUMANS AND SPIRITS. I WASN'T ABLE TO BRIDGE THAT DIVIDE. I *FAILED*.
NOW THERE'S A DIVIDE BETWEEN BENDERS AND NON-BENDERS. I'M NOT SURE HOW TO FIX THAT EITHER.
HEY, YOU BRIDGED THAT DIVIDE WITH ME, DIDN'T YOU? YOU'RE A BENDER, I'M A NON-BENDER AND WE'RE FRIENDS. IT GIVES YOU A LITTLE BIT OF HOPE, DOESN'T IT?
YES, A LITTLE HOPE.

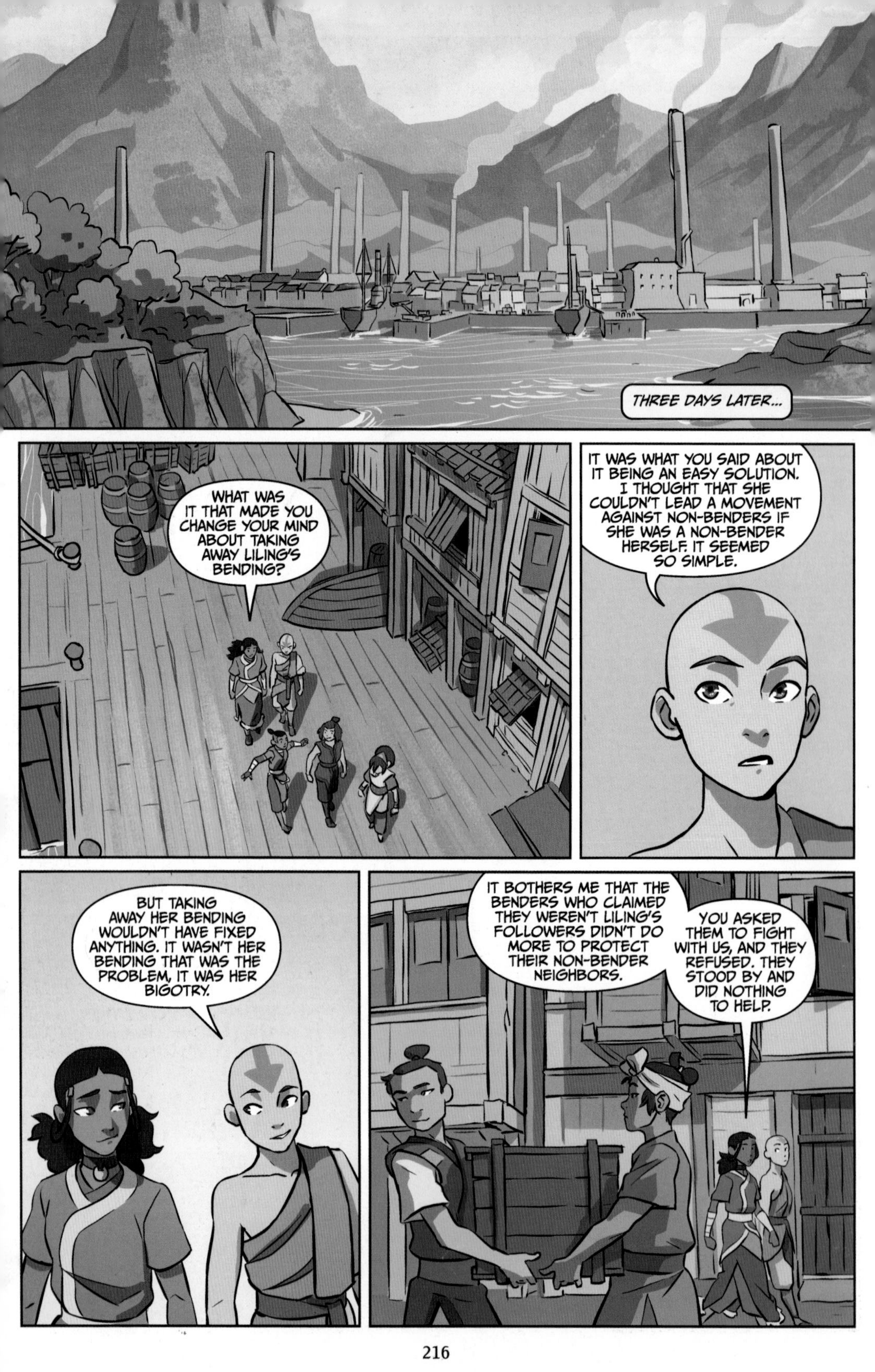
THREE DAYS LATER...
WHAT WAS IT THAT MADE YOU CHANGE YOUR MIND ABOUT TAKING AWAY LILING'S BENDING?
IT WAS WHAT YOU SAID ABOUT IT BEING AN EASY SOLUTION. I THOUGHT THAT SHE COULDN'T LEAD A MOVEMENT AGAINST NON-BENDERS IF SHE WAS A NON-BENDER HERSELF. IT SEEMED SO SIMPLE.
BUT TAKING AWAY HER BENDING WOULDN'T HAVE FIXED ANYTHING. IT WASN'T HER BENDING THAT WAS THE PROBLEM, IT WAS HER BIGOTRY.
IT BOTHERS ME THAT THE BENDERS WHO CLAIMED THEY WEREN'T LILING'S FOLLOWERS DIDN'T DO MORE TO PROTECT THEIR NON-BENDER NEIGHBORS.
YOU ASKED THEM TO FIGHT WITH US, AND THEY REFUSED. THEY STOOD BY AND DID NOTHING TO HELP.

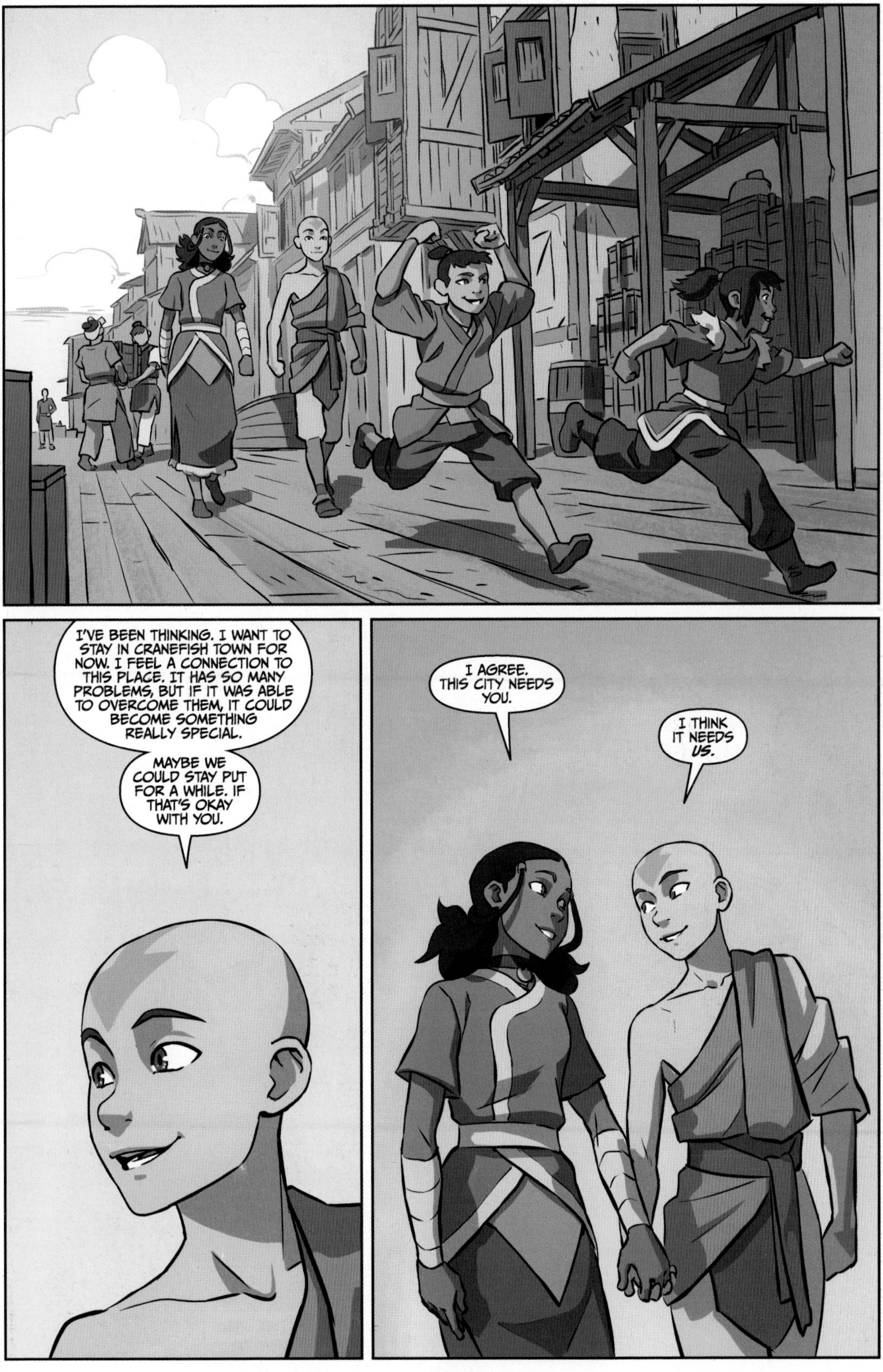
I'VE BEEN THINKING. I WANT TO STAY IN CRANEFISH TOWN FOR NOW. I FEEL A CONNECTION TO THIS PLACE. IT HAS SO MANY PROBLEMS, BUT IF IT WAS ABLE TO OVERCOME THEM, IT COULD BECOME SOMETHING REALLY SPECIAL.
MAYBE WE COULD STAY PUT FOR A WHILE. IF THAT'S OKAY WITH YOU.
I AGREE. THIS CITY NEEDS YOU.
I THINK IT NEEDS *US*.

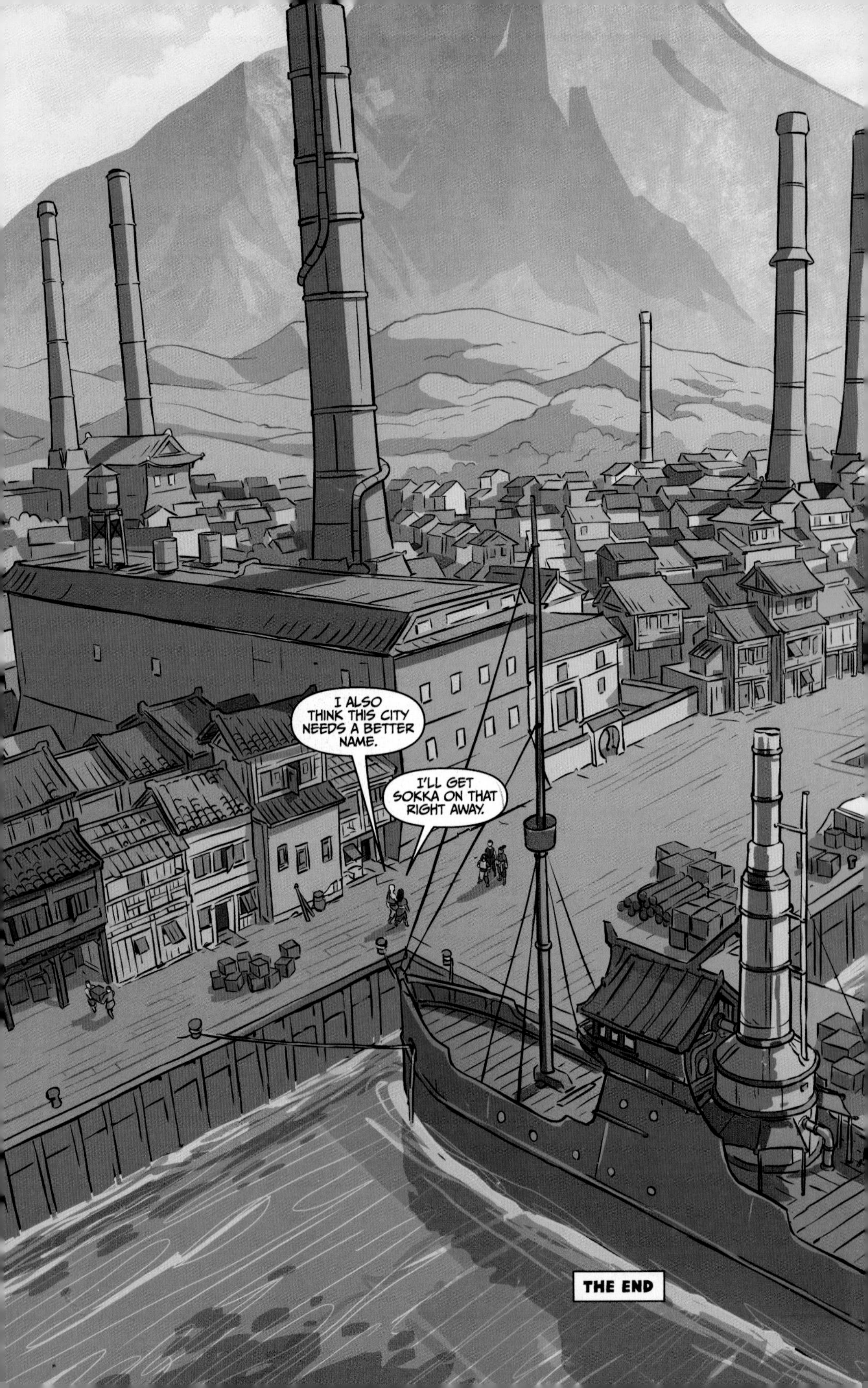
I ALSO THINK THIS CITY NEEDS A BETTER NAME.
I'LL GET SOKKA ON THAT RIGHT AWAY.
THE END

Avatar: The Last Airbender—Imbalance Sketchbook

Artwork and captions by Peter Wartman

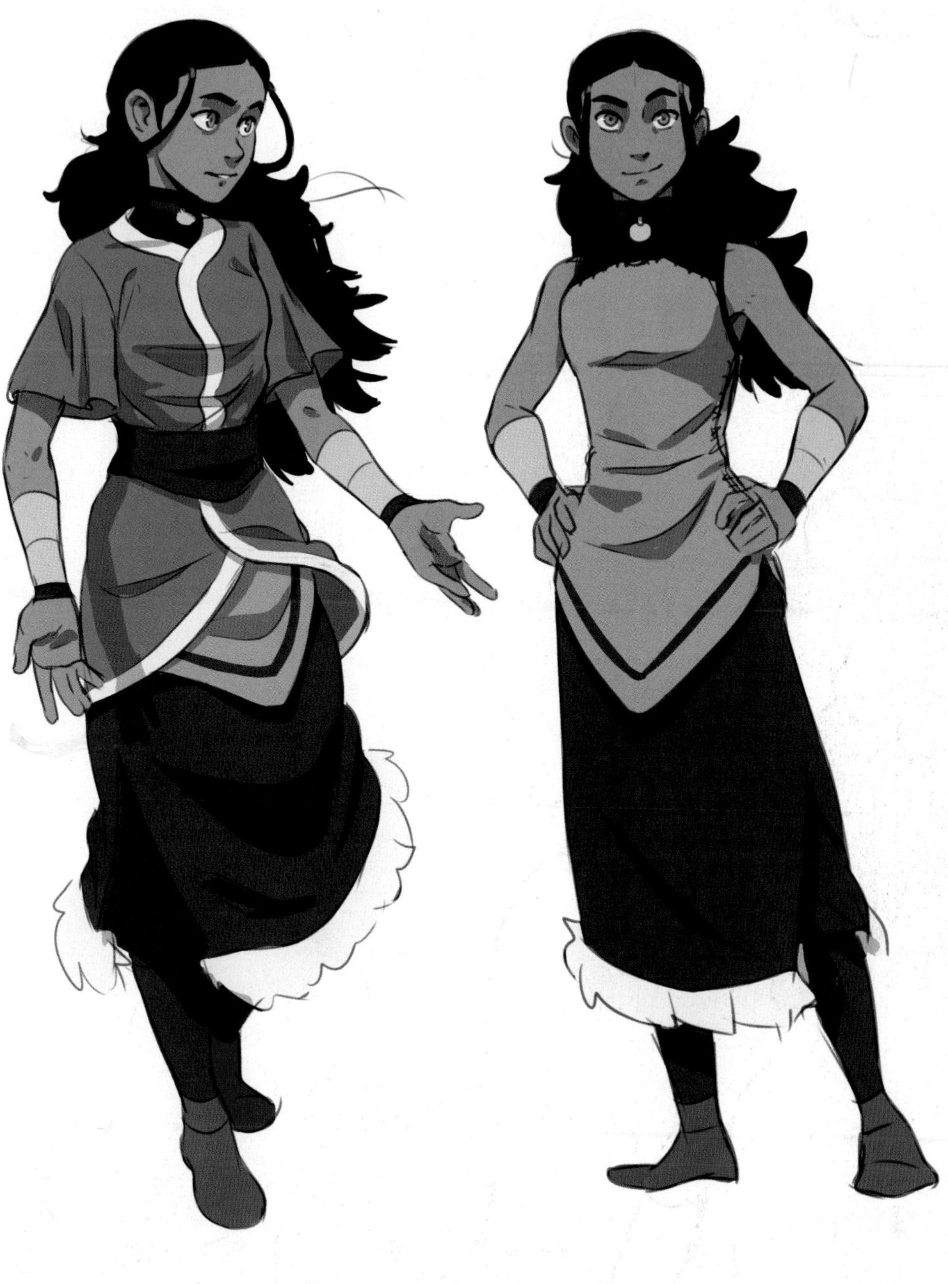

These two drawings were early concepts for Katara's look in the comic. I ended up going with something close to this, although I changed her undershirt a little.

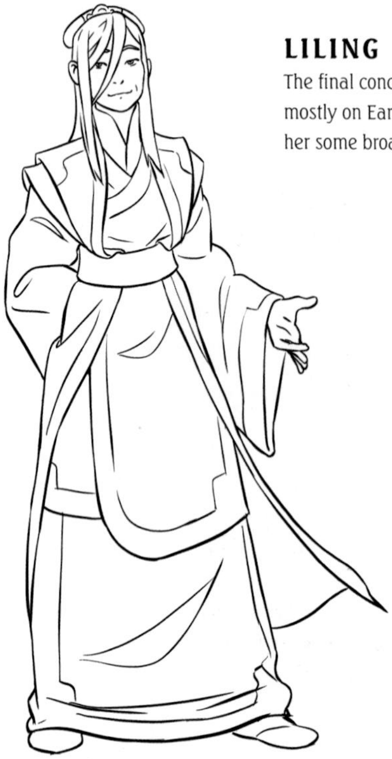

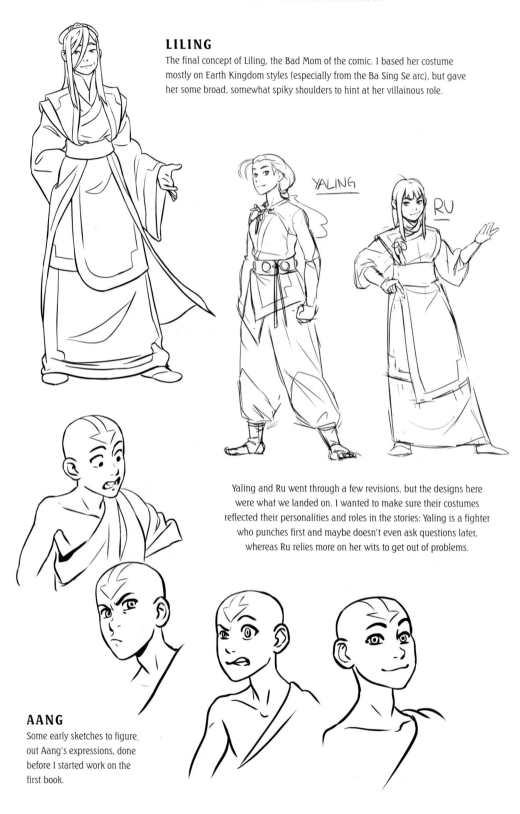

LILING

The final concept of Liling, the Bad Mom of the comic. I based her costume mostly on Earth Kingdom styles (especially from the Ba Sing Se arc), but gave her some broad, somewhat spiky shoulders to hint at her villainous role.

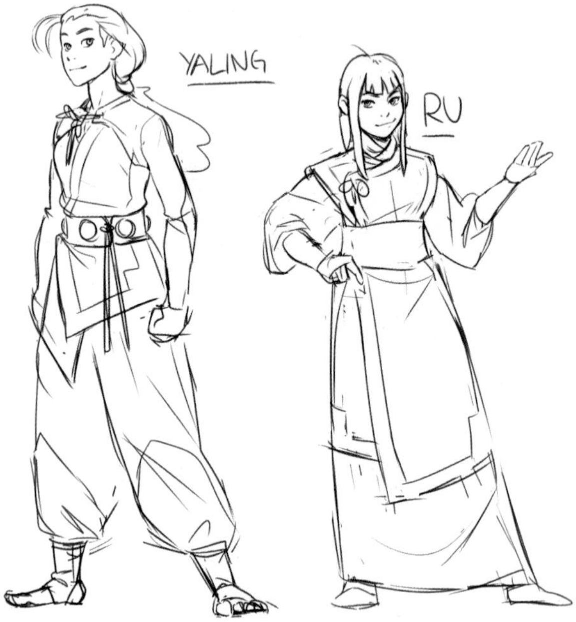
YALING
RU

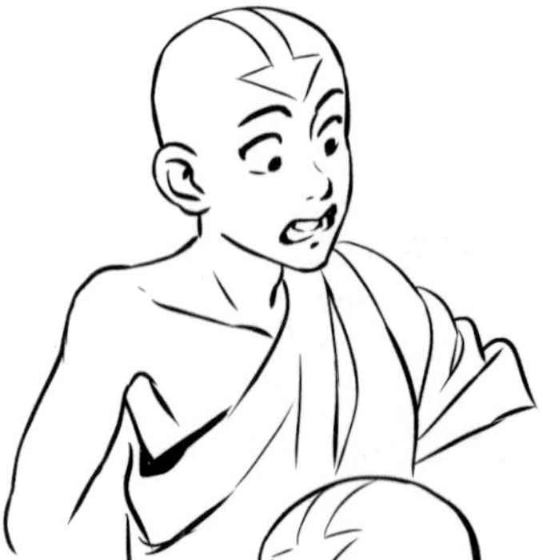

Yaling and Ru went through a few revisions, but the designs here were what we landed on. I wanted to make sure their costumes reflected their personalities and roles in the stories: Yaling is a fighter who punches first and maybe doesn't even ask questions later, whereas Ru relies more on her wits to get out of problems.

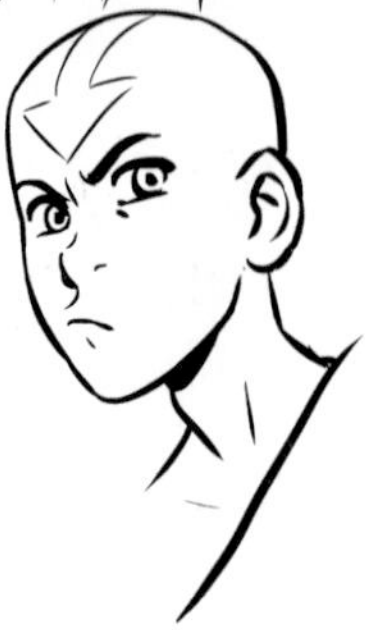

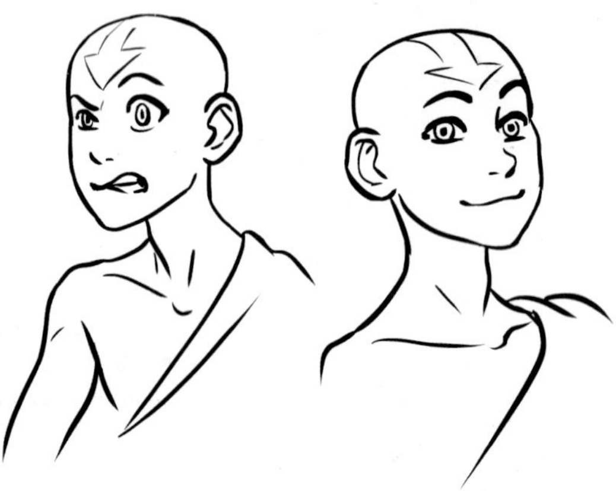

AANG

Some early sketches to figure out Aang's expressions, done before I started work on the first book.

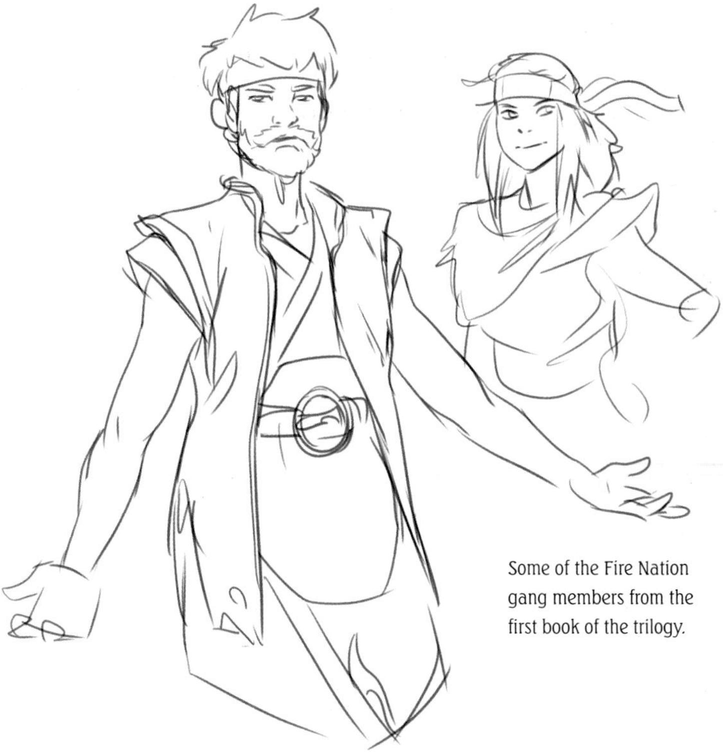

Some of the Fire Nation gang members from the first book of the trilogy.

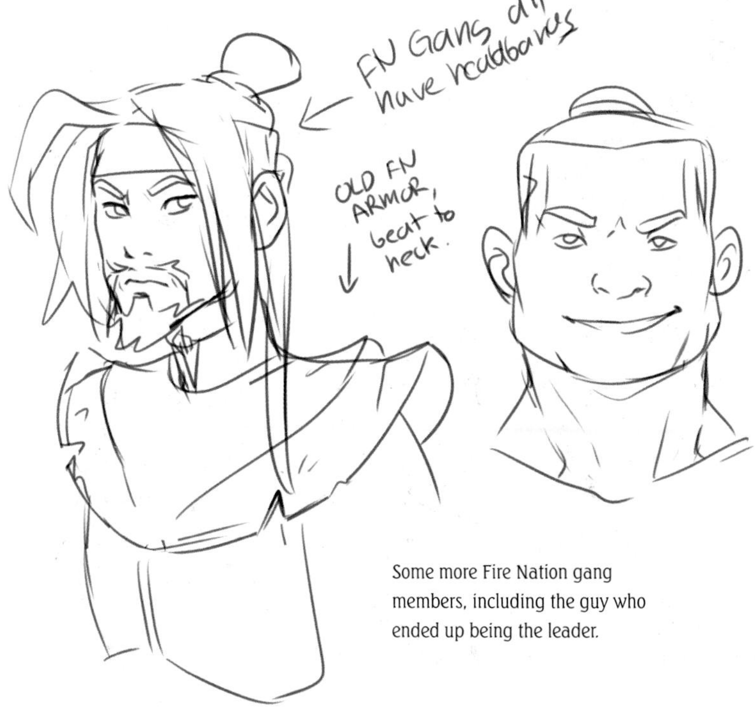
FN Gangs all have headbands
OLD FN ARMOR, beat to heck.

Some more Fire Nation gang members, including the guy who ended up being the leader.

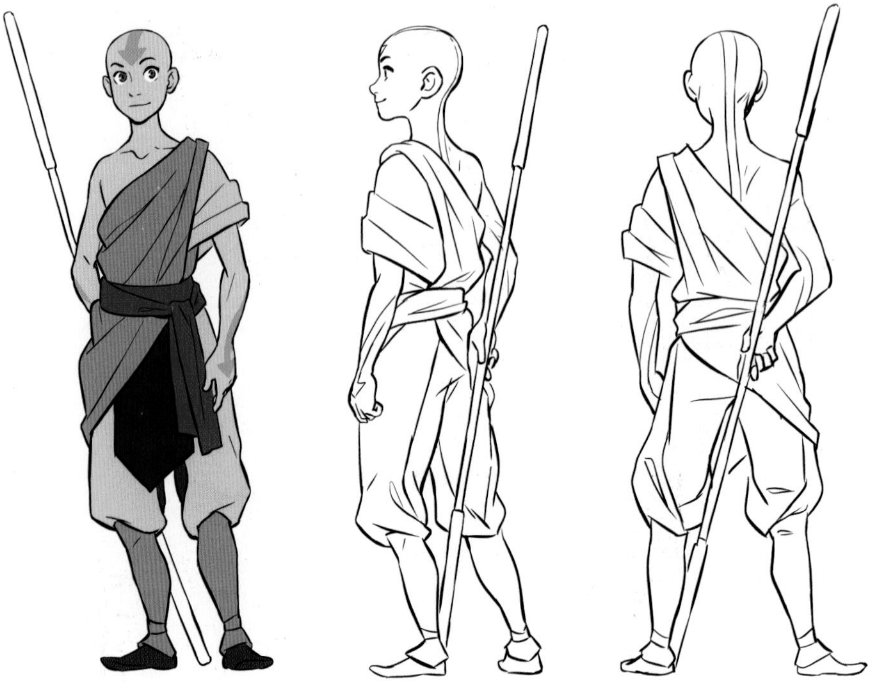

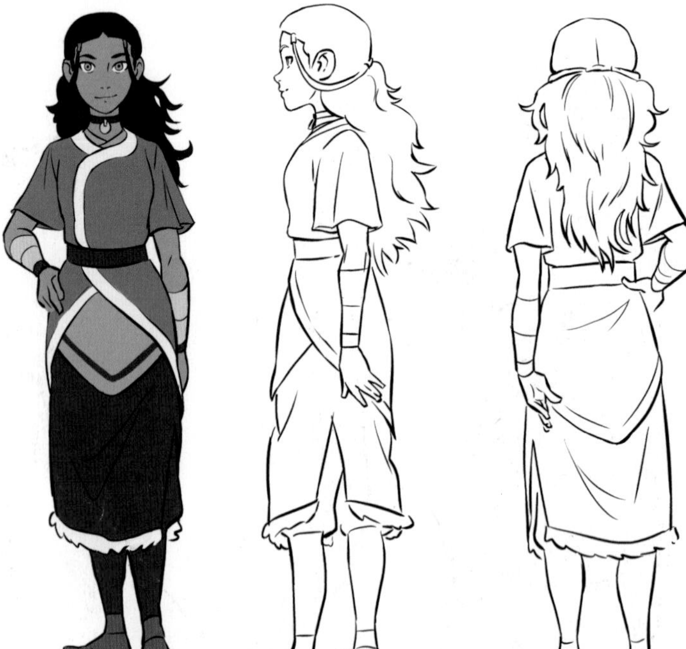

Turnarounds for most of the main characters as they appear in *Imbalance*, which were also the first thing I really did for the project. Mostly I stuck close to what the show (and later Guruhiru) depicted, but some characters (like Katara) took me a little longer.

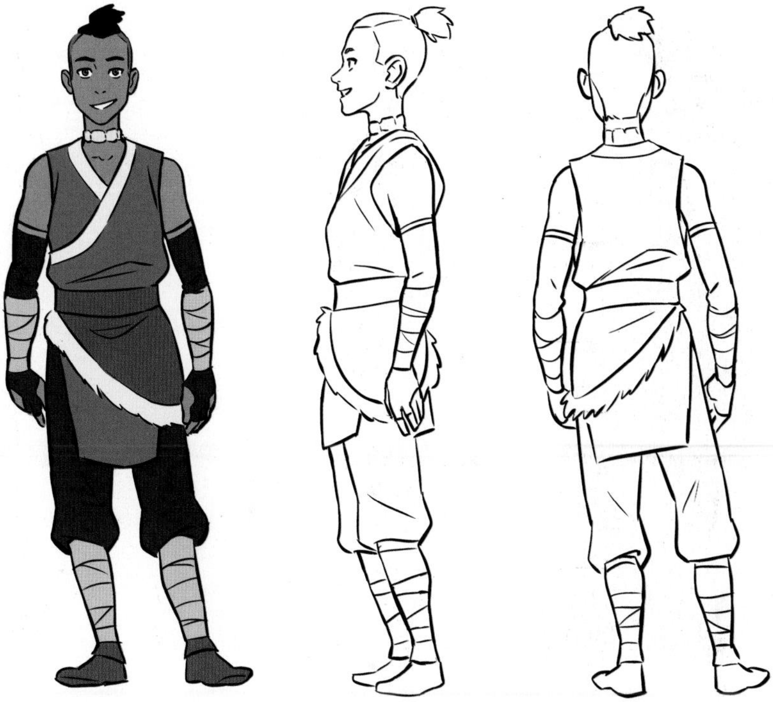

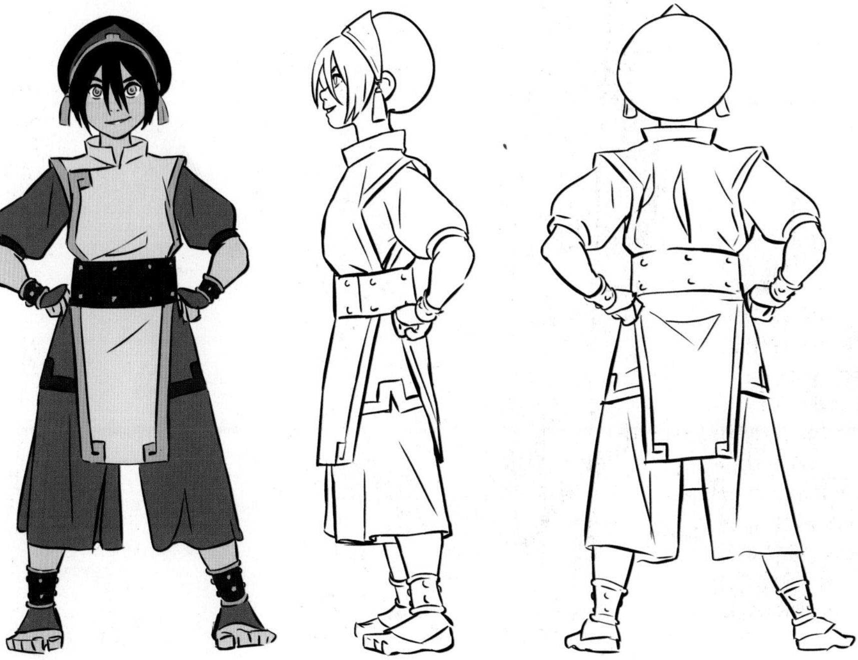

Some initial explorations for rundown buildings in Cranefish Town.

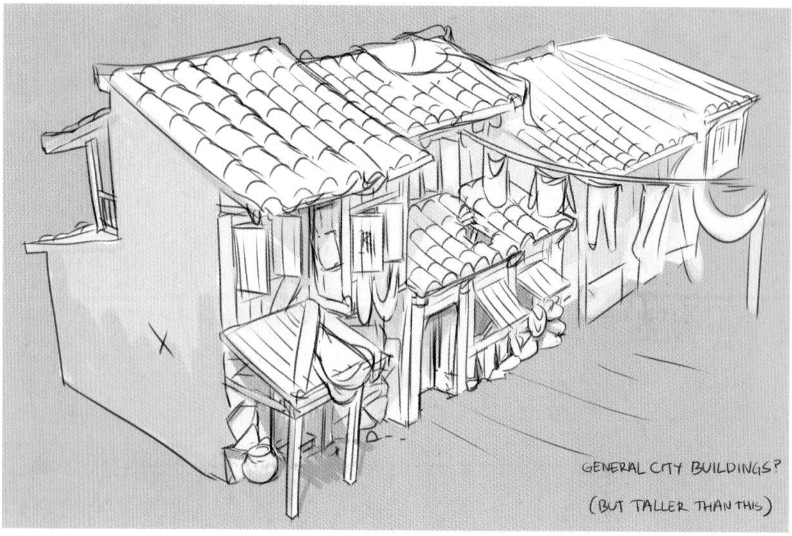
GENERAL CITY BUILDINGS?
(BUT TALLER THAN THIS)

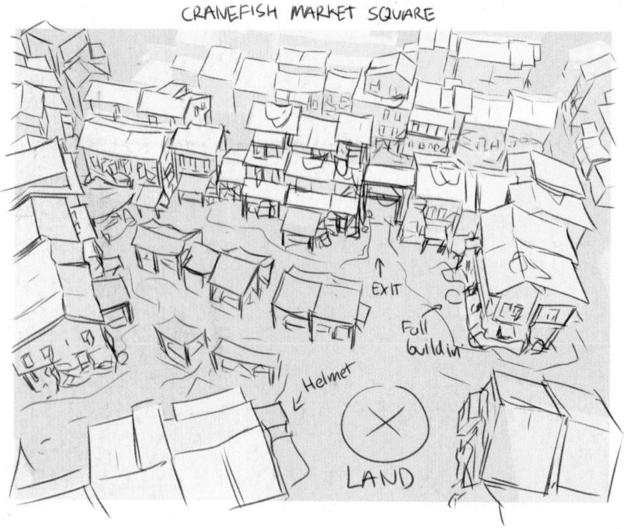
CRANEFISH MARKET SQUARE
EXIT
Full buildin'
Helmet
LAND

A sketch of the market from early in the first book. I created simple 3D models in a program called Blender for most of the backgrounds in *Imbalance*, which I used as a base to draw over.

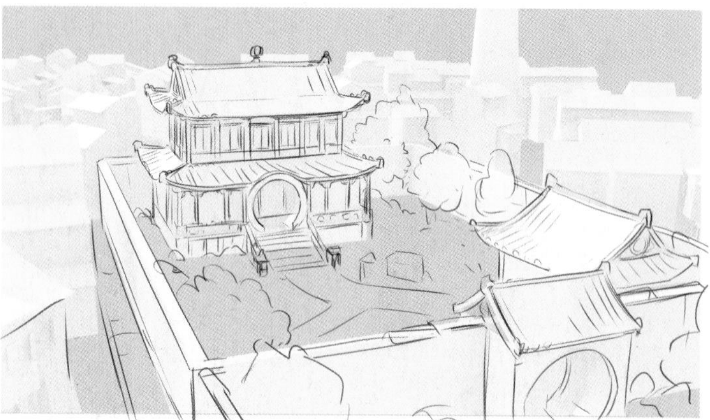

Design for Liling's house. You can see more clearly the 3D models I used in the background here. These models were especially handy for scenes we returned to several times (like Liling's house), as it ensured that buildings were placed consistently.